POINTS OF DEPARTURE

A Collection of Short Fiction

PRENTICE-HALL ENGLISH LITERATURE SERIES
Maynard Mack, *Editor*

PRENTICE-HALL INTERNATIONAL, INC., *London*
PRENTICE-HALL OF AUSTRALIA, PTY. LTD., *Sydney*
PRENTICE-HALL OF CANADA, LTD., *Toronto*
PRENTICE-HALL OF INDIA PRIVATE LIMITED, *New Delhi*
PRENTICE-HALL OF JAPAN, INC., *Tokyo*

POINTS OF DEPARTURE

A Collection of Short Fiction

HERBERT GOLDSTONE
University of Connecticut

IRVING CUMMINGS
University of Connecticut

THOMAS CHURCHILL

PRENTICE-HALL, INC., *Englewood Cliffs, New Jersey*

© 1971 by Prentice-Hall, Inc., Englewood Cliffs, New Jersey. *All rights reserved. No part of this book may be reproduced in any form or by any means without permission in writing from the publisher.*

13-684670-X

Library of Congress Catalog Card Number: 76–136195

Printed in the United States of America

Current printing (last number):
10 9 8 7 6 5 4 3 2 1

Acknowledgments

We would like to extend our appreciation for the use of:

the quote from "Fern Hill" *on p. 20 from* Dylan Thomas COLLECTED POEMS. Copyright 1946 by New Directions Publishing Corporation. Reprinted by permission of New Directions Publishing Corporation and of J. M. Dent & Sons Ltd. and the Trustees for the Copyrights of the late Dylan Thomas.

the quote from THE DEATH OF THE HEART *on p. 21 from* DEATH OF THE HEART by Elizabeth Bowen. Copyright 1938 by Elizabeth Bowen. Reprinted by permission of Alfred A. Knopf, Inc.

Acknowledgments v

the quote from THE QUIET AMERICAN *on p. 21 from* Graham Greene's THE QUIET AMERICAN. Copyright 1955 by Graham Greene. Reprinted by permission of The Viking Press, Inc., William Heinemann Ltd., and the author.

the quote from The Cherry Orchard on p. 68 and for the quote from The Three Sisters on p. 346. From The Cherry Orchard and The Three Sisters from SIX PLAYS OF CHEKHOV: NEW ENGLISH VERSIONS AND INTRODUCTIONS by Robert W. Corrigan. © 1962 by Robert W. Corrigan. Reprinted by permission of Holt, Rinehart and Winston, Inc.

the quote from LETTERS TO A YOUNG POET *on p. 68.* Reprinted from LETTERS TO A YOUNG POET by Rainer Maria Rilke. Translation by M. D. Herter Norton. By permission of W. W. Norton & Company, Inc. Copyright 1934 by W. W. Norton & Company, Inc. Renewed 1962 by M. D. Herter Norton. Revised Edition Copyright 1954 by W. W. Norton & Company, Inc.

the quote from "Easter 1916" *on p. 69.* Reprinted with permission of The Macmillan Company from "Easter 1916" by William Butler Yeats. Copyright 1924 by The Macmillan Company, renewed 1952 by Bertha Georgie Yeats.

the quote from Racine's PHAEDRA *on p. 68 from* Robert Lowell's translation of Racine's PHAEDRA. Copyright © 1960, 1961 by Robert Lowell. Reprinted by permission of Farrar, Straus and Giroux, Inc.

the quote from "Man and Wife" *on p. 102 from* Anne Sexton, "Man and Wife" from LIVE OR DIE. Copyright 1966 by Anne Sexton. Reprinted by permission of Houghton Mifflin Company.

the quote from ULYSSES *on p. 102 and for the one on p. 347 from* ULYSSES by James Joyce. Copyright 1914, 1918 by Margaret Caroline Anderson. Copyright 1934 by The Modern Library, Inc. Copyright 1942, 1946 by Nora Joseph Joyce. New Edition, corrected and reset 1961. Reprinted by permission of Random House, Inc.

the quote from Man and Superman by George Bernard Shaw on p. 102. By permission of The Society of Authors, London, on behalf of the Bernard Shaw Estate.

the song "Popeye the Sailor Man" *on p. 157.* © Famous Music Corp.

the quote from "Provide, Provide" *on p. 157.* From "Provide, Provide" from THE POETRY OF ROBERT FROST edited by Edward Connery Lathem. Copyright © 1964 by Lesley Frost Ballantine. Copyright © 1969 by Holt, Rinehart and Winston, Inc. Reprinted by permission of Holt, Rinehart and Winston, Inc.

the quote from THE HOUSE ON THE HILL *on p. 221.* From THE HOUSE ON THE HILL by Cesare Pavese. By permission of Walker & Co., New York.

vi Acknowledgments

the quote from "The Meadow Mouse" *on p. 265 from* "The Meadow Mouse" copyright © 1963 by Beatrice Roethke as Administratrix of the Estate of Theodore Roethke, from THE COLLECTED POEMS OF THEODORE ROETHKE. Reprinted by permission of Doubleday & Company, Inc.

the quote from "Spring and All" *on p. 265 from* William Carlos Williams THE COLLECTED EARLIER POEMS. Copyright 1938 by William Carlos Williams. Reprinted by permission of New Directions Publishing Corporation.

the quote from Waiting for Godot *on p. 347.* Translated from the original French text by Samuel Beckett. Reprinted by permission of Grove Press, Inc. Copyright © 1954 by Grove Press.

the quote from HOW TO WRITE SHORT STORIES *on p. 402.* Reprinted with the permission of Charles Scribner's Sons from HOW TO WRITE SHORT STORIES by Ring Lardner (1924).

the quote from ALL THE KING'S MEN *on p. 403 from* Robert Penn Warren ALL THE KING'S MEN. Copyright 1946 by Harcourt Brace Jovanovich, Inc. Reprinted by permission of Harcourt Brace Jovanovich, Inc.

the quote from Sophocles' Oedipus *on p. 403 from* Sophocles' Oedipus the King. Translated by David Grene. Copyright © 1942 by the University of Chicago. From THE COMPLETE GREEK TRAGEDIES, edited by David Grene and Richmond Lattimore. Reprinted with the permission of the University of Chicago Press and of David Grene.

Preface

AMERICAN WRITERS AND STORIES written within the last twenty-five years dominate this collection. Many stories are familiar, many are fresh or at least relatively so in anthologies. The stories are grouped around eight general topics—innocence, love, marriage, identity, war, brotherhood, belief, and obligation. We are aware that the selection and the arrangement of the stories may not be pleasing to many who examine this book, but we would like to explain briefly our intentions.

Selection and arrangement are procedures which modify each other. We started with a desire to make a collection of stories likely to engage the interest and attention of freshmen and sophomores and adaptable to classes in which the reading and study of short stories might also involve writing assignments. Our own experiences as teachers have convinced us that approaching stories with the question "What's the story about?" is a valid way and the most effective way to lead students to the means and ends of short fiction (indeed of any art). Our starting point, then, was to select stories that might loosely yet not misleadingly or impertinently be considered as variations on a series of topics. Our recognition of the topics developed mutually with the choice of stories: as we explored the literature, topics suggested themselves, and, conversely, a more or less clear idea about a topic set us looking for appropriate stories. We decided that most of the stories and the topics themselves ought to be, if not timely, at least likely to reflect students' interests; thus, the emphasis on recent American writing.

These were our major considerations. Within these limits we tried to achieve a wide variety of techniques and forms and even to accommodate our own enthusiasms and preferences. We felt no obligations to represent a writer because he is a master; we could list several writers whom we admire but who are not here.

This range in quality, technique, and form is matched by our efforts to make for flexibility even within our grouping by themes or topics. Instead of silently and without comment presenting the stories, imposing no apparent structure on the collection, we decided to capitalize on the structure, to suggest ways in which our arrangement by topics can be a means of opening up discussion and appreciation. We do not pretend that all the stories within a group hammer on one theme or one perspective. The presence of Elizabeth Bowen's "A Queer Heart" in the group about innocence is one sign of this. (We finally gave up, though, in searching for a war story that we liked and that would celebrate those virtues discussed by William James in his call for a Moral Equivalent to War.) We know that the greatness of "Death of a Traveling Salesman," of "Tell Me a Riddle," of "Rothschild's Fiddle" cannot be confined by any rubric, but we elect to *approach* them, respectively, through the gates of identity, belief, and obligation.

We have tried to enrich, not inhibit, our topical arrangement by two other devices: by affixing to each group a rubric which is in the form of a question or which raises a questioning mood; and by introducing each group of stories with a few of the quotations that buzzed in our minds as we worked. We have leaned toward the satiric and the pungent, the indirect and the evocative and the epigraph, but we have not always scrupulously avoided the obvious and the emphatic. We hope our serious amusement in deciding on which fragments to include will be suggestive to teachers and students.

The apparatus is unobtrusive and suggestive, not systematic. The introductory essay on reading short stories does not seek to develop a method or to imply a theory of the ideal form of the short story. It explores some of the connections between short stories and the experience and interests of students; it suggests some of the ways artists create those connections; and it introduces some of the terms most useful in discussing the workings of the short story.

At the back of the books are questions and biographical notes. The questions and problems are of three kinds. First there are sets of ques-

Preface ix

tions for discussion and writing assignments aimed at critical reading of sixteen of the stories; second there are ten writing assignments which suggest other interesting and pertinent uses of the stories; third, there are five more general, open ended topics leading to longer papers. Here again the variety of questions and problems opens up possibilities and does not imply one way to respond or to understand. The biographical notes seek at least to identify the writer in place and time, and to do more than that when the writer is one whose stature and achievement demand attention.

Finally we have suggested one other possibility for students of short fiction. Several of the stories are followed by comments by the authors. Some of these comments are reprints. Some of them came in response to our requests; for these our gratitude is immeasureable. Altogether these comments—theoretical, or practical, or genetic—suggest something of the interests and intentions of the artist himself.

Like all anthologists we regret the omisson of those other stories that might have been included: the ones we wanted but for one reason or another could not get permission to include, the ones we thought about including but had to omit because a book can only be so big, and especially the ones that would have been here if we had only known about them. We are grateful to many who have helped us in preparing the book, particularly to three daughters—Beth and Ann Goldstone and Jean Cummings, and to Mrs. Paula Cohn of Prentice-Hall.

HERBERT GOLDSTONE
IRVING CUMMINGS
THOMAS CHURCHILL

Contents

On Reading Short Stories   1

I   WHAT WAS INNOCENCE?   **20**

     James Joyce, An Encounter   23
     Frank O'Connor, First Confession   31
     Elizabeth Bowen, A Queer Heart   40
     William Faulkner, That Evening Sun   50

II   "THIS THING CALLED LOVE"   **68**

     William Carlos Williams, The Knife of the Times   71
     Guy de Maupassant, Two Little Soldiers   75
     Katherine Mansfield, A Dill Pickle   82
     Sean O'Faolain, Childybawn   89

Contents

III "TO SPEAK OF MARRIAGE . . ." 102

J. F. Powers, The Valiant Waman 105
D. H. Lawrence, Two Blue Birds 115
R. V. Cassill, Fracture 130
Katherine Anne Porter, The Jilting of Granny Weatherall 145

IV WHO AM I? 156

Thomas Churchill, The Home Stretch 159
Nancy Huddleston Packer, Oh Jerusalem 172
Joyce Carol Oates, In the Region of Ice 188
Eudora Welty, Death of a Traveling Salesman 206

V "OH WHAT A LOVELY WAR" 220

Ambrose Bierce, Chickamauga 223
Harris Downey, The Hunters 230
Isaac Rosenfeld, The Brigadier 247
Isaac Babel, Crossing Into Poland 256
Luigi Pirandello, War 259

VI ARE ALL MEN BROTHERS? 264

Flannery O'Connor, Revelation 267
Philip Roth, Defender of the Faith 288
Albert Camus, The Guest 317
Doris Lessing, The Black Madonna 330

VII WHAT CAN A MAN BELIEVE IN? 346

Jordon Pecile, A Piece of Polenta 349

Anton Chekhov, Rothschild's Fiddle   362
Ryunosuke Akutagawa, In a Grove   372
Heinrich Böll, Murke's Collected Silences   381

VIII   HOW MUCH CAN A MAN PAY?   **402**

Donald Barthelme, A Shower of Gold   405
Ralph Ellison, King of the Bingo Game   414
Lawrence Sargent Hall, The Ledge   424
Tillie Olsen, Tell Me a Riddle   441

Some Questions and Problems   **477**

Biographical Notes   **500**

POINTS OF DEPARTURE

A Collection of Short Fiction

On Reading Short Stories

UNLIKE THE CHARACTER IN MOLIERE'S PLAY, *The Middle-Class Gentleman*, who discovers to his amazement and joy that he has been speaking prose all his life, most of us realize how much of our time we have spent reading stories. From Dr. Seuss to Steinbeck, from Boccaccio to Chekhov, and from Aesop's to Thurber's Fables, we are likely to have had a rich, varied diet of fiction. But we may not realize that our very familiarity makes us overlook some considerations that are important if we want to extend our understanding and appreciation.

To begin with, the sheer range of the short story—in length alone, not to mention subject matter, structure, style, or method of narration—is extraordinary. Consider, for example, this difference in two of the stories in this collection, William Carlos Williams' "The Knife of the Times," which runs to four pages, and Tillie Olsen's "Tell Me a Riddle," which goes almost to thirty-five. Mr. Williams' story concerns a middle-aged, highly respectable woman's double discovery: first, that an equally respectable friend of many years' standing has developed strong homosexual feelings for her;

1

and, second, that the woman (named Ethel) finds herself, much to her own surprise, interested and tempted to respond. From our description so far, we might expect a complex, and perhaps theatrical story, the equivalent in fiction of a Jean Genêt play. The story, however, is straightforward and plain, with a simple sequence of events presented casually and quickly, and the author remains in the background. These very economies make what could have been lurid natural, as though these women could accept such feelings as facts of life. To expand, complicate, and intensify would create another story, not the one Mr. Williams is telling. In Mrs. Olsen's story, a dying old woman is both recounting her present reactions as she visits her various relatives for the last time, and ruminating about her past life, which she remembers in fitful snatches. Again, the author keeps to the background; most of the action emerges through the reactions of the old woman, which sometimes represent a straightforward account of what is happening, sometimes her associations with the events, sometimes her reflections about their meaning, and sometimes nearly prophetic visionary utterances that she struggles to express. In subject matter, scope, and technique the story has an epiclike spaciousness and complexity as it explores a whole lifetime of experience and poses questions about ultimate values. Possibly for these reasons some critics regard this story as one of the great works of short fiction of this past decade.

For all their differences, however, "The Knife of the Times" and "Tell Me A Riddle" are both forms of short fiction. They take place in a particular locale, or *setting*, private or public; they have a sequence of events or *plot* which involves personages who are not mere stick figures but are *characters* with distinctive qualities of personality and/or embody different viewpoints; they use language with some distinction, whether it is in a factual, dramatic, or poetically evocative *style;* they are narrated to us by someone, either outside the story, or in it, or both; and through the interplay of all these elements—*setting, plot, character, style,* and method of narration (or what technically we call *point of view*)—they are projecting a *theme*—an image or view of human experience.

Each story is accordingly doing something different and within its own terms equally effective. As the very list of writers in our opening paragraph indicates, short fiction is eclectic, fantastically so. While eclecticism creates difficulties, particularly for those who wish everything to be "nice and tidy," it permits authors great freedom. They can use contrasting techniques, pursue widely varied interests, or even explore similar interests differently, as the very structure of this book reveals. Because short fiction is so eclectic, we as readers have to be wary in generalizing about what stances authors, past or present, are taking, what techniques they are utilizing, and what values they are affirming or questioning. Instead, we need to focus on individual stories, which we want to read openly and freely—either separately or, as we propose, through comparisons and contrasts of various kinds—to discover some of their distinctive qualities.

To enhance our discoveries, we need to remind ourselves regularly that stories exist to be enjoyed. If we don't read to enjoy and enjoy what we read, we have not understood what fiction is about. As Robert M. Adams explains:

> . . . it won't do to become too portentous over the matter of modern fiction. Short stories, and for that matter, long stories, may profit from exegesis, but they are written to be available to other and more direct modes of appreciation. The reason they are stories, and not essays or aphorisms or lyrical cries, lies in a primitive passion shared by both tellers and readers of stories, to follow with sympathy and delight the actions of a fellow human. However layered its ironies, however subtle its moral insights or complex its verbal textures, no story is worth a hoot which doesn't somehow stir that delight.[1]

By "primitive passion" Adams means a strong, intuitive feeling common to all people, regardless of education, age, background, temperament or experience, which even underlies intellectual excitement or psychological understanding, and without which these others, though very important, would be incomplete. Story actions may involve exciting outward changes in people or their situations, as our fascination with adventure or detective stories confirms. But story actions may be slight, almost commonplace, and we may find ourselves fascinated by them merely because they are happening

---

[1] Robert M. Adams, "Introduction," *The Modern Image: Outstanding Stories From the Hudson Review*, ed. Frederick Morgan (New York: W. W. Norton & Company, Inc.), p. 13.

to men and women, "fellow humans." A good writer may raise this "primitive passion" by focusing our attention on unexceptional people in such a way as to make their actions surprisingly significant and moving. Guy de Maupassant tells in "Two Little Soldiers" of two simple French farmers doing their service in the army; they are friends, barely distinguishable in their taciturn stolidity, and certainly not the kind of people usually noticed by others. They meet a young farm girl, and we begin to be aware of a difference between the two soldiers. These three inarticulate, perhaps less than ordinary people find themselves in a dilemma of love and friendship that they seem scarcely aware of, and when one of the three dies, a death as inarticulate as everything else about the three, they seem not to understand themselves. Yet the story has absorbed readers' attention for decades. And why? Because the author has awakened in his readers an interest in the actions of the three characters, has told a story which, whatever else it does, moves in a convincing and covert manner and finally surprises us. It surprises us, not because its ending in a death is a clever trick, but because its ending is unexpected until it happens. But having happened, we realize with a shudder that it was always possible.

"Two Little Soldiers" satisfies that primitive passion for action because it presents a story, not just a series of events. First two, then three characters, of a certain kind, do certain things, and because they are the kinds of people they are, certain consequences flow from their actions. The characters and actions reflect each other and form a sequence or order with a beginning, middle, and end. This order or *plot* is not immediately apparent because what happens does not initially seem to be significant, but the plot is felt as we read. We see, after we have finished the story, that the inarticulateness of the characters was not just realistic detail but was a necessary condition of the story; we see that the ever so slight differences between the two men were not merely variations for variety's sake but were hints of the fundamental differences between the two on which the story turns. These stolid, uncommunicative, apparently simple characters are not explained away by the author, nor do they seem really to understand themselves, but when we finish de Maupassant's story we are both satisfied and moved; we are satisfied because everything hangs together to make a whole, and we are moved that these characters should become victims of their own decent impulses and their naïveté. But action need not be external—meetings, secrets, engagements—it may be largely internal as in Katherine Mansfield's "A Dill Pickle." Two people who at one time were lovers meet unexpectedly after not seeing each other for several years. They sit in a cafe and chat casually about what they are doing now, though with occasional glances back to their past. For the girl (through whose inward reactions we follow what is going on) these glances stir up so many frustrated hopes and romantic memories that she begins to hope wildly for some dramatic restoration of that past. As this fails to happen, she is left with new unhappiness, but also with a clearer understanding of herself and her former lover. Some outer action takes place, for without it the girl's reactions might be difficult to sustain; but the center of the story is the girl's consciousness. There, as Emily Dickinson wrote in one of her poems, "is where the meanings are."

The meanings of de Maupassant's "Two Little Soldiers" arise partly from the fact that we observe a series of events, reported with little comment, and with almost no information about what goes on in the minds of the soldiers. But in Miss Mansfield's "A Dill Pickle" the external events are chiefly important because they contribute to our experience of the girl's perceptions and responses. The way each of the authors tells his story is, therefore, one of the ways he creates his meanings. We say, "tell me a story"; the effect and the meanings of a short story often depend upon our recognizing whom the author chooses to tell the story or upon our recognizing that the focus, the center, may be on events or on some character or character's response to those events.

Consequently we speak of the *point of view*. Both de Maupassant and Katherine Mansfield employ the third person point of view; that is, someone tells us a story about other people. But the narrator of "Two Little Soldiers" remains largely outside his story, somewhat removed and aloof. We could say that most of the meanings of that story arise from the interplay between the events the narrator reports and occasionally comments on and his curiously sympathetic but still detached and cool attitude toward the events. The narrator of "A Dill Pickle," on the other hand, is far less apparent. Although this narrator reports actions and conversation, almost always she presents these things as they occur to the girl. Moreover, she freely enters into the thoughts, recollections and hopes in the girl's mind.

Fiction writers, especially in the last century, have consistently experimented with point of view because of their awareness of its impact upon meaning. Therefore, the possibilities inherent within point of view remain open; though no rules or formulas govern its uses, we may recognize in general five sorts—three variations of the third person, and two of the first person: (1) stories told to us by a third person who remains outside of the story and presents little or no direct comment on the events (as in "The Knife of the Times" or "Two Little Soldiers"); (2) stories told in the third person, but by a narrator who seems almost omniscient as he freely comments, enters in and out of the thoughts and feelings of any or all of the characters (as in "Two Blue Birds," by D. H. Lawrence); (3) stories told in the third person, but by a narrator who confines himself to presenting events and thoughts as they are experienced by one character (as in "A Dill Pickle," and in Katherine Anne Porter's "The Jilting of Granny Weatherall"); (4) stories told in the first person, by an "I" who is also the chief character in the story (as in Frank O'Connor's "First Confession" and Jordon Pecile's "A Piece of Polenta"); and (5) stories told in the first person, by an "I" who is more of an observer or who seems, at least, not so much the dramatic center of the story as another character (as in Mrs. Packer's "Oh Jerusalem" or in Faulkner's "That Evening Sun," where either Quentin, the "I" of the story, or Nancy may be regarded as the chief character).

These five uses of point of view do not exhaust all the possibilities, but they indicate the chief variations. Each method of narration has its own capacity for creating immediacy, attitude, focus, and implication. Its advantages and limitations cannot really be set forth in the abstract; we can only be aware of how a point of view works on us in a particular story. Nor is it wise to assume that a good story is always rigorous, pure, and simple in handling point of view. Sometimes a story retains its power and effect even though we may feel that the author has mishandled the point of view; for some readers Ambrose Bierce's "Chickamauga" is spoiled because the author shifts from the limited third person narrator (see the third type in the preceding paragraph) to the omniscient narrator (see the second type in the preceding paragraph). On the other hand, in some stories there is no question but that the author has intentionally mixed points of view as one means for achieving his effect. Akutagawa's "In a Grove" depends for its provocative power upon its mélange of precisely defined and discordant first person narratives and third person reports. Tillie Olsen's "Tell Me a Riddle" shifts rather freely its points of view; the author's "impure" experimenting helps to make this story at once one of a private life and of a representative cultural figure.

Let us now return to Robert Adams' remark that "we follow with sympathy and delight the actions of a fellow human." *Sympathy* indicates not just pleasure or interest in what happens to others but both concern and empathy in varying proportions. To sympathize means (1) to care enough about what happens to others that we feel implicated with them, and (2) to so identify with their responses that we can at least accept them and even, it is to be hoped, understand them. Sympathy as we describe it presupposes a great deal on the part of both writer and reader, but it is a necessary part of their mutual involvement, as Nancy Huddleston Packer's "Oh Jerusalem" makes clear.

The plot action in this story seems slight, involving, as it does, merely a social call which a young Jewish physician and his new wife, make upon his father's sister and her husband. But the consequences are not slight because the wife is Gentile and the uncle and aunt have only now reluctantly extended this first invitation. Told to us through the eyes of the young wife, who is both an observer and a victim, the story centers on the ostensible efforts of the uncle (Maurice) to show his "tolerance." But the harder he tries, the more he embarrasses and hurts everyone: the niece, whom he keeps calling a *shiksa* (the Yiddish word for Gentile, which expresses a special kind of condescension or even contempt); his nephew, the doctor; his wife (Sarah), with whom he can't resist quarreling whenever the occasion presents itself; and even himself. The uncle's efforts are so destructive because he has ambivalent feelings about his own Jewish identity. As a young man he tried hard to escape from the ghetto but lacked the will—and the good fortune—to do so. As a result, he had to return and experience the bitterness of his failure. Worse yet, his relatives found it very difficult to accept him as a Jew. For some he was not Jewish enough in his beliefs and actions; for others, he was too Jewish. Deeply frustrated, he expressed his ambivalent feelings by quarreling with all comers. Moreover, once he begins expressing these feelings, as he does when the couple arrives, he simply can't stop. Though he does not know it and cannot admit it, he is also making clear how much he needs them.

Now to the question: how does Mrs. Packer arouse sympathy? First of all, by conveying through her narrator the strong, conflicting feelings of the other characters as they find themselves implicated in the uncle's plight. Toward the end of the story the uncle, worn out from all his attacks, momentarily reveals himself in all his helplessness. In doing so, he embarrasses everyone, himself included:

> He sat still, only his crossed leg bobbing to the echoed rhythm of his voice. When finally in the silence he lifted his head, he looked sick and foolish and shrewd. And we were ashamed to see him.
>
> As if she had been waiting for just that moment, Aunt Sarah went over to him. She put her hand on his shoulder, and I thought that that first kind touch was the goal, the inevitable purpose of all her rage, repeated endlessly over twenty-eight years of embarrassment and quarrel.
>
> "Look, you'd better go," she said to us. "He talks too much and then he's ashamed and then he's tired."

Second, Mrs. Packer arouses sympathy by her talent for characterization. In Uncle Maurice she has created an interesting, possibly memorable, character. Callous, self-righteous, aggressive, and hopelessly opinionated, he challenges most of our notions of what constitutes sympathy. Yet, confused, defensive, and candid as he is, he invites it; but, as his response to his wife's overtures of tenderness reveals, he flatly rejects it. Long after we finish reading the story, we can still feel Uncle Maurice attacking everyone around him (and, by implication, ourselves as readers); yet we can also sense how unhappy this embittered man is, especially when he has the occasion to honestly judge himself. Even after Aunt Sarah, as revealed in the passage quoted from the story, treats him gently, Uncle Maurice can't stop: "he seemed to be mustering strength for a final attack of words." And this remark by his niece is right, for his "attack" shows the best and worst of him:

> "You paid your call from duty. Next time come to visit. No chicken sandwiches, we'll have gefilte fish. We're Jews, nothing more, nothing less, and proud of it. Accept us or not, we don't care. I'm not prejudiced. Who am I to judge my nephew and his wife? Judge yourself, but who can do that? We see people looking at us is how we judge ourselves. You think I'm looking at you but I'm not. I look only at the son of my friend and I smile at you as he smiled at me. You didn't choose easy to be William, but remember Jerusalem. There I go, talking too much. But I'm not going to cut out my tongue if nobody likes me talking. Not my wife, not my nephew, not the shiksa."

Considering how effectively this speech reveals Maurice's conflicts, we might feel that it is enough to account for interesting and fascinating characters in a story. But this is not so because the basis for interesting characters, like interesting stories, may be very different.

One obvious difference is between what are often called *static* characters and *developing* characters. By static we mean those who remain unchanged regardless of what happens in the story. J. F. Powers' "The Valiant Woman" provides a fine example of such a character in the person of Mrs. Stoner, the housekeeper for the kindly, patient Father Firman. Though Father Firman may be the head of his parish, he simply has no control over his housekeeper. She takes ferocious pleasure in beating him at bridge every night, insulting his guests, and complaining about her miserable life. Like a broken phonograph record, she repeats the same sound over and over. Because Mrs. Stoner is so rigid and stupid, the story is touching, for Father Firman is too kind and stoical to fire her. Instead, like one of the Wife of Bath's long-suffering husbands, he simply endures her. On the other hand, the main character in Chekhov's "Rothschild's Fiddle" changes noticeably. He does so because of the stunning impact which his wife's illness and subsequent death make upon him. Yakov, the main character, is a skilled coffin maker and a talented amateur violinist. But his talents seem meaningless to him because he has lived a hard, grubby life and has shown little, if any, feeling for his wife. As Yakov takes his mortally ill wife to a doctor who treats her as though she were an animal, Yakov realizes that for years he had treated his wife even more shabbily. After her death, Yakov begins to realize how empty his life has been. For almost the first time he experiences feelings of love and joy, particularly in playing his violin. It is true that playing his violin and bequeathing it (before his death) to another musician (whom previously he had treated badly) represent the only overt change Yakov exhibits. Yet paradoxically this very fact emphasizes how much Yakov has changed *inwardly* because now he no longer cares what others think. For the first time, as he is dying, he has begun to live, but only he knows this, yet that is all that is necessary.

A second difference is between *realistic* and *nonrealistic* characters. By realistic we generally mean those who remind us of ordinary people in ordinary life. Such characters may be interesting because they reveal ordinary people so much more clearly and dramatically than may possibly be true in life itself, where we have only confused impressions. Or, such characters may be interesting just because of the way their environment registers its impact upon them. Flannery O'Connor's "Revelation" presents a group of small-town Southerners gossiping away in a hot, stuffy doctor's waiting room. By means of this situation, Miss O'Connor forcefully reveals just how such people can unwittingly be prejudiced and in such different ways. Yet, these characters are not mean or depraved, nor conversely are they really, underneath, tenderhearted and well-meaning. The truth is that they are confused and provincial. Through their interaction, Miss O'Connor makes their drabness and ignorance interesting and disturbing. Moreover, by the contrast in attitudes of the lower middle class, the middle middle class, and the Black day laborers, she pointedly reveals how economic and social position do affect character.

On the other hand, characters may be interesting because they are *not* like ordinary people. Instead, as is true of the old grandmother in "Tell Me A Riddle," they may seem like larger than life figures. This is so because characters like the grandmother have had so much more life experience than most people and react vigorously and critically to that experience. Such characters, whom we call *representational,* show us what are some of the possibilities of human nature, even if these are seldom realized. But there are other ways in which literary characters may be radically different from ordinary people. There can be characters who personify particular attitudes or values. In this respect they may seem limited, even one dimensional, for virtually the entire personality consists of this one trait. Yet a distinct advantage results because it is possible to see how many ramifications such a trait may have and how it may dominate a person's existence.

D. H. Lawrence's "Two Blue Birds" portrays a very strange relationship involving a successful novelist, his proud beautiful wife, and his apparently selfless secretary. Though husband and wife insist they love each other, they live apart most of the year; the wife has a villa in southern France where she has affairs with other men (though all the time she is ostensibly thinking of her husband). He, on the other hand, lives farther north in the country, where he spends his time assiduously dictating his novels to his secretary who, along with her mother and sister, cater to his every whim. Only during the summer does the wife grace her husband with her presence. While the three main characters are distinct, they are virtually one dimensional for they represent variations in vanity and cruelty. Through such rigorous limitation Lawrence sacrifices the depth of three or even two dimensional characters. But in doing so he is able to show how powerful and complex these emotions really are. If *all* is not vanity in the story, certainly Lawrence shows us how much of a person's emotional life it can determine.

Yet if interesting characters can vary greatly, still there are some features that they have in common and that are best examined by our looking again at Uncle Maurice.

In the first place, Uncle Maurice is brought vividly before us as a presence; and, as a character in Pinter's *The Birthday Party* remarks, "What a presence!" The very first paragraph of the story brings him to life:

> Uncle Moshe-Morris-Maurice was sitting on the sofa with his feet flat on the floor and his hands lightly on his knees. He gave the impression of having waited for us in that pose for a long and trying time. Plump and nervous, he was like a bumblebee poised on a sofa.

The last sentence in particular suggests at once how menacing he is, and yet how small. In addition, we can see in the first two sentences that he is like an actor waiting for his cue, a good actor, since he is so well prepared. But we also see that posing isn't easy for him, so that we realize how difficult his role is. While the word play on his name does not constitute physical detail, it corroborates the rest. Is he Jewish Moshe or would-be Gentile Maurice? Or both? Or neither?

Besides the physical presence of a character, there needs to be a rationale for what he does, some pattern of behavior. The rationale or pattern may not appear to the character himself and it may not be spelled out explicitly by the author; but it will be apparent to the reader. This does not mean that characters must act consistently. Often their very inconsistency is a significant part of their nature. There may be, in short, a rationale of contradiction—as again with Moshe-Maurice.

Given Uncle Maurice's position as a younger brother who wished to emulate an older one who did manage to free himself from the Polish ghetto, we can understand why he has such conflicting feelings about his Jewishness. And since he himself failed to escape and was personally so unappealing, we can understand his bitterness toward fellow Jews who have remained in the ghetto as well as toward those who have escaped. Besides family and environment, there is the added difficulty in his marriage. As he points out, a person with his nature and background needed a wife who was meek and quiet. But Aunt Sarah is aggressive and even unrelenting, so that he has to defend himself against her as well. Yet precisely what he fails to realize is how much he wants Aunt Sarah's love, while he stubbornly resists it.

Finally, Maurice, like a majority of interesting characters, exists, both as an individual and as a type. Or, as Robert Scholes suggests in his handbook, *Elements of Fiction*, as a character he embodies two distinct yet related creative impulses.[2] One is that which particularizes: Maurice is an individual with a stance and personality all his own. In any group of Jews he might stand out because he is garrulous, confused, and compulsive in acting out his unresolved identity conflict; and also, as his last speech reveals, because he is so theatrical and articulate, even when he doesn't understand what he says.

[2] Robert Scholes, *Elements of Fiction* (New York: Oxford University Press, 1968), pp. 19–20.

The other impulse is that which generalizes. Because he is Moshe-Morris-Maurice, his ambivalent feelings about Jewishness are representative of many who have identity conflicts. What is more, despite all his willfulness, he realizes that his is not a pointless life, but that his very failures represent an effort to confront basic forces which others who are persecuted simply ignore. For these reasons he assumes a significance larger than himself. If he is not the prophetic figure he sometimes envisages himself to be, he is also *not* just "a bumblebee perched on a sofa."

Besides the reasons already given for enjoying short stories, we would add three others, two of which we have already discussed briefly. One is *setting*—the environment, locale, or milieu in which the action takes place. In some stories the setting may justifiably be sketchy because it plays only a minor role. But in "The Guest," by Albert Camus, the setting—a hard and isolated mountainous region of Algeria—is as important to the total effect of the story as the dilemma of the main character, Daru. In fact part of our understanding of Daru's problems and of his feelings and actions arises from our awareness of the landscape in which he chooses to act and live. The snow, the rocks, the desolation, and the isolation help to define Daru's conflicting attitudes towards his fellow men. At first there is his consciousness of his superiority to others as he lives alone in his schoolhouse, closed because of a snow storm. But the arrival of a gendarme with an Arab prisoner forces a different perspective on his isolation and his relations with others, for he is obliged to assume responsibility for sheltering the prisioner over night and for getting him to the authorities in a town beyond the mountains. Alone at night with the prisoner Daru attempts to withdraw into himself, to remain aloof from the Arab. But as he watches the sleeping Arab he feels that "it bothered him . . . by imposing on him a sort of brotherhood he knew well but refused to accept in the present circumstances."

Daru's apprehensions are well grounded because as he watches the sleeping prisoner he begins to sympathize with him. Then, at the climax of the story, Daru acts out a curious and ambiguous scene with the Arab, and we become aware of them as two small creatures in an immense and rocky landscape. At the end of the story we read: "Daru looked at the sky, the plateau, and, beyond, the invisible lands stretching all the way to the sea. In this vast landscape he had loved so much he was alone." The little room in the schoolhouse and the "vast landscape" are insistently presented to us, and this setting becomes a vital and inseparable part of the story's perpective on the ideal of human brotherhood.

The second is *style*—the kinds of feeling or the controlling attitudes toward his material that the narrator expresses through his descriptive detail and comment. Lawrence Sargent Hall's "The Ledge" owes much of its impact to the suggestive detail and the subtle comments about the main character that the author presents. The story describes the brave but futile efforts of a proud, self-reliant Maine fisherman to save the lives of his son and his nephew, whom he has taken duck hunting with him on Christmas Day. The expedition begins auspiciously but ends tragically. With an unexpected storm coming up and the tide coming in, and no other persons in the vicinity to rescue the party, all three hunters seem doomed. "Nevertheless, the fisherman plants himself in the water, orders his son to climb on his shoulders, and gets the boy to agree that when the water reaches him, he will take his chances by swimming." Proud of the boys because they react courageously and reveal their affection for him, the fisherman prepares for his death, determined to remain alert and self-controlled to the end. As the fisherman stands in the freezing water, knowing that he is losing all sensation, the author makes him into a tragic figure by his selection of descriptive detail and his restrained admiration for the doomed man:

> Freezing seas swept by, flooding inexorably up and up as the earth sank away imperceptibly beneath them. The boy called out once to his cousin. There was no answer. The fisherman, marvelling on a terror without voice, was dumbly glad when the boy did not call again. His own boots were long full of water. With no sensation left in his straddling legs he dared not move them. So long as the seas came sidewise against his hips, and then sidewise against his shoulders, he might balance—no telling how long. The upper half of him was what felt frozen. His legs, disengaged from his nerves and his will, he came to regard quite scientifically. They were the absurd, precarious axis around which reeled the surged universal tumult. The waves would come on and on; he could not visualize how many tossing reinforcements lurked in the night beyond—inexhaustible numbers, and he wept in supernatural fury at each

because it was higher, till he transcended hate and took them, swaying like a convert, one by one as they lunged against him and away aimlessly into their own undisputed, wild realm.

This passage, near the end of "The Ledge," invests a simple scene with uncommon grandeur. At the same time the contrast between the fisherman's legs and his "supernatural fury," on the one hand, and the violence of the water, on the other, is a climactic variation on a pattern working throughout the story. In responding to this pattern we are perceiving the third of these sources of enjoyment in stories, that part of the whole meaning we call the *theme*. By theme we mean, first of all, the subject matter. This may be—as the organization of our book indicates—such topics as innocence, love, marriage, or war. Without being aware of the subject (or subjects) about which an author is writing, it is difficult to say anything at all about the meaning of a story. On the other hand, if all we can say about Harris Downey's "The Hunters," Ambrose Bierce's "Chickamauga," or Isaac Babel's "Crossing Into Poland" is that they deal with war, we have said precious little. Even if we go further and say that all three stories show how much suffering war brings, we are still talking in general terms. We have not suggested what might be unique to each story. To suggest this uniqueness, we need to consider theme as embodying the particular implications or ramifications of the subject that the author concentrates on and the attitudes toward human nature or human experience with which he explores his subject or which underlie his treatment of his subject.

Both Luigi Pirandello's "War" and Isaac Rosenfeld's "The Brigadier," for example, concern themselves with the confusion and suffering that war brings about. Moreover, they resemble each other more closely than do many other war stories (which also deal with suffering and confusion) because both reveal how contradictory human behavior is and how little human beings understand themselves. Yet each has its special vision of contradiction and bewilderment.

In Rosenfeld's story a general recounts to us his incredibly persistent efforts to find some way to shorten a long, confusing, and destructive war whose end seems nowhere in sight. The war has been going on so long that the general has risen all the way from private to his present position, and the war is so confusing that neither side has any idea where the battle lines are or who is winning. Disturbed by these conditions, the general believes that if only he understood the enemy in his true nature he could fight him more effectively. In his logical and thorough manner, the brigadier first reads widely all the available histories of the enemy. Then he interrogates enemy prisoners, lives with some of them himself at close quarters, and even comes to regard one as a close personal friend. When he realizes that the enemy and his own forces have much in common, the brigadier begins to study himself intently so that he won't confuse the enemy with himself.

From what we have mentioned so far, we might consider the general at most as a determined and naïve idealist. But when we look more closely, we see how dangerously the general abuses his intelligence. In studying the enemy, he is firmly convinced that he can discover his essence. So he begins analyzing the enemy as though the enemy were a quantity or an abstraction. But as he sees the enemy wounded in the hospitals, he realizes that the enemy really differs very little from himself. Instead, however, of concluding that both sides are merely helpless human beings, he now feels more impelled than ever to track down the differences, *however narrow*, which constitute the essence of his side and theirs. When the enemy fail to reveal these differences, he orders them all killed and prides himself on having been so thorough. By the end of the story, though with no one paying any attention to him, and as far from his solution as ever, he still retains his heady confidence and even his joy in his work!

Whereas Rosenfeld's story takes place in a war remote in time and place, Pirandello's occurs in an all too well known war and in an everyday setting. In a second-class compartment on a small Italian local train traveling north from Rome during World War I, a group of middle-aged people are trying to pass the long night hours in conversation. Since all of the passengers have children fighting in the war, parental concern dominates their conversation, or, we should say, their arguments, since all speak as though they were presenting legal briefs. And what briefs! Not only do their ideas contradict one another, but the passengers' actions completely undercut what they are saying.

For example, one of the main characters is an old man who

(as Pirandello reveals through descriptive imagery) is in great physical distress. Yet the old man argues eloquently that parents have no right to concern themselves with their children's suffering. Instead, children have a right to live their lives as they choose, which is just as natural as it is for people to eat, or defend their native country. Since someone has to defend the native land, and since many young people have chosen to go to war for that purpose, parents should appreciate the fact that their children have chosen freely and even can enjoy what they have done. As the old man points out, his own son, just before his death, wrote to let him know he had no regrets about dying. For this reason, the old man does not mourn his son's death. Yet it never dawns on the old man that his analogies may have been specious, that his son was simply a blind patriot, or that his own feelings for his son matter. Even more pathetic, the old man doesn't realize that his eloquence and verbal assurance completely belie his physical misery. When an old woman sitting nearby asks him in astonishment, is it true that his son has died, the old man begins to weep hysterically. He breaks down because only now can he confront his feelings about his son's death. Until this moment he has lived a kind of schizophrenic existence in which his intellect and feelings were divorced from each other.

While both stories reveal how self-centered and irrational people can be, striking differences exist. Pirandello's characters at first glance seem more irrational and helpless than does the general, but they at least have deep feelings which they ultimately confront. Moreover, for all their egocentrism, they try to empathize with others and share their grief. As their reasoned arguments become more ridiculous, their shared suffering affirms their common humanity. In contrast, Rosenfeld's general, who understands much more of human nature than these bewildered parents, uses his knowledge only to isolate himself more and more from his fellowmen and even his own better self. By the end of the story, he becomes a sophisticated version of Adolf Eichmann, with a fantastic talent for self deception and moral confusion. His last comments show how blind he is:

> To know the enemy! It is the whole purpose and nature of our war, its ultimate meaning, its glory and its greatness. Already

I have succeeded in my own character, for I have become my task in my whole being. Nothing comes between me and the work I do. I have triumphed in my character and in my person, but I must still triumph over the enemy. Sometimes I see his armies standing before me, clearly revealed in their dark, powerful mass, and I rush out of the schoolhouse, out of our office, and I feel that in a moment, but one moment more, I will know the truth. And when I hear our gunfire from the front that winds around us in all directions, I know that if my faith is only great enough, the knowledge will come to me and I will win.

The point, however, is not that one story is better than the other, but that each writer presents *different facets* of war and human nature, and does so *concretely* and *comprehensively*. Anton Chekhov, the great modern Russian writer, in one of his letters, illuminates for us what theme really means in works of fiction:

Moscow, October 27, 1888

In conversation with my literary colleagues I always insist that it is not the artist's business to solve problems that require a specialist's knowledge. It is a bad thing if a writer tackles a subject he does not understand. We have specialists for dealing with special questions: it is their business to judge of the commune, of the future, of capitalism, of the evils of drunkenness, of boots, of the diseases of women. An artist must judge only of what he understands, his field is just as limited as that of any other specialist—I repeat this and insist on it always. That in his sphere there are no questions, but only answers, can be maintained only by those who have never written and have had no experience of thinking in images. An artist observes, selects, guesses, combines—and this in itself presupposes a problem: unless he had set himself a problem from the very first there would be nothing to conjecture and nothing to select. To put it briefly, I will end by using the language of psychiatry: if one denies that creative work involves problems and purposes, one must admit that an artist creates without premeditation or intention, in a state of aberration; therefore, if an author boasted to me of having written a novel without a preconceived design, under a sudden inspiration, I should call him mad.

You are right in demanding that an artist should take an intelligent attitude to his work, but you confuse two things: *solving a problem and stating a problem correctly*. It is only the second that is obligatory for the artist. In "Anna Karenina" and "Evgeni Onegin" not a single problem is solved, but they satisfy you completely because all the problems in these works are correctly stated. It is the business of the judge to put the right questions, but the answers must be given by the jury according to their own lights.

"No I am not Prince Hamlet nor was meant to be—" sighs T. S. Eliot's J. Alfred Prufrock, painfully aware of his own limitations. Similarly, we as readers are not Chekhov. Yet we can, if we respond openly and thoughtfully to an author's work, participate in the life he has created. The life we read about is not our own, but it makes ours richer through our sympathetic involvement.*

* We suggest that you now read the author's comments that follow Flannery O'Connor's "Revelation," R. V. Cassill's "Fracture," Thomas Churchill's "The Home Stretch," Nancy Huddleston Packer's "Oh Jerusalem," Joyce Carol Oates' "In the Region of Ice," Harris Downey's "The Hunters," Doris Lessing's "The Black Madonna," and Jordon Pecile's "A Piece of Polenta." Our gratitude to the last seven for sending us their comments is great.

I

WHAT WAS INNOCENCE?

Oh   as I was young   and easy in the mercy of his means,
       Time held me green and dying
Though I sang in my chains like the sea.

                DYLAN THOMAS
                "Fern Hill"

She's fifteen—going on thirty.

                ANONYMOUS

Speak roughly to your little boy,
And beat him when he sneezes:
He does it only to annoy,
Because he knows it teases.

                LEWIS CARROLL
                Alice in Wonderland

The innocents are so few that two of them seldom meet—
when they do meet, their victims lie strewn all around.

    ELIZABETH BOWEN
    The Death of the Heart

The great thing about innocence is that you *can* lose it.

    ANONYMOUS

Innocence is like a dumb leper who has lost his bell, wandering the world, meaning no harm. . . . Innocence is a kind of insanity.

    GRAHAM GREENE
    The Quiet American

  Though nothing can bring back the hour
Of splendor in the grass, of glory in the flower.

    WILLIAM WORDSWORTH
    "Intimations Ode"

James Joyce

An Encounter[*]

IT WAS JOE DILLON who introduced the Wild West to us. He had a little library made up of old numbers of *The Union Jack, Pluck* and *The Halfpenny Marvel*. Every evening after school we met in his back garden and arranged Indian battles. He and his fat young brother Leo, the idler, held the loft of the stable while we tried to carry it by storm; or we fought a pitched battle on the grass. But, however well we fought, we never won siege or battle and all our bouts ended with Joe Dillon's war dance of victory. His parents went to eight-o'clock mass every morning in Gardiner Street and the peaceful odour of Mrs. Dillon was prevalent in the hall of the house. But he played too fiercely for us who were younger and more timid. He looked like some kind of an Indian when he capered round the garden, an old tea-cosy on his head, beating a tin with his fist and yelling:

[*] From DUBLINERS by James Joyce. Originally published by B. W. Huebsch, Inc., in 1916. Copyright © 1967 by the Estate of James Joyce. All rights reserved. Published by permission of The Viking Press, Inc.

23

"Ya! yaka, yaka, yaka!"

Everyone was incredulous when it was reported that he had a vocation for the priesthood. Nevertheless it was true.

A spirit of unruliness diffused itself among us and, under its influence, differences of culture and constitution were waived. We banded ourselves together, some boldly, some in jest and some almost in fear: and of the number of these latter, the reluctant Indians who were afraid to seem studious or lacking in robustness, I was one. The adventures related in the literature of the Wild West were remote from my nature but, at least, they opened doors of escape. I liked better some American detective stories which were traversed from time to time by unkempt fierce and beautiful girls. Though there was nothing wrong in these stories and though their intention was sometimes literary they were circulated secretly at school. One day when Father Butler was hearing the four pages of Roman History clumsy Leo Dillon was discovered with a copy of *The Halfpenny Marvel*.

"This page or this page? This page? Now, Dillon, up! 'Hardly had the day' . . . Go on! What day? 'Hardly had the day dawned' . . . Have you studied it? What have you there in your pocket?"

Everyone's heart palpitated as Leo Dillon handed up the paper and everyone assumed an innocent face. Father Butler turned over the pages, frowning.

"What is this rubbish?" he said. *"The Apache Chief!* Is this what you read instead of studying your Roman History? Let me not find any more of this wretched stuff in this college. The man who wrote it, I suppose, was some wretched fellow who writes these things for a drink. I'm surprised at boys like you, educated, reading such stuff. I could understand it if you were . . . National School boys. Now, Dillon, I advise you strongly, get at your work or . . ."

This rebuke during the sober hours of school paled much of the glory of the Wild West for me and the confused puffy face of Leo Dillon awakened one of my consciences. But when the restraining influence of the school was at a distance I began to hunger again for wild sensations, for the escape which those chronicles of disorder alone seemed to offer me. The mimic warfare of the evening became at last as wearisome to me as the routine of school in the morning because I wanted real adventures to happen to myself. But real adventures, I reflected, do not happen to people who remain at home: they must be sought abroad.

The summer holidays were near at hand when I made up my mind to break out of the weariness of school-life for one day at least. With Leo Dillon and a boy named Mahony I planned a day's miching. Each of us saved up sixpence. We were to meet at ten in the morning on the Canal Bridge. Mahony's big sister was to write an excuse for him and Leo Dillon was to tell his brother to say he was sick. We arranged to go along the Wharf Road until we came to the ships, then to cross in the ferryboat and walk out to see the Pigeon House. Leo Dillon was afraid we might meet Father Butler or someone out of the college; but Mahony asked, very sensibly, what would Father Butler be doing out at the Pigeon House. We were reassured: and I brought the first stage of the plot to an end by collecting sixpence from the other two, at the same time showing them my own sixpence. When we were making the last arrangements on the eve we were all vaguely excited. We shook hands, laughing, and Mahony said:

"Till to-morrow, mates!"

That night I slept badly. In the morning I was first-comer to the bridge as I lived nearest. I hid my books in the long grass near the ashpit at the end of the garden where nobody ever came and hurried along the canal bank. It was a mild sunny morning in the first week of June. I sat up on the coping of the bridge admiring my frail canvas shoes which I had diligently pipeclayed overnight and watching the docile horses pulling a tramload of business people up the hill. All the branches of the tall trees which lined the mall were gay with little light green leaves and the sunlight slanted through them on to the water. The granite stone of the bridge was beginning to be warm and I began to pat it with my hands in time to an air in my head. I was very happy.

When I had been sitting there for five or ten minutes I saw Mahony's grey suit approaching. He came up the hill, smiling, and clambered up beside me on the bridge. While we were waiting he brought out the catapult which bulged from his inner pocket and explained some improvements which he had made in it. I asked him why he had brought it and he told me he had brought it to have some gas with the birds. Mahony used slang freely, and spoke of Father Butler as Old Bunser. We waited on for a quarter of an hour more but still there was no sign of Leo Dillon. Mahony, at last, jumpod down and said:

"Come along. I knew Fatty'd funk it."

"And his sixpence . . . ?" I said.

"That's forfeit," said Mahony. "And so much the better for us—a bob and a tanner instead of a bob."

We walked along the North Strand Road till we came to the Vitriol Works and then turned to the right along the Wharf Road. Mahony began to play the Indian as soon as we were out of public sight. He chased a crowd of ragged girls, brandishing his unloaded catapult and, when two ragged boys began, out of chivalry, to fling stones at us, he proposed that we should charge them. I objected that the boys were too small, and so we walked on, the ragged troop screaming after us: "*Swaddlers! Swaddlers!*" thinking that we were Protestants because Mahony, who was dark-complexioned, wore the silver badge of a cricket club in his cap. When we came to the Smoothing Iron we arranged a siege; but it was a failure because you must have at least three. We revenged ourselves on Leo Dillon by saying what a funk he was and guessing how many he would get at three o'clock from Mr. Ryan.

We came then near the river. We spent a long time walking about the noisy streets flanked by high stone walls, watching the working of cranes and engines and often being shouted at for our immobility by the drivers of groaning carts. It was noon when we reached the quays and, as all the labourers seemed to be eating their lunches, we bought two big currant buns and sat down to eat them on some metal piping beside the river. We pleased ourselves with the spectacle of Dublin's commerce—the barges signalled from far away by their curls of woolly smoke, the brown fishing fleet beyond Ringsend, the big white sailing-vessel which was being discharged on the opposite quay. Mahony said it would be right skit to run away to sea on one of those big ships and even I, looking at the high masts, saw, or imagined, the geography which had been scantily dosed to me at school gradually taking substance under my eyes. School and home seemed to recede from us and their influences upon us seemed to wane.

We crossed the Liffey in the ferryboat, paying our toll to be transported in the company of two labourers and a little Jew with a bag. We were serious to the point of solemnity, but once during the short voyage our eyes met and we laughed. When we landed we watched the discharging of the graceful three-master which we had observed from the other quay. Some bystanders said that she was a Norwegian vessel. I went to the stern and tried to decipher the legend upon it but, failing to do so, I came back and examined the foreign sailors to see had any of them green eyes for I had some confused notion. . . . The sailors' eyes were blue and grey and even black. The only sailor whose eyes could have been called green was a tall man who amused the crowd on the quay by calling out cheerfully every time the planks fell:

"All right! All right!"

When we were tired of this sight we wandered slowly into Ringsend. The day had grown sultry, and in the windows of the grocers' shops musty biscuits lay bleaching. We bought some biscuits and chocolate which we ate sedulously as we wandered through the squalid streets where the families of the fishermen live. We could find no dairy and so we went into a huckster's shop and bought a bottle of raspberry lemonade each. Refreshed by this, Mahony chased a cat down a lane, but the cat escaped into a wide field. We both felt rather tired and when we reached the field we made at once for a sloping bank over the ridge of which we could see the Dodder.

It was too late and we were too tired to carry out our project of visiting the Pigeon House. We had to be home before four o'clock lest our adventure should be discovered. Mahony looked regretfully at his catapult and I had to suggest going home by train before he regained any cheerfulness. The sun went in behind some clouds and left us to our jaded thoughts and the crumbs of our provisions.

There was nobody but ourselves in the field. When we had lain on the bank for some time without speaking I saw a man approaching from the far end of the field. I watched him lazily as I chewed one of those green stems on which girls tell fortunes. He came along by the band slowly. He walked with one hand upon his hip and in the other hand he held a stick with which he tapped the turf lightly. He was shabbily dressed in a suit of greenish-black and wore what we used to call a jerry hat with a high crown. He seemed to be fairly old for his moustache was ashen-grey. When he passed at our feet he glanced up at us quickly and then continued his way. We followed him with our eyes and saw that when he had gone on for perhaps fifty paces he turned about and began to retrace his steps. He walked towards us very slowly, always tapping the ground with his stick, so slowly that I thought he was looking for something in the grass.

He stopped when he came level with us and bade us good-day. We answered him and he sat down beside us on the slope slowly and with great care. He began to talk of the weather, saying that it would be a very hot summer and adding that the seasons had changed greatly since he was a boy—a long time ago. He said that the happiest time of one's life was undoubtedly one's schoolboy days and that he would give anything to be young again. While he expressed these sentiments which bored us a little we kept silent. Then he began to talk of school and of books. He asked us whether we had read the poetry of Thomas Moore or the works of Sir Walter Scott and Lord Lytton. I pretended that I had read every book he mentioned so that in the end he said:

"Ah, I can see you are a bookworm like myself. Now," he added, pointing to Mahony who was regarding us with open eyes, "he is different; he goes in for games."

He said he had all Sir Walter Scott's works and all Lord Lytton's works at home and never tired of reading them. "Of course," he said, "there were some of Lord Lytton's works which boys couldn't read." Mahony asked why couldn't boys read them—a question which agitated and pained me because I was afraid the man would think I was as stupid as Mahony. The man, however, only smiled. I saw that he had great gaps in his mouth between his yellow teeth. Then he asked us which of us had the most sweethearts. Mahony mentioned lightly that he had three totties. The man asked me how many I had. I answered that I had none. He did not believe me and said he was sure I must have one. I was silent.

"Tell us," said Mahony pertly to the man, "how many have you yourself?"

The man smiled as before and said that when he was our age he had lots of sweethearts.

"Every boy," he said, "has a little sweetheart."

His attitude on this point struck me as strangely liberal in a man of his age. In my heart I thought that what he said about boys and sweethearts was reasonable. But I disliked the words in his mouth and I wondered why he shivered once or twice as if he feared something or felt a sudden chill. As he proceeded I noticed that his accent was good. He began to speak to us about girls, saying what nice soft hair they had and how soft their hands were and how all girls were not so good as they seemed to be if one only knew. There was nothing he liked, he said, so much as looking at a nice young girl, at her nice white hands and her beautiful soft hair. He gave me the impression that he was repeating something which he had learned by heart or that, magnetised by some words of his own speech, his mind was slowly circling round and round in the same orbit. At times he spoke as if he were simply alluding to some fact that everybody knew, and at other times he lowered his voice and spoke mysteriously as if he were telling us something secret which he did not wish others to overhear. He repeated his phrases over and over again, varying them and surrounding them with his monotonous voice. I continued to gaze towards the foot of the slope, listening to him.

After a long while his monologue paused. He stood up slowly, saying that he had to leave us for a minute or so, a few minutes, and, without changing the direction of my gaze, I saw him walking slowly away from us towards the near end of the field. We remained silent when he had gone. After a silence of a few minutes I heard Mahony exclaim:

"I say! Look what he's doing!"

As I neither answered nor raised my eyes Mahony exclaimed again:

"I say . . . He's a queer old josser!"

"In case he asks us for our names," I said, "let you be Murphy and I'll be Smith."

We said nothing further to each other. I was still considering whether I would go away or not when the man came back and sat down beside us again. Hardly had he sat down when Mahony, catching sight of the cat which had escaped him, sprang up and pursued her across the field. The man and I watched the chase. The cat escaped once more and Mahony began to throw stones at the wall she had escaladed. Desisting from this, he began to wander about the far end of the field, aimlessly.

After an interval the man spoke to me. He said that my friend was a very rough boy and asked did he get whipped often at school. I was going to reply indignantly that we were not National School boys to be whipped, as he called it; but I remained silent. He began to speak on the subject of chastising boys. His mind, as if magnetised again by his speech, seemed to circle slowly round and round its new centre. He said that when boys were that kind they ought to be whipped and well whipped. When a boy was rough and unruly there was nothing would do him any good but a good sound whipping. A slap on the hand or a box on the ear was no good: what he wanted was to get a nice warm whipping. I was surprised at this sentiment and involuntarily glanced up at his face. As I did so I met the gaze of a pair of bottle-green eyes peering at me from under a twitching forehead. I turned my eyes away again.

The man continued his monologue. He seemed to have forgotten his recent liberalism. He said that if ever he found a boy talking to girls or having a girl for a sweetheart he would whip him and whip him; and that would teach him not to be talking to girls. And if a boy had a girl for a sweetheart and told lies about it then he would give him such a whipping as no boy ever got in this world. He said that there was nothing in this world he would like so well as that. He described to me how he would whip such a boy as if he were unfolding some elaborate mystery. He would love that, he said, better than anything in this world; and his voice, as he led me monotonously through the mystery, grew almost affectionate and seemed to plead with me that I should understand him.

I waited till his monologue paused again. Then I stood up abruptly. Lest I should betray my agitation I delayed a few moments pretending to fix my shoe properly and then, saying that I was obliged to go, I bade him good-day. I went up the slope calmly but my heart was beating quickly with fear that he would seize me by the ankles. When I reached the top of the slope I turned round and, without looking at him, called loudly across the field:

"Murphy!"

My voice had an accent of forced bravery in it and I was ashamed of my paltry stratagem. I had to call the name again before Mahony saw me and hallooed in answer. How my heart beat as he came running across the field to me! He ran as if to bring me aid. And I was penitent; for in my heart I had always despised him a little.

Frank O'Connor

First Confession*

ALL THE TROUBLE BEGAN when my grandfather died and my grandmother—my father's mother—came to live with us. Relations in the one house are a strain at the best of times, but, to make matters worse, my grandmother was a real old countrywoman and quite unsuited to the life in town. She had a fat, wrinkled old face, and, to Mother's great indignation, went round the house in bare feet— the boots had her crippled, she said. For dinner she had a jug of porter and a pot of potatoes with—sometimes—a bit of salt fish, and she poured out the potatoes on the table and ate them slowly, with great relish, using her fingers by way of a fork.

Now, girls are supposed to be fastidious, but I was the one who suffered most from this. Nora, my sister, just sucked up to the old woman for the penny she got every Friday out of the old-age pension, a thing I could not do. I was too honest, that was my trouble; and when I was playing with Bill Connell, the sergeant-

* Copyright 1951 by Frank O'Connor. Reprinted from THE STORIES OF FRANK O'CONNOR by permission of Alfred A. Knopf, Inc.

31

major's son, and saw my grandmother steering up the path with the jug of porter sticking out from beneath her shawl I was mortified. I made excuses not to let him come into the house, because I could never be sure what she would be up to when we went in.

When Mother was at work and my grandmother made the dinner I wouldn't touch it. Nora once tried to make me, but I hid under the table from her and took the bread-knife with me for protection. Nora let on to be very indignant (she wasn't, of course, but she knew Mother saw through her, so she sided with Gran) and came after me. I lashed out at her with the bread-knife, and after that she left me alone. I stayed there till Mother came in from work and made my dinner, but when Father came in later Nora said in a shocked voice: "Oh, Dadda, do you know what Jackie did at dinner-time?" Then, of course, it all came out; Father gave me a flaking; Mother interfered, and for days after that he didn't speak to me and Mother barely spoke to Nora. And all because of that old woman! God knows, I was heart-scalded.

Then, to crown my misfortunes, I had to make my first confession and communion. It was an old woman called Ryan who prepared us for these. She was about the one age with Gran; she was well-to-do, lived in a big house on Montenotte, wore a black cloak and bonnet, and came every day to school at three o'clock when we should have been going home, and talked to us of hell. She may have mentioned the other place as well, but that could only have been by accident, for hell had the first place in her heart.

She lit a candle, took out a new half-crown, and offered it to the first boy who would hold one finger—only one finger!—in the flame for five minutes by the school clock. Being always very ambitious I was tempted to volunteer, but I thought it might look greedy. Then she asked were we afraid of holding one finger—only one finger!—in a little candle flame for five minutes and not afraid of burning all over in roasting hot furnaces for all eternity. "All eternity! Just think of that! A whole lifetime goes by and it's nothing, not even a drop in the ocean of your sufferings." The woman was really interesting about hell, but my attention was all fixed on the half-crown. At the end of the lesson she put it back in her purse. It was a great disappointment; a religious woman like that, you wouldn't think she'd bother about a thing like a half-crown.

Another day she said she knew a priest who woke one night to find a fellow he didn't recognize leaning over the end of his bed. The priest was a bit frightened—naturally enough—but he asked the fellow what he wanted, and the fellow said in a deep, husky voice that he wanted to go to confession. The priest said it was an awkward time and wouldn't it do in the morning, but the fellow said that the last time he went to confession, there was one sin he kept back, being ashamed to mention it, and now it was always on his mind. Then the priest knew it was a bad case, because the fellow was after making a bad confession and committing a mortal sin. He got up to dress, and just then the cock crew in the yard outside, and—lo and behold!—when the priest looked round there was no sign of the fellow, only a smell of burning timber, and when the priest looked at his bed didn't he see the print of two hands burned in it? That was because the fellow had made a bad confession. This story made a shocking impression on me.

But the worst of all was when she showed us how to examine our conscience. Did we take the name of the Lord, our God, in vain? Did we honour our father and our mother? (I asked her did this include grandmothers and she said it did.) Did we love our neighbours as ourselves? Did we covet our neighbour's goods? (I thought of the way I felt about the penny that Nora got every Friday.) I decided that, between one thing and another, I must have broken the whole ten commandments, all on account of that old woman, and so far as I could see, so long as she remained in the house I had no hope of ever doing anything else.

I was scared to death of confession. The day the whole class went I let on to have a toothache, hoping my absence wouldn't be noticed; but at three o'clock, just as I was feeling safe, along comes a chap with a message from Mrs. Ryan that I was to go to confession myself on Saturday and be at the chapel for communion with the rest. To make it worse, Mother couldn't come with me and sent Nora instead.

Now, that girl had ways of tormenting me that Mother never knew of. She held my hand as we went down the hill, smiling sadly and saying how sorry she was for me, as if she were bringing me to the hospital for an operation.

"Oh, God help us!" she moaned. "Isn't it a terrible pity you weren't a good boy? Oh, Jackie, my heart bleeds for you! How will you ever think of all your sins? Don't forget you have to tell him about the time you kicked Gran on the shin."

"Lemme go!" I said, trying to drag myself free of her. "I don't want to go to confession at all."

"But sure, you'll have to go to confession, Jackie," she replied in the same regretful tone. "Sure, if you didn't, the parish priest would be up to the house, looking for you. 'Tisn't, God knows, that I'm not sorry for you. Do you remember the time you tried to kill me with the bread-knife under the table? And the language you used to me? I don't know what he'll do with you at all, Jackie. He might have to send you up to the bishop."

I remember thinking bitterly that she didn't know the half of what I had to tell—if I told it. I knew I couldn't tell it, and understood perfectly why the fellow in Mrs. Ryan's story made a bad confession; it seemed to me a great shame that people wouldn't stop criticizing him. I remember that steep hill down to the church, and the sunlit hillsides beyond the valley of the river, which I saw in the gaps between the houses like Adam's last glimpse of Paradise.

Then, when she had manoeuvred me down the long flight of steps to the chapel yard, Nora suddenly changed her tone. She became the raging malicious devil she really was.

"There you are!" she said with a yelp of triumph, hurling me through the church door. "And I hope he'll give you the penitential psalms, you dirty little caffler."

I knew then I was lost, given up to eternal justice. The door with the coloured-glass panels swung shut behind me, the sunlight went out and gave place to deep shadow, and the wind whistled outside so that the silence within seemed to crackle like ice under my feet. Nora sat in front of me by the confession box. There were a couple of old women ahead of her, and then a miserable-looking poor devil came and wedged me in at the other side, so that I couldn't escape even if I had the courage. He joined his hands and rolled his eyes in the direction of the roof, muttering aspirations in an anguished tone, and I wondered had he a grandmother too. Only a grandmother could account for a fellow behaving in that heartbroken way, but he was better off than I, for he at least could go and confess his sins; while I would make a bad confession and then die in the night and be continually coming back and burning people's furniture.

Nora's turn came, and I heard the sound of something slamming, and then her voice as if butter wouldn't melt in her mouth, and then another slam, and out she came. God, the hypocrisy of women! Her eyes were lowered, her head was bowed, and her hands were joined very low down on her stomach, and she walked up the aisle to the side altar looking like a saint. You never saw such an exhibition of devotion; and I remembered the devilish malice with which she had tormented me all the way from our door, and wondered were all religious people like that, really. It was my turn now. With the fear of damnation in my soul I went in, and the confessional door closed of itself behind me.

It was pitch-dark and I couldn't see priest or anything else. Then I really began to be frightened. In the darkness it was a matter between God and me, and He had all the odds. He knew what my intentions were before I even started; I had no chance. All I had ever been told about confession got mixed up in my mind, and I knelt to one wall and said: "Bless me, father, for I have sinned; this is my first confession." I waited for a few minutes, but nothing happened, so I tried it on the other wall. Nothing happened there either. He had me spotted all right.

It must have been then that I noticed the shelf at about one height with my head. It was really a place for grown-up people to rest their elbows, but in my distracted state I thought it was probably the place you were supposed to kneel. Of course, it was on the high side and not very deep, but I was always good at climbing and managed to get up all right. Staying up was the trouble. There was room only for my knees, and nothing you could get a grip on but a sort of wooden moulding a bit above it. I held on to the moulding and repeated the words a little louder, and this time something happened all right. A slide was slammed back; a little light entered the box, and a man's voice said: "Who's there?"

"Tis me, father," I said for fear he mightn't see me and go away again. I couldn't see him at all. The place the voice came from was under the moulding, about level with my knees, so I took a good grip of the moulding and swung myself down till I saw the astonished face of a young priest looking up at me. He had to put his head on one side to see me, and I had to put mine on one side to see him, so we were more or less talking to one another upside-down. It struck me as a queer way of hearing confessions, but I didn't feel it my place to criticize.

"Bless me, father, for I have sinned; this is my first confession," I rattled off all in one breath, and swung myself down the least shade more to make it easier for him.

"What are you doing up there?" he shouted in an angry voice, and the strain the politeness was putting on my hold of the moulding, and the shock of being addressed in such an uncivil tone, were too much for me. I lost my grip, tumbled, and hit the door an unmerciful wallop before I found myself flat on my back in the middle of the aisle. The people who had been waiting stood up with their mouths open. The priest opened the door of the middle box and came out, pushing his biretta back from his forehead; he looked something terrible. Then Nora came scampering down the aisle.

"Oh, you dirty little caffler!" she said. "I might have known you'd do it. I might have known you'd disgrace me. I can't leave you out of my sight for one minute."

Before I could even get to my feet to defend myself she bent down and gave me a clip across the ear. This reminded me that I was so stunned I had even forgotten to cry, so that people might think I wasn't hurt at all, when in fact I was probably maimed for life. I gave a roar out of me.

"What's all this about?" the priest hissed, getting angrier than ever and pushing Nora off me. "How dare you hit the child like that, you little vixen?"

"But I can't do my penance with him, father," Nora cried, cocking an outraged eye up at him.

"Well, go and do it, or I'll give you some more to do," he said, giving me a hand up. "Was it coming to confession you were, my poor man?" he asked me.

"'Twas, father," said I with a sob.

"Oh," he said respectfully, "a big hefty fellow like you must have terrible sins. Is this your first?"

"'Tis, father," said I.

"Worse and worse," he said gloomily. "The crimes of a lifetime. I don't know will I get rid of you at all today. You'd better wait now till I'm finished with these old ones. You can see by the looks of them they haven't much to tell."

"I will, father," I said with something approaching joy.

The relief of it was really enormous. Nora stuck out her tongue at me from behind his back, but I couldn't even be bothered retorting. I knew from the very moment that man opened his mouth that he was intelligent above the ordinary. When I had time to think, I saw how right I was. It only stood to reason that a fellow confessing after seven years would have more to tell than people that went every week. The crimes of a lifetime, exactly as he said. It was only what he expected, and the rest was the cackle of old women and girls with their talk of hell, the bishop, and the penitential psalms. That was all they knew. I started to make my examination of conscience, and barring the one bad business of my grandmother it didn't seem so bad.

The next time, the priest steered me into the confession box himself and left the shutter back the way I could see him get in and sit down at the further side of the grille from me.

"Well, now," he said, "what do they call you?"

"Jackie, father," said I.

"And what's a-trouble to you, Jackie?"

"Father," I said, feeling I might as well get it over while I had him in good humour, "I had it all arranged to kill my grandmother."

He seemed a bit shaken by that, all right, because he said nothing for quite a while.

"My goodness," he said at last, "that'd be a shocking thing to do. What put that into your head?"

"Father," I said, feeling very sorry for myself, "she's an awful woman."

"Is she?" he asked. "What way is she awful?"

"She takes porter, father," I said, knowing well from the way Mother talked of it that this was a mortal sin, and hoping it would make the priest take a more favourable view of my case.

"Oh, my!" he said, and I could see he was impressed.

"And snuff, father," said I.

"That's a bad case, sure enough, Jackie," he said.

"And she goes round in her bare feet, father," I went on in a rush of self-pity, "and she knows I don't like her, and she gives pennies to Nora and none to me, and my da sides with her and flakes me, and one night I was so heart-scalded I made up my mind I'd have to kill her."

"And what would you do with the body?" he asked with great interest.

"I was thinking I could chop that up and carry it away in a barrow I have," I said.

"Begor, Jackie," he said, "do you know you're a terrible child?"

"I know, father," I said, for I was just thinking the same thing myself. "I tried to kill Nora too with a bread-knife under the table, only I missed her."

"Is that the little girl that was beating you just now?" he asked.

" 'Tis, father."

"Someone will go for her with a bread-knife one day, and he won't miss her," he said rather cryptically. "You must have great courage. Between ourselves, there's a lot of people I'd like to do the same to but I'd never have the nerve. Hanging is an awful death."

"Is it, father?" I asked with the deepest interest—I was always very keen on hanging. "Did you ever see a fellow hanged?"

"Dozens of them," he said solemnly. "And they all died roaring."

"Jay!" I said.

"Oh, a horrible death!" he said with great satisfaction. "Lots of the fellows I saw killed their grandmothers too, but they all said 'twas never worth it."

He had me there for a full ten minutes talking, and then walked out the chapel yard with me. I was genuinely sorry to part with him, because he was the most entertaining character I'd ever met in the religious line. Outside, after the shadow of the church, the sunlight was like the roaring of waves on a beach; it dazzled me; and when the frozen silence melted and I heard the screech of trams on the road my heart soared. I knew now I wouldn't die in the night and come back, leaving marks on my mother's furniture. It would be a great worry to her, and the poor soul had enough.

Nora was sitting on the railing, waiting for me, and she put on a very sour puss when she saw the priest with me. She was mad jealous because a priest had never come out of the church with her.

"Well," she asked coldly, after he left me, "what did he give you?"

"Three Hail Marys," I said.

"Three Hail Marys?" she repeated incredulously. "You mustn't have told him anything."

"I told him everything," I said confidently.

"About Gran and all?"

"About Gran and all."

(All she wanted was to be able to go home and say I'd made a bad confession.)

"Did you tell him you went for me with the bread-knife?" she asked with a frown.

"I did to be sure."

"And he only gave you three Hail Marys?"

"That's all."

She slowly got down from the railing with a baffled air. Clearly, this was beyond her. As we mounted the steps back to the main road she looked at me suspiciously.

"What are you sucking?" she asked.

"Bullseyes."

"Was it the priest gave them to you?"

" 'Twas."

"Lord God," she wailed bitterly, "some people have all the luck! 'Tis no advantage to anybody trying to be good. I might just as well be a sinner like you."

Elizabeth Bowen

A Queer Heart*

MRS. CADMAN GOT OUT OF THE BUS BACKWARDS. No amount of practice ever made her more agile; the trouble she had with her big bulk amused everyone, and herself. Gripping the handles each side of the bus door so tightly that the seams of her gloves cracked, she lowered herself cautiously, like a climber, while her feet, overlapping her smart shoes, uneasily scrabbled at each step. One or two people asked why the bus made, for one passenger, such a long, dead stop. But on the whole she was famous on this line, for she was constantly in and out of town. The conductor waited behind her, smiling, holding her basket, arms wide to catch her if she should slip.

Having got safe to the ground, Mrs. Cadman shook herself like a satisfied bird. She took back her shopping-basket from the conductor and gave him a smile instead. The big, kind, scarlet bus once more ground into movement, off up the main road hill: it

* From LOOK AT ALL THOSE ROSES by Elizabeth Bowen. Copyright 1941 and renewed 1969 by Elizabeth Bowen. Reprinted by permission of Alfred A. Knopf, Inc.

made a fading blur in the premature autumn dusk. Mrs. Cadman almost waved after it, for with it went the happy part of her day. She turned down the side road that led to her gate. A wet wind of autumn, smelling of sodden gardens, blew in her face and tilted her hat. Leaves whirled along it, and one lime leaf, as though imploring shelter, lodged in her fur collar. Every gust did more to sadden the poor trees. This was one of those roads outside growing provincial cities that still keep their rural mystery. They seem to lead into something still not known. Traffic roars past one end, but the other end is in silence: you see a wood, a spire, a haughty manor gate, or your view ends with the turn of an old wall. Here some new, raw-looking villas stood with spaces between them; in the spaces were orchards and market-gardens. A glass-house roof reflected the wet grey light; there was a shut chapel farther along. And, each standing back in half an acre of ground, there were two or three stucco houses with dark windows, sombre but at the same time ornate, built years ago in this then retired spot. Dead lime leaves showered over their grass plots and evergreens. Mrs. Cadman's house, Granville, was one of these: its name was engraved in scrolls over the porch. The solid house was not large, and Mrs. Cadman's daughter, Lucille, could look after it with a daily help.

The widow and her daughter lived here in the state of cheerless meekness Lucille considered suitable for them now. *Mr.* Cadman had liked to have everything done in style. But twelve years ago he had died, travelling on business, in an hotel up in the North. Always the gentleman, he had been glad to spare them this upset at home. He had been brought back to the Midlands for his impressive funeral, whose size showed him a popular man. How unlike Mr. Cadman was Rosa proving herself. One can be most unfriendly in one's way of dying. Ah, well, one chooses one's husband; one's sister is dealt out to one by fate.

Mrs. Cadman, thumb on the latch of her own gate, looked for a minute longer up and down the road—deeply, deeply unwilling to go in. She looked back at the corner where the bus had vanished, and an immense sigh heaved up her coat lapels and made a cotton carnation, pinned to the fur, brush a fold of her chin. Laced, hooked, buttoned so tightly into her clothes, she seemed to need to deflate herself by these sudden sighs, by yawns or by those explosions of laughter that often vexed Lucille. Through her face—embedded in fat but still very lively, as exposed, as ingenuous as a little girl's—you could see some emotional fermentation always at work in her. Her smiles were frequent, hopeful and quick. Her pitching walk was due to her tight shoes.

When she did go in she went in with a sort of rush. She let the door bank back on the hall wall, so that the chain rattled and an outraged clatter came from the letter-box. Immediately, she knew she had done wrong. Lucille, appalled, looked out of the dining-room. "*Shisssssh!* How can you, mother?" she said.

"Ever so sorry, dear," said Mrs. Cadman, cast down.

"She'd just dropped off," said Lucille. "After her bad night and everything. It really does seem hard."

Mrs. Cadman quite saw that it did. She glanced nervously up the stairs, then edged into the dining-room. It was not cheerful in here: a monkey puzzle, too close to the window, drank the last of the light up; the room still smelt of dinner; the fire smouldered resentfully, starved for coal. The big mahogany furniture lowered, with no shine. Mrs. Cadman, putting her basket down on the table, sent an uncertain smile across at Lucille, whose glasses blankly gleamed high up on her long face. She often asked herself where Lucille could have come from. *Could* this be the baby daughter she had borne, and tied pink bows on, and christened a pretty name? In the sun in this very bow window she had gurgled into sweet-smelling creases of Lucille's neck—one summer lost in time.

"You *have* been an age," Lucille said.

"Well, the shops were quite busy. I never *saw*," she said with irrepressible pleasure, "I never *saw* so many people in town!"

Lucille, lips tighter than ever shut, was routing about, unpacking the shopping basket, handling the packages. Chemist's and grocer's parcels. Mrs. Cadman watched her with apprehension. Then Lucille pounced; she held up a small, soft parcel in frivolous wrappings. "Oho," she said. "So you've been in at Babbington's?"

"Well, I missed one bus, so I had to wait for the next. So I just popped in there a minute out of the cold. And, you see, I've been wanting a little scarf——"

"Little scarf!" said Lucille. "I don't know what to make of you, mother. I don't really. How *could* you, at such a time? How you ever could have the heart!" Lucille, standing the other side of the table, leaned across it, her thin weight on her knuckles. This brought her face near her mother's. "Can't you understand?" she said. "Can't you take *anything* in? The next little scarf *you'll* need to buy will be black!"

"What a thing to say!" exclaimed Mrs. Cadman, profoundly offended. "With that poor thing upstairs now, waiting to have her tea."

"Tea? She can't take her tea. Why, since this morning she can't keep a thing down."

Mrs. Cadman blenched and began unbuttoning her coat. Lucille seemed to feel that her own prestige and Aunt Rosa's entirely hung on Aunt Rosa's approaching death. You could feel that she and her aunt had thought up this plan together. These last days had been the climax of their complicity. And there was Mrs. Cadman—as ever, as usual—put in the wrong, frowned upon, out of things. Whenever Rosa arrived to stay, Mrs. Cadman had no fun in her home, and now Rosa was leaving for ever it seemed worse. A perverse kick of the heart, a flicker of naughtiness, made Mrs. Cadman say: "Oh, well, while there's life there's hope."

Lucille said: "If you won't face it, you won't. But I just say it does fall heavy on me . . . We had the vicar round here this afternoon. He was up with Aunt for a bit, then he looked in and said he did feel I needed a prayer too. He said he thought I was wonderful. He asked where you were, and he seemed to wonder you find the heart to stay out so long. I thought from his manner he wondered a good deal."

Mrs. Cadman, with an irrepressible titter, said: "Give him something to think about! Why if I'd ha' shown up that vicar'd have popped out as fast as he popped in. Thinks I'd make a mouthful of him. Why, I've made him bolt down the street. Well, well. He's not *my* idea of a vicar. When your father and I first came here we had a rural dean. Oh, he was as pleasant as anything."

Lucille, with the air of praying for Christian patience, folded her lips. Jabbing her fingers down the inside of her waistbelt, she more tightly tucked in her tight blouse. She liked looking like Mrs. Noah—no, *Miss* Noah. "The doctor's not been again. We're to let him know of any change."

"Well, let's do the best we can," said Mrs. Cadman. "But don't keep on *talking*. You don't make things any better, keeping on going on. My opinion is one should keep bright to the last. When my time comes, oh, I would like a cherry face."

"It's well for you . . ." began Lucille. She bit the remark off and, gathering up the parcels, stalked scornfully out of the dining-room. Without comment she left exposed on the table a small carton of goodies Mrs. Cadman had bought to cheer herself up with and had concealed in the toe of the shopping bag. Soon, from the kitchen came the carefully muffled noises of Lucille putting away provisions and tearing the wrappings off the chemist's things. Mrs. Cadman, reaching out for the carton, put a peppermint into each cheek. She, oh so badly, wanted a cup of tea but dared not follow Lucille into the kitchen in order to put the kettle on.

Though, after all, Granville *was* her house. . . .

You would not think it was her house—not when Rosa was there. While Lucille and her mother were *tête à tête* Lucille's disapproval was at least fairly tacit. But as soon as Rosa arrived on one of these yearly autumn visits—always choosing the season when Mrs. Cadman felt in her least good form, the fall of the leaf— the aunt and niece got together and found everything wrong. Their two cold natures ran together. They found Mrs. Cadman lacking; they forbade the affection she would have offered them. They censured her the whole time. Mrs. Cadman could date her real alienation from Lucille from the year when Rosa's visits began. During Mr. Cadman's lifetime Rosa had never come for more than an afternoon. Mr. Cadman had been his wife's defence from her sister—a great red kind of rumbustious fortification. He had been a man who kept every chill wind out. Rosa, during those stilted afternoon visits, had adequately succeeded in conveying that she found marriage *low*. She might just have suffered a pious marriage; she openly deprecated this high living, this state of fleshly bliss. In order not to witness it too closely she lived on in lodgings in her native town . . . But once widowhood left her sister exposed, Rosa started flapping round Granville like a doomful bird. She instituted these yearly visits, which, she made plain at the same time, gave her not much pleasure. The journey was tedious, and by breaking her habits, leaving her lodgings, Rosa was, out of duty, putting herself about. Her joyless and intimidating visits had, therefore, only one object—to protect the interests of Lucille.

Mrs. Cadman had suspected for some time that Rosa had something the matter with her. No one looks as yellow as that for nothing. But she was not sufficiently intimate with her sister to get down to the cosy subject of insides. This time, Rosa arrived looking worse than ever, and three days afterwards had collapsed. Lucille said now she had known her aunt was poorly. Lucille said now she had always known. "But of course you wouldn't notice, mother," she said.

Mrs. Cadman sat down by the fire and, gratefully, kicked off her tight shoes. In the warmth her plump feet uncurled, relaxed, expanded like sea-anemones. She stretched her legs out, propped her heels on the fender and wiggled her toes voluptuously. They went on wiggling of their own accord: they seemed to have an independent existence. Here, in her home, where she felt so "put wrong" and chilly, they were like ten stout, confidential friends. She said, out loud: "Well, *I* don't know what I've done."

The fact was: Lucille and Rosa resented her. (She'd feel better when she had had her tea.) She should *not* have talked as she had about the vicar. But it seemed so silly, Lucille having just him. She did wish Lucille had a better time. No young man so much as paused at the gate. Lucille's aunt had wrapped her own dank virginity round her like someone sharing a mackintosh.

Mrs. Cadman had had a good time. A real good time always lasts: you have it with all your nature and all your nature stays living with it. She had been a pretty child with long, blonde hair that her sister Rosa, who was her elder sister, used to tweak when they were alone in their room. She had grown used, in that childish attic bedroom, to Rosa's malevolent silences. Then one had grown up, full of great uppish curves. Hilda Cadman could sing. She had sung at parties and sung at charity concerts, too. She had been invited from town to town, much fêted in business society. She had sung in a dress cut low at the bosom, with a rose or carnation tucked into her hair. She had drunk port wine in great red rooms blazing with chandeliers. Mr. Cadman had whisked her away from her other gentlemen friends, and not for a moment had she regretted it. Nothing had been too good for her: she had gone on singing. She had felt warm air on her bare shoulders; she still saw the kind, flushed faces crowding round. Mr. Cadman and she belonged to the jolly set. They all thought the world of her, and she thought the world of them.

Mrs. Cadman, picking up the poker, jabbed the fire into a spurt of light. It does not do any good to sit and think in the dark.

The town was not the same now. They had all died, or lost their money, or gone. But you kept on loving the town for its dear old sake. She sometimes thought: Why not move and live at the seaside, where there would be a promenade and a band? But she knew her nature clung to the old scenes; where you had lived, you lived—your nature clung like a cat. While there was *something* to look at she was not one to repine. It kept you going to keep out and about. Things went, but then new things came in their place. You can't cure yourself of the habit of loving life. So she drank up the new pleasures—the big cafés, the barging buses, the cinemas, the shops dripping with colour, almost all built of glass. She could be perfectly happy all alone in a café, digging into a cream bun with a fork, the band playing, smiling faces all round. The old faces had not gone: they had dissolved, diluted into the ruddy blur through which she saw everything.

Meanwhile, Lucille was hard put to it, living her mother down. Mother looked ridiculous, always round town like that.

Mrs. Cadman heard Lucille come out of the kitchen and go upstairs with something rattling on a tray. She waited a minute more, then sidled into the kitchen, where she cautiously started to make tea. The gas-ring, as though it were a spy of Lucille's, popped loudly when she applied the match.

"Mother, she's asking for you."

"Oh, dear—do you mean she's——?"

"She's much more herself this evening," Lucille said implacably.

Mrs. Cadman, at the kitchen table, had been stirring sugar into her third cup. She pushed her chair back, brushed crumbs from her bosom and followed Lucille like a big, unhappy lamb. The light was on in the hall, but the stairs led up into the shadow: she had one more start of reluctance at their foot. Autumn draughts ran about in the top storey: up there the powers of darkness all seemed to mobilize. Mrs. Cadman put her hand on the banister knob. "Are you sure she *does* want to see me? Oughtn't she to stay quiet?"

"You should go when she's asking. You never know. . . ."

Breathless, breathing unevenly on the top landing, Mrs. Cadman pushed open the spare-room—that was the sick-room—door. In there—in here—the air was dead, and at first it seemed very dark. On the ceiling an oil-stove printed its flower-pattern; a hooded lamp, low down, was turned away from the bed. On that dark side of the lamp she could just distinguish Rosa, propped up, with the sheet drawn to her chin.

"Rosa?"

"Oh, it's you?"

"Yes; it's me, dear. Feeling better this evening?"

"Seemed funny, you not coming near me."

"They said for you to keep quiet."

"My own sister . . . You never liked sickness, did you? Well, I'm going. I shan't trouble you long."

"Oh, don't talk like that!"

"I'm glad to be going. Keeping on lying here . . . We all come to it. Oh, give over crying, Hilda. Doesn't do any good."

Mrs. Cadman sat down, to steady herself. She fumbled in her lap with her handkerchief, perpetually, clumsily knocking her elbows against the arms of the wicker chair. "It's such a shame," she said. "It's such a pity. You and me, after all . . ."

"Well, it's late for all that now. Each took our own ways." Rosa's voice went up in a sort of ghostly sharpness. "There were things that couldn't be otherwise. I've tried to do right by Lucille. Lucille's a good girl, Hilda. You should ask yourself if you've done right by her."

"Oh, for shame, Rosa," said Mrs. Cadman, turning her face through the dark towards that disembodied voice. "For shame, Rosa, even if you *are* going. You know best what's come between her and me. It's been you and her, you and her. I don't know where to turn sometimes——"

Rosa said: "You've got a shallow heart."

"How should you know? Why, you've kept at a distance from me ever since we were tots. Oh, I know I'm a great silly, always after my fun, but I never took what was yours; I never did harm to you. I don't see what call we have got to judge each other. You didn't want my life that I've had."

Rosa's chin moved: she was lying looking up at her sister's big rippling shadow, splodged up there by the light of the low lamp. It is frightening, having your shadow watched. Mrs. Cadman said: "But what did I do to you?"

"I *could* have had a wicked heart," said Rosa. "A vain, silly heart like yours. I could have fretted, seeing you take everything. One thing, then another. But I was shown. God taught me to pity you. God taught me my lesson . . . You wouldn't even remember that Christmas tree."

"What Christmas tree?"

"No, you wouldn't even remember. Oh, I thought it was lovely. I could have cried when they pulled the curtains open, and there it was, all blazing away with candles and silver and everything——"

"Well, isn't that funny? I——"

"No; you've had all that pleasure since. All of us older children couldn't take it in, hardly, for quite a minute or two. It didn't look real. Then I looked up, and there was a fairy doll fixed on the top, right on the top spike, fixed on to a star. I set my heart on her. She had wings and long, fair hair, and she was shining away. I couldn't take my eyes off her. They cut the presents down; but she wasn't for anyone. In my childish blindness I kept praying to God. If I am not to have her, I prayed, let her stay there."

"And what did God do?" Hilda said eagerly.

"Oh, He taught me and saved me. You were a little thing in a blue sash; you piped up and asked might you have the doll."

"Fancy me! Aren't children awful!" said Mrs. Cadman. "Asking like that."

"They said: 'Make her sing for it.' They were taken with you. So you piped up again, singing. You got her, all right. I went off where they kept the coats. I've thanked God ever since for what I had to go through! I turned my face from vanity from that very night. I had been shown."

"Oh, what a shame!" said Hilda. "Oh, I think it was cruel; you poor little mite."

"No; I used to see that doll all draggled about the house till no one could bear the sight of it. I said to myself; that's how those things end. Why, I'd learnt more in one evening than you've ever learnt in your life. Oh, yes, I've watched you, Hilda. Yes, and I've pitied you."

"Well, you showed me no pity."

"You asked for no pity—all vain and set up."

"No wonder you've been against me. Fancy me not knowing. I didn't *mean* any harm—why, I was quite a little thing. I don't even remember."

"Well, you'll remember one day. When you lie as I'm lying you'll find that everything comes back. And you'll see what it adds up to."

"Well, if I do?" said Hilda. I haven't been such a baby; I've seen things out in my own way; I've had my ups and downs. It hasn't been all jam." She got herself out of the armchair and came and stood uncertainly by the foot of the bed. She had a great wish to reach out and turn the hooded lamp round, so that its light could fall on her sister's face. She felt she should *see* her sister, perhaps for the first time. Inside the flat, still form did implacable disappointment, then, stay locked? She wished she could give Rosa some little present. Too late to give Rosa anything pretty now: she looked back—it had always, then, been too late? She thought: you poor queer heart; you queer heart, eating yourself out, thanking God for the pain. She thought: I did that to her; then what have I done to Lucille?

She said: "You're ever so like me, Rosa, really, aren't you? Setting our hearts on things. When you've got them you don't notice. No wonder you wanted Lucille . . . You did ought to have had that fairy doll."

William Faulkner

That Evening Sun*

I

MONDAY IS NO DIFFERENT from any other weekday in Jefferson now. The streets are paved now, and the telephone and electric companies are cutting down more and more of the shade trees—the water oaks, the maples and locusts and elms—to make room for iron poles bearing clusters of bloated and ghostly and bloodless grapes, and we have a city laundry which makes the rounds on Monday morning, gathering the bundles of clothes into bright-colored, specially-made motor cars: the soiled wearing of a whole week now flees apparitionlike behind alert and irritable electric horns, with a long diminishing noise of rubber and asphalt like tearing silk, and even the Negro women who still take in white people's washing after the old custom, fetch and deliver it in automobiles.

But fifteen years ago, on Monday morning the quiet, dusty,

---

* Copyright 1931 and renewed 1959 by William Faulkner. Reprinted from COLLECTED STORIES OF WILLIAM FAULKNER by permission of Random House, Inc.

shady streets would be full of Negro women with, balanced on their steady, turbaned heads, bundles of clothes tied up in sheets, almost as large as cotton bales, carried so without touch of hand between the kitchen door of the white house and the blackened washpot beside a cabin door in Negro Hollow.

Nancy would set her bundle on the top of her head, then upon the bundle in turn she would set the black straw sailor hat which she wore winter and summer. She was tall, with a high, sad face sunken a little where her teeth were missing. Sometimes we would go a part of the way down the lane and across the pasture with her, to watch the balanced bundle and the hat that never bobbed nor wavered, even when she walked down into the ditch and up the other side and stooped through the fence. She would go down on her hands and knees and crawl through the gap, her head rigid, uptilted, the bundle steady as a rock or a balloon, and rise to her feet again and go on.

Sometimes the husbands of the washing women would fetch and deliver the clothes, but Jesus never did that for Nancy, even before father told him to stay away from our house, even when Dilsey was sick and Nancy would come to cook for us.

And then about half the time we'd have to go down the lane to Nancy's cabin and tell her to come on and cook breakfast. We would stop at the ditch, because father told us not to have anything to do with Jesus—he was a short black man, with a razor scar down his face—and we would throw rocks at Nancy's house until she came to the door, leaning her head around it without any clothes on.

"What yawl mean, chunking my house?" Nancy said. "What you little devils mean?"

"Father says for you to come on and get breakfast," Caddy said. "Father says it's over a half an hour now, and you've got to come this minute."

"I ain't studying no breakfast," Nancy said. "I going to get my sleep out."

"I bet you're drunk," Jason said. "Father says you're drunk. Are you drunk, Nancy?"

"Who says I is?" Nancy said. "I got to get my sleep out. I ain't studying no breakfast."

So after a while we quit chunking the cabin and went back home. When she finally came, it was too late for me to go to school.

So we thought it was whisky, until that day they arrested her again and they were taking her to jail and they passed Mr. Stovall. He was the cashier in the bank and a deacon in the Baptist church, and Nancy began to say:

"When you going to pay me, white man? When you going to pay me, white man? It's been three times now since you paid me a cent—" Mr. Stovall knocked her down, but she kept on saying, "When you going to pay me, white man? It's been three times now since—" until Mr. Stovall kicked her in the mouth with his heel and the marshal caught Mr. Stovall back, and Nancy lying in the street, laughing. She turned her head and spat out some blood and teeth and said, "It's been three times now since he paid me a cent."

That was how she lost her teeth, and all that day they told about Nancy and Mr. Stovall, and all that night the ones that passed the jail could hear Nancy singing and yelling. They could see her hands holding to the window bars, and a lot of them stopped along the fence, listening to her and to the jailer trying to make her stop. She didn't shut up until almost daylight, when the jailer began to hear bumping and scraping upstairs and he went up there and found Nancy hanging from the window bar. He said that it was cocaine and not whisky, because no nigger would try to commit suicide unless he was full of cocaine, because a nigger full of cocaine wasn't a nigger any longer.

The jailer cut her down and revived her; then he beat her, whipped her. She had hung herself with her dress. She had fixed it all right, but when they arrested her she didn't have on anything except a dress and so she didn't have anything to tie her hands with and she couldn't make her hands let go of the window ledge. So the jailer heard the noise and ran up there and found Nancy hanging from the window, stark naked, her belly already swelling out a little, like a little balloon.

When Dilsey was sick in her cabin and Nancy was cooking for us, we could see her apron swelling out; that was before father told Jesus to stay away from the house. Jesus was in the kitchen, sitting behind the stove, with his razor scar on his black face like a piece of dirty string. He said it was a watermelon that Nancy had under her dress.

"It never come off of your vine, though," Nancy said.

"Off of what vine?" Caddy said.

"I can cut down the vine it did come off of," Jesus said.
"What makes you want to talk like that before these chillen?" Nancy said. "Whyn't you go on to work? You done et. You want Mr. Jason to catch you hanging around his kitchen, talking that way before these chillen?"
"Talking what way?" Caddy said. "What vine?"
"I can't hang around white man's kitchen," Jesus said. "But white man can hang around mine. White man can come in my house, but I can't stop him. When white man want to come in my house, I ain't got no house. I can't stop him, but he can't kick me outen it. He can't do that."
Dilsey was still sick in her cabin. Father told Jesus to stay off our place. Dilsey was still sick. It was a long time. We were in the library after supper.
"Isn't Nancy through in the kitchen yet?" mother said. "It seems to me that she has had plenty of time to have finished the dishes."
"Let Quentin go and see," father said. "Go and see if Nancy is through, Quentin. Tell her she can go on home."
I went to the kitchen. Nancy was through. The dishes were put away and the fire was out. Nancy was sitting in a chair, close to the cold stove. She looked at me.
"Mother wants to know if you are through," I said.
"Yes," Nancy said. She looked at me. "I done finished." She looked at me.
"What is it?" I said. "What is it?"
"I ain't nothing but a nigger," Nancy said. "It ain't none of my fault."
She looked at me, sitting in the chair before the cold stove, the sailor hat on her head. I went back to the library. It was the cold stove and all, when you think of a kitchen being warm and busy and cheerful. And with a cold stove and the dishes all put away, and nobody wanting to eat at that hour.
"Is she through?" mother said.
"Yessum," I said.
"What is she doing?" mother said.
"She's not doing anything. She's through."
"I'll go and see," father said.
"Maybe she's waiting for Jesus to come and take her home," Caddy said.

"Jesus is gone," I said. Nancy told us how one morning she woke up and Jesus was gone.

"He quit me," Nancy said. "Done gone to Memphis, I reckon. Dodging them city *po*-lice for a while, I reckon."

"And a good riddance," father said. "I hope he stays there."

"Nancy's scaired of the dark," Jason said.

"So are you," Caddy said.

"I'm not," Jason said.

"Scairy cat," Caddy said.

"I'm not," Jason said.

"You, Candace!" mother said. Father came back.

"I am going to walk down the lane with Nancy," he said. "She says that Jesus is back."

"Has she seen him?" mother said.

"No. Some Negro sent her word that he was back in town. I won't be long."

"You'll leave me alone, to take Nancy home?" mother said. "Is her safety more precious to you than mine?"

"I won't be long," father said.

"You'll leave these children unprotected, with that Negro about?"

"I'm going too," Caddy said. "Let me go, Father."

"What would he do with them, if he were unfortunate enough to have them?" father said.

"I want to go, too," Jason said.

"Jason!" mother said. She was speaking to father. You could tell that by the way she said the name. Like she believed that all day father had been trying to think of doing the thing she wouldn't like the most, and that she knew all the time that after a while he would think of it. I stayed quiet, because father and I both knew that mother would want him to make me stay with her if she just thought of it in time. So father didn't look at me. I was the oldest. I was nine and Caddy was seven and Jason was five.

"Nonsense," father said. "We won't be long."

Nancy had her hat on. We came to the lane. "Jesus always been good to me," Nancy said. "Whenever he had two dollars, one of them was mine." We walked in the lane. "If I can just get through the lane," Nancy said, "I be all right then."

The lane was always dark. "This is where Jason got scared on Hallowe'en," Caddy said.

"I didn't," Jason said.

"Can't Aunt Rachel do anything with him?" father said. Aunt Rachel was old. She lived in a cabin beyond Nancy's, by herself. She had white hair and she smoked a pipe in the door, all day long; she didn't work any more. They said she was Jesus' mother. Sometimes she said she was and sometimes she said she wasn't any kin to Jesus.

"Yes, you did," Caddy said. "You were scairder than Frony. You were scairder than T. P. even. Scairder than niggers."

"Can't nobody do nothing with him," Nancy said. "He say I done woke up the devil in him and ain't but one thing going to lay it down again."

"Well, he's gone now," father said. "There's nothing for you to be afraid of now. And if you'd just let white men alone."

"Let what white men alone?" Caddy said. "How let them alone?"

"He ain't gone nowhere," Nancy said. "I can feel him. I can feel him now, in this lane. He hearing us talk, every word, hid somewhere, waiting. I ain't seen him, and I ain't going to see him again but once more, with that razor in his mouth. That razor on that string down his back, inside his shirt. And then I ain't going to be even surprised."

"I wasn't scaired," Jason said.

"If you'd behave yourself, you'd have kept out of this," father said. "But it's all right now. He's probably in St. Louis now. Probably got another wife by now and forgot all about you."

"If he has, I better not find out about it," Nancy said. "I'd stand there right over them, and every time he wropped her, I'd cut that arm off. I'd cut his head off and I'd slit her belly and I'd shove—"

"Hush," father said.

"Slit whose belly, Nancy?" Caddy said.

"I wasn't scaired," Jason said. "I'd walk right down this lane by myself."

"Yah," Caddy said. "You wouldn't dare to put your foot down in it if we were not here too."

II

Dilsey was still sick, so we took Nancy home every night until mother said, "How much longer is this going on? I to be left alone in this big house while you take home a frightened Negro?"

We fixed a pallet in the kitchen for Nancy. One night we waked up, hearing the sound. It was not singing and it was not crying, coming up the dark stairs. There was a light in mother's room and we heard father going down the hall, down the back stairs, and Caddy and I went into the hall. The floor was cold. Our toes curled away from it while we listened to the sound. It was like singing and it wasn't like singing, like the sounds that Negroes make.

Then it stopped and we heard father going down the back stairs, and we went to the head of the stairs. Then the sound began again, in the stairway, not loud, and we could see Nancy's eyes halfway up the stairs, against the wall. They looked like cat's eyes do, like a big cat against the wall, watching us. When we came down the steps to where she was, she quit making the sound again, and we stood there until father came back up from the kitchen, with his pistol in his hand. He went back down with Nancy and they came back with Nancy's pallet.

We spread the pallet in our room. After the light in mother's room went off, we could see Nancy's eyes again. "Nancy," Caddy whispered, "are you asleep, Nancy?"

Nancy whispered something. It was oh or no, I don't know which. Like nobody had made it, like it came from nowhere and went nowhere, until it was like Nancy was not there at all; that I had looked so hard at her eyes on the stairs that they had got printed on my eyeballs, like the sun does when you have closed your eyes and there is no sun. "Jesus," Nancy whispered. "Jesus."

"Was it Jesus?" Caddy said. "Did he try to come into the kitchen?"

"Jesus," Nancy said. Like this: Jeeeeeeeeeeeeeeesus, until the sound went out, like a match or a candle does.

"It's the other Jesus she means," I said.

"Can you see us, Nancy?" Caddy whispered. "Can you see our eyes too?"

"I ain't nothing but a nigger," Nancy said. "God knows. God knows."

"What did you see down there in the kitchen?" Caddy whispered. "What tried to get in?"

"God knows," Nancy said. We could see her eyes. "God knows."

Dilsey got well. She cooked dinner. "You'd better stay in bed a day or two longer," father said.

"What for?" Dilsey said. "If I had been a day later, this place would be to rack and ruin. Get on out of here now, and let me get my kitchen straight again."

Dilsey cooked supper too. And that night, just before dark, Nancy came into the kitchen.

"How do you know he's back?" Dilsey said. "You ain't seen him."

"Jesus is a nigger," Jason said.

"I can feel him," Nancy said. "I can feel him laying yonder in the ditch."

"Tonight?" Dilsey said. "Is he there tonight?"

"Dilsey's a nigger too," Jason said.

"You try to eat something," Dilsey said.

"I don't want nothing," Nancy said.

"I ain't a nigger," Jason said.

"Drink some coffee," Dilsey said. She poured a cup of coffee for Nancy. "Do you know he's out there tonight? How come you know it's tonight?"

"I know," Nancy said. "He's there, waiting. I know. I done lived with him too long. I know what he is fixing to do fore he know it himself."

"Drink some coffee," Dilsey said. Nancy held the cup to her mouth and blew into the cup. Her mouth pursed out like a spreading adder's, like a rubber mouth, like she had blown all the color out of her lips with blowing the coffee.

"I ain't a nigger," Jason said. "Are you a nigger, Nancy?"

"I hellborn, child," Nancy said. "I won't be nothing soon. I going back where I come from soon."

III

She began to drink the coffee. While she was drinking, holding the cup in both hands, she began to make the sound again. She made the sound into the cup and the coffee sploshed out onto her hands and her dress. Her eyes looked at us and she sat there, her elbows on her knees, holding the cup in both hands, looking at us across the wet cup, making the sound. "Look at Nancy," Jason said. "Nancy can't cook for us now. Dilsey's got well now."

"You hush up," Dilsey said. Nancy held the cup in both hands, looking at us, making the sound, like there were two of them: one looking at us and the other making the sound. "Whyn't you let Mr. Jason telefoam the marshal?" Dilsey said. Nancy stopped then, holding the cup in her long brown hands. She tried to drink some coffee again, but it sploshed out of the cup, onto her hands and her dress, and she put the cup down. Jason watched her.

"I can't swallow it," Nancy said. "I swallows but it won't go down me."

"You go down to the cabin," Dilsey said. "Frony will fix you a pallet and I'll be there soon."

"Won't no nigger stop him," Nancy said.

"I ain't a nigger," Jason said. "Am I, Dilsey?"

"I reckon not," Dilsey said. She looked at Nancy. "I don't reckon so. What you going to do, then?"

Nancy looked at us. Her eyes went fast, like she was afraid there wasn't time to look, without hardly moving at all. She looked at us, at all three of us at one time. "You member that night I stayed in yawls' room?" she said. She told about how we waked up early the next morning, and played. We had to play quiet, on her pallet, until father woke up and it was time to get breakfast. "Go and ask your maw to let me stay here tonight," Nancy said. "I won't need no pallet. We can play some more."

Caddy asked mother. Jason went too. "I can't have Negroes sleeping in the bedrooms," mother said. Jason cried. He cried until mother said he couldn't have any dessert for three days if he didn't stop. Then Jason said he would stop if Dilsey would make a chocolate cake. Father was there.

"Why don't you do something about it?" mother said. "What do we have officers for?"

"Why is Nancy afraid of Jesus?" Caddy said. "Are you afraid of father, mother?"

"What could the officers do?" father said. "If Nancy hasn't seen him, how could the officers find him?"

"Then why is she afraid?" mother said.

"She says he is there. She says she knows he is there tonight."

"Yet we pay taxes," mother said. "I must wait here alone in this big house while you take a Negro woman home."

"You know that I am not lying outside with a razor," father said.

"I'll stop if Dilsey will make a chocolate cake," Jason said. Mother told us to go out and father said he didn't know if Jason would get a chocolate cake or not, but he knew what Jason was going to get in about a minute. We went back to the kitchen and told Nancy.

"Father said for you to go home and lock the door, and you'll be all right," Caddy said. "All right from what, Nancy? Is Jesus mad at you?" Nancy was holding the coffee cup in her hands again, her elbows on her knees and her hands holding the cup between her knees. She was looking into the cup. "What have you done that made Jesus mad?" Caddy said. Nancy let the cup go. It didn't break on the floor, but the coffee spilled out, and Nancy sat there with her hands still making the shape of the cup. She began to make the sound again, not loud. Not singing and not unsinging. We watched her.

"Here," Dilsey said. "You quit that, now. You get aholt of yourself. You wait here. I going to get Versh to walk home with you." Dilsey went out.

We looked at Nancy. Her shoulders kept shaking, but she quit making the sound. We watched her. "What's Jesus going to do to you?" Caddy said. "He went away."

Nancy looked at us. "We had fun that night I stayed in yawls' room, didn't we?"

"I didn't," Jason said. "I didn't have any fun."

"You were asleep in mother's room," Caddy said. "You were not there."

"Let's go down to my house and have some more fun," Nancy said.

"Mother won't let us," I said. "It's too late now."

"Don't bother her," Nancy said. "We can tell her in the morning. She won't mind."

"She wouldn't let us," I said.

"Don't ask her now," Nancy said. "Don't bother her now."

"She didn't say we couldn't go," Caddy said.

"We didn't ask," I said.

"If you go, I'll tell," Jason said.

"We'll have fun," Nancy said. "They won't mind, just to my house. I been working for yawl a long time. They won't mind."

"I'm not afraid to go," Caddy said. "Jason is the one that's afraid. He'll tell."

"I'm not," Jason said.

"Yes, you are," Caddy said. "You'll tell."

"I won't tell," Jason said. "I'm not afraid."

"Jason ain't afraid to go with me," Nancy said. "Is you, Jason?"

"Jason is going to tell," Caddy said. The lane was dark. We passed the pasture gate. "I bet if something was to jump out from behind that gate, Jason would holler."

"I wouldn't," Jason said. We walked down the lane. Nancy was talking loud.

"What are you talking so loud for, Nancy?" Caddy said.

"Who; me?" Nancy said. "Listen at Quentin and Caddy and Jason saying I'm talking loud."

"You talk like there was five of us here," Caddy said. "You talk like father was here too."

"Who; me talking loud, Mr. Jason?" Nancy said.

"Nancy called Jason 'Mister,'" Caddy said.

"Listen how Caddy and Quentin and Jason talk," Nancy said.

"We're not talking loud," Caddy said. "You're the one that's talking like father—"

"Hush," Nancy said; "hush, Mr. Jason."

"Nancy called Jason 'Mister' aguh—"

"Hush," Nancy said. She was talking loud when we crossed the ditch and stooped through the fence where she used to stoop through with the clothes on her head. Then we came to her house. We were going fast then. She opened the door. The smell of the house was like the lamp and the smell of Nancy was like the wick, like they were waiting for one another to begin to smell. She lit the lamp and closed the door and put the bar up. Then she quit talking loud, looking at us.

"What're we going to do?" Caddy said.

"What do yawl want to do?" Nancy said.

"You said we could have some fun," Caddy said.

There was something about Nancy's house; something you could smell besides Nancy and the house. Jason smelled it, even. "I don't want to stay here," he said. "I want to go home."

"Go home, then," Caddy said.

"I don't want to go by myself," Jason said.

"We're going to have some fun," Nancy said.
"How," Caddy said.
Nancy stood by the door. She was looking at us, only it was like she had emptied her eyes, like she had quit using them. "What do you want to do?" she said.
"Tell us a story," Caddy said. "Can you tell a story?"
"Yes," Nancy said.
"Tell it," Caddy said. We looked at Nancy. "You don't know any stories."
"Yes," Nancy said. "Yes, I do."
She came and sat in a chair before the hearth. There was a little fire there. Nancy built it up, when it was already hot inside. She built a good blaze. She told a story. She talked like her eyes looked, like her eyes watching us and her voice talking to us did not belong to her. Like she was living somewhere else, waiting somewhere else. She was outside the cabin. Her voice was inside and the shape of her, the Nancy that could stoop under a barbed wire fence with a bundle of clothes balanced on her head as though without weight, like a balloon, was there. But that was all. "And so this here queen come walking up to the ditch, where that bad man was hiding. She was walking up to the ditch, and she say, 'If I can just get past this here ditch,' was what she say . . ."
"What ditch?" Caddy said. "A ditch like that one out there? Why did a queen want to go into a ditch?"
"To get to her house," Nancy said. She looked at us. "She had to cross the ditch to get into her house quick and bar the door."
"Why did she want to go home and bar the door?" Caddy said.

IV

Nancy looked at us. She quit talking. She looked at us. Jason's legs stuck straight out of his pants where he sat on Nancy's lap. "I don't think that's a good story," he said. "I want to go home."
"Maybe we had better," Caddy said. She got up from the floor. "I bet they are looking for us right now." She went toward the door.
"No," Nancy said. "Don't open it." She got up quick and passed Caddy. She didn't touch the door, the wooden bar.
"Why not?" Caddy said.

"Come back to the lamp," Nancy said. "We'll have fun. You don't have to go."

"We ought to go," Caddy said. "Unless we have a lot of fun." She and Nancy came back to the fire, the lamp.

"I want to go home," Jason said. "I'm going to tell."

"I know another story," Nancy said. She stood close to the lamp. She looked at Caddy, like when your eyes look up at a stick balanced on your nose. She had to look down to see Caddy, but her eyes looked like that, like when you are balancing a stick.

"I won't listen to it," Jason said. "I'll bang on the floor."

"It's a good one," Nancy said. "It's better than the other one."

"What's it about?" Caddy said. Nancy was standing by the lamp. Her hand was on the lamp, against the light, long and brown.

"Your hand is on that hot globe," Caddy said. "Don't it feel hot to your hand?"

Nancy looked at her hand on the lamp chimney. She took her hand away, slow. She stood there, looking at Caddy, wringing her long hand as though it were tied to her wrist with a string.

"Let's do something else," Caddy said.

"I want to go home," Jason said.

"I got some popcorn," Nancy said. She looked at Caddy and then at Jason and then at me and then at Caddy again. "I got some popcorn."

"I don't like popcorn," Jason said. "I'd rather have candy."

Nancy looked at Jason. "You can hold the popper." She was still wringing her hand; it was long and limp and brown.

"All right," Jason said. "I'll stay a while if I can do that. Caddy can't hold it. I'll want to go home again if Caddy holds the popper."

Nancy built up the fire. "Look at Nancy putting her hands in the fire," Caddy said. "What's the matter with you, Nancy?"

"I got popcorn," Nancy said. "I got some." She took the popper from under the bed. It was broken. Jason began to cry.

"Now we can't have any popcorn," he said.

"We ought to go home, anyway," Caddy said. "Come on, Quentin."

"Wait," Nancy said; "wait. I can fix it. Don't you want to help me fix it?"

"I don't think I want any," Caddy said. "It's too late now."

"You help me, Jason," Nancy said. "Don't you want to help me?"

"No," Jason said. "I want to go home."

"Hush," Nancy said; "hush. Watch. Watch me. I can fix it so Jason can hold it and pop the corn." She got a piece of wire and fixed the popper.

"It won't hold good," Caddy said.

"Yes, it will," Nancy said. "Yawl watch. Yawl help me shell some corn."

The popcorn was under the bed too. We shelled it into the popper and Nancy helped Jason hold the popper over the fire.

"It's not popping," Jason said. "I want to go home."

"You wait," Nancy said. "It'll begin to pop. We'll have fun then." She was sitting close to the fire. The lamp was turned up so high it was beginning to smoke.

"Why don't you turn it down some?" I said.

"It's all right," Nancy said. "I'll clean it. Yawl wait. The popcorn will start in a minute."

"I don't believe it's going to start," Caddy said. "We ought to start home, anyway. They'll be worried."

"No," Nancy said. "It's going to pop. Dilsey will tell um yawl with me. I been working for yawl long time. They won't mind if yawl at my house. You wait, now. It'll start popping any minute now."

Then Jason got some smoke in his eyes and he began to cry. He dropped the popper into the fire. Nancy got a wet rag and wiped Jason's face, but he didn't stop crying.

"Hush," she said. "Hush." But he didn't hush. Caddy took the popper out of the fire.

"It's burned up," she said. "You'll have to get some more popcorn, Nancy."

"Did you put all of it in?" Nancy said.

"Yes," Caddy said. Nancy looked at Caddy. Then she took the popper and opened it and poured the cinders into her apron and began to sort the grains, her hands long and brown, and we watching her.

"Haven't you got any more?" Caddy said.

"Yes," Nancy said; "yes. Look. This here ain't burnt. All we need to do is—"

"I want to go home," Jason said. "I'm going to tell."

"Hush," Caddy said. We all listened. Nancy's head was already turned toward the barred door, her eyes filled with red lamplight. "Somebody is coming," Caddy said.

Then Nancy began to make that sound again, not loud, sitting there above the fire, her long hands dangling between her knees; all of a sudden water began to come out on her face in big drops, running down her face, carrying in each one a little turning ball of firelight like a spark until it dropped off her chin. "She's not crying," I said.

"I ain't crying," Nancy said. Her eyes were closed. "I ain't crying. Who is it?"

"I don't know," Caddy said. She went to the door and looked out. "We've got to go now," she said. "Here comes father."

"I'm going to tell," Jason said. "Yawl made me come."

The water still ran down Nancy's face. She turned in her chair. "Listen. Tell him. Tell him we going to have fun. Tell him I take good care of yawl until in the morning. Tell him to let me come home with yawl and sleep on the floor. Tell him I won't need no pallet. We'll have fun. You member last time how we had so much fun?"

"I didn't have fun," Jason said. "You hurt me. You put smoke in my eyes. I'm going to tell."

V

Father came in. He looked at us. Nancy did not get up.

"Tell him," she said.

"Caddy made us come down here," Jason said. "I didn't want to."

Father came to the fire. Nancy looked up at him. "Can't you go to Aunt Rachel's and stay?" he said. Nancy looked up at father, her hands between her knees. "He's not here," father said. "I would have seen him. There's not a soul in sight."

"He in the ditch," Nancy said. "He waiting in the ditch yonder."

"Nonsense," father said. He looked at Nancy. "Do you know he's there?"

"I got the sign," Nancy said.

"What sign?"

"I got it. It was on the table when I come in. It was a hogbone, with blood meat still on it, laying by the lamp. He's out there. When yawl walk out that door, I gone."

"Gone where, Nancy?" Caddy said.

"I'm not a tattletale," Jason said.

"Nonsense," father said.

"He out there," Nancy said. "He looking through that window this minute for yawl to go. Then I gone."

"Nonsense," father said. "Lock up your house and we'll take you on to Aunt Rachel's."

"'Twont do no good," Nancy said. She didn't look at father now, but he looked down at her, at her long, limp, moving hands. "Putting it off won't do no good."

"Then what do you want to do?" father said.

"I don't know," Nancy said. "I can't do nothing. Just put it off. And that don't do no good. I reckon it belong to me. I reckon what I going to get ain't no more than mine."

"Get what?" Caddy said. "What's yours?"

"Nothing," father said. "You all must get to bed."

"Caddy made me come," Jason said.

"Go on to Aunt Rachel's," father said.

"It won't do no good," Nancy said. She sat before the fire, her elbows on her knees, her long hands between her knees. "When even your own kitchen wouldn't do no good. When even if I was sleeping on the floor in the room with your chillen, and the next morning there I am, and blood—"

"Hush," father said. "Lock the door and put out the lamp and go to bed."

"I scared of the dark," Nancy said. "I scared for it to happen in the dark."

"You mean you're going to sit right here with the lamp lighted?" father said. Then Nancy began to make the sound again, sitting before the fire, her long hands between her knees. "Ah, damnation," father said. "Come along, chillen. It's past bedtime."

"When yawl go home, I gone," Nancy said. She talked quieter now, and her face looked quiet, like her hands. "Anyway, I got my coffin money saved up with Mr. Lovelady." Mr. Lovelady was a short, dirty man who collected the Negro insurance, coming around to the cabins or the kitchens every Saturday morning, to collect fifteen cents. He and his wife lived at the hotel. One morning his wife committed suicide. They had a child, a little girl. He and the child went away. After a week or two he came back alone. We would see him going along the lanes and the back streets on Saturday mornings.

"Nonsense," father said. "You'll be the first thing I'll see in the kitchen tomorrow morning."

"You'll see what you'll see, I reckon," Nancy said. "But it will take the Lord to say what that will be."

VI

We left her sitting before the fire.

"Come and put the bar up," father said. But she didn't move. She didn't look at us again, sitting quietly there between the lamp and the fire. From some distance down the lane we could look back and see her through the open door.

"What, Father?" Caddy said. "What's going to happen?"

"Nothing," father said. Jason was on father's back, so Jason was the tallest of all of us. We went down into the ditch. I looked at it, quiet. I couldn't see much where the moonlight and the shadows tangled.

"If Jesus is hid here, he can see us, can't he?" Caddy said.

"He's not there," father said. "He went away a long time ago."

"You made me come," Jason said, high; against the sky it looked like father had two heads, a little one and a big one. "I didn't want to."

We went up out of the ditch. We could still see Nancy's house and the open door, but we couldn't see Nancy now, sitting before the fire with the door open, because she was tired. "I just done got tired," she said. "I just a nigger. It ain't no fault of mine."

But we could hear her, because she began just after we came up out of the ditch, the sound that was not singing and not unsinging. "Who will do our washing now, Father?" I said.

"I'm not a nigger," Jason said, high and close above father's head.

"You're worse," Caddy said, "you are a tattletale. If something was to jump out, you'd be scairder than a nigger."

"I wouldn't," Jason said.

"You'll cry," Caddy said.

"Caddy," father said.
"I wouldn't!" Jason said.
"Scairy cat," Caddy said.
"Candace!" father said.

II

"THIS THING CALLED LOVE..."

Trofimov:
 I don't believe in such trivialities. We're above love.
Madame Lyubov: And I suppose I'm below love.

>> ANTON CHEKHOV
>> *The Cherry Orchard*

(I) felt my ancient venomous
passion tear my body limb from limb:
naked, Venus was clawing down her victim.

>> RACINE, *Phaedra*
>> translated by Robert Lowell

Love consists in this, that two solitudes protect and touch each other.

>> RAINER MARIA RILKE
>> *Letters to a Young Poet*

I can love her and her and you and you,
I can love any, so she be not true.

>   JOHN DONNE
>   "The Indifferent"

And what if excess of love
Bewildered them till they died?

>   WILLIAM BUTLER YEATS
>   "Easter 1916"

William Carlos Williams

The Knife of the Times*

AS THE YEARS PASSED the girls who had been such intimates as children still remained true to one another. Ethel by now had married. Maura had married; the one having removed to Harrisburg, the other to New York City. And both began to bring up families. Ethel especially went in for children. Within a very brief period, comparatively speaking, she had three of them, then four, then five and finally six. And through it all, she kept in constant touch with her girlhood friend, dark-eyed Maura, by writing long intimate letters.

At first these had been newsy chit chat, ending always however in continued protestations of that love which the women had enjoyed during their childhood. Maura showed them to her husband and both enjoyed their full newsy quality dealing as they did with people and scenes with which both were familiar.

But after several years, as these letters continued to flow, there

* William Carlos Williams THE FARMERS' DAUGHTERS. Copyright 1932 by William Carlos Williams. Reprinted by permission of New Directions Publishing Corporation.

came a change in them. First the personal note grew more confidential. Ethel told about her children, how she had had one after the other—to divert her mind, to distract her thoughts from their constant brooding. Each child would raise her hopes of relief, each anticipated delivery brought only renewed disappointment. She confided more and more in Maura. She loved her husband; it was not that. In fact, she didn't know what it was save that she, Ethel, could never get her old friend Maura out of her mind.

Until at last the secret was out. It is you, Maura, that I want. Nothing but you. Nobody but you can appease my grief. Forgive me if I distress you with this confession. It is the last thing in this world that I desire. But I cannot contain myself longer.

Thicker and faster came the letters. Full love missives they were now without the least restraint.

Ethel wrote letters now such as Maura wished she might at some time in her life have received from a man. She was told that all these years she had been dreamed of, passionately, without rival, without relief. Now, surely, Maura did not dare show the letters to her husband. He would not understand.

They affected her strangely, they frightened her, but they caused a shrewd look to come into her dark eyes and she packed them carefully away where none should ever come upon them. She herself was occupied otherwise but she felt tenderly toward Ethel, loved her in an old remembered manner—but that was all. She was disturbed by the turn Ethel's mind had taken and thanked providence her friend and she lived far enough apart to keep them from embarrassing encounters.

But, in spite of the lack of adequate response to her advances, Ethel never wavered, never altered in her passionate appeals. She begged her friend to visit her, to come to her, to live with her. She spoke of her longings, to touch the velvet flesh of her darling's breasts, her thighs. She longed to kiss her to sleep, to hold her in her arms. Franker and franker became her outspoken lusts. For which she begged indulgence.

Once she implored Maura to wear a silk chemise which she was sending, to wear it for a week and return it to her, to Ethel, unwashed, that she might wear it in her turn constantly upon her.

Then, after twenty years, one day Maura received a letter from

Ethel asking her to meet her—and her mother, in New York. They were expecting a sister back from Europe on the *Mauretania* and they wanted Maura to be there—for old time's sake.

Maura consented. With strange feelings of curiosity and not a little fear, she stood at the gate of the Pennsylvania station waiting for her friend to come out at the wicket on the arrival of the Harrisburg express. Would she be alone? Would her mother be with her really? Was it a hoax? Was the woman crazy, after all? And, finally, would she recognize her?

There she was and her mother along with her. After the first stare, the greetings on all sides were quiet, courteous and friendly. The mother dominated the moment. Her keen eyes looked Maura up and down once, then she asked the time, when would the steamer dock, how far was the pier and had they time for lunch first?

There was plenty of time. Yes, let's lunch. But first Ethel had a small need to satisfy and asked Maura if she would show her the way. Maura led her friend to the Pay Toilets and there, after inserting the coin, Ethel opened the door and, before Maura could find the voice to protest, drew her in with herself and closed the door after her.

What a meeting! What a release! Ethel took her friend into her arms and between tears and kisses, tried in some way, as best she could, to tell her of her happiness. She fondled her old playmate, hugged her, lifted her off her feet in the eager impressment of her desire, whispering into her ear, stroking her hair, her face, touching her lips, her eyes; holding her, holding her about as if she could never again release her.

No one could remain cold to such an appeal, as pathetic to Maura as it was understandable and sincere, she tried her best to modify its fury, to abate it, to control. But, failing that, she did what she could to appease her old friend. She loved Ethel, truly, but all this show was beyond her. She did not understand it, she did not know how to return it. But she was not angry, she found herself in fact in tears, her heart touched, her lips willing.

Time was slipping by and they had to go.

At lunch Ethel kept her foot upon the toe of Maura's slipper. It was a delirious meal for Maura with thinking of old times, watching the heroic beauty of the old lady and, while keeping up a chatter of small conversation, intermixed with recollections, to respond secretly as best she could to Ethel's insistent pressures.

At the pier there was a long line waiting to be admitted to the enclosure. It was no use—Ethel from behind constantly pressed her body against her embarrassed friend, embarrassed not from lack of understanding or sympathy, but for fear lest one of the officers and Customs inspectors who were constantly watching them should detect something out of the ordinary.

But the steamer was met, the sister saluted; the day came to an end and the hour of parting found Ethel still keeping close, close to the object of her lifelong adoration.

What shall I do? thought Maura afterward on her way home, on the train alone. Ethel had begged her to visit her, to go to her, to spend a week at least with her, to sleep with her. Why not?

Guy de Maupassant

Two Little Soldiers

EVERY SUNDAY, as soon as they were free, the two little soldiers would set out walking.

They turned to the right on leaving the barracks, and crossed Courbevoie with long, quick strides, as if on military march; then, on passing the last houses, they continued at a calmer pace, on the bare, dusty road which leads to Bezons.

They were little and thin, lost in their coats, which were too big and too long, with sleeves which covered the hands, bothered by the too-big red trousers, which forced them to separate their legs if they wanted to walk fast. And under the tall, stiff shakos, one could scarcely see a small bit of face, two poor hollow Breton faces, simple with an almost animal-like innocence, with calm, sweet blue eyes.

They never spoke during the walk, the same idea, which took the place of conversation, stirring in their heads; for they had found, at the edge of the little woods of Champioux, a place which reminded them of their home, and they felt at ease nowhere else.

At the crossing of the roads of Colombes and Chatou, on arriving under the trees, they would take off their shakos, which weighed on the head, and dry their brows.

They always stopped a little on the bridge of Bezons to look at the Seine. They would stay there two or three minutes, bent over, leaning on the parapet; or they would consider the great basin of Argenteuil, where glided the white, leaning sails of the clippers, which, perhaps, reminded them of the Breton sea, the port of Vannes, whose neighbors they were, and of the boats which went on across Morbihan, toward the open sea.

As soon as they had crossed the Seine, they would buy their provisions from the shops of the pork butcher and the baker, and from the town wine shop. A piece of sausage, four sous' worth of bread, and a liter of *petit-bleu*, carried in handkerchiefs, constituted their supply. But as soon as they had left the village, they would slow their pace, and begin to talk.

Before them a barren plain, spotted here and there with a clump of trees, led to the woods, the little woods which, they thought, resembled those of Kermarivan. Blades of oats bordered the narrow path, lost in the fresh verdure of the coming crops; and Jean Kerderen would always say to Luc le Ganidec, "It's just like near Plunivon."

"Yes, it's just like it."

They would go on, side by side, their spirits filled with vague remembrances of their own country, full of awakened images, naïve images like the colored pictures one buys for a sou. They would see again the corner of a field, a hedge, a bit of heath, a crossroads, a granite cross.

Every time, too, they would stop near a stone which marked the boundary of a property, because it looked somewhat like the dolmen of Locneuven.

On reaching the first clump of trees, Luc le Ganidec would break off a switch, a hazel switch; and he would begin, quite gently, to peel back the bark, thinking of the people back home.

Jean Kerderen carried the provisions.

From time to time, Luc would mention a name, or recall an episode of childhood, briefly in order to give them time to dream. And their own country, the dear, faraway country, would repossess them little by little, would envelop them, would send to them, across the distance, its forms, its noises, its known horizons, its odors, the odor of the green heath where the sea air ran.

They no longer smelled the exhalations of the Parisian stables by which the earth of the suburbs is manured, but the perfume of the blooming thorn broom which the salt breeze gathers and carries away. And the sails of the boats appearing above the banks seemed to them the sails of coasting vessels seen beyond the long plain which stretched from their homes to the edge of the waves.

They walked slowly, Luc le Ganidec and Jean Kerderen, happy and sad, haunted by a sweet melancholy, the slow and penetrating melancholy of a caged animal that remembers.

And by the time Luc had finished peeling the bark from the thin switch, they would have arrived at the corner of the woods where they had lunch every Sunday.

They would find the two bricks which they had hidden in a thicket, and would light a little fire of twigs to cook their sausage on the point of a knife.

And when they had finished, eaten their bread to the last crumb and drunk their wine to the last drop, they would remain seated in the grass, side by side, not speaking, eyes far away, eyelids heavy, fingers crossed as at mass, their red legs stretched out beside the poppies of the field; and the leather of their shakos and the brass of their buttons shining under the burning sun would make the larks overhead stop singing.

Toward noon, they would begin to turn their glance, now and then, toward the village of Bezons, for the milkmaid.

Every Sunday she passed before them on her way to milk the cow and bring it home, the only cow in the neighborhood out at grass. It was pastured in a small field at the edge of the woods, beyond them.

They would soon see the girl, the only human being moving on the plain, and they would feel gladdened by the brilliant reflections thrown by the tin bucket under the flame of the sun. They never spoke to her. They were merely glad to see her, without realizing why.

She was a great, vigorous girl, reddened and burned by the heat of bright days, a great, bold girl of the Parisian countryside.

One time, seeing them seated at the accustomed place, she said to them, "Hello—so you're always here?"

Luc le Ganidec, the more daring, stammered: "Yes, we're here to rest."

That was all. But the following Sunday, she laughed on seeing them, laughing with the patronizing benevolence of a shrewd woman who understood their timidity, and asked: "What are you doing like that? Are you watching the grass grow?"

Luc, brightening, smiled too: "Maybe."

She replied: "What! It doesn't go fast."

Still laughing, he said: "Well, no."

She went on. But on returning with her pail full of milk, she stopped in front of them again, and said to them: "Do you want a drop? It'll remind you of home."

With the instinctive knowledge of belonging to the same stock, perhaps far from home herself, she had divined and touched their feeling.

They were both moved.

Then she poured out some milk, not without difficulty, into the neck of the bottle in which they had carried the wine; and Luc drank first, in little sips, stopping now and then to see that he didn't get more than his share. Then he gave the bottle to Jean.

She remained standing before them, her hands on her hips, the pail on the ground at her feet, glad for the pleasure she had given them.

Then, going away, she called: "Well, so long till Sunday!"

And as long as they could see her, their eyes followed her tall silhouette which receded, which diminished, which seemed to sink into the verdure of the earth.

When, the next week, they left the barracks, Jean said to Luc, "Shouldn't we buy her something nice?"

And they were embarrassed before the problem of choosing a tidbit for the milkmaid.

Luc thought of a piece of pork sausage, but Jean, because he loved sweets, preferred some candy. His idea carried, and they bought at a grocer's two sous' worth of white and red bonbons.

They ate their lunch faster than usual, agitated by their expectancy.

Jean saw her first. "There she is," he said.

Luc replied: "Yes. There she is."

On seeing them, still far off, she laughed, and called: "Is it going to suit you?"

They answered together: "How about you?"

Then she chatted with them, speaking of simple things which interested them, the weather, the crops, the folks she worked for.

They scarcely dared to offer their bonbons which melted gently in Jean's pocket.

Luc at last nerved himself and murmured, "We've brought you something."

"What is it?" she demanded.

Then Jean, red to the ears, reached for the thin cone of paper, and held it out to her.

She began eating the little pieces of candy which she rolled from one cheek to the other, and which made bumps under the flesh. The two soldiers, seated before her, regarded her, moved and enchanted.

Then she went to milk her cow and, on returning, again gave them some milk.

They thought of her all week and spoke of her many times. The next Sunday she sat down beside them to chat longer, and all three, side by side, their eyes far away, their knees held in clasped hands, recounted little events and little details of the villages where they had been born, while the cow, over there, seeing that the girl had stopped on the way, stretched out her heavy head, with the damp nostrils, and lowed protractedly to call her.

The girl soon accepted the invitation to eat a little with them and to drink a little wine. Often she would bring them some plums in her pocket, for the plum season had come. Her presence enlivened the two little Breton soldiers, who chattered like two birds.

Now, on a Tuesday, Luc le Ganidec asked for leave, something which he had never done before, and did not return until ten in the evening.

Jean, disturbed, racked his head for the reason for his comrade's absence.

The following Friday, Luc, having borrowed ten sous from his cot neighbor, asked and obtained permission for another leave of some hours.

And when he set out with Jean for the Sunday walk, he had a roguish, nervous air, all changed. Kerderen did not understand, but he vaguely suspected something, without guessing what it might be.

They didn't speak a word until they had reached the usual place, where they had worn out the grass by always sitting in the same spot; and they ate slowly. Neither one was hungry.

Soon the girl appeared. They watched her coming as they did

every Sunday. When she was near, Luc got up and took two steps. She set her pail on the ground, and embraced him. She embraced him passionately, throwing her arms about his neck, without concerning herself with Jean, without noticing that he was there, without seeing him.

And he felt lost, poor Jean, so lost that he did not understand it, his soul agitated, his heart broken.

Then the girl sat near Luc, and they began to chatter.

Jean did not look at them. He divined now why his comrade had gone out twice during the week, and he felt within himself a burning sadness, a sort of wound, that rending which treacheries make.

Luc and the girl got up to go together to change the cow.

Jean followed them with his eyes. He saw them move away, side by side. His comrade's red trousers made a blazing spot in the path. It was Luc who picked up the mallet and drove in the stake which held the animal.

The girl sank down to milk, while he absently caressed the animal's sharp backbone. Then they left the pail on the grass, and disappeared under the trees.

Jean saw nothing more than the wall of leaves through which they had entered; and he felt so troubled that, had he tried to rise, he would certainly have fallen.

He stayed still, stupefied by amazement and suffering, with a suffering deep and simple. He longed to weep, to get away, to hide, never to see anybody again.

Suddenly, he saw them coming out of the thicket. They came slowly holding hands, the way engaged couples do in the villages. It was Luc who carried the pail.

They kissed again at parting, and the girl, after having cast a friendly farewell and a knowing smile to Jean, went away. She did not think of offering him any milk that day.

The two little soldiers remained side by side, motionless as always, silent and calm, the placidity of their faces showing nothing of what troubled their hearts. The sun set. The cow, sometimes, lowed, regarding them from the distance.

At the usual hour, they got up to return.

Luc was peeling a switch. Jean carried the empty bottle. He left it at the wine shop of Bezons. Then they reached the bridge, and, as every Sunday, stopped at the middle for some moments to watch the water flow.

Jean leaned forward; he leaned forward more and more on the iron balustrade, as though he had seen something in the current which attracted him.

Luc said to him: "Maybe you'd like a drink of it?"

As he spoke the last word, Jean's head overbalanced his body, the lifted legs described a circle in the air, and the little red and blue soldier fell like a stone, entered the water, and disappeared.

Luc, his throat paralyzed with anguish, tried in vain to cry out. He saw something moving farther on; then his comrade's head broke the surface of the river, only to disappear again.

Farther on yet, he saw, again, a single hand which reached from the water, and plunged in again. That was all.

The boatmen who came hurrying did not find the body that day.

Luc returned to the barracks alone, running, his head in a whirl, and told of the accident, his eyes and voice full of tears, blowing his nose from time to time: "He leaned—he—he leaned—so far—so far his head tumbled over—and—and—look at him falling there—he's falling—"

He could not go on, his emotion strangled him so. If he had only known—

Katherine Mansfield

A Dill Pickle*

AND THEN, AFTER SIX YEARS, she saw him again. He was seated at one of those little bamboo tables decorated with a Japanese vase of paper daffodils. There was a tall plate of fruit in front of him, and very carefully, in a way she recognised immediately as his "special" way, he was peeling an orange.

He must have felt that shock of recognition in her, for he looked up and met her eyes. Incredible! He didn't know her! She smiled; he frowned. She came towards him. He closed his eyes an instant, but opening them his face lit up as though he had struck a match in a dark room. He laid down the orange and pushed back his chair, and she took her little warm hand out of her muff and gave it to him.

"Vera!" he exclaimed. "How strange. Really, for a moment I

---

* Copyright 1920 by Alfred A. Knopf, Inc. and renewed 1948 by John Middleton Murry. Reprinted from THE SHORT STORIES OF KATHERINE MANSFIELD by permission of the publisher.

didn't know you. Won't you sit down? You've had lunch? Won't you have some coffee?"

She hesitated, but of course she meant to.

"Yes, I'd like some coffee." And she sat down opposite him.

"You've changed. You've changed very much," he said, staring at her with that eager, lighted look. "You look so well. I've never seen you look so well before."

"Really?" She raised her veil and unbuttoned her high fur collar. "I don't feel very well. I can't bear this weather, you know."

"Ah, no. You hate the cold. . . ."

"Loathe it." She shuddered. "And the worst of it is that the older one grows . . ."

He interrupted her. "Excuse me," and tapped on the table for the waitress. "Please bring some coffee and cream." To her: "You are sure you won't eat anything? Some fruit, perhaps. The fruit here is very good."

"No, thanks. Nothing."

"Then that's settled." And smiling just a hint too broadly he took up the orange again. "You were saying—the older one grows—"

"The colder," she laughed. But she was thinking how well she remembered that trick of his—the trick of interrupting her—and how it used to exasperate her six years ago. She used to feel then as though he, quite suddenly, in the middle of what she was saying, put his hand over her lips, turned from her, attended to something different, and then took his hand away, and with just the same slightly too broad smile, gave her his attention again. . . . Now we are ready. That is settled.

"The colder!" He echoed her words, laughing too. "Ah, ah. You still say the same things. And there is another thing about you that is not changed at all—your beautiful voice—your beautiful way of speaking." Now he was very grave; he leaned towards her, and she smelled the warm; stinging scent of the orange peel. "You have only to say one word and I would know your voice among all other voices. I don't know what it is—I've often wondered—that makes your voice such a—haunting memory. . . . Do you remember that first afternoon we spent together at Kew Gardens? You were so surprised because I did not know the names of any flowers. I am still just as ignorant for all your telling me. But whenever it is very fine and warm, and I see some bright colours—it's awfully strange—I heard your voice saying: 'Geranium, marigold and verbena.' And I feel those three words are all I recall of some forgotten, heavenly language. . . . You remember that afternoon?"

"Oh, yes, very well." She drew a long, soft breath, as though the paper daffodils between them were almost too sweet to bear. Yet, what had remained in her mind of that particular afternoon was an absurd scene over the tea-table. A great many people taking tea in a Chinese pagoda, and he behaving like a maniac about the wasps—waving them away, flapping at them with his straw hat, serious and infuriated out of all proportion to the occasion. How delighted the sniggering tea drinkers had been. And how she had suffered.

But now, as he spoke, that memory faded. His was the truer. Yes, it had been a wonderful afternoon, full of geranium and marigold and verbena, and—warm sunshine. Her thoughts lingered over the last two words as though she sang them.

In the warmth, as it were, another memory unfolded. She saw herself sitting on a lawn. He lay beside her, and suddenly, after a long silence, he rolled over and put his head in her lap.

"I wish," he said, in a low, troubled voice, "I wish that I had taken poison and were about to die—here now!"

At that moment a little girl in a white dress, holding a long, dripping white lily, dodged from behind a bush, stared at them, and dodged back again. But he did not see. She leaned over him.

"Ah, why do you say that? I could not say that."

But he gave a kind of soft moan, and taking her hand he held it to his cheek.

"Because I know I am going to love you too much—far too much. And I shall suffer so terribly, Vera, because you never, never will love me."

He was certainly far better looking now than he had been then. He had lost all that dreamy vagueness and indecision. Now he had the air of a man who has found his place in life, and fills it with a confidence and an assurance which was, to say the least, impressive. He must have made money, too. His clothes were admirable, and at that moment he pulled a Russian cigarette-case out of his pocket.

"Won't you smoke?"

"Yes, I will." She hovered over them. "They look very good." "I think they are. I get them made for me by a little man in St. James's Street. I don't smoke very much. I'm not like you—but when I do, they must be delicious, very fresh cigarettes. Smoking isn't a habit with me; it's a luxury—like perfume. Are you still so fond of perfumes? Ah, when I was in Russia . . ."

She broke in: "You've really been to Russia?"

"Oh yes. I was there for over a year. Have you forgotten how we used to talk of going there?"

"No, I've not forgotten."

He gave a strange half-laugh and leaned back in his chair. "Isn't it curious. I have really carried out all those journeys that we planned. Yes, I have been to all those places that we talked of, and stayed in them long enough to—as you used to say—'air oneself' in them. In fact, I have spent the last three years of my life travelling all the time. Spain, Corsica, Siberia, Russia, Egypt. The only country left is China, and I mean to go there, too, when the war is over."

As he spoke, so lightly, tapping the end of his cigarette against the ash-tray, she felt the strange beast that had slumbered so long within her bosom stir, stretch itself, yawn, prick up its ears, and suddenly bound to its feet, and fix its longing, hungry stare upon those far-away places. But all she said was, smiling gently: "How I envy you."

He accepted that. "It has been," he said, "very wonderful—especially Russia. Russia was all that we had imagined, and far, far more. I even spent some days on a river boat on the Volga. Do you remember that boatman's song that you used to play?"

"Yes." It began to play in her mind as she spoke.

"Do you ever play it now?"

"No, I've no piano."

He was amazed at that. "But what has become of your beautiful piano?"

She made a little grimace. "Sold. Ages ago."

"But you were so fond of music," he wondered.

"I've no time for it now," said she.

He let it go at that. "That river life," he went on, "is something quite special. After a day or two you cannot realise that you have ever known another. And it is not necessary to know the language

—the life of the boat creates a bond between you and the people that's more than sufficient. You eat with them, pass the day with them, and in the evening there is that endless singing."

She shivered, hearing the boatman's song break out again loud and tragic, and seeing the boat floating on the darkening river with melancholy trees on either side. . . . "Yes, I should like that," said she, stroking her muff.

"You'd like almost everything about Russian life," he said warmly. "It's so informal, so impulsive, so free without question. And then the peasants are so splendid. They are such human beings—yes, that is it. Even the man who drives your carriage has—has some real part in what is happening. I remember the evening a party of us, two friends of mine and the wife of one of them, went for a picnic by the Black Sea. We took supper and champagne and ate and drank on the grass. And while we were eating the coachman came up. 'Have a dill pickle,' he said. He wanted to share with us. That seemed to me so right, so—you know what I mean?"

And she seemed at that moment to be sitting on the grass beside the mysteriously Black Sea, black as velvet, and rippling against the banks in silent, velvet waves. She saw the carriage drawn up to one side of the road, and the little group on the grass, their faces and hands white in the moonlight. She saw the pale dress of the woman outspread and her folded parasol, lying on the grass like a huge pearl crochet-hook. Apart from them, with his supper in a cloth on his knees, sat the coachman. "Have a dill pickle," said he, and although she was not certain what a dill pickle was, she saw the greenish glass jar with a red chilli like a parrot's beak glimmering through. She sucked in her cheeks; the dill pickle was terribly sour. . . .

"Yes, I know perfectly what you mean," she said.

In the pause that followed they looked at each other. In the past when they had looked at each other like that they had felt such a boundless understanding between them that their souls had, as it were, put their arms round each other and dropped into the same sea, content to be drowned, like mournful lovers. But now, the surprising thing was that it was he who held back. He who said:

"What a marvellous listener you are. When you look at me with those wild eyes I feel that I could tell you things that I would never breathe to another human being."

Was there just a hint of mockery in his voice or was it her fancy? She could not be sure.

"Before I met you," he said, "I had never spoken of myself to anybody. How well I remember one night, the night that I brought you the little Christmas tree, telling you all about my childhood. And of how I was so miserable that I ran away and lived under a cart in our yard for two days without being discovered. And you listened, and your eyes shone, and I felt that you had even made the little Christmas tree listen too, as in a fairy story."

But of that evening she had remembered a little pot of caviare. It had cost seven and sixpence. He could not get over it. Think of it—a tiny jar like that costing seven and sixpence. While she ate it he watched her, delighted and shocked.

"No, really, that is eating money. You could not get seven shillings into a little pot that size. Only think of the profit they must make. . . ." And he had begun some immensely complicated calculations. . . . But now good-bye to the caviare. The Christmas tree was on the table, and the little boy lay under the cart with his head pillowed on the yard dog.

"The dog was called Bosun," she cried delightedly.

But he did not follow. "Which dog? Had you had a dog? I don't remember a dog at all."

"No, no. I mean the yard dog when you were a little boy." He laughed and snapped the cigarette-case to.

"Was he? Do you know I had forgotten that. It seems such ages ago. I cannot believe that it is only six years. After I had recognised you to-day—I had to take such a leap—I had to take a leap over my whole life to get back to that time. I was such a kid then." He drummed on the table. "I've often thought how I must have bored you. And now I understand so perfectly why you wrote to me as you did—although at the time that letter nearly finished my life. I found it again the other day, and I couldn't help laughing as I read it. It was so clever—such a true picture of me." He glanced up. "You're not going?"

She had buttoned her collar again and drawn down her veil.

"Yes, I am afraid I must," she said, and managed a smile. Now she knew that he had been mocking.

"Ah no, please," he pleaded. "Don't go just for a moment," and he caught up one of her gloves from the table and clutched at it as if that would hold her. "I see so few people to talk to nowadays, that I have turned into a sort of barbarian," he said. "Have I said something to hurt you?"

"Not a bit," she lied. But as she watched him draw her glove through his fingers, gently, gently, her anger really did die down, and besides, at the moment he looked more like himself of six years ago. . . .

"What I really wanted then," he said softly, "was to be a sort of carpet—to make myself into a sort of carpet for you to walk on so that you need not be hurt by the sharp stones and the mud that you hated so. It was nothing more positive than that—nothing more selfish. Only I did desire, eventually, to turn into a magic carpet and carry you away to all those lands you longed to see."

As he spoke she lifted her head as though she drank something; the strange beast in her bosom began to purr. . . .

"I felt that you were more lonely than anybody else in the world," he went on, "and yet, perhaps, that you were the only person in the world who was really, truly alive. Born out of your time," he murmured, stroking the glove, "fated."

Ah, God! What had she done! How had she dared to throw away her happiness like this. This was the only man who had ever understood her. Was it too late? Could it be too late? *She* was that glove that he held in his fingers. . . .

"And then the fact that you had no friends and never had made friends with people. How I understand that, for neither had I. Is it just the same now?"

"Yes," she breathed. "Just the same. I am as alone as ever."

"So am I," he laughed gently, "just the same."

Suddenly with a guick gesture he handed her back the glove and scraped his chair on the floor. "But what seemed to me so mysterious then is perfectly plain to me now. And to you, too, of course. . . . It simply was that we were such egoists, so self-engrossed, so wrapped up in ourselves that we hadn't a corner in our hearts for anybody else. Do you know," he cried, naïve and hearty, and dreadfully like another side of that old self again, "I began studying a Mind System when I was in Russia, and I found that we were not peculiar at all. It's quite a well-known form of . . ."

She had gone. He sat there, thunder-struck, astounded beyond words. . . . And then he asked the waitress for his bill.

"But the cream has not been touched," he said. "Please do not charge me for it."

Sean O'Faolain

Childybawn*

WHEN BENJY SPILLANE'S MOTHER got a letter signed "A True Friend" informing her that Benjy had been "carrying on" for years with a young lady in the bank she at once sank beneath all the appropriate maternal emotions. She saw her treasure looted, her future imperiled, her love deceived. She saw her poor, foolish child beguiled, his innocence undermined, his sanity destroyed. At this time Benjy was just turned forty-one, a cheerful man-about-town with a winey face like a Halloween turnip with a candle inside it, a pair of merry, bull's eyes, a hint of gray at his temples; and his overcoat hung down straight from his paunch as if he was going to have a baby. He was an accountant at the bank, his rank and his cubicle next to the manager's.

For two weeks Benjy could not go out for a walk, or open a letter at the breakfast table without evoking long, anxious, secretive

* Copyright © 1954, 1957 by Sean O'Faolain. From THE FINEST STORIES OF SEAN O'FAOLAIN, by permission of Atlantic-Little, Brown and Co.

looks from his mother. At last she could stand it no longer, and put the question point-blank to him.

"Benjy, lovey, is it true what I heard? That you're thinking of getting married? Not, of course, childybawn, that anything would give me more joy than to see you settled down. But, of course you have time enough, too, and I'd love to see you happy. It isn't a thing you'd rush into, you know."

Benjy's eyes were normally *à fleur de tête*. At this they protruded as if he had goiter. His little mouth was open like a toy fish. Then he hooted loudly.

"Me? Married? In the name of God where did you get that yarn?"

"I dunno now what put it into my head," she said, her heart beginning to glow with relief and joy. "I wonder could it be something that ould jade Ma Looney said to me the other night at the chapel? About how I'd soon be losing you, or something like that. She was always a bad-minded ould rip."

"Well you can tell her from me she's talking through her left leg. I know, Mammy, when I'm well off," and he slapped her knee. "Aren't you better to me than any wife? And amn't I as good as a second husband to you?"

Which, natural functions apart, was quite true; for, like all Irish mothers, she had him fastened to her with hoops of comfort, and he was so devoted to her that his young lady at the bank once told him that it made her sick to see the pair of them together. So, she thought no more about it, beyond petting and spoiling him worse than ever, until she got another letter, this time signed "A Well Wisher." It came a few days after he came home from his Easter holidays and it informed her that the young lady at the bank had gone with him to Paris and Cannes. At this she began to steam open his correspondence. Since Benjy and his lady-love were at the same bank it was over a month before she was rewarded. She was scarlet before she finished the first sentence:—"Darling Benjy Wenjy, your poor little Angela is in bed with the flu, and isn't it a shame, a show, and a scandal that 'tis only the flu I'm in bed with . . ." As she watched Benjy reading the letter that evening over dinner, with a foolish smile on his fat face, she wished that his Angela would get double-pneumonia and never rise from her bed again.

The first thing she did was to toddle off to her father-confessor. He annoyed her exceedingly by advising her to pray for her son's early marriage. She thanked him; she said she would; but she had no intention of doing anything of the kind; firstly because it was the last thing she wanted herself, and secondly because she had to face the fact that it was the last thing Benjy wanted either. She thought up a much more satisfying plan. She had always had an intense devotion to Saint Monica the mother of Saint Augustine, and she now started to make a novena to the pair of them. She hung up their pictures in Benjy's bedroom. One day she went so far as to borrow a copy of the *Confessions of Saint Augustine* from the Free Library, and laid it casually under the *Sporting Chronicle* on Benjy's armchair. It was the night he usually took her to the pictures, so when she said she was a bit tired and would rather stay at home he naturally sat down on the book.

"Hello!" he said, lugging it out. "Where did you get this?"

"That?" she said, peering at it over her specs. "Wisha, I dunno now where did I get that? Ah, yes! I remember now I got it in the Free Library. I suppose 'tis edifying but. Anyway the old print is too small for my poor eyes."

"Would you like me to read a bit of it for you?" said Benjy, who used sometimes to read aloud to her on their nights at home.

"If you like," she said without enthusiasm.

He humored her, but after a few pages he began to ruffle the pages.

"Why doesn't he come to the point?" he asked impatiently. "This is all craw-thumping stuff. There's not as much as a bottle of stout in it yet. I mean what did he do anyway after all his old guff?"

"Not much, then," she said, and gazed sadly into the fire. "God help the poor creature!" she sighed. "That's all I have to say—God help her!"

"God help who?" said Benjy. "Oh, but you're right! Didn't he go off with a woman or something?" and he began to turn the pages more hopefully.

"I'm referring to Monica," said his mother severely. "He broke his poor mother's heart. But," she said cheerfully, "he mended it again, God bless him and protect him. When he turned from his bad ways! Ah, that was a lovely scene, the two of them sitting in the window, and the sun going down over the sea. Hand in hand. Mother and son. Lovely! Lovely! Lovely!"

"You seem to have the book off by heart. We didn't come to that at all yet."

"Yerrah, what book, childybawn! I don't need any book. Amn't I going to the special anniversary sermon on him every year for the last forty years down in Saint Augustine's? And that was another lovely scene, the day in the orchard. When the poor boy was feeling down in the dumps. His conscience at him, I suppose. And the Voice said Tolle lege, Tolle lege. And there and then he took up the book, and what did he read in the first line?" She fixed her eye on Benjy, who was looking at her in astonishment out of his cheerful, ruddy, turnip face, and she let him have it full blast:— "'Not in rioting nor in wantonness, not in chambering nor in drunkenness, but put ye on the garment of the Lord Jesus Christ.'" (She said it so dramatically that Benjy thought she was going to begin the next sentence with Dearly Beloved Brethren.) "Aha!" she went on. "That was when the arrow struck him. As it strikes each and every one of us sooner or later. Even the hardest hearted amongst us. 'I come,' says the Lord, 'like a thief in the night seeking whom I may devour!'"

Benjy looked at her sourly.

"There was a great preacher lost in you," he said, and went on looking for the spicy bit.

She was silent for a while. He had succeeded in finding a not-too-bad description of what he took to be a bull-fight so he did not see the sharp looks she was giving him. Then he heard her say, lightly, to nobody in particular:

"I was at confession today."

Benjy grunted. That was nothing new.

"Father Benignus I went to. Over at the Capuchins."

Benjy was now deeply interested in the bull-fight so he said nothing to this either.

"He says he knows you."

At this Benjy looked up.

"Me? I never laid eyes on him." And he looked down again.

"He laid eyes on you then. He says he knows you as well as a bad ha'penny."

Benjy laid down the book; the craw-thumping stuff had begun again.

"Oho? So ye were talking about me?" with an ominous note in his voice which she nervously observed and dared to ignore.

"No! No! Sure, amn't I telling you it was inside in confession? 'Twas only just how we were talking about poor Saint Augustine."

"Is that so?" says Benjy, giving her a long look. "Tell me! Is there, by any chance, any other priest who knows me like that?"

"Father Semple at the South Chapel told me he often saw you at the bank. And Father Milvey up in the Lough Chapel says you have a great future if you'll only mind your p's and q's."

At that Benjy flared:

"I see you have me well bell-a-ragged around the town! I suppose you're telling them all that I'm a trial and a torment to you?"

"Oh! Benjy! What a dreadful thing you're after saying! All I ever said to anyone, and I'd say it to the Pope himself, is that you're the best son ever trod shoe-leather. As you are! So far as I know!" A hurt came into her voice as she added: "What do I know about your affairs? Only what you tell me." A long pause. "Your life is your own." A still longer pause. "To make or to mar."

"I think," said Benjy, after a long silence, "I'll take the ould dog out for a walk."

He got no farther than the local, where he had a couple of brooding drinks. He needed them. So did she, and had them. For it was one of her little habits—which she never mentioned to Benjy, it would be only troubling the poor boy—to have a nip of brandy every night, or if the poor heart was weak or overexcited, maybe two. She felt so much better after them that she was able to put on her specs again and have a look in his *Sporting Chronicle* for tomorrow's starters at Leopardstown: an old County Kildare woman, she had never lost her interest in the nags.

The Monica regimen went on for about three months. During all that time she never said a single word of reproach to him. Every morning she said goodby to him with a sad smile. She welcomed him home every evening with a fond, pathetic kiss, going down then on her knees in spite of all his protests to remove his galoshes. He was never so well looked after. She used to heat the seat of his trousers at the fire every morning before letting him put them on. But she stopped going to the pictures. She said she had no heart for them. Instead she would sit opposite him saying the Rosary. If he said anything cheerful she would let out a deep sigh. He found it hard to concentrate on his *Sporting Chronicle*. After about three months of this both their nerves were so shaken that when he was going to Biarritz for his summer holidays he gave himself away to her by assuring her three times that he was going alone. She decided to call in the help of the bank manager.

"But, my dear Mrs. Spillane," he said to her, when she had finished her extraordinary story, "what on earth can I do? The private lives of my staff are no concern of mine—provided, of course, that there isn't any public scandal, and that it doesn't interfere with the affairs of the bank. I can assure you that your son is an exemplary official. In fact, what you tell me astonishes me. Have you any proof of it?"

She couldn't mention that she had been opening his letters, so she side-stepped that one. What she did say was:—

"Amn't I his mother? And let me tell you that, if you're astonished, I'm more astonished, to think you'd allow lassies like that one to be working in a respectable bank like this. 'Tis against Nature to have women in banks. 'Tis against God! Banks, indeed! I know another name some people would give them, with straps like that one waiting to put their claws into the first poor innocent boy they can capture!"

This rattled him. He had married a lady bank-clerk himself and had lived to regret it.

"Mrs. Spillane, your son is not a boy. He is a grown man. And you are doing him no good at all with this kind of talk. Your son will probably become a Manager himself one day, but it's unlikely unless he gets married. Now, wouldn't the very best solution to all this be if your *boy* were to marry this young lady?"

She rose up before him to her full height: a small, humpty-dumpty old woman, with misery in her pale-blue eyes, and hatred in her voice, then she said:—

"I'd rather see him in his pools of blood at my feet than see him married to that Jezebel!"

The day after he came back from Biarritz he fell down at her feet spouting blood from a burst ulcer, and was rushed off to the hospital. Before they started to operate they brought the priest to him, and by then Benjy was in no state—moral, physical, or strategical—to resist his administrations. It was a close shave, they barely pulled him through, and by the time he was recuperating he was a changed man. The day Mrs. Spillane passed a bold-looking strap on the stairs of the Nursing Home, her eyes as red as her painted lips from crying, and walked in to find Benjy reading *The Life of the Curé d'Ars*, of his own free will, she knew that mother love had triumphed at last.

2

After that Benjy developed a great regard for Saint Augustine. Every evening, now, side by side, he and his mother sat in the bay-window of their little villa watching the sun slowly draw its light away from the bay. He never went out of evenings except on works of charity with the Saint Vincent de Pauls. He gave up the liquor. He banned the *Sporting Chronicle*. The only visitors were other fellows from the S.V.deP's., or Father Benignus from the Capuchin priory, or Father Semple from the South Chapel, or the curate who had salvaged him in the Nursing Home. One night when he saw his mother reading a novel called *Her Scarlet Lover* he got up, went to his shelves, and with a sad little smile he handed her a new biography of a Peruvian Jesuit who used to flagellate himself with whips made of old safety-razor blades. There was an embarrassing moment another night when he came home a bit early from his charitable rounds, moved a cushion, found a half-empty bottle of Hennessey's Three Star, and got a definite smell of brandy in the air. Not that he said anything. Nor did he a few evenings later when, with a wry memory of his past follies, he took up that morning's paper to have a look at the racing page and found that day's starters at Hurst Park all checked off pro and con in pencil, with the odds written in beside them. But he began to remember things; he even began to brood—the steak that night had been a bit tough and she had brought him Bordeaux instead of Burgundy. He remembered how, about a year back, he had come one morning on a little heap of colored betting-slips behind D'Alton's six-volume History of Ireland on his bookshelves, and hastily and fearfully burned them as his own. He became aware that she was backbiting Ma Looney:—

"God forgive me," she was saying. "I ran into that ould jade Ma Looney this morning after Mass, and it didn't do me a haporth of good. That one is always detracting and backbiting. Oh, an envious jade! Do you remember the time she wanted to persuade me, right go wrong, that you were getting married? Pure jealousy, that's what it was! She's eaten up with it. Do you know now what that one is . . ."

In his years of wickedness Benjy would have listened to her with an indulgent smile. She saw him looking at her now as coldly as if she was a strange woman in a bus. She faltered, shuffled, petered out, and suggested humbly to him that he might like to take the dog for a walk. He did. She profited by his absence: two quick ones. The next night he profited by hers when she toddled off to confession: he rooted the house upside down. He found two empty brandy bottles; eight more betting tickets; her grocer's bills with several incriminating items; and the three anonymous letters. With a sad heart he put them all back where he found them.

"The poor old divil," he was saying to himself. "What a lousy, lonely, empty life I've driven her to! God! I've been a bastard to her!"

That night when she came home he had a new bottle of Three Star ready for her. She took a great deal of persuading before she would accept a teeny, little night-cap. She took less and less persuading every night after, but always she took the nip from him, humbly, cringingly. He began to collect racing-tips for her at the bank.

"You should put a bob on now and again," he would say, with his cheery hoot of laughter. "There's no harm in it, Mammy! 'Twill only amuse you."

After that it was a joy to him to see her handing out her shilling to him every morning with a cackle of laughter at her own folly— until the day she won at ten-to-one on an outsider. In her excitement she let out a wail:—

"Oh, what misfortune I had, that I didn't put ten bob on him!"

With a shock he thought that maybe she always used to put half-a-crown on her fancy before. He cursed his meanness.

"Never mind," he comforted her. "Sure, 'tis only fun. I mean what do you want the money for?"

"Oho then and oho then," she said fretfully, "we could all do with the money. 'Tis all right for you, you don't have to worry about it. Housekeeping isn't what it was when you were a boy."

"Mammy, are the accounts a worry to you? Would you prefer me to take them off your chest?"

"No, no, no!" she cried at once. "No worry at all! What would the worry be? Chuchuchu! For goodness sake, what worry?"

All the same he dropped into the grocer's the next morning on his way to the bank. He came out trembling. Not a bill paid for six months. The butcher had the same story for him. All that morning at the bank he was distracted by misery at the thought of the poor old creature crimping for money while he had been gallivanting with her ladyship in Paris and Biarritz and Cannes. At his lunch-hour he went sadly into Joe Rosenberg's betting-office to put her shilling on a horse called Silver Lining. It was Joe who took the bob. He looked at it, looked at Benjy, and said:

"Mr. Spillane, could I have a word with you for a minute?"

Much surprised at being addressed by name, Benjy passed the lifted lid of the counter to where Joe's big, fat hand was already slowly turning the pages of a ledger. Benjy's stomach was slowly turning over with it. Sure enough, when Joe had smoothened out a page with his big fingers that looked as if they had been worn flat by delving in his money-satchel, Benjy saw her name at the top of the page. His eye raced down to the foot of the page. A total, in the red, of £125. 17. 6.

"I thought you didn't know," said Joe, seeing the look in his face. Then, slowly tapping out *The Dead March* with his fingers across the total. "I suppose my money is safe with you?"

"You'll get it," said Benjy, knowing well that Joe knew well that it was as much as his job was worth to plead the Gaming Act and disown the debt. He saw that there was no bet under two pounds, several for a fiver, and there was one wild splurge of a tenner.

"What did she back that day?" he asked, and Joe had to laugh.

"Do you remember that old four-year-old mare of Billy Morgan's at Punchestown last year?"

"Jasus!" Benjy moaned. "Sure they're looking for her yet. You'll have to take it in installments, Joe. Give her no more credit."

When he got back to the bank he had to sit down. When he saw Angela's legs as she sailed down the aisle, the seam of her black nylons as straight and swelling as the line of a yacht, he thought his ulcer was going to burst all over again. Twice during that afternoon he caught her flirting gaily with the teller in the next cubicle and he got so dizzy that he had to hold on to the desk. That night, as he ate his dinner opposite his mother, the silence lay heavy between them like a gramophone record that has not been started. He waited until they were by the fire to let it go.

"Mammy," he said, leading with his left and ready with the right for her answer, "would it upset you very much if I got married?"

She turned joyfully to him.

"Oh, Benjy! Isn't that great news? Who is the lucky girl?"

"A young lady I know at the bank," said Benjy, giving her the right, and waiting with the left for the knock-out. "Her name is Angela."

He found his two hands being grasped and kissed.

"Childybawn, I'm simply delighted. How soon will it be?"

"You seem," he said, taken aback, "to be bloody anxious to get rid of me?"

"No! No, Benjy love! No!" And she began to sniffle. "Only you've been so cross with me this last six months there's no pleasing you."

"Cross?" he roared. "Cross? Am I hearing things? Was I cross about the brandy? Was I cross about the grocer's bills? Or about the butcher? And what about your hundred and twenty-five pounds, seventeen shillings, and six pence that you owe Joe Rosenberg?"

She crouched down in her chair, her two withered hands clasped before her and stared at him in horror.

"Oh, Benjy!" she fluttered. "Is that all you found out?"

You could have counted out one hundred and twenty-five pounds, seventeen shillings, and six pennies before Benjy could close his mouth and control his wandering paws.

"Sacred Heart!" he whispered at last. "What else is there?"

Her snuffle rose into a wail.

"There's the bloody old money-lenders!"

And as Benjy sank back into his armchair and gazed at the ceiling, as helpless as a man in a barber's chair, her wail sirened up into a bawl, and through the bawling and sniffling he heard;—

"I only wish to God you got married years and years ago. Ever since you took to. That old piety of yours. You've made my life a misery. Giving me thimblefuls of brandy like a baby. Making me bet in measly ould bobs. Picking and prying at me. From morning to night. Watching every penny I spend. Go on!" she bawled. "Go on, and get married! And torment some other misfortunate woman. The way you're tormenting me."

Benjy's eyes roved patiently all over the ceiling as if he were in search of the answer to the Mystery of Life. Not finding it in any part of the ceiling he looked out at the sky. He sought for it in the grass of the garden. At last he sought for it in her face, and at the sight of it, all puckered up comically like a baby with the gripe he burst into laughter. He laughed and he laughed.

"Honest to God, Mammy," he howled, "you ought to be put in the budget. You bloody ould rip of hell you!"

She clutched his two hands and drew him toward her.

"Oh, childybawn, they're the first natural words you said to me in six months! Go on! Abuse me! I deserve it!"

He detached himself from her, got up, and looked down at her, flooding with pity at the thought of what the two of them had been through since the Easter before. He patted her hand and said,

"I'm going for a walk."

He was back in ten minutes with a new bottle of Hennessey. He got out the tumblers and slapped out two hard ones. He put one in her fist, he sat on the arm of her chair, he put his arm around her shoulder and he made her clink glasses. She was beginning to protest when his look stopped her. The two of them were soon laughing like children or lovers, and discussing his wedding like any natural mother and son the world over.

An hour later, well fortified, he put on his hat and coat and went down to Angela's digs. She was in slacks, and shapely in them; and only that he was not too sure of his ground he would have loved to squeeze the life out of her. Instead she led him into the back parlor, closed the door, walked over to him and slapped his face. She called him a creeping rat, a cringing worm, and a bloody mammy's darling. She asked him did he think she could be picked up and dropped again at his own sweet will. She told him she wouldn't marry him if he was the last man on earth. She asked him did he think she was a common trollop. She asked him why didn't he go and marry his mother since he was so bloody fond of her. To none of this Benjy was in a position to give a truthful, or indeed any, answer. She slapped his face once more. Then she burst into floods of tears on his shoulder. At a quarter to two in the morning the landlady came down in her dressing gown and threw him out, battered, exhausted, but affianced.

When his old mother died, about five years later, he married Angela. He was then a tender forty-six. But, as he said when a bachelor pal teased him at the wedding for marrying so young:—
"That's all very fine, but, damn it all! I mean to say, a fellow has to have *some* regard for his mammy!!"

III

"TO SPEAK OF MARRIAGE..."

We are not lovers,
We do not even know each other.
We look alike
but we have nothing to say.
We are like pigeons . . .

> ANNE SEXTON
> "Man and Wife"

—and how he kissed me under the Moorish wall and I thought well as well him as another and then I asked him with my eyes to ask again yes—

> JAMES JOYCE
> *Ulysses*

What we have done this afternoon is to renounce happiness, renounce freedom, renounce tranquillity, above all renounce the romantic possibilities of an unknown future for the cares of a household and a family . . .

> Jack Tanner announcing his marriage
> GEORGE BERNARD SHAW
> *Man and Superman*

If some marriages are made in heaven,
others are unmade in hell.

        ANONYMOUS

True and false fears let us refrain,
Let us love nobly, and live, and add again
Years and years unto years till we attain
To write threescore . . .

        JOHN DONNE
        "The Anniversary"

It is not good for man to be alone. Some would have the sense hereof to be in respect of procreation only; and *Austin* [Augustine] contests that manly friendship in all other regards had been a more becoming solace for *Adam* than to spend so many secret years in an empty world with one woman. But our writers severely reject this crabbed opinion; and defend that there is a peculiar comfort in the married state besides the genial bed, which no other society affords.

        JOHN MILTON
        Tetrachordon

J. F. Powers

The Valiant Woman*

THEY HAD COME to the dessert in a dinner that was a shambles. "Well, John," Father Nulty said, turning away from Mrs. Stoner and to Father Firman, long gone silent at his own table. "You've got the bishop coming for confirmations next week."

"Yes," Mrs. Stoner cut in, "and for dinner. And if he don't eat any more than he did last year—"

Father Firman, in a rare moment, faced it. "Mrs. Stoner, the bishop is not well. You know that."

"And after I fixed that fine dinner and all," Mrs. Stoner pouted in Father Nulty's direction.

"I wouldn't feel bad about it, Mrs. Stoner," Father Nulty said. "He never eats much anywhere."

"It's funny. And that new Mrs. Allers said he ate just fine when he was there," Mrs. Stoner argued, and then spit out, "but she's a damned liar!"

---

* "The Valiant Woman" copyright 1947 by J. F. Powers, from the book PRINCE OF DARKNESS AND OTHER STORIES by J. F. Powers. Reprinted by permission of Doubleday & Company, Inc.

105

Father Nulty, unsettled but trying not to show it, said, "Who's Mrs. Allers?"

"She's at Holy Cross," Mrs. Stoner said.

"She's the housekeeper," Father Firman added, thinking Mrs. Stoner made it sound as though Mrs. Allers were the pastor there.

"I swear I don't know what to do about dinner this year," Mrs. Stoner said.

Father Firman moaned. "Just do as you've always done, Mrs. Stoner."

"Huh! And have it all to throw out! Is that any way to do?"

"Is there any dessert?" Father Firman asked coldly.

Mrs. Stoner leaped up from the table and bolted into the kitchen, mumbling. She came back with a birthday cake. She plunged it in the center of the table. She found a big wooden match in her apron pocket and thrust it at Father Firman.

"I don't like this bishop," she said. "I never did. And the way he went and cut poor Ellen Kennedy out of Father Doolin's will!"

She went back into the kitchen.

"Didn't they talk a lot of filth about Doolin and the housekeeper?" Father Nulty asked.

"I should think they did," Father Firman said. "All because he took her to the movies on Sunday night. After he died and the bishop cut her out of the will, though I hear he gives her a pension privately, they talked about the bishop."

"I don't like this bishop at all," Mrs. Stoner said, appearing with a cake knife. "Bishop Doran—there was the man!"

"We know," Father Firman said. "All man and all priest."

"He did know real estate," Father Nulty said.

Father Firman struck the match.

"Not on the chair!" Mrs. Stoner cried, too late.

Father Firman set the candle burning—it was suspiciously large and yellow, like a blessed one, but he could not be sure. They watched the fluttering flame.

"I'm forgetting the lights!" Mrs. Stoner said, and got up to turn them off. She went into the kitchen again.

The priests had a moment of silence in the candle-light.

"Happy birthday, John," Father Nulty said softly. "Is it fifty-nine you are?"

"As if you didn't know, Frank," Father Firman said, "and you the same but one."

Father Nulty smiled, the old gold of his incisors shining in the flickering light, his collar whiter in the dark, and raised his glass of water, which would have been wine or better in the bygone days, and toasted Father Firman.

"Many of 'em, John."

"Blow it out," Mrs. Stoner said, returning to the room. She waited by the light switch for Father Firman to blow out the candle.

Mrs. Stoner, who ate no desserts, began to clear the dishes into the kitchen, and the priests, finishing their cake and coffee in a hurry, went to sit in the study.

Father Nulty offered a cigar.

"John?"

"My ulcers, Frank."

"Ah, well, you're better off." Father Nulty lit the cigar and crossed his long black legs. "Fish Frawley has got him a Filipino, John. Did you hear?"

Father Firman leaned forward, interested. "He got rid of the woman he had?"

"He did. It seems she snooped."

"Snooped, eh?"

"She did. And gossiped. Fish introduced two town boys to her, said, 'Would you think these boys were my nephews?' That's all, and the next week the paper had it that his two nephews were visiting him from Erie. After that, he let her believe he was going East to see his parents, though both are dead. The paper carried the story. Fish returned and made a sermon out of it. Then he got the Filipino."

Father Firman squirmed with pleasure in his chair. "That's like Fish, Frank. He can do that." He stared at the tips of his fingers bleakly. "You could never get a Filipino to come to a place like this."

"Probably not," Father Nulty said. "Fish is pretty close to Minneapolis. Ah, say, do you remember the trick he played on us all in Marmion Hall!"

"That I'll not forget!" Father Firman's eyes remembered. "Getting up New Year's morning and finding the toilet seats all painted!"

"*Happy Circumcision!* Hah!" Father Nulty had a coughing fit.

When he had got himself together again, a mosquito came and sat on his wrist. He watched it a moment before bringing his heavy hand down. He raised his hand slowly, viewed the dead mosquito, and sent it spinning with a plunk of his middle finger.

"Only the female bites," he said.

"I didn't know that," Father Firman said.

"Ah, yes . . ."

Mrs. Stoner entered the study and sat down with some sewing—Father Firman's black socks.

She smiled pleasantly at Father Nulty. "And what do you think of the atom bomb, Father?"

"Not much," Father Nulty said.

Mrs. Stoner had stopped smiling. Father Firman yawned.

Mrs. Stoner served up another: "Did you read about this communist convert, Father?"

"He's been in the Church before," Father Nulty said, "and so it's not a conversion, Mrs. Stoner."

"No? Well, I already got him down on my list of Monsignor's converts."

"It's better than a conversion, Mrs. Stoner, for there is more rejoicing in heaven over the return of . . . uh, he that was lost, Mrs. Stoner, is found."

"And that congresswoman, Father?"

"Yes. A convert—she."

"And Henry Ford's grandson, Father. I got him down."

"Yes, to be sure."

Father Firman yawned, this time audibly, and held his jaw.

"But he's one only by marriage, Father," Mrs. Stoner said. "I always say you got to watch those kind."

"Indeed you do, but a convert nonetheless, Mrs. Stoner. Remember, Cardinal Newman himself was one."

Mrs. Stoner was unimpressed. "I see where Henry Ford's making steering wheels out of soybeans, Father."

"I didn't see that."

"I read it in the *Reader's Digest* or some place."

"Yes, well . . ." Father Nulty rose and held his hand out to Father Firman. "John," he said. "It's been good."

"I heard Hirohito's next," Mrs. Stoner said, returning to converts.

"Let's wait and see, Mrs. Stoner," Father Nulty said.

The priests walked to the door.

"You know where I live, John."

"Yes. Come again, Frank. Good night."

Father Firman watched Father Nulty go down the walk to his car at the curb. He hooked the screen door and turned off the porch light. He hesitated at the foot of the stairs, suddenly moved to go to bed. But he went back into the study.

"Phew!" Mrs. Stoner said. "I thought he'd never go. Here it is after eight o'clock."

Father Firman sat down in his rocking chair. "I don't see him often," he said.

"I give up!" Mrs. Stoner exclaimed, flinging the holey socks upon the horsehair sofa. "I'd swear you had a nail in your shoe."

"I told you I looked."

"Well, you ought to look again. And cut your toenails, why don't you? Haven't I got enough to do?"

Father Firman scratched in his coat pocket for a pill, found one, swallowed it. He let his head sink back against the chair and closed his eyes. He could hear her moving about the room, making the preparations: and how he knew them—the fumbling in the drawer for a pencil with a point, the rip of the page from his daily calendar, and finally the leg of the card table sliding up against his leg.

He opened his eyes. She yanked the floor lamp alongside the table, setting the bead fringe tinkling on the shade, and pulled up her chair on the other side. She sat down and smiled at him for the first time that day. Now she was happy.

She swept up the cards and began to shuffle with the abandoned virtuosity of an old riverboat gambler, standing them on end, fanning them out, whirling them through her fingers, dancing them halfway up her arms, cracking the whip over them. At last they lay before him tamed into a neat deck.

"Cut?"

"Go ahead," he said. She liked to go first.

She gave him her faint, avenging smile and drew a card, cast it aside for another which he thought must be an ace from the way she clutched it face down.

She was getting all the cards, as usual, and would have been invincible if she had possessed his restraint and if her cunning had been of a higher order. He knew a few things about leading and lying back that she would never learn. Her strategy was attack, forever attack, with one baffling departure: she might sacrifice certain tricks as expendable if only she could have the last ones, the heartbreaking ones, if she could slap them down one after another, shatteringly.

She played for blood, no bones about it, but for her there was no other way; it was her nature, as it was the lion's, and for this reason he found her ferocity pardonable, more a defect of the flesh, venial, while his own trouble was all in the will, mortal. He did not sweat and pray over each card as she must, but he did keep an eye out for reneging and demanded a cut now and then just to aggravate her, and he was always secretly hoping for aces.

With one card left in her hand, the telltale trick coming next, she delayed playing it, showing him first the smile, the preview of defeat. She laid it on the table—so! She held one more trump than he had reasoned possible. Had she palmed it from somewhere? No, she would not go that far; that would not be fair, was worse than reneging, which so easily and often happened accidentally, and she believed in being fair. Besides he had been watching her.

God smote the vines with hail, the sycamore trees with frost, and offered up the flocks to the lightning—but Mrs. Stoner! What a cross Father Firman had from God in Mrs. Stoner! There were other housekeepers as bad, no doubt, walking the rectories of the world, yes, but . . . yes. He could name one and maybe two priests who were worse off. One, maybe two. Cronin. His scraggly blonde of sixty—take her, with her everlasting banging on the grand piano, the gift of the pastor; her proud talk about the goiter operation at the Mayo Brothers', also a gift; her honking the parish Buick at passing strange priests because they were all in the game together. She was worse. She was something to keep the home fires burning. Yes sir. And Cronin said she was not a bad person really, but what was he? He was quite a freak himself.

For that matter, could anyone say that Mrs. Stoner was a bad person? No. He could not say it himself, and he was no freak. She had her points, Mrs. Stoner. She was clean. And though she cooked poorly, could not play the organ, would not take up the collection in an emergency, and went to card parties, and told all— even so, she was clean. She washed everything. Sometimes her underwear hung down beneath her dress like a paratrooper's pants, but it and everything she touched was clean. She washed constantly. She was clean.

She had her other points, to be sure—her faults, you might say. She snooped—no mistake about it—but it was not snooping for snooping's sake; she had a reason. She did other things, always with a reason. She overcharged on rosaries and prayer books, but that was for the sake of the poor. She censored the pamphlet rack, but that was to prevent scandal. She pried into the baptismal and matrimonial records, but there was no other way if Father was out, and in this way she had once uncovered a bastard and flushed him out of the rectory, but that was the perverted decency of the times. She held her nose over bad marriages in the presence of the victims, but that was her sorrow and came from having her husband buried in a mine. And he had caught her telling a bewildered young couple that there was only one good reason for wanting to enter into a mixed marriage—the child had to have a name, and that—that was what?

She hid his books, kept him from smoking, picked his friends (usually the pastors of her colleagues), bawled out people for calling after dark, had no humor, except at cards, and then it was grim, very grim, and she sat hatchet-faced every morning at Mass. But she went to Mass, which was all that kept the church from being empty some mornings. She did annoying things all day long. She said annoying things into the night. She said she had given him the best years of her life. Had she? Perhaps—for the miner had her only a year. It was too bad, sinfully bad, when he thought of it like that. But all talk of best years and life was nonsense. He had to consider the heart of the matter, the essence. The essence was that housekeepers were hard to get, harder to get than ushers, than willing workers, than organists, than secretaries—yes, harder to get than assistants or vocations.

And she was a *saver*—saved money, saved electricity, saved string, bags, sugar, saved—him. That's what she did. That's what she said she did, and she was right, in a way. In a way, she was usually right. In fact, she was always right—in a way. And you could never get a Filipino to come way out here and live. Not a young one anyway, and he had never seen an old one. Not a Filipino. They liked to dress up and live.

Should he let it drop about Fish having one, just to throw a scare into her, let her know he was doing some thinking? No. It would be a perfect cue for the one about a man needing a woman to look after him. He was not up to that again, not tonight.

Now she was doing what she liked most of all. She was making a grand slam, playing it out card for card, though it was in the bag, prolonging what would have been cut short out of mercy in gentle company. Father Firman knew the agony of losing.

She slashed down the last card, a miserable deuce trump, and did in the hapless king of hearts he had been saving.

"Skunked you!"

She was awful in victory. Here was the bitter end of their long day together, the final murderous hour in which all they wanted to say—all he wouldn't and all she couldn't—came out in the cards. Whoever won at honeymoon won the day, slept on the other's scalp, and God alone had to help the loser.

"We've been at it long enough, Mrs. Stoner," he said, seeing her assembling the cards for another round.

"Had enough, huh!"

Father Firman grumbled something.

"No?"

"Yes."

She pulled the table away and left it against the wall for the next time. She went out of the study carrying the socks, content and clucking. He closed his eyes after her and began to get under way in the rocking chair, the nightly trip to nowhere. He could hear her brewing a cup of tea in the kitchen and conversing with the cat. She made her way up the stairs, carrying the tea, followed by the cat, purring.

He waited, rocking out to sea, until she would be sure to be through in the bathroom. Then he got up and locked the front door (she looked after the back door) and loosened his collar going upstairs.

In the bathroom he mixed a glass of antiseptic, always afraid of pyorrhea, and gargled to ward off pharyngitis.

When he turned on the light in his room, the moths and beetles began to batter against the screens, the lighter insects humming. . . .

Yes, and she had the guest room. How did she come to get that? Why wasn't she in the back room, in her proper place? He knew, if he cared to remember. The screen in the back room—it let in mosquitoes, and if it didn't do that she'd love to sleep back there, Father, looking out at the steeple and the blessed cross on top, Father, if it just weren't for the screen, Father. Very well, Mrs.

Stoner, I'll get it fixed or fix it myself. Oh, could you now, Father? I could, Mrs. Stoner, and I will. In the meantime you take the guest room. Yes, Father, and thank you, Father, the house ringing with amenities then. Years ago, all that. She was a pie-faced girl then, not really a girl perhaps, but not too old to marry again. But she never had. In fact, he could not remember that she had even tried for a husband since coming to the rectory, but, of course, he could be wrong, not knowing how they went about it. God! God save us! Had she got her wires crossed and mistaken him all these years for *that*? *That!* Him! Suffering God! No. That was going too far. That was getting morbid. No. He must not think of that again, ever. No.

But just the same she had got the guest room and she had it yet. Well, did it matter? Nobody ever came to see him any more, nobody to stay overnight anyway, nobody to stay very long . . . not any more. He knew how they laughed at him. He had heard Frank humming all right—before he saw how serious and sad the situation was and took pity—humming, "Wedding Bells Are Breaking Up That Old Gang of Mine." But then they'd always laughed at him for something—for not being an athlete, for wearing glasses, for having kidney trouble . . . and mail coming addressed to Rev. and Mrs. Stoner.

Removing his shirt, he bent over the table to read the volume left open from last night. He read, translating easily, "*Eisdem licet cum illis* . . . Clerics are allowed to reside only with women about whom there can be no suspicion, either because of a natural bond (as mother, sister, aunt) or of advanced age, combined in both cases with good repute."

Last night he had read it, and many nights before, each time as though this time to find what was missing, to find what obviously was not in the paragraph, his problem considered, a way out. She was not mother, not sister, not aunt, and *advanced age* was a relative term (why, she was younger than he was) and so, eureka, she did not meet the letter of the law—but, alas, how she fulfilled the spirit! And besides it would be a slimy way of handling it after all her years of service. He could not afford to pension her off, either.

He slammed the book shut. He slapped himself fiercely on the back, missing the wily mosquito, and whirled to find it. He took a magazine and folded it into a swatter. Then he saw it—oh, the preternatural cunning of it!—poised in the beard of St. Joseph on the bookcase. He could not hit it there. He teased it away, wanting it to light on the wall, but it knew his thoughts and flew high away. He swung wildly, hoping to stun it, missed, swung back, catching St. Joseph across the neck. The statue fell to the floor and broke.

Mrs. Stoner was panting in the hall outside his door.

"What is it!"

"Mosquitoes!"

"What is it, Father? Are you hurt?"

"Mosquitoes—damn it! And only the female bites!"

Mrs. Stoner, after a moment, said, "Shame on you, Father. She needs the blood for her eggs."

He dropped the magazine and lunged at the mosquito with his bare hand.

She went back to her room, saying, "Pshaw, I thought it was burglars murdering you in your bed."

He lunged again.

D. H. *Lawrence*

Two Blue Birds*

THERE WAS A WOMAN who loved her husband, but she could not live with him. The husband, on his side, was sincerely attached to his wife, yet he could not live with her. They were both under forty, both handsome and both attractive. They had the most sincere regard for one another, and felt, in some odd way, eternally married to one another. They knew one another more intimately than they knew anybody else, they felt more known to one another than to any other person.

Yet they could not live together. Usually, they kept a thousand miles apart, geographically. But when he sat in the greyness of England, at the back of his mind, with a certain grim fidelity, he was aware of his wife, her strange yearning to be loyal and faithful, having her gallant affairs away in the sun, in the south. And she, as she drank her cocktail on the terrace over the sea, and turned her

---

* From THE COMPLETE SHORT STORIES OF D. H. LAWRENCE, VOL. II. Copyright 1922 by Thomas B. Seltzer, Inc., renewed 1950 by Frieda Lawrence. Reprinted by permission of The Viking Press, Inc.

grey, sardonic eyes on the heavy dark face of her admirer, whom she really liked quite a lot, she was actually preoccupied with the clear-cut features of her handsome young husband, thinking of how he would be asking his secretary to do something for him, asking in that good-natured, confident voice of a man who knows that his request will be only too gladly fulfilled.

The secretary, of course, adored him. She was *very* competent, quite young, and quite good-looking. She adored him. But then all his servants always did, particularly his women-servants. His men-servants were likely to swindle him.

When a man has an adoring secretary, and you are the man's wife, what are you to do? Not that there was anything "wrong"—if you know what I mean!—between them. Nothing you could call adultery, to come down to brass tacks. No, no! They were just the young master and his secretary. He dictated to her, she slaved for him and adored him, and the whole thing went on wheels.

He didn't "adore" her. A man doesn't need to adore his secretary. But he depended on her. "I simply rely on Miss Wrexall." Whereas he could never rely on his wife. The one thing he knew finally about *her* was that she didn't intend to be relied on.

So they remained friends, in the awful unspoken intimacy of the once-married. Usually each year they went away together for a holiday, and, if they had not been man and wife, they would have found a great deal of fun and stimulation in one another. The fact that they were married, had been married for the last dozen years, and couldn't live together for the last three or four, spoilt them for one another. Each had a private feeling of bitterness about the other.

However, they were awfully kind. He was the soul of generosity, and held her in real, tender esteem, no matter how many gallant affairs she had. Her gallant affairs were part of her modern necessity. "After all, I've got to *live*. I can't turn into a pillar of salt in five minutes just because you and I can't live together! It takes years for a woman like me to turn into a pillar of salt. At least I hope so!"

"Quite!" he replied. "Quite! By all means put them in pickle, make pickled cucumbers of them, before you crystallize out. That's my advice."

He was like that: so awfully clever and enigmatic. She could more or less fathom the idea of the pickled cucumbers, but the "crystallizing out"—what did that signify? And did he mean to suggest that he himself had been well pickled and that further immersion was for him unnecessary, would spoil his flavour? Was that what he meant? And herself, was she the brine and the vale of tears?

You never knew how catty a man was being, when he was really clever and enigmatic, withal a bit whimsical. He was adorably whimsical, with a twist of his flexible, vain mouth, that had a long upper lip, so fraught with vanity! But then a handsome, clear-cut, histrionic young man like that, how could he help being vain? The women made him so.

Ah, the women! How nice men would be if there were no other women!

And how nice the women would be if there were no other men! That's the best of a secretary. She may have a husband, but a husband is the mere shred of a man compared to a boss, a chief, a man who dictates to you and whose words you faithfully write down and then transcribe. Imagine a wife writing down anything her husband said to her! But a secretary! Every *and* and *but* of his she preserves for ever. What are candied violets in comparison!

Now it is all very well having gallant affairs under the southern sun, when you know there is a husband whom you adore dictating to a secretary whom you are too scornful to hate whom you rather despise, though you allow she has her good points, away north in the place you ought to regard as home. A gallant affair isn't much good when you've got a bit of grit in your eye. Or something at the back of your mind.

What's to be done? The husband, of course, did not send his wife away.

"You've got your secretary and your work," she said. "There's no room for me."

"There's a bedroom and a sitting-room exclusively for you," he replied. "And a garden and half a motor-car. But please yourself entirely. Do what gives you most pleasure."

"In that case," she said, "I'll just go south for the winter."

"Yes, do!" he said. "You always enjoy it."

"I always do," she replied.

They parted with a certain relentlessness that had a touch of wistful sentiment behind it. Off she went to her gallant affairs, that were like the curate's egg, palatable in parts. And he settled down to work. He said he hated working, but he never did anything else. Ten or eleven hours a day. That's what it is to be your own master!

So the winter wore away, and it was spring, when the swallows homeward fly, or northward, in this case. This winter, one of a series similar, had been rather hard to get through. The bit of grit in the gallant lady's eye had worked deeper in the more she blinked. Dark faces might be dark, and icy cocktails might lend a glow; she blinked her hardest to blink that bit of grit away, without success. Under the spicy balls of the mimosa she thought of that husband of hers in his library, and of that neat, competent but *common* little secretary of his, forever taking down what he said!

"How a man can *stand* it! How *she* can stand it, common little thing as she is, I don't know!" the wife cried to herself.

She meant this dictating business, this ten hours a day intercourse, *à deux*, with nothing but a pencil between them, and a flow of words.

What was to be done? Matters, instead of improving, had grown worse. The little secretary had brought her mother and sister into the establishment. The mother was a sort of cook-housekeeper, the sister was a sort of upper maid—she did the fine laundry, and looked after "his" clothes, and valeted him beautifully. It was really an excellent arrangement. The old mother was a splendid plain cook, the sister was all that could be desired as a valet de chambre, a fine laundress, an upper parlour-maid, and a table-waiter. And all economical to a degree. They knew his affairs by heart. His secretary flew to town when a creditor became dangerous, and she *always* smoothed over the financial crisis.

"He," of course, had debts, and he was working to pay them off. And if he had been a fairy prince who could call the ants to help him, he would not have been more wonderful than in securing this secretary and her family. They took hardly any wages. And they seemed to perform the miracle of loaves and fishes daily.

"She," of course, was the wife who loved her husband, but helped him into debt, and she still was an expensive item. Yet when she appeared at her "home," the secretarial family received her with most elaborate attentions and deference. The knight returning from the Crusades didn't create a greater stir. She felt like Queen Elizabeth at Kenilworth, a sovereign paying a visit to her faithful subjects. But perhaps there lurked always this hair in her soup! Won't they be glad to be rid of me again!

But they protested No! No! They had been waiting and hoping and praying she would come. They had been pining for her to be there, in charge: the mistress, "his" wife. Ah, "his" wife!

"His" wife! His halo was like a bucket over her head.

The cook-mother was "of the people," so it was the upper-maid daughter who came for orders.

"What will you order for tomorrow's lunch and dinner, Mrs. Gee?"

"Well, what do you usually have?"

"Oh, we want *you* to say."

"No, what do you *usually* have?"

"We don't have anything fixed. Mother goes out and chooses the best she can find, that is nice and fresh. But she thought you would tell her now what to get."

"Oh, I don't know! I'm not very good at that sort of thing. Ask her to go on just the same; I'm quite sure she knows best."

"Perhaps you'd like to suggest a sweet?"

"No, I don't care for sweets—and you know Mr. Gee doesn't. So don't make one for me."

Could anything be more impossible! They had the house spotless and running like a dream; how could an incompetent and extravagant wife dare to interfere, when she saw their amazing and almost inspired economy! But they ran the place on simply nothing!

Simply marvellous people! And the way they strewed palm-branches under her feet!

But that only made her feel ridiculous.

"Don't you think the family manage very well?" he asked her tentatively.

"Awfully well! Almost romantically well!" she replied. "But I suppose you're perfectly happy?"

"I'm perfectly comfortable," he replied.

"I can see you are," she replied. "Amazingly so! I never knew such comfort! Are you sure it isn't bad for you?"

She eyed him stealthily. He looked very well, and extremely

handsome, in his histrionic way. He was shockingly well-dressed and valeted. And he had that air of easy *aplomb* and good humour which is so becoming to a man, and which he only acquires when he is cock of his own little walk, made much of by his own hens.

"No!" he said, taking his pipe from his mouth and smiling whimsically round at her. "Do I look as if it were bad for me?"

"No, you don't," she replied promptly: thinking, naturally, as a woman is supposed to think nowadays, of his health and comfort, the foundation, apparently, of all happiness.

Then, of course, away she went on the backwash.

"Perhaps for your work, though, it's not so good as it is for *you*," she said in a rather small voice. She knew he couldn't bear it if she mocked at his work for one moment. And he knew that rather small voice of hers.

"In what way?" he said, bristles rising.

"Oh, I don't know," she answered indifferently. "Perhaps it's not good for a man's work if he is too comfortable."

"I don't know about *that!*" he said, taking a dramatic turn round the library and drawing at his pipe. "Considering I work, actually, by the clock, for twelve hours a day, and for ten hours when it's a short day, I don't think you can say I am deteriorating from easy comfort."

"No, I suppose not," she admitted.

Yet she did think it, nevertheless. His comfortableness didn't consist so much in good food and a soft bed, as in having nobody, absolutely nobody and nothing, to contradict him. "I do like to think he's got nothing to aggravate him," the secretary had said to the wife.

"Nothing to aggravate him!" What a position for a man! Fostered by women who would let nothing "aggravate" him. If anything would aggravate his wounded vanity, this would!

So thought the wife. But what was to be done about it? In the silence of midnight she heard his voice in the distance, dictating away, like the voice of God to Samuel, alone and monotonous, and she imagined the little figure of the secretary busily scribbling shorthand. Then in the sunny hours of morning, while he was still in bed—he never rose till noon—from another distance came that sharp insect-noise of the typewriter, like some immense grasshopper chirping and rattling. It was the secretary, poor thing, typing out his notes.

That girl—she was only twenty-eight—really slaved herself to skin and bone. She was small and neat, but she was actually worn out. She did far more work than he did, for she had not only to take down all those words he uttered, she had to type them out, make three copies, while he was still resting.

"What on earth she gets out of it," thought the wife, "I don't know. She's simply worn to the bone, for a very poor salary, and he's never kissed her, and never will, if I know anything about him."

Whether his never kissing her—the secretary, that is—made it worse or better, the wife did not decide. He never kissed anybody. Whether she herself—the wife, that is—wanted to be kissed by him, even that she was not clear about. She rather thought she didn't.

What on earth did she want then? She was his wife. What on earth did she want of him?

She certainly didn't want to take him down in shorthand and type out again all those words. And she didn't really want him to kiss her; she knew him too well. Yes, she knew him too well. If you know a man too well, you don't want him to kiss you.

What then? What did she want? Why had she such an extraordinary hang-over about him? Just because she was his wife? Why did she rather "enjoy" other men—and she was relentless about enjoyment—without ever taking them seriously? And why must she take him so damn seriously, when she never really "enjoyed" him?

Of course she *had* had good times with him, in the past, before— ah! before a thousand things, all amounting really to nothing. But she enjoyed him no more. She never even enjoyed being with him. There was a silent, ceaseless tension between them, that never broke, even when they were a thousand miles apart.

Awful! That's what you call being married! What's to be done about it? Ridiculous, to know it all and not do anything about it!

She came back once more, and there she was, in her own house, a sort of super-guest, even to him. And the secretarial family devoting their lives to him.

Devoting their lives to him! But actually! Three women pouring out their lives for him day and night! And what did they get in return? Not one kiss! Very little money, because they knew all about his debts, and had made it their life-business to get them paid off! No expectations! Twelve hours' work a day! Comparative isolation, for he saw nobody!

And beyond that? Nothing! Perhaps a sense of uplift and importance because they saw his name and photograph in the newspapers sometimes. But would anybody believe that it was good enough?

Yet they adored it! They seemed to get a deep satisfaction out of it, like people with a mission. Extraordinary!

Well, if they did, let them. They were, of course, rather common, "of the people"; there might be a sort of glamour in it for them.

But it was bad for him. No doubt about it. His work was getting diffuse and poor in quality—and what wonder! His whole tone was going down—becoming commoner. Of course it was bad for him.

Being his wife, she felt she ought to do something to save him. But how could she? That perfectly devoted, marvellous secretarial family, how could she make an attack on them? Yet she'd love to sweep them into oblivion. Of course they were bad for him: ruining his work, ruining his reputation as a writer, ruining his life. Ruining him with their slavish service.

Of course she ought to make an onslaught on them! But how *could* she? Such devotion! And what had she herself to offer in their place? Certainly not slavish devotion to him, nor to his flow of words! Certainly not!

She imagined him stripped once more naked of secretary and secretarial family, and she shuddered. It was like throwing the naked baby in the dust-bin. Couldn't do that!

Yet something must be done. She felt it. She was almost tempted to get into debt for another thousand pounds and send in the bill, or have it sent in to him, as usual.

But no! Something more drastic!

Something more drastic, or perhaps more gentle. She wavered between the two. And wavering, she first did nothing, came to no decision, dragged vacantly on from day to day, waiting for sufficient energy to take her departure once more.

It was spring! What a fool she had been to come up in spring! And she was forty! What an idiot of a woman to go and be forty!

She went down the garden in the warm afternoon, when birds were whistling loudly from the cover, the sky being low and warm, and she had nothing to do. The garden was full of flowers: he loved them for their theatrical display. Lilac and snowball bushes, and laburnum and red may, tulips and anemones and coloured daisies. Lots of flowers! Borders of forget-me-nots! Bachelor's buttons! What absurd names flowers had! She would have called them blue dots and yellow blobs and white frills. Not so much sentiment, after all!

There is a certain nonsense, something showy and stagey, about spring, with its pushing leaves and chorus-girl flowers, unless you have something corresponding inside you. Which she hadn't.

Oh, heaven! Beyond the hedge she heard a voice, a steady rather theatrical voice. Oh, heaven! He was dictating to his secretary, in the garden. Good God, was there nowhere to get away from it!

She looked around: there was indeed plenty of escape. But what was the good of escaping? He would go on and on. She went quietly towards the hedge, and listened.

He was dictating a magazine article about the modern novel. "What the modern novel lacks is architecture." Good God! Architecture! He might just as well say: What the modern novel lacks is whalebone, or a teaspoon, or a tooth stopped.

Yet the secretary took it down, took it down, took it down! No, this could not go on! It was more than flesh and blood could bear.

She went quietly along the hedge, somewhat wolf-like in her prowl, a broad, strong woman in an expensive mustard-coloured silk jersey and cream-coloured pleated skirt. Her legs were long and shapely, and her shoes were expensive.

With a curious wolf-like stealth she turned the hedge and looked across at the small, shaded lawn where the daisies grew impertinently. "He" was reclining in a coloured hammock under the pink-flowering horse-chestnut tree, dressed in white serge with a fine yellow-coloured linen shirt. His elegant hand dropped over the side of the hammock and beat a sort of vague rhythm to his words. At a little wicker table the little secretary, in a green knitted frock, bent her dark head over her note-book, and diligently made those awful shorthand marks. He was not difficult to take down, as he dictated slowly, and kept a sort of rhythm, beating time with his dangling hand.

"In every novel there must be one outstanding character with which we always sympathize—with *whom* we always sympathize—even though we recognize its—even when we are most aware of the human frailties——"

Every man his own hero, thought the wife grimly, forgetting that every woman is intensely her own heroine.

But what did startle her was a blue bird dashing about near the feet of the absorbed, shorthand-scribbling little secretary. At least it was a blue-tit, blue with grey and some yellow. But to the wife it seemed blue, that juicy spring day, in the translucent afternoon. The blue bird, fluttering round the pretty but rather *common* little feet of the little secretary.

The blue bird! The blue bird of happiness! Well, I'm blest, thought the wife. Well, I'm blest!

And as she was being blest, appeared another blue bird—that is, another blue-tit—and began to wrestle with the first blue-tit. A couple of blue birds of happiness, having a fight over it! Well, I'm blest!

She was more or less out of sight of the human preoccupied pair. But "he" was disturbed by the fighting blue birds, whose little feathers began to float loose.

"Get out!" he said to them mildly, waving a dark-yellow handkerchief at them. "Fight your little fight, and settle your private affairs, elsewhere, my dear little gentlemen."

The little secretary looked up quickly, for she had already begun to write it down. He smiled at her his twisted whimsical smile.

"No, don't take that down," he said affectionately. "Did you see those two tits laying into one another?"

"No!" said the little secretary, gazing brightly round, her eyes half-blinded with work.

But she saw the queer, powerful, elegant, wolf-like figure of the wife, behind her, and terror came into her eyes.

"I did!" said the wife, stepping forward with those curious, shapely, she-wolf legs of hers, under the very short skirt.

"Aren't they extraordinary vicious little beasts?" said he.

"Extraordinarily!" she re-echoed, stooping and picking up a little breast-feather. "Extraordinarily! See how the feathers fly!"

And she got the feather on the tip of her finger, and looked at it. Then she looked at the secretary, then she looked at him. She had a queer, werewolf expression between her brows.

"I think," he began, "these are the loveliest afternoons, when there's no direct sun, but all the sounds and the colours and the scents are sort of dissolved, don't you know, in the air, and the whole thing is steeped, steeped in spring. It's like being on the inside; you know how I mean, like being inside the egg and just ready to chip the shell."

"Quite like that!" she assented without conviction.

There was a little pause. The secretary said nothing. They were waiting for the wife to depart again.

"I suppose," said the latter, "you're awfully busy, as usual?"

"Just about the same," he said, pursing his mouth deprecatingly. Again the blank pause, in which he waited for her to go away again.

"I know I'm interrupting you," she said.

"As a matter of fact," he said, "I was just watching those two blue-tits."

"Pair of little demons!" said the wife, blowing away the yellow feather from her finger-tip.

"Absolutely!" he said.

"Well, I'd better go, and let you get on with your work," she said.

"No hurry!" he said, with benevolent nonchalance. "As a matter of fact, I don't think it's a great success, working out of doors."

"What made you try it?" said the wife. "You know you never could do it."

"Miss Wrexall suggested it might make a change. But I don't think it altogether helps, do you, Miss Wrexall?"

"I'm sorry," said the little secretary.

"Why should *you* be sorry?" said the wife, looking down at her as a wolf might look down half-benignly at a little black-and-tan mongrel. "You only suggested it for his good, I'm sure!"

"I thought the air might be good for him," the secretary admitted.

"Why do people like you never think about yourselves?" the wife asked.

The secretary looked her in the eye.

"I suppose we do, in a different way," she said.

"A *very* different way!" said the wife ironically. "Why don't you make *him* think about *you?*" she added slowly, with a sort of drawl. "On a soft spring afternoon like this, you ought to have him dictating poems to you, about the blue birds of happiness fluttering round your dainty little feet. I know *I* would, if I were his secretary."

There was a dead pause. The wife stood immobile and statuesque, in an attitude characteristic of her, half turning back to the little secretary, half averted. She half turned her back on everything.

The secretary looked at him.

"As a matter of fact," he said, "I was doing an article on the Future of the Novel."

"I know that," said the wife. "That's what's so awful! Why not something lively in the life of the novelist?"

There was a prolonged silence, in which he looked pained, and somewhat remote, statuesque. The little secretary hung her head. The wife sauntered slowly away.

"Just where were we, Miss Wrexall?" came the sound of his voice.

The little secretary started. She was feeling profoundly indignant. Their beautiful relationship, his and hers, to be so insulted!

But soon she was veering downstream on the flow of his words, too busy to have any feelings, except one of elation at being so busy.

Tea-time came; the sister brought out the tea-tray into the garden. And immediately, the wife appeared. She had changed, and was wearing a chicory-blue dress of fine cloth. The little secretary had gathered up her papers and was departing, on rather high heels.

"Don't go, Miss Wrexall," said the wife.

The little secretary stopped short, then hesitated.

"Mother will be expecting me," she said.

"Tell her you're not coming. And ask your sister to bring another cup. I want you to have tea with us."

Miss Wrexall looked at the man, who was reared on one elbow in the hammock, and was looking enigmatical, Hamletish.

He glanced at her quickly, then pursed his mouth in a boyish negligence.

"Yes, stay and have tea with us for once," he said. "I see strawberries, and I know you're the bird for them."

She glanced at him, smiled wanly, and hurried away to tell her mother. She even stayed long enough to slip on a silk dress.

"Why, how smart you are!" said the wife, when the little secretary reappeared on the lawn, in chicory-blue silk.

"Oh, don't look at my dress, compared to yours!" said Miss Wrexall. They were of the same colour, indeed!

"At least you earned yours, which is more than I did mine," said the wife, as she poured tea. "You like it strong?"

She looked with her heavy eyes at the smallish, birdy, blue-clad, overworked young woman, and her eyes seemed to speak many inexplicable dark volumes.

"Oh, as it comes, thank you," said Miss Wrexall, leaning nervously forward.

"It's coming pretty black, if you want to ruin your digestion," said the wife.

"Oh, I'll have some water in it, then."

"Better, I should say."

"How'd the work go—all right?" asked the wife, as they drank tea, and the two women looked at each other's blue dresses.

"Oh!" he said, "As well as you can expect. It was a piece of pure flummery. But it's what they want. Awful rot, wasn't it, Miss Wrexall?"

Miss Wrexall moved uneasily on her chair.

"It interested me," she said, "though not so much as the novel."

"The novel? Which novel?" said the wife. "Is there another new one?"

Miss Wrexall looked at him. Not for words would she give away any of his literary activities.

"Oh, I was just sketching out an idea to Miss Wrexall," he said.

"Tell us about it!" said the wife. "Miss Wrexall, *you* tell us what it's about."

She turned on her chair and fixed the little secretary.

"I'm afraid"—Miss Wrexall squirmed—"I haven't got it very clearly myself, yet."

"Oh, go along! Tell us what you *have* got then!"

Miss Wrexall sat dumb and very vexed. She felt she was being baited. She looked at the blue pleatings of her skirt.

"I'm afraid I can't," she said.

"Why are you afraid you can't? You're so *very* competent. I'm sure you've got it all at your finger-ends. I expect you write a good deal of Mr. Gee's books for him, really. He gives you the hint, and you fill it all in. Isn't that how you do it?" She spoke ironically, and as if she were teasing a child. And then she glanced down at the fine pleatings of her own blue skirt, very fine and expensive.

"Of course you're not speaking seriously?" said Miss Wrexall, rising on her mettle.

"Of course I am! I've suspected for a long time—at least, for some time—that you write a good deal of Mr. Gee's books for him, from his hints."

It was said in a tone of raillery, but it was cruel.

"I should be terribly flattered," said Miss Wrexall, straightening herself, "if I didn't know you were only trying to make me feel a fool."

"Make you feel a fool? My dear child!—why, nothing could be farther from me! You're twice as clever and a million times as competent as I am. Why, my dear child, I've the greatest admiration for you! I wouldn't do what you do, not for all the pearls in India. I *couldn't,* anyhow——"

Miss Wrexall closed up and was silent.

"Do you mean to say my books read as if——" he began, rearing up and speaking in a harrowed voice.

"I do!" said the wife. "*Just* as if Miss Wrexall had written them from your hints. I *honestly* thought she did—when you were too busy——"

"How very clever of you!" he said.

"Very!" she cried. "Especially if I was wrong!"

"Which you were," he said.

"How very extraordinary!" she cried. "Well, I am once more mistaken!"

There was a complete pause.

It was broken by Miss Wrexall, who was nervously twisting her fingers.

"You want to spoil what there is between me and him, I can see that," she said bitterly.

"My dear, but what *is* there between you and him?" asked the wife.

"I was *happy* working with him, working for him! I was happy working for him!" cried Miss Wrexall, tears of indignant anger and chagrin in her eyes.

"My dear child!" cried the wife, with simulated excitement, "go *on* being happy working with him, go on being happy while you can! If it makes you happy, why then, enjoy it! Of course! Do you think I'd be so cruel as to want to take it away from you?— working with him? *I* can't do shorthand and typewriting and double-entrance book-keeping, or whatever it's called. I tell you,

I'm utterly incompetent. I never earn anything. I'm the parasite on the British oak, like the mistletoe. The blue bird doesn't flutter round my feet. Perhaps they're too big and trampling."

She looked down at her expensive shoes.

"If I *did* have a word of criticism to offer," she said, turning to her husband, "it would be to you, Cameron, for taking so much from her and giving her nothing."

"But he gives me everything, everything!" cried Miss Wrexall. "He gives me everything!"

"What do you mean by everything?" said the wife, turning on her sternly.

Miss Wrexall pulled up short. There was a snap in the air and a change of currents.

"I mean nothing that *you* need begrudge me," said the little secretary rather haughtily. "I've never made myself cheap."

There was a blank pause.

"My God!" said the wife. "You don't call that being cheap? Why, I should say you got nothing out of him at all, you only give! And if you don't call that making yourself cheap—my God!"

"You see, we see things different," said the secretary.

"I should say we do!—*thank God!*" rejoined the wife.

"On whose behalf are you thanking God?" he asked sarcastically.

"Everybody's, I suppose! Yours, because you get everything for nothing, and Miss Wrexall's, because she seems to like it, and mine because I'm well out of it all."

"You *needn't* be out of it all," cried Miss Wrexall magnanimously, "if you didn't *put* yourself out of it all."

"Thank you, my dear, for your offer," said the wife, rising. "But I'm afraid no man can expect *two* blue birds of happiness to flutter round his feet, tearing out their little feathers!"

With which she walked away.

After a tense and desperate interim, Miss Wrexall cried:

"And *really*, need any woman be jealous of *me?*"

"Quite!" he said.

And that was all he did say.

R. V. Cassill

Fracture*

"I WON'T HAVE HIM in the house any more," she said. "I know that sounds like I'm getting old and mean and middle class and all that. But I simply don't want him here again. Is that unreasonable, hon?"

And the odd, characteristic thing about Margaret's ultimatum was that it didn't climax a discussion with her husband, who sat among the papers he had brought from the office, quiet as a well-fed Buddha. They didn't argue. Had they ever argued seriously? He couldn't remember a time. The ultimatum came at the end of an interior discussion so detailed that one suspected a regular little courtroom inside her head, where the advocates of conflicting views were allowed to confront, scowl, and grimace at each other.

So Worth thought. He had mentioned Harold at dinner. "Don Carpenter had a time with Harold yesterday," he said. "Seems Harold was coming over to his place for something. Well, Harold

* From STORIES FROM EPOCH, Baxter Hathaway, ed. (Cornell University Press, 1966). Reprinted by permission of R.V. Cassill.

called to say that he'd got stuck in a bar on 83rd and wondered if Don would pick him up. When Don got there Harold was out in front heckling a parade of school children. I guess he was in wild shape—not shaved and you know how he looks with a beard on that green depraved face of his. Everytime a bunch of kids in costume would pass him he'd say loudly, 'Ain't that gawd dam cute?' Don says that there was a big circle around him, an empty place where women had pulled back away from him with their babies, kind of watching him uneasily out of the corners of their eyes."

"Oh good Lord," Margaret said.

"Then—this is the rich part—Don took him home and it seems that Don's uncle had just dropped in too. Don went out to the kitchen to mix a drink. Harold followed him out and said in a very loud voice, 'Where'd you get that ugly ball-headed sonofabitch? Uncle huh? Uncle Shmunkle.' Don's mother came tearing out and made Don get Harold out of the house."

"I admit," Margaret said, "that I don't see what's funny about it. Harold's just pathological. He ought to be locked up. There's nothing funny about a sick man. Harold is disgusting."

"Oh well," Worth said. The matter seemed to drop, but he knew it was being argued further in her mind. Since they had left the table and come to the living room, sitting with Margaret had been like sitting in a theater where the curtain for some reason is not yet raised. The action has evidently begun and sometimes the curtain is bulged or fretted by the movement of the actors. There is suspense but no sound until suddenly the stage manager resolves the conflict, says, "I won't have him in the house," banishes the contentious pleader so that when the curtain does go up the stage is vacant—but very orderly. Reason has swept it clean. The closed session has found results which may be published. Margaret has made up her mind.

"Whatever you want," Worth said. "I can take Harold—usually I can take him—or leave him alone. If you don't want him here. . . ." He shifted in his chair to settle back in contentment with her and the life they worked out together. She makes up her mind, he thought, just the way she set about fixing up this apartment, considering each of the rather drab possibilities and finally imposing sweet reason on what had been a hodgepodge of dowdiness when they moved in. Two years ago when they came to the city they had no choice but to take this fantastically old-fashioned apartment in a gone-to-seed neighborhood. And now look at it. The brown and purple drapes were gone. The lighting was rearranged. Painting the walls in the best modern way, working their furniture into place so it seemed to fit not only the dimensions of the room but the very habits of their living together had transformed the grotesqueness that seemed, God knows, to have been built into these rooms to a gray, white and ivory order in which their large Braque reproduction fitted as smoothly as the parts of a gyro compass. When he came home in the evening there was a kind of soothing each time he passed from the battered street to the precision of their apartment. This orderliness was Margaret's way with all things. His comfort was all her doing.

Of course it was all her doing, and yet it was an important part of her orderliness that she should ask, when the question had really been tied up and disposed of, "Is that unreasonable?" Her arrangements would be incomplete without his approval. And of course he gave it.

"It isn't at all, darling. There is no point in injuring ourselves trying to be courteous to Harold. He doesn't live in a mental world where courtesy makes any difference anyhow." Worth yawned. "You're the one to say. It's your home. He's your family friend."

"Well," she said, and obviously this was a point she had dispatched far back in her silent debate. "I don't think his coming from the same town makes an obligation at all. No . . . there are so many things about him that I can't stand. Like the change he picked up in the bar the other day. I don't think he was so drunk he didn't know whose it was. I would have called him to book for that."

"I should have," Worth said. "My fault, dear. I could have pointed out to him quietly that it was ours. It didn't seem worth mentioning at the time."

"How much was it?"

"Seven or eight dollars. I should have. . . ."

"I won't have you blame yourself," Margaret said. "It simply isn't your fault. You always act in a good sane way. But there goes Harold with our seven or eight dollars. So. . . . Then his harping at the Courtneys. 'The Courtneys are sonsofbitches, the

Courtneys are sonsofbitches.' I think I told him rather stiffly that the Courtneys are friends of ours. He didn't pay any attention to me. That's too much. He says the same things about us to other people, for no reason. Did we ever give him any reason? I admit nobody believes him, but it scares me to know he's talking like that about us."

"I doubt if he talks about us," Worth said.

"How can you be sure?"

"I think he likes us. Poor Harold."

"OK, Worth. There's no way to be sure. Let's drop that point. But about a month ago—I didn't tell you this—I caught him stealing a bottle out of the closet right there. He looked like a mean little kid. I thought he was going to hit me when I caught him. I was truly scared. You were in the kitchen and I almost screamed."

"Oh not Harold. Harold wouldn't hurt a fly."

She came over and sat on the arm of the chair. Her plaid wool skirt rubbed his arm. He smelled the briskly clean smell of the wool. "Is it really all right with you if we don't have Harold here again? I mean not let him in if he comes? He'll be here knocking at our door sometime and we'll have to tell him he can't come in. I'll do it. I wouldn't expect you to because you're so softhearted. But is it really OK if I tell him NO he can't come in?"

"Sure." He smiled, pulled her down to him so he could rub her forehead with his nose. "After all, our marriage would be a poor partnership if we couldn't talk and arrange things like this. Let Harold go."

"You're so good," Margaret said. "You're good to everyone and I'm not like that. I'm just not made that way," she said in a childlike voice. He pecked happily at her cheek.

Presently when she had gone to the kitchen he had a pleasant vision of her in this part of her self-created setting, her blade-slender figure among the gray and white planes of the kitchen furniture. The warm brown gray of the walls was one of the colors that Margaret had mixed herself. A real triumph of taste.

Thinking of her in her simple and spotless kitchen and thinking how much the simplicity and severity of it pleased her, he wondered what had got into him that evening when he had thought of buying her the bracelet. Her thirtieth birthday was not very far off. This year he had not known what to get her. Since he'd come back from the ETO, birthday presents had been quite simple for her. Clothes that she had halfway picked for herself—pausing just far enough short of actual selection so he'd have an area of choice to make it his gift—or something for the apartment. They were settled now and her wardrobe was well rounded. It would have to be something different this year. Still the bracelet had been been a wild impulse, clear off the track.

The jewelry she liked was the sort which had the plain beauty of a microscope or a camera or some other instrument of precision. Her jewel box looked like an instrument case. Silver went with her clothes. He supposed the cool color of silver was really meant for her.

The bracelet fitted none of these conditions. He had noticed it in the window of a shop just at the edge of their neighborhood. The shop window was stuck full of junk, bracelets and rings and necklaces that were completely tasteless. At first glance this bracelet was the same kind of thing. There were spars of gold angling out of the band like the grains in a head of barley. It was oddly made. There were three coils of gold wire ending in the spars and the clasp fastened by wrapping these coils together like a spring. When his eye had stopped on it among the other junky pieces it had occurred to him that it had a quality of its own. It looked genuinely like a savage ornament, and it seemed to him Margaret might like it for its outright contrast to the other jewelry she owned.

Now that seemed a bad idea. Still he would not make up his mind. A bit of contrast quite unexpectedly given might please Margaret more than he knew.

Later that evening they talked more about Harold. She had passed judgment and even the specter of him should have been banished out of the apartment. It hadn't gone yet. She was restless. She might have been feeling that in her efforts at justice something had been overlooked. At last she said, "About Harold. Do you really agree with me? I can't be sure of myself. I knew Harold when he was a little boy, and I used to remember that I thought—after I left home, I mean—that he wasn't like the rest of the Parsons, not so stuck up. Maybe now that I have the chance to be nasty to him I'm paying back the Parsons family for the way they used to be. And if he's the only good one in the lot. . . . He is awfully poor, don't you suppose?"

"I suppose."
"And he is an artist."
"Not really. I don't think he works at all. He talks big about a book he's writing. Nobody has ever seen a page of it."
"I don't want to hurt him because there's something malicious in me," she said. "I want to be right."
"Now, darling, you gave your reasons like a little lawyer. They seem adequate. You could probably find more if you thought longer."
"Only, am I sure?" she said.
"Hon, it's all settled. Good-bye to Harold."
She sighed her contentment, twisted down in the couch so the breeze from the window would not touch her head any more.
"Thank you for keeping me straight, friend. I couldn't stand to have him come here any more," she said.

Thursday evening on their way home from the movies they stopped in the neighborhood bar and found Harold there. He had been waiting for them, it turned out, after he had called their apartment and got no answer.

They had not noticed him when they came in; they had taken their usual table back by the empty dance floor and had been served their drinks. They sipped and then there was a moment of silence. Worth was wondering if he ought to give his wife the bracelet which he had, after all, bought for her birthday. That odd gold bracelet was right now in his inside coat pocket, wrapped in a tissue-paper parcel. There were only two more days until her birthday and they had never made much of waiting to show the presents they had for each other. Now he was feeling that he might be able to explain well his reasons for buying something so out of character —so garish—for her. He might make a few amusing observations on the subject which she would remember and which would associate themselves ever after with the gift.

Then all at once Harold was standing over them. His shocking face peered down at them woefully. "Hello. I know I made a big ass out of myself the last time I saw you," he said. "Gawd. I can't drink decently and I know it. What's that got to do with it? No excuse. I made an ass out of myself. Period. See? I don't even know how to apologize decently. Oh forget it. Jesus." His face in the bar lights looked decayed and his clothes smelled with a combination of wet wool, urine, and tobacco smells. "Can I sit down?" he asked. "Or do you want me to get to hell away from you?"

Worth threw a smile to his wife and said, "Sit down, please. What will you drink?"

"Listen," Harold said doggedly, like a child who drives himself to say something which is not only painful but which seems to him to verge on nonsense as well. "May I sit down, Margy? I know what I did, too. I know I got some of your money the other night. God. I don't know how I did it. Did I . . . ? I guess not. Forget it. I know I didn't have any and then the next morning right in my breast pocket I found six dollars. How much was it now? I want you to tell the truth." He pushed a handful of dollar bills across the table, fifteen or twenty of them, wrinkled so much the pile stood an inch thick. "Please now, tell me."

"Never mind," Margaret said sharply. "We've forgotten about it."

"No, no, please tell me."

He's going to cry, Worth thought, and that isn't necessary.

"Here's the whiskey. Drink up, everybody. It was change from a ten, Harold, about eight and a quarter," he said.

After he took the money they drank in silence. A boy and girl left their stools at the bar and came back to the dance floor. The boy put a quarter in the jukebox, turned to the girl with an almost imperceptible shrug of invitation. Her body rose to meet him as the music began. She went on tiptoe against him. The music had been chosen for the season—to say it was April, to make blatantly clear what the wind on the streets was all for.

"Jesus," Harold said. "Too much noise. We can't talk here. I hate to ask. . . . Forget it. Can we go up to your place for a nightcap? Here's the pitch. I've got to talk to you people tonight. That's not a joke."

"Well. . . ." Margaret seemed to be deliberating.

"I know what you must think of me," Harold said.

"We'll do it this way," Worth said. "Margaret's tired, but you and I will run down to your place for a while. For one drink. I've got to be at the office tomorrow and that's no joke either."

The street, when they went out with Harold, seemed by accident or miracle to have changed from what it was twenty minutes before. Perhaps because the bar was so dark, there seemed to be a luminosity in the air that they had not noticed, as if the air were full of a million sequins. When they had come from the theater the street was empty. Now a whole parade of boys and girls moved up the block—not exactly conjured by magic, because it was time for intermission at the Y dance, but magically making the night big and disquieting.

"I'll be home by twelve," Worth said; and at that moment as he looked around he was startled by his wife's face, her look of frightened determination.

"If it's only for that long"—she laughed—"I'll come too. If I may, Harold?"

Why? It was too silly, Worth thought, to believe that she was afraid Harold would lead him astray. He could not account for it.

"Please," Harold said. "I'm glad you're coming. The two of you together is what I need to get me out of my rut. I mean you people are such a team. Nuts. I mean I like you sooo." Delighted now, he made them hold the cab while he went back inside to get an extra pint.

They had been fooled and taken in, there was no doubt of that. In their moment of compassion in the bar Harold had made a demand on them they could not refuse. Who could tell what desperate thing he might do if they would not help him? He had looked so terribly wasted and shaky. Now, climbing the stairs to his apartment, his drunken unbearable arrogance was loose again. The taxi ride had given him time to drink half the pint like a happy child drinking pop.

"You might know them sonofabitching Courtneys," he said to Margaret. "You know what that bitch Alice Courtney said to me the other day? 'Harold, you're malodious,' she said. I ought to let her have it right in the mouth. So she thinks I'm a bum, so what? Forget it." He had grabbed Margaret's arm—his black fingernails pinching into the cloth of her coat—and was dragging her up the stairs at his own headlong pace, thrusting his ugly happy face toward her, ignoring her anger. "Yeah. That bitch. You know who she's playing around with while that fag husband of hers goes out with his fag pals? I'll tell you. . . ."

"Oh!"—the convulsive, revolted sigh of Margaret's breath.

It seemed to Worth that his wife would turn at any moment and march righteously toward home; and he thought later that she might have done so if they had not come then to Harold's door and into what he had always referred to as his apartment.

The shock of seeing it—the immediate acid shock—must have restored anyone from the notion that Harold was more to be blamed than pitied. There was a studio couch unfolded in the room with a brown blanket rumpled across it, crumbs and grease spots on the blue couch upholstery, and no sign of any linens. In front of the couch was a long coffee table crowded with beer cans from which the roaches poured as the light went on. Among the cans were crusts and slivers of meat. There was a chair in the room. There were three skillets and some dirty plates in the opposite corner on the floor. Something that looked like an egg had been trampled into the linoleum.

"It's lovely, Harold, lovely," Margaret exclaimed. Her voice rang with triumph. After all, her excursion over here was not in vain. To see this den of corruption was revenge for the embarrassments he had caused her. "Maid's day off?"

He stood blinking in the harsh light from the ceiling fixture. He had not counted on the room's being this way. His befuddled face suggested that gnomes must have come in while he was gone and lived the hell out of his room. "It's kind of messy," he said in a diminished voice. "Glasses. We've got to have glasses. You see any?"

"I'll look under the couch," Margaret said. While he went out to get some she asked Worth, "Are you going to sit *down* here?" She pulled her wool skirt against her hips as if it were iron that she was fitting close for protection. She moved away from the couch. It might have jumping bugs.

Worth said, "Kilroy was here. Before that Raskolnikov had this suite, I suppose. What the hell? Let's sit down and have a drink anyway. Maybe he does have something on his mind he needs to talk about. You take the chair. I'll sit on the couch."

"He doesn't need us."

"We'll see."

"Worth, doesn't this bother you? I don't understand you."

"I wouldn't want to live here. It's interesting."

"If you could tell me why. . . . It's just filthy."

Down the hall they heard Harold speaking and heard a woman's voice—a bawdy, bubbling, fat-woman's voice—answer him with a joke.

"Don't needle him about it," Worth said.

The glasses Harold brought were greasy. Beads of cold water huddled on their surfaces. He divided the whiskey and took an armful of the beer cans from the table so they would have a place to set their drinks.

"It's a mess," Harold said. "But let me explain something—it's always this way." When he laughed very heartily at his joke the laughter turned into prolonged coughing. He rubbed his lips with his fist after he coughed and rubbed his fist on the cover of the studio couch. Margaret set her glass down hard. After seeing the slime on his lips she had no intention of drinking from any of his glasses.

"Have you been doing any work, Harold?" Worth asked. "We hardly know what you're doing these days. The novel you were. . . ."

"I haven't committed it yet," Harold said. "I been thinking about it. I may make it oral." His eyes were swinging to cover every detail of the room, as though some arrangement of the papers piled on the floor, the cans, the skillets, and the milk cartons behind the door might hold a pattern which he did not yet know. "Needs a woman's touch, don't it? But nothing like I do. Pretty Sarah is the girl. That's what I have to talk to you Joes about." Again he coughed and rubbed his mouth. "Women, shmimmen. I had a babe and now she's gone."

"Sounds like a blues number," Worth said.

"Don't it? Listen I wrote some song lyrics yesterday. Tell me what you think of this." He began humming the tune of *Night and Day*. "Hell, I don't remember. It was about a guy whose girl left him and it's spring, see?"

"Never mind," Worth said. "Tell your story. You had a girl and she's left you."

Margaret's face tightened even more. She had never looked colder, more like a disapproving schoolteacher. She was carried by the intensity of her disapproval to a foolish question. "Here?"

"Here, shmere," Harold said. He was jolly drunk enough to ignore what Margaret might think of him. "You know her, Worth, old boy. You ought to know her. Found her when I came to hunt you one day. Never did find you. Found her. She works at your office. Out in the pen in front where they got this acre of pretty girls. Pounds a typewriter. Pretty Sarah LeRoy is the one I mean."

"You're joking," Worth said. "LeRoy's a kid. She can't be more than. . . ."

"Well, she's seventeen."

"Good God, Harold."

"Now wait. I ain't so old myself. Relative matter of course. I'm only twenty-seven and the baby of the family. Right, Margaret? Margaret knew me when I was a baby at the breast."

He kept on talking, a harsh croon intended obviously for himself, but pointless and perhaps impossible to him unless he had them there to sit as though he were telling them something. Worth did not listen. He was thinking about Sarah LeRoy. Such a pretty little kid. The starched white of her blouses every morning, the skin that kept fluctuating in color whenever he talked to her, her pleasant eagerness to get work done just right for him, "Yes, Mr. Hough. Yes," the hands that looked so clean and creamy but not yet shaped like a grown woman's hands, the smooth fall of her hair brushed neat for school, he thought, a pretty little maid from school. His idea of her had been so fixed that what he was hearing from Harold stabbed at him like the discovery of a betrayal.

". . . Damn near three months," Harold was saying. "Through the winter when it was cold. Happy as little old puppies. Bang, Slam, one day she hits me right in the mouth. 'Only reason you want to marry me is you think you ought to.' 'Right,' I said. I was real smart. Whatta quick comeback that was. So bang, slam, she let me have it while I was lying flat on my back in bed. Out the door she goes without even waiting to pack her douche bag. I shouldn't have said that to her because this weather is so nice. I sure need her because. . . ."

"Please," Margaret said. "You have no right to tell us things like that. Oh come on, Worth. I can't stand any more of this."

"Sure wish I could coax her back," Harold said. "She was so pretty, so beautiful, so lovely." He lay over against the arm of the studio couch, breathing heavily through his mouth. His tongue lay for a second against his ugly lips. "Listen, Worth, old boy, she won't even let me come near to her. I chased her on the street one day, and she ran up to a big fat mean-looking cop. That's a fact. You hear me, Worth? Here's what I want you to do. . . ."

Margaret was at the door, her gloved hand resting on the frame and her whole body inclined for immediate exit. "Worth . . . ," she said.

"Coming."

Harold said, "What I want you to do is talk to her for me."

"I'm sorry, Harold."

"Now listen, Worth, I know what I'm talking about. She thinks you're brains from the belly up. That's a fact. She told me. You're her boss. Now listen, you talk to her. Tell her old Harold's cleaned up and quit drinking. If you get a rise out of her, I will, too. Anyway talk to her sensible. Tell her. . . . I mean she's an adult. Don't give her any Sunny School guff. Just tell her old Harold. . . ." Then gently his voice stopped. His hand with the fingers spread and cupped moved caressingly over the arm of the couch. His face in their last glimpse looked sick and moldy as the room, but young, like a debauched-child's face.

Their taxi moved for what seemed a very long time through streets of velvety darkness. Over and over Worth thought, Not Sarah LeRoy. It seemed impossible to him and then impossible that he should have been so wrong about her. He had been thinking of her as he would have thought of a daughter, and she was living with a man almost his own age.

Once when they stopped at a traffic light and the cab was lit from the store windows on the corner he noticed Margaret watching him distantly. "You're not going to, are you?" she said.

"Going to what?"

"Going to talk to this tramp about Harold?"

"No. Of course not, darling. She's not a tramp, though. We mustn't jump to any judgments."

"Living with *Harold* in that sty? Oh no." He could not see her face, but he felt her shudder.

He smiled to himself. He had the melancholy and lonely notion that he was assailed from all sides by the grotesque emotions of other people. "Now, darling," he said, "love and cleanliness are not necessarily mutually dependent, whatever the soap ads say." As he spoke it seemed that the cab might as well be the basket of a balloon carrying him miles above the earth while down below the earth was twinkling with the thousand garrulous lights of April. How comic and melancholy to ride at that height saying reasonable things to the empty air.

"Love!" Margaret said. "I've heard everything now."

She went to bed as soon as they got home. "Don't stay up too late," she said.

When he saw the light go out in the bedroom he got a small glass of whiskey from the cupboard. Something soft that the wind carried beat twice against the window. He went to the window and looked down. It was too late now for anyone to be on the street. The upreaching branches of the trees below him swayed as though they were a scaffold that might sometime—soon—collapse all at once to show him the secret and filthy processes of spring among the roots. In the meantime it seemed that this fragile scaffold was supporting him at a lonely height. If the wind rose more, he might hear the snap of branches giving way, letting him drop.

"Margaret," he called. "Margaret? Tonight *was* good-bye to Harold. Never again." He called this out jovially. He went to the bedroom door, wanting to talk to her. If the two of them could really agree and think together they might keep their lofty and precarious perch above the mess that the Harolds and LeRoys made of their lives. He peered toward the dark bed. "Margaret?"

"All right," she said. "I heard you. Please. I'm too tired to talk about it tonight any more."

But I have to talk about it, dear Margaret, he thought. Tonight all this has jarred me loose. He went back toward the window and this time, as he approached it, was sharply aware of his own reflection emerging on it—the reflection of his white shirt; his head, hands and trousers being darker hardly registered on the transparent pane. The white animate shape jiggled on the glass. Then in a trick of vision it seemed to be moving against the cover on Harold's couch, an immaculate substance on the dirty blanket. As though it were one of Sarah LeRoy's white blouses he was staring at.

Sarah LeRoy—how wrong could he be about someone? For a long time he thought he had her figured out perfectly, and he was quite wrong. From his height in the air he had never seen her as a woman at all. He had missed the simplest fact in the world. A surge of self-pity struck him, the realization that his cleverness had someway cheated him.

He drank and then without thinking lifted his hand to the pocket where the bracelet lay wrapped in its soft paper. His fingers tightened on it and he felt its spring give under the pressure.

Margaret's bracelet for her thirtieth birthday. No. He saw now why he had bought this gaudy bit of jewelry. It was not for Margaret.

He was pinching the bracelet together as though he were already fitting it to someone's wrist.

"Sarah LeRoy," he whispered in amazement. "I'll be damned." Harold seemed to him, just then, very lucky. He envied Harold everything—his enemies, his dirty room, his mammoth drunks, his cough, his Sarah. He saw now why Margaret had wanted so much to get Harold cleanly out of their way. She had been afraid sometime he might envy Harold. She had known what that envy would mean to him; she had known what he was just beginning to grasp— that envy would never lead him to imitate Harold, nor even actually give the bracelet to Sarah, but that it would swing a cold light on his own imcompleteness. He saw—or thought he saw—how every limitation in Margaret's life had been placed carefully, like a spar to shore over and hide from him his own matching frailty, and his heart was stung with a treacherous wish to wake her and tell her he understood. At the same time he knew that the time itself for such communication had been spent as ransom against his terrible need.

He opened the window a little as if the stable air of the room were choking him. A flat tongue of wind came in, sliding its secret dampness and urgency against him with a tremor, and on its motion he heard the crackle of branches breaking.

AUTHOR'S NOTE ON "FRACTURE"

The post-publication history of this piece has been more illuminating for me, perhaps, than the insights that preceded or accompanied its composition. It sprang from a doubly exasperating acquaintance with a young man. He wasted my time and I pitied him for his troubles, and yet in some curious way I envied him. These contradictory tendencies sufficed as material for writing the story, dictating that invention of detail and circumstance which is always part of transferring one's observations from life into fiction. But once the story was done and printed it began to dawn on me—and was pointed out to me by recurring comment —that what had seemed a fairly singular relationship was, in fact, but part of a continuing and spreading disharmony between my generation and its successors. It became clear that my unhappy and dissolute character was a sort of natural prototype for the self-styled Beat Generation. And they begat the Flower Children. And when I think of the story now, many years after it was written, I do not think of this or that episode or detail it contains. Rather, it all coalesces into a fragment of handwriting on the wall: Thou shalt not be at ease with the young. Really, it is a painful story for me to recollect. It is my sharpest, and perhaps saddest, formulation of the conflict doomed to exist between aging and young people.

Katherine Anne Porter

The Jilting of Granny Weatherall*

SHE FLICKED HER WRIST neatly out of Doctor Harry's pudgy careful fingers and pulled the sheet up to her chin. The brat ought to be in knee breeches. Doctoring around the country with spectacles on his nose! "Get along now, take your schoolbooks and go. There's nothing wrong with me."

Doctor Harry spread a warm paw like a cushion on her forehead where the forked green vein danced and made her eyelids twitch. "Now, now, be a good girl, and we'll have you up in no time."

"That's no way to speak to a woman nearly eighty years old just because she's down. I'd have you respect your elders, young man."

"Well, Missy, excuse me." Doctor Harry patted her cheek. "But I've got to warn you, haven't I? You're a marvel, but you must be careful or you're going to be good and sorry."

---

* Copyright, 1930, 1958, by Katherine Anne Porter. Reprinted from her volume, FLOWERING JUDAS AND OTHER STORIES by permission of Harcourt Brace Jovanovich, Inc.

"Don't tell me what I'm going to be. I'm on my feet now, morally speaking. It's Cornelia. I had to go to bed to get rid of her."

Her bones felt loose, and floated around in her skin, and Doctor Harry floated like a balloon around the foot of the bed. He floated and pulled down his waistcoat and swung his glasses on a cord. "Well, stay where you are, it certainly can't hurt you."

"Get along and doctor your sick," said Granny Weatherall. "Leave a well woman alone. I'll call for you when I want you. . . . Where were you forty years ago when I pulled through milk-leg and double pneumonia? You weren't even born. Don't let Cornelia lead you on," she shouted, because Doctor Harry appeared to float up to the ceiling and out. "I pay my own bills, and I don't throw my money away on nonsense!"

She meant to wave good-by, but it was too much trouble. Her eyes closed of themselves, it was like a dark curtain drawn around the bed. The pillow rose and floated under her, pleasant as a hammock in a light wind. She listened to the leaves rustling outside the window. No, somebody was swishing newspapers: no, Cornelia and Doctor Harry were whispering together. She leaped broad awake, thinking they whispered in her ear.

"She was never like this, *never* like this!" "Well, what can we expect?" "Yes, eighty years old. . . ."

Well, and what if she was? She still had ears. It was like Cornelia to whisper around doors. She always kept things secret in such a public way. She was always being tactful and kind. Cornelia was dutiful; that was the trouble with her. Dutiful and good: "So good and dutiful," said Granny, "that I'd like to spank her." She saw herself spanking Cornelia and making a fine job of it.

"What'd you say, Mother?"

Granny felt her face tying up in hard knots.

"Can't a body think, I'd like to know?"

"I thought you might want something."

"I do. I want a lot of things. First off, go away and don't whisper."

She lay and drowsed, hoping in her sleep that the children would keep out and let her rest a minute. It had been a long day. Not that she was tired. It was always pleasant to snatch a minute now and then. There was always so much to be done, let me see: tomorrow. Tomorrow was far away and there was nothing to trouble about. Things were finished somehow when the time came; thank God there was always a little margin over for peace: then a person could spread out the plan of life and tuck in the edges orderly. It was good to have everything clean and folded away, with the hair brushes and tonic bottles sitting straight on the white embroidered linen: the day started without fuss and the pantry shelves laid out with rows of jelly glasses and brown jugs and white stone-china jars with blue whirligigs and words painted on them: coffee, tea, sugar, ginger, cinnamon, allspice: and the bronze clock with the lion on top nicely dusted off. The dust that lion could collect in twenty-four hours! The box in the attic with all those letters tied up, well, she'd have to go through that tomorrow. All those letters—George's letters and John's letters and her letters to them both—lying around for the children to find afterwards made her uneasy. Yes, that would be tomorrow's business. No use to let them know how silly she had been once.

While she was rummaging around she found death in her mind and it felt clammy and unfamiliar. She had spent so much time preparing for death there was no need for bringing it up again. Let it take care of itself now. When she was sixty she had felt very old, finished, and went around making farewell trips to see her children and grandchildren, with a secret in her mind: This is the very last of your mother, children! Then she made her will and came down with a long fever. That was all just a notion like a lot of other things, but it was lucky too, for she had once for all got over the idea of dying for a long time. Now she couldn't be worried. She hoped she had better sense now. Her father had lived to be one hundred and two years old and had drunk a noggin of strong hot toddy on his last birthday. He told the reporters it was his daily habit, and he owed his long life to that. He had made quite a scandal and was very pleased about it. She believed she'd just plague Cornelia a little.

"Cornelia! Cornelia!" No footsteps, but a sudden hand on her cheek. "Bless you, where have you been?"

"Here, Mother."

"Well, Cornelia, I want a noggin of hot toddy."

"Are you cold, darling?"

"I'm chilly, Cornelia. Lying in bed stops the circulation. I must have told you that a thousand times."

Well, she could just hear Cornelia telling her husband that Mother was getting a little childish and they'd have to humor her. The thing that most annoyed her was that Cornelia thought she was deaf, dumb, and blind. Little hasty glances and tiny gestures tossed around her and over her head saying, "Don't cross her, let her have her way, she's eighty years old," and she sitting there as if she lived in a thin glass cage. Sometimes Granny almost made up her mind to pack up and move back to her own house where nobody could remind her every minute that she was old. Wait, wait, Cornelia, till your own children whisper behind your back!

In her day she had kept a better house and had got more work done. She wasn't too old yet for Lydia to be driving eighty miles for advice when one of the children jumped the track, and Jimmy still dropped in and talked things over: "Now, Mammy, you've a good business head, I want to know what you think of this? . . ." Old. Cornelia couldn't change the furniture around without asking. Little things, little things! They had been so sweet when they were little. Granny wished the old days were back again with the children young and everything to be done over. It had been a hard pull, but not too much for her. When she thought of all the food she had cooked, and all the clothes she had cut and sewed, and all the gardens she had made—well, the children showed it. There they were, made out of her, and they couldn't get away from that. Sometimes she wanted to see John again and point to them and say, Well, I didn't do so badly, did I? But that would have to wait. That was for tomorrow. She used to think of him as a man, but now all the children were older than their father, and he would be a child beside her if she saw him now. It seemed strange and there was something wrong in the idea. Why, he couldn't possibly recognize her. She had fenced in a hundred acres once, digging the post holes herself and clamping the wires with just a Negro boy to help. That changed a woman. John would be looking for a young woman with the peaked Spanish comb in her hair and the painted fan. Digging post holes changed a woman. Riding country roads in the winter when women had their babies was another thing: sitting up nights with sick horses and sick Negroes and sick children and hardly ever losing one. John, I hardly ever lost one of them! John would see that in a minute, that would be something he could understand, she wouldn't have to explain anything!

It made her feel like rolling up her sleeves and putting the whole place to rights again. No matter if Cornelia was determined to be everywhere at once, there were a great many things left undone on this place. She would start tomorrow and do them. It was good to be strong enough for everything, even if all you made melted and changed and slipped under your hands, so that by the time you finished you almost forgot what you were working for. What was it I set out to do? she asked herself intently, but she could not remember. A fog rose over the valley, she saw it marching across the creek swallowing the trees and moving up the hill like an army of ghosts. Soon it would be at the near edge of the orchard, and then it was time to go in and light the lamps. Come in, children, don't stay out in the night air.

Lighting the lamps had been beautiful. The children huddled up to her and breathed like little calves waiting at the bars in the twilight. Their eyes followed the match and watched the flame rise and settle in a blue curve, then they moved away from her. The lamp was lit, they didn't have to be scared and hang on to mother any more. Never, never, never more. God, for all my life I thank Thee. Without Thee, my God, I could never have done it. Hail, Mary, full of grace.

I want you to pick all the fruit this year and see that nothing is wasted. There's always someone who can use it. Don't let good things rot for want of using. You waste life when you waste good food. Don't let things get lost. It's bitter to lose things. Now, don't let me get to thinking, not when I am tired and taking a little nap before supper. . . .

The pillow rose about her shoulders and pressed against her

heart and the memory was being squeezed out of it: oh, push down the pillow, somebody: it would smother her if she tried to hold it. Such a fresh breeze blowing and such a green day with no threats in it. But he had not come, just the same. What does a woman do when she has put on the white veil and set out the white cake for a man and he doesn't come? She tried to remember. No, I swear he never harmed me but in that. He never harmed me but in that . . . and what if he did? There was the day, the day, but a whirl of dark smoke rose and covered it, crept up and over into the bright field where everything was planted so carefully in orderly rows. That was hell, she knew hell when she saw it. For sixty years she had prayed against remembering him and against losing her soul in the deep pit of hell, and now the two things were mingled in one and the thought of him was a smoky cloud from hell that moved and crept in her head when she had just got rid of Doctor Harry and was trying to rest a minute. Wounded vanity, Ellen, said a sharp voice in the top of her mind. Don't let your wounded vanity get the upper hand of you. Plenty of girls get jilted. You were jilted, weren't you? Then stand up to it. Her eyelids wavered and let in streamers of blue-gray light like tissue paper over her eyes. She must get up and pull the shades down or she'd never sleep. She was in bed again and the shades were not down. How could that happen? Better turn over, hide from the light, sleeping in the light gave you nightmares. "Mother, how do you feel now?" and a stinging wetness on her forehead. But I don't like having my face washed in cold water!

Hapsy? George? Lydia? Jimmy? No, Cornelia, and her features were swollen and full of little puddles. "They're coming, darling, they'll all be here soon." Go wash your face, child, you look funny.

Instead of obeying, Cornelia knelt down and put her head on the pillow. She seemed to be talking but there was no sound. "Well, are you tongue-tied? Whose birthday is it? Are you going to give a party?"

Cornelia's mouth moved urgently in strange shapes. "Don't do that, you bother me, daughter."

"Oh, no, Mother. Oh, no. . . ."

Nonsense. It was strange about children. They disputed your every word. "No what, Cornelia?"
"Here's Doctor Harry."
"I won't see that boy again. He just left five minutes ago."
"That was this morning, Mother. It's night now. Here's the nurse."
"This is Doctor Harry, Mrs. Weatherall. I never saw you look so young and happy!"
"Ah, I'll never be young again—but I'd be happy if they'd let me lie in peace and get rested."

She thought she spoke up loudly, but no one answered. A warm weight on her forehead, a warm bracelet on her wrist, and a breeze went on whispering, trying to tell her something. A shuffle of leaves in the everlasting hand of God, He blew on them and they danced and rattled. "Mother, don't mind, we're going to give you a little hypodermic." "Look here, daughter, how do ants get in this bed? I saw sugar ants yesterday." Did you send for Hapsy too?

It was Hapsy she really wanted. She had to go a long way back through a great many rooms to find Hapsy standing with a baby on her arm. She seemed to herself to be Hapsy also, and the baby on Hapsy's arm was Hapsy and himself and herself, all at once, and there was no surprise in the meeting. Then Hapsy melted from within and turned flimsy as gray gauze and the baby was a gauzy shadow, and Hapsy came up close and said, "I thought you'd never come," and looked at her very searchingly and said, "You haven't changed a bit!" They leaned forward to kiss, when Cornelia began whispering from a long way off, "Oh, is there anything you want to tell me? Is there anything I can do for you?"

Yes, she had changed her mind after sixty years and she would like to see George. I want you to find George. Find him and be sure to tell him I forgot him. I want him to know I had my husband just the same and my children and my house like any other woman. A good house too and a good husband that I loved and fine children out of him. Better than I hoped for even. Tell him I was given back everything he took away and more. Oh, no, oh, God, no, there was something else besides the house and the man and the children. Oh, surely they were not all? What was it? Something not given back. . . . Her breath crowded down under her ribs and grew into a monstrous frightening shape with cutting edges; it bored up into her head, and the agony was unbelievable: Yes, John, get the Doctor now, no more talk, my time has come.

When this one was born it should be the last. The last. It should have been born first, for it was the one she had truly wanted. Everything came in good time. Nothing left out, left over. She was strong, in three days she would be as well as ever. Better. A woman needed milk in her to have her full health.

"Mother, do you hear me?"

"I've been telling you—"

"Mother, Father Connolly's here."

"I went to Holy Communion only last week. Tell him I'm not so sinful as all that."

"Father just wants to speak to you."

He could speak as much as he pleased. It was like him to drop in and inquire about her soul as if it were a teething baby, and then stay on for a cup of tea and a round of cards and gossip. He always had a funny story of some sort, usually about an Irishman who made his little mistakes and confessed them, and the point lay in some absurd thing he would blurt out in the confessional showing his struggles between native piety and original sin. Granny felt easy about her soul. Cornelia, where are your manners? Give Father Connolly a chair. She had her secret comfortable understanding with a few favorite saints who cleared a straight road to God for her. All as surely signed and sealed as the papers for the new Forty Acres. Forever . . . heirs and assigns forever. Since the day the wedding cake was not cut, but thrown out and wasted. The whole bottom dropped out of the world, and there she was blind and sweating with nothing under her feet and the walls falling away. His hand had caught her under the breast, she had not fallen, there was the freshly polished floor with the green rug on it, just as before. He had cursed like a sailor's parrot and said, "I'll kill him for you." Don't lay a hand on him, for my sake leave something to God. "Now, Ellen, you must believe what I tell you. . . ."

So there was nothing, nothing to worry about any more, except sometimes in the night one of the children screamed in a nightmare, and they both hustled out shaking and hunting for the matches and calling, "There, wait a minute, here we are!" John, get the doctor now, Hapsy's time has come. But there was Hapsy standing by the bed in a white cap. "Cornelia, tell Hapsy to take off her cap. I can't see her plain."

Her eyes opened very wide and the room stood out like a picture she had seen somewhere. Dark colors with the shadows rising toward the ceiling in long angles. The tall black dresser gleamed with nothing on it but John's picture, enlarged from a little one, with John's eyes very black when they should have been blue. You never saw him, so how do you know how he looked? But the man insisted the copy was perfect, it was very rich and handsome. For a picture, yes, but it's not my husband. The table by the bed had a linen cover and a candle and a crucifix. The light was blue from Cornelia's silk lampshades. No sort of light at all, just frippery. You had to live forty years with kerosene lamps to appreciate honest electricity. She felt very strong and she saw Doctor Harry with a rosy nimbus around him.

"You look like a saint, Doctor Harry, and I vow that's as near as you'll ever come to it."

"She's saying something."

"I heard you, Cornelia. What's all this carrying-on?"

"Father Connolly's saying—"

Cornelia's voice staggered and bumped like a cart in a bad road. It rounded corners and turned back again and arrived nowhere. Granny stepped up in the cart very lightly and reached for the reins, but a man sat beside her and she knew him by his hands, driving the cart. She did not look in his face, for she knew without seeing, but looked instead down the road where the trees leaned over and bowed to each other and a thousand birds were singing a Mass. She felt like singing too, but she put her hand in the bosom of her dress and pulled out a rosary, and Father Connolly murmured Latin in a very solemn voice and tickled her feet. My God, will you stop that nonsense? I'm a married woman. What if he did run away and leave me to face the priest by myself? I found another a whole world better. I wouldn't have exchanged my husband for anybody except St. Michael himself, and you may tell him that for me with a thank you in the bargain.

Light flashed on her closed eyelids, and a deep roaring shook her. Cornelia, is that lightning? I hear thunder. There's going to be a storm. Close all the windows. Call the children in. . . . "Mother, here we are, all of us." "Is that you, Hapsy?" "Oh, no, I'm Lydia. We drove as fast as we could." Their faces drifted above her, drifted away. The rosary fell out of her hands and Lydia put it back. Jimmy tried to help, their hands fumbled together, and Granny closed two fingers around Jimmy's thumb. Beads wouldn't do, it must be something alive. She was so amazed her thoughts ran round and round. So, my dear Lord, this is my death and I wasn't even thinking about it. My children have come to see me die. But I can't, it's not time. Oh, I always hated surprises. I wanted to give Cornelia the amethyst set—Cornelia, you're to have the amethyst set, but Hapsy's to wear it when she wants, and, Doctor Harry, do shut up. Nobody sent for you. Oh, my dear Lord, do wait a minute. I meant to do something about the Forty Acres. Jimmy doesn't need it and Lydia will later on, with that worthless husband of hers. I meant to finish the altar cloth and send six bottles of wine to Sister Borgia for her dyspepsia. I want to send six bottles of wine to Sister Borgia, Father Connolly, now don't let me forget.

Cornelia's voice made short turns and tilted over and crashed. "Oh, Mother, oh, Mother, oh, Mother. . . ."

"I'm not going, Cornelia. I'm taken by surprise. I can't go."

You'll see Hapsy again. What about her? "I thought you'd never come." Granny made a long journey outward, looking for Hapsy. What if I don't find her? What then? Her heart sank down and down, there was no bottom to death, she couldn't come to the end of it. The blue light from Cornelia's lampshade drew into a tiny point in the center of her brain, it flickered and winked like an eye, quietly it fluttered and dwindled. Granny lay curled down within herself, amazed and watchful, staring at the point of light that was herself; her body was now only a deeper mass of shadow in an endless darkness and this darkness would curl around the light and swallow it up. God, give a sign!

For the second time there was no sign. Again no bridegroom and the priest in the house. She could not remember any other sorrow because this grief wiped them all away. Oh, no, there's nothing more cruel than this—I'll never forgive it. She stretched herself with a deep breath and blew out the light.

IV

WHO AM I?

I'm nobody—who are you?
>> EMILY DICKINSON

Who is it that can tell me who I am?
>> King Lear, in
>> Shakespeare's *King Lear*, 1, 12, 250

I celebrate myself and sing myself,
And what I assume you shall assume,
For every atom belonging to me as good belongs to you . . .
I too am not a bit tamed, I too am untranslatable,
I sound my barbaric yawp over the roofs of the world.
>> WALT WHITMAN
>> "Song of Myself"

I yam what I yam
And tha's all I yam
I'm Popeye the Sailor Man.

    Song, "Popeye The Sailor Man"

The witch that came (the withered hag)
To wash the steps with pail and rag
Was once the beauty Abishag,
The picture pride of Hollywood.

Too many fall from great and good
For you to doubt the likelihood.

    ROBERT FROST
    "Provide, Provide"

Thomas Churchill

The Home Stretch*

I

GRANNY WAS IN THE LIVING ROOM playing solitaire at the coffee table my stepfather had made out of an old frame and a piece of Philippine mahogany. I had been aware of her before I read my mother's warning note because of the loud clacking noise she made shuffling the deck, which was the more noticeable because you could never erase from that sound the image of her, nearly blind and half-mad, erratically dealing out the last days of her life. She played constantly, and as she dealt and worried the cards, mumbled words that arose from some opaque ferocity within the workings of her mind. She spit the words out, "Shut*up!*" and "St*up*pit, now!" Sometimes an outraged denial—"No, I did *not!*"—that more than once had led me to imagine unflattering but vivid scenes from her past.

I stood in the doorway to the living room, eyeing her balding

---

* "The Home Stretch." Reprinted by permission of Thomas Churchill.

head, while her eyes, pitifully magnified by the great but useless lenses of her glasses, swept the room but did not take me in. She stared perhaps no closer than my left shoulder and fiercely demanded, "Overweight?" I started at this challenge and glanced down at my meagre frame, though I knew she couldn't be speaking of me.

My stepfather's chair groaned as I settled into it, but Granny was nearly deaf as well as purblind and took no notice. We were side by side, the cards lay in confusion under her crawling hands; some had been nibbled at the corners. She seemed transfixed by the fireplace directly in front of her, whose coals had evidently taken on the status of an arena, for as she stared she began to run her fingers along her hair in a gesture that was more agitated than smoothing. Now she whispered contemptuously and as though to imitate a heavy whiskey voice, "*That* little half-mile track?"

Somehow this stolen look into her past stayed with me and redeemed her in my eyes. I wasn't really fond of her, mostly because she was my stepfather's mother and at that time he and I weren't getting along. They were quite different, though: where he was furtive and austere, she was forthright (when she was sane); where he was thrifty and almost priggish, she spent her tiny pension on Pall Malls and scotch and a lanolin dressing that she rubbed by the hour into her dying scalp. At times one could find in her tirades a towering but painful kind of humor. She was nearly six feet tall, walked with a long, white cane that she handled the way a skier does a ski pole, and wore a hat with a wide brim that disguised her enormous brow and wafted above her magnified eyes. She could terrify you. During one of her earlier difficult periods she had chased the next door neighbor from the front porch shouting, "Get out of here, you big cow!" and the woman, who had come to console her, positively flew. The strange thing was, that neighbor *was* a cow in a way. Always browsing her way into everyone else's business. I got trouble from Granny that same night at supper. She was extremely touchy about her handbag, a big black leather thing. All of her possessions were in there, and God knew what proportion of her ego. It was not a stable meal. My mother fell into a fit of near hysteria, she was actually giggling and wiping her eyes, and lucky for her my stepfather thought she was crying. But he was angry with her anyway. After dinner Granny swayed toward my end of the table and suddenly began belting me with the bag. "Can't you get up and give a lady a seat?" she cried. My stepfather took her away, but Mother and I stayed at the table, petrified, then giggling, biting our lips until the tears flowed. He came back and seeing us red eyed said we should learn to control ourselves.

Getting back, until the time I sat at her side peeping, I suppose, into her past, straining to see the strange track laid out as she must have done there in the embers of our modest fireplace, I had not liked her very much. Before then she was principally equated in my mind with extra burden for Mother, though she was certainly not what you would call an open door, or at all single-motived.

And they moved her into my room while I was living at home going to school. In the middle of the night she would sometimes awake, and no amount of persuasion could steer her from the conviction that there was a Nigger in bed with her, or two or three, and once an entire quartet. She would plead with us to get them out of there and was so pathetically convincing that Mother's own connection with reality began to slip, and one morning I found myself comforting her in my drawers—I had run from the bathroom when I heard her scream and swear—and Granny was at the breakfast table blandly saying that we were going to have to do something with Marge. She had told my mother The Voices, with whom she constantly and openly fought, were trying to get her to kill Joey, my younger brother, but that Granny wouldn't hear of it. That made us very angry with her.

But it was hard to keep her in a home, which we tried once or twice. She always hated the people and the food. Her condition was strictly organic; hardening of the arteries caused hallucinations of varying intensity. Sometimes she was all right, other times half the lewd and criminal world cavorted in the crumbling vault of her mind.

It was not just that I disapproved of her, she was also an unhappy enigma, a figure for our own emotional schizophrenia. We were not a loving family, and as she sat at our table yammering at her horde of derelict images, the rest of us ate in silence. This was the time of my stepfather's great truce with me. When I was twenty, twenty-one, we had fought. Now I was twenty-two and still hanging around. He had gone to sea at seventeen and, scarcely believing that anyone could be as dependent as I, would ask my younger brother to pass him things that lay just off the port side of my plate. Just as he was pointedly avoiding me, Granny might suddenly and incongruously say, "Shut*tup!*" which always made me want to laugh and cry at once. How that senile crone could undermine our incivility!

We were always under pressure with her about the house, and I can remember the relief everyone felt when she ventured out alone on a weekend to visit her pals in the Klondike Hotel in downtown Seattle. There was Mrs. Ned and Helen Klaeble, very old, both with green eyeshades. I once caught a glimpse of the three of them sitting around a table in the Klondike when I paused, waiting for a bus out from under the impossible Northwest rain. I had simply peered through the window of a sad hotel and there she was, intimate, laughing I think. Maybe she was telling them something terribly funny that had happened at our home that week. Funnier, perhaps to her and her friends than to us. And on another occasion, about a month before I confronted her in the living room, I came upon her waiting on the same corner for a bus. She stood there with the wind beating about her hat, so completely alone in her faded red coat and the tall cane. Weird, oh, so weird. There was a moment when I thought, if I walk just as I am walking now I'll miss that bus, but then some instinct—I hope to God, humane—forced me into a jog, and I caught her elbow just as the bus hissed to a stop. She wheeled, violent and terrified. Christ, her look could kill you. No approach, no matter how politic or gentle, could keep her from revealing that horrified surprise, as though you were Jack the Ripper himself, but always this look would subside and change into a smile that was so clearly grateful and welcome that you felt the effort was worth it after all. Nothing to do with Boy Scout gratification, it was just that momentarily you saw the woman behind the mask, and she was nice to see.

We sat near the back of the bus across from the rear door. She was not bad to talk with away from home. She hadn't the deaf person's habit of shouting in conversation. And somehow she heard pretty well when you were close and she was sure of her ground.

"My, you scared me, Billy," she said, letting go of my arm which she had proudly and rather desperately squeezed as we made our way down the aisle.

"Who did you think it was?" She always brought out a weary frankness in me. I couldn't help judging her, I guess it was, but for no reason that was very clear.

"Oh, there are so many bums around that place." Her voice was high but not piercing, and had a saccharine quality. "That hotel used to be quality."

"How was your day?"

"We had a *fine* time. I've known Mrs. Klaeble for years, you know." After a moment she added, "She's not Jewish."

This was a usual beginning but her repetitiveness was not tedious that day. Having just come from her visit, her meagre experience with her cronies seemed more interesting than when she gave accounts of her trip at home. There I scarcely ever listened, now I found myself asking what she and Mrs. Klaeble had done together when they were younger.

She needed this repeated, then pondered her answer. The whole problem amused her. "We were in business together," she said, and I couldn't miss her tone: rather coy she was.

It occurred to me to be bawdy, to pin her down in a way that would make her think that I saw her reticence as being based upon something risqué in her past. But I hesitated. Why had I thought to carry on that way? Precisely because on reflection I saw that I had associated her tone with bawdiness, not coyness. I looked at her. Could one really see through forty years of grief and excess, a lifetime of wrinkles and blotches, see behind those saurian eyes to the woman she might have been? I thought I caught a glimpse of someone I would like to know.

I decided to risk it: "What was the business?"

She laughed then took off the heavy glasses to wipe her eyes. "That was during prohibition," she said vaguely. "Seattle was quite a town . . . quite a town." Now she fished a Pall Mall from her leaden bag and offered me her lighter. She had a number of them and I had never noticed this one before. It was jade and white and depicted a Japanese girl in a kimono.

"Bootlegging?" I asked, carefully lighting the fag, and going coy myself.

"Oh, everything was hard to get in those days," she said. Her hands came together demurely in her lap. ". . . story of the world," she went on imprecisely, "everyone bought and sold . . . bought

. . ." then froze up for what must have been five minutes, a state I wished she had held, for she emerged from her silence in such violent discourse with The Voices that I riveted my eyes to the floor in embarrassment.

That night I smoked my first cigarette. I sat softly creaking from side to side in my stepfather's easy chair, staring out at the Sound in the dark. The cigarette was a Pall Mall. I thought and thought about Granny but got no closer than I had ever been. She remained a puzzle, as strange and unreal as on the day I overheard her criticizing her too-heavy jockey and peering into that disappointing track—three days before we sent her away.

II

The telephone went off right beside me and I picked up the receiver. It was the Home in Tacoma. They said Granny had chased another patient down a flight of stairs, and that the man was in critical condition but his daughter wasn't pressing charges because Granny had broken her back. They wanted instructions as to what to do with the body. My mother and stepfather weren't around. It was a Friday and a friend and I were planning an overnight fishing trip into the Cascades. My younger brother sat at the kitchen table playing Monopoly with some friends, and I told him Granny had died and that he should inform his parents as soon as they got home, then I left. I lived in an apartment with two or three others and had only stopped by to pick up some fishing gear. I drove away from the house slowly, alternately cold and hysterical as I imagined her last day. I dressed that moment up and packed it into me, sitting very private and smug behind the wheel of my car. Stopping for lights I had the feeling people were sneaking wondering glances at me: to be the *only* one to know how she had died. . . . "A bloody and a sudden end, Gunshot or a noose—" I felt a few twinges of conscience for not sticking around and telling them, but I covered this over by reflecting how good it was that I felt so little sense of loss; and of course to think of cancelling the fishing trip was out of the question, even artificial. But I was damned if I was going to be a bore about her death. Then it occurred to me that there would be a funeral. I couldn't go to that. I was leaving for a lookout's job in Oregon that Monday. Surely they would see that I was too far from her by now, and from them, and not embarrass me by asking me to stay for the funeral.

My sister set me straight as to the proper way to feel about Granny's death. She had been successfully married all the time Granny was living with us and used periodically to tell Mother and me that we had her all wrong. *She* had no trouble communicating with Granny. She and my brother-in-law came down from Canada for the funeral, and she called me on Sunday while I slouched in my apartment listening to some corrupting piano music. Debussy, I think.

"Why is it the more educated you get, the more heartless you seem to become?" she wondered.

Then I did become a bore about Granny's death. Had she read *The Loved One?* I asked. Yes, and what had that to do with it?

Then she said: "You're going to the funeral, aren't you?"

Sweetheart, I wanted to say. No! I don't be*lieve* in funerals. Instead I said, "I have to report to work on Monday."

"Surely they'll understand. A death in the family . . ." trailing off as though the conversation were beginning to offend her. What I said next was crummy at best, and she didn't like it. I said that I would lose ten or fifteen bucks, maybe, missing a day of work. I'm not sure she even replied to that, and I went on to add that I was a student, mumbling . . . needed every dime I could get. God. She always has that effect on me.

Monday morning. The funeral would begin at three and Mother, my sister and I were placed in the kitchen, as we so often had been in the past, amid the dishes and sunlight of a borrowed house. Always the kitchen, it is the one place that seems as though it should bring us together. Here we have memory that goes back to the 'forties, the war, yet Mother fools around with broom and dustpan, deferring in some strange mother's way to the children of her first marriage, long since gone, broken. My sister looks out the open window to the backyard with her hands idly at work in the soapy water, disengaged from her innermost thoughts. I assume an attitude of nonchalance that is at once an anticipation of some correcting word from them, and a criticism of what I find to be their too rigid lives, half sitting on the sideboard while I dry a dish carelessly. It is sunny and warm, a lovely day in June. Granny's "things" lie piled with monolithic certainty upon the kitchen table: dresses, packs of cards, jewelry, lighters, defeated old woman's shoes. Her red overcoat enfolds a chair and the cane is propped against it. There is a heavy, musky scent in the air and it is not of gillyflowers or violets.

I was about to make pronouncements. Everything that came forth arose from earlier monologues, practiced in the mind, practiced in taverns with my roommates, waiting for such a time as this to leap unexpected upon anyone opposed who might give me an ear. Having been formed in imaginary conflict with my edition of the suburban mind, of what seemed counterparts of my family and their friends, my views would seem overtrim, or, at worst, non sequiturs. Nothing my mother and sister said called for the kind of reaction I offered. Their demand was simple, they wanted me to come to that funeral. Granny would have wanted me to. My dislike of mortuaries seemed off the point to them, but especially to my mother. My sister knew what I was talking about but did not like the implication that she was one of *them*.

"I just hate the idea of a rotten funeral, that's all." I had laid aside the towel and dish and taken up a battered pack of Bicycles. I opened the deck and fanned out the cards, remembering that as an undergraduate I'd been a pretty decent poker player.

Mother eyed me. "Well, what are people supposed to do, just leave their loved ones laying around in the streets?"

I gasped in panic, nearly dropping the cards.

"He doesn't like you using that term," my sister said.

"What?"

"Never mind." They watched me lay a Jack on the table, spin it about and flick it under a fold of Granny's coat. "Annie, you know what I'm talking about if you'd just ad*mit* it."

"Oh, look, just come along, will you? I see your point, but it's just . . . what's *done*. I don't care how that sounds, either. It's a family thing—people have them, that's all."

"Look, what's more permanent than death?" I asked, putting down a King where the Jack had been.

"More death," she answered.

Mother looked up-in-the-air with us both. How did it turn out that she had two smart-aleck kids?

"—nothing more permanent than death, and these clowns in the mortuary places paint people all up and stick them full of that freezing guck and they're supposed to last for all time! The idea's preposterous. Christ!" I turned up another King, then rubbed my thumb along the edge of the deck more studiously.

"Formaldehyde, big shot."

"We saw Gramma last night and she looks just like she did when she was alive."

"Oh, booey," I said with sweeping gesture. "Mom, what's the point? Graves, graves—everywhere you look there's graveyards. If everyone gets buried . . . if they buried everyone, just didn't stop, you know . . . in a hundred years there won't be any room for the live ones. All we'd have is graveyards!"

I concluded on a note of such ringing triumph that momentarily even I was stunned, but Mother shot me down in a trice: "We're not burying her, Billy, she's being cremated."

They didn't have me for long, though. After a moment I said, "Want to see a trick?" Annie turned from the sink. Mother came up, interested but cautious, sniffing for trouble. Granny had been a great winner at her lonely game. How often—*too* often, I had thought—I heard her call out to me, "I beat the Chinaman again, Billy. I'm so lucky tonight." Mother and Annie drew chairs, and standing I dealt out three cards. "That's an Ace, that's a King, and mine's a Queen," I said. We turned them over and I was right on the mark.

Mother was baffled but impressed; she liked tricks. Annie said, "He's got the stupid deck stacked."

I shuffled the cards. "Here. Pick out any face card or ace and hand it to me face down. I'll tell you what it is without looking at it." She complied and out of five cards I guessed only one. They stared at me, disappointed and embarrassed. "I thought I was on to her . . . I thought I had the secret," I mumbled, feeling my ears beginning to flame, and then staggered on brutally and compulsively, ". . . the Braille Method."

For a time we heard the morning ferry traffic whizzing along Fauntleroy Avenue, then Mother began to sweep again and Annie's fists dropped from the edge of the table to her lap. "God", she managed at last, "you thought she cheated at solitaire! It's too much."

If I could have held us there and explained . . . but you never can. The garage door slumped open and my mother's face collapsed. "Put them away," she hissed.

"What for?"

"Just put them away! You oughten to be touching them, anyway."

As it turned out I went along, self-reproving for a time for being so callous, until it turned out that what my heroes said about funerals was actually true. My relatives really did insist that Granny's head, propped skull-like on that insidious pillow, looked perfectly natural. There was a vivid unreality about the day. I remember that Mother was just beginning to wear false teeth, and I had got a new pair of glasses—better for the viewing—I mean from the lookout tower. Mother went out after lunch and got her hair cut. It had always hung to her shoulders, now it was frizzed and clinging to her head in the best suburban style. My own was much longer than usual in anticipation of a fallow, hair and beard growing summer in solitude.

A day of cockeyed images: whenever I looked at my reflection in the glass I saw with dismaying clarity a scintillating fink, lenses sparkling, hair newly washed but left unoiled for the purity of the occasion, an innocent but ultimately stupid, soft surprise revealed on my face. Seeing Mother offered no relief, there was the cropped hair and a new smile. She wasn't the mother I had known nor I her son. After the service she ran with a muffled cry straight past me to my brother-in-law, who comforted her in his arms.

I believe the standard line is, I never felt anything for Granny except guilty that I couldn't feel anything. I tried this out on my sister and she only turned away. We were left momentarily adrift standing beside the corpse in the back room, while the others milled about in the chapel. It was agonizing for both of us that we could not somehow close the gap between us, and I reached automatically for a cigarette in my nervousness.

"Don't smoke now, please . . . you smoke too much, anyway—"
"Come on, Annie, is this goddamned place supposed to be sacred, or something?" I jammed the butt into the dirt of a potted plant. "Fits right in with that wildly mediocre performance of Reverend Bigot-face."

"You really are being tiresome." She was trying to be tough but held a hankie ready in her hand.

"That's right. Why not go really primitive and toss in a little memento for the dead?" I held up the jade and white lighter which she eyed while her mouth grew tighter, pursing up.

"Go ahead, if it helps you."

She had called my bluff so I reached to put the lighter on the satin pillow beside Granny's ear, but as I placed it there my sister squeezed my hand until her fingernails bit into the flesh.

"It's her own," I explained, trying to bring us over to firmer ground.

"Really?" Her eyes were shifting all over my face, and when she saw me grip my injured hand, looked as though she might panic.

I felt a sudden rising anger—"Did you really think you knew her?"

"Evidently not."

"Did you know she kept a whole stable of horses?" That was a guess (or a lie); she may have had from one to twenty.

"No. You knew her so well, why didn't you ever tell us about her?" The reproach hung there. She wanted me back in the safe and rather human harbor she and her husband had always held open to me.

"There was more—" But I didn't tell her, instead I tried idealizing Granny, saying that she knew about Life and pettiness.

"Yes, there's plenty of that!" Tears rolled onto her lashes, and the shock I felt told me that she loved me, which made the water well in my eyes as well, and I hated it. "We just don't know you, Bill," she brought out, leaning on my arm as Granny had done that day in the bus. "I know funerals are lousy. We know you wanted to leave. I feel bad about it now—"

I got the lighter out of the coffin fast after that. The bastard mortician was coming to burn Granny up, glasses and all.

That night I went with some friends of my youth to one of those peculiarly depressing, pre-discotheque taverns—all guys and chicks, humadum non-jazz, phoney "live" paintings produced by the first local boy on pot, hardly any light, one or two who were separating from their wives or husbands. All of Seattle, or at least everything I'd ever found dismally trying-to-be-hip about Seattle, was in that bar.

Later I lay down on Granny's old bed which I used when I was home, but found that the beer did not make me sleepy. It had the effect of putting me through one of my frequent rolling fits—right side, stomach, left side, back—nothing can make you sleep when you're seeing more clearly, or more vividly, in the dark than in the morning light. Of course I dozed off and perhaps slept soundly for a time, but I woke out of a sweat-producing dream to hear my stepfather softly clumping down the stairs. My room was in the basement, his car was lodged across the hall, and it occurred to me with a jab of pain that he must want to murder me. The guilt Granny had inspired!

And though I knew it was mad to invent a fear of this kind, I lay in real terror, planning my moves, my heart pounding. Surely that door would not open, but I kept my half-closed eye on the doorknob anyhow. It was just light enough and I had just enough vision to see the slightest movement of the knob. This had to be the maddest kind of fantasy, obviously built on self-hatred; yet I peered through the half light, ground my teeth—and then, by god, the crazy knob began to turn! I could *not* cry out. I just lay there, frozen, waiting for the rush of air as the door swung open and he made for me. Fifty-six years old and cardiacal vs. twenty-three and heartwhole. How could he possibly hurt me? The door slowly swung, retreated an inch, then came wider open. I slipped the covers higher, up to my ears, but I left enough opening to see that it was not my stepfather but my mother. For a moment I was so elated I considered ballooning the covers and roaring at her, but I continued to peep, silently, and unnoticed. She came padding across the room and placed an envelope on the nightstand, pausing in her retreat only to examine my handkerchief. She closed the door as softly as she had opened it. I heard them leave in the car and all was quiet in the house. Then I tried to sleep but that was impossible. What had my goofy mother left on the nightstand? It was no good pretending not to be curious. I rose and took up the envelope.

What I found drove me temporarily insane. It was a ten dollar bill.

Oh, Christ, Mother. Oh, *Sis*ter! I ground it into a ball, popped open my lighter and was ready to send that latter-day bribe to oblivion. But the sudden flame held me and I remembered that afternoon before the fireplace. I tossed the bill on the bed and lit a cigarette instead. Slumping down I puffed for half a minute, coughed, hacked, a few tears came, and as the cigarette burned close to my fingers I knew how small the world must have appeared to my grandmother. Out of gratitude to her insight, I closed my hand on the ten spot.

ON "THE HOME STRETCH"

Most of the events in the story are either invented or transmuted from experience, though, obviously, it would still have to be called autobiographical. Two events, however—Granny's saying, "That little half-mile track?" and the narrator's being bought after the fact—are less "transmuted" than "real." On these two incidents, primarily, I built the story—running it back and forth like a flag on one of those clothes lines that works between pulleys. There are moments in one's life, at least in my life, which one knows must sooner or later be turned into fiction, because in living them they seem so *like* fiction. When my grandmother made that remark—to me in one sense because I was sitting beside her even though she did not know it, but really to some race-going companion of years ago—a door creaked open and I shuttered but did not know that I was entering a life that previously I had seen as having little to do with me. Because I spied on her and she said what she said, it was as though we were both brought in on the action—something like that. I passed her remark on to friends and invented a past for her that made her seem pretty grand, though corrupt, but left me out of it. Nothing hereditary there, I reminded them. Then, I don't know how many years later, came the payoff: "Here's cash for being a lousy mourner." Or, less complicatedly, "You must really be desperate for money to want to miss this event of all family events." What it had to mean—fictionally, and therefore, really, since all past time is a fiction—was that I was her grandson, her jockey, her go-between after all. This may sound like a protest in excess of the facts as they appear, or, worse, like overplotting, but that's the way I see it; and better to know who you are than miss the point that most experience, if well remembered, has a way of tying you to the ordinary, the gross, and at rare times to what is human and worthwhile.

Nancy Huddleston Packer

Oh Jerusalem*

UNCLE MOISHE-MOSES-MORRIS-MAURICE WAS SITTING on the sofa with his feet flat on the floor and his hands lightly on his knees. He gave the impression of having waited for us in that pose for a long and trying time. Plump and nervous, he was like a bumblebee poised on a sofa.

Ours was a visit of duty, a time to be endured, undertaken solely out of a sense of behaving rightly. Uncle Maurice and Aunt Sarah had claims on us through my husband's dead father, Aunt Sarah's brother. I had never before met either of them, but of course I had heard about them.

Uncle Maurice was an embarrassment to the family and a comic figure to the world. He was full of words and postures, wit and foolishness. He was both volatile and calculated and no one trusted him. At the funeral of my husband's father, Uncle Maurice had planted himself in the very center of grief, mourned loudest and longest and lamented that he had lost even more than the dead

* Reprinted by permission of Nancy Huddleston Packer.

man, his brother-in-law. But more than brother-in-law: his other self, his self-respect, his conscience. He used exactly those words and for some members of the family he made sorrow for a good man a false and shameful thing.

As for Aunt Sarah, best to say that she was a woman who had a great deal to put up with and did not always do it gracefully.

When William and I had married, four months before our visit, quietly and away from New York, we had received a telegram from Uncle Maurice. "Your father would say, If I forget thee, Oh Jerusalem, let my right had forget her cunning." William had assured me his father would have said no such thing. But I felt the telegram to be intentionally threatening and yet clownish.

Back in New York, we had made a series of calls on William's family, for me to see and be seen. They were pleasant undemanding little calls, perhaps to be repeated once a year. Uncle Maurice and Aunt Sarah had been slow to invite us and so when they finally did, for a Sunday afternoon, we were quick to accept.

"You see," said William, "they don't object so much."

What we had thought they objected to was the fact that William had married a Christian.

Once sure that we had seen his expectant waiting pose, Uncle Maurice rushed toward the front door of his apartment and held out a hand to each of us.

"Me," he said, "I'm glad to see you, I don't care what." As if according to plan, he shoved us urgently toward particular chairs on either side of the sofa, nodding and smiling all the while. "Sit down. Sit down. Let's not stand around all day, in my house there are plenty of chairs."

Aunt Sarah, taller than he and equally plump, had remained at the door, still holding the knob. Uncle Maurice had jerked us out of her care and she resented it but apparently had no recourse but to join the group, which, finally, shaking her head, she did.

"It's an honor to have you here," said Uncle Maurice. "It isn't every day our nephew the doctor visits us. He's a busy man." He looked at William shrewdly, assessing the damage of his thrust, and then smiled. "And yet when I see the son I think of the father, a man I loved better than a brother. I forgive the no visits."

"He was my brother," said Aunt Sarah.

"We were boys together," went on Uncle Maurice. "Born in

the same town at the same time. He came to this country a year before I did. And three years later, my wife." He winked at Aunt Sarah and nodded. "But not then my wife, only his baby sister. She's been on my knee in more ways than one."

"I'm listening," I said, "but I can't hear any accent, at all."

He was pleased at that. "My youngest son says it's there. The accent. Still sometimes for fun I say born in New York and nobody calls me liar. Only a son could hear it. William's father came a year ahead, but you could hear the accent. Always the *w* was a *v*."

"Don't make fun," said Aunt Sarah. "The accent isn't everything." She sat quite still, with her fingers tensely and awkwardly at the belthooks of her elegant gray dress, and she watched her husband.

"Would I make fun of him?" asked Uncle Maurice. Shaking his head, pretending bewilderment, he turned to William. "Would I laugh at your father?"

"No," said William, in his thoughtful reassuring tone. "I can't think that you would. You were too close."

Uncle Maurice turned back to his wife. "Are we to have no refreshments, Sarah? You prepare all day for the visit and then we have nothing?"

"Nobody has prepared all day," said Aunt Sarah. "You talk too much."

Uncle Maurice laughed, happy with his anger turned to teasing. "You see, William? After twenty-eight years of marriage if I speak I talk too much. Unless I just say Yes ma'am. Train your wife early. A mean husband is a good marriage to these women. They don't like us when we're so easy."

"Easy," repeated Aunt Sarah. "My God. What would hard have been?"

William laughed, showing me the way to deal with this sudden ill humor. "Nothing changes," he said. "The same Uncle Maurice, the same Aunt Sarah, even the same old quarrel." We all laughed then, even Aunt Sarah. And indeed the quarrel seemed so old and so used and habitual that they were not ashamed and I was not embarrassed. Somehow the fact that they were relaxed enough to go on with their own relationship made our visit seem easier.

"That woman is Eddie Arcaro for twenty-eight years," said

Uncle Maurice with pleasure, "and I am the horse. Your people wouldn't have stood it," he said to me in mock envy. "A bloody nose on Saturday night or Reno. And, God help us, some of us these days too. But Alabama, not Reno. Down one morning and back the next, free as birds. We can't take time from our business, the almighty dollar, you think. Does marriage mean nothing these days? Bourbon or scotch? In spite of my wife I offer you my side of the refreshments."

"Scotch," I said, automatically. I looked at William, and with an almost imperceptible gesture of his hand he told me that he too had heard the almighty dollar but that we should both let it go by.

"Clever shiksa," said Uncle Maurice. "The scotch is at worse mediocre, but the bourbon, who knows? In this house you can be safe."

"All right, then," said William, "bourbon."

Uncle Maurice stood up and carefully worked his way around the coffee table and between the chairs. As he got alongside his wife, he invited us to watch his playfulness. He patted Aunt Sarah on the shoulder. "Pretending she has not been preparing all day the refreshments and then not bringing them out for us to enjoy. If we have refreshments, bring them out. If not, apologize and don't argue with your husband. Your own brother, our nephew's father, said how many times don't argue with your husband."

"He said a lot of things you don't follow either," said Aunt Sarah in a dull and graceless voice.

"Did he say don't feed your guests?"

With a face glinting with satisfaction, Uncle Maurice left the room. After a moment, Aunt Sarah followed him.

"The almighty dollar," I said, shaking my head.

"I won't let it bother me," said William, "if you won't let it bother you. We won't let it bother us if they won't let it bother them." But his expression was wary and I reached across the table to touch his hand.

"He's really not so bad," I said. "He's kind of cute."

"What a word," said William.

Uncle Maurice, bearing drinks, came back into the room. And shortly Aunt Sarah followed him. She was carrying a large silver tray, carrying it before her like an offering, not even allowing the edge of it to rest against her body. Little pieces of steak marinated for hours and broiled quickly in a hot oven. A plate of chicken sandwiches ice cold from the refrigerator. Cauliflower, carrots, celery and radishes, crisp and clean, carved and curled, and a lovely subtle cheese mixture molded into a double ring. The pride she felt in her skill and her strange shame of caring warred on her face. At first I was amused, then uncomfortable. Faintly William frowned. It seemed unfair that our casual visit, our visit intended only to manipulate their good graces, cost them so much. To make up for our indifference, we praised her highly, and regretted the condescension of that praise.

Uncle Maurice looked at the tray with pride. "That's my wife," he said. "A born cook but too proud to admit it. Eat up, eat up, and see what we are really like." Encouraging us with nods and gestures and example, he forced each dish on us and watched for our approval.

"Judge a man," he said, "by what he allows to go in his stomach. Me, I eat anything. I'm not prejudiced. Ancient laws I left in the old country. What I like, I eat. What I don't like, I don't eat and that isn't much. Jews are a fat people, you may have noticed, because we like to eat."

"I'm not fat," said William.

His voice fell on silence. Instinctively we both knew that his idle words were a mistake. Uncle Maurice looked at each of us, and at his wife.

"You have a shiksa cook," he said. "But for us none of your overcooked roast beef eaten only to get us to the next meal. We eat for pleasure and grow fat with pleasure."

"Why so proud right now?" asked Aunt Sarah. "You always tell me to reduce."

"I tease you," said Uncle Maurice sharply. "You can't take a joke. Every pound you have I'm proud of. Look at our niece, skinny as a rail. Not that I mind, I like it," he went on to me, "but your people think we're stingy and won't spend money. How account for our weight then? That costs money. I've had a thousand meals in gentile homes and gone away hungry. Eat, they said, but what was there to eat?"

"Please, Maurice," said Aunt Sarah. "Don't talk like that. He doesn't mean it."

Signals passed between William and me. Endure, endure, he

said, it won't last long. I don't mind, I said, don't you. William gestured. A clown. Yes, a clown.

"Oh it was enough all right," said Uncle Maurice quickly. He leaned toward me, showing his good will. "The food, I'm not complaining, don't think that. They were my friends, the Christians, and I broke bread in their homes. Fine people, too, without prejudice, like yourself, like me. I was like a brother in the family. A step-brother. No, I don't mean that, I'm kidding, making a joke for my niece."

"It isn't a good joke," said Aunt Sarah. "Who can understand your jokes? Don't make them." She spoke in a warning tone and watched him with suspicion.

Uncle Maurice ignored her. "I don't say scratch a gentile deep enough and you find an anti-semite. When we say that, we ask for it. It's our fault. I say scratch a gentile and if he itches you find a friend. It's a Christian world and if you find friends among them that's good. Walk careful and carry a big stick like the president said. But be willing. Not all Jews can do it. I can. They think they're too good for it. And when trouble comes they wonder why. They speak yiddish in the goyim's faces and call them stupid. I say go to Israel or make friends, and who wants to hammer on sand? My nephew is a smart man, he knows the ways of the world. What's better than a friend? A little shiksa wife. Not that he married you for that, a girl like you. You're no fool. God grant we should have as clever among us. Not that we don't, don't get that idea, we do."

His words were coming too fast and I had no responses ready. William seemed as badgered and perplexed as I. We did nothing. We sat there listening and wanting not to hear.

"Maurice," said Aunt Sarah, in a tone that pretended to make light of what he had said. "Please, no more about mixed marriage. It's not a good topic. Accept it or don't accept, but let it alone. Too much talk talk talk," she finished, smiling sourly.

"I am not talk talk talk," said Uncle Maurice. "I am explaining. I want the shiksa niece to feel comfortable. If our nephew visited her family, wouldn't you want them to give him ease? If he visited."

"We visit," said William. "It's all right, don't worry."

"Well, then, maybe what my wife says is true," said Uncle Maurice, still rapid but now quiet. "Maybe the shiksa thinks I insult when I don't. For once maybe Sarah has a point. I'm a loudmouth, I guess. Look, I apologize, I've offended talking too much."

"No," I said. "Why should I be offended? Did I miss something? I like to hear you talk." William gave approval but Aunt Sarah, too late, shook her head at me, as if to say don't encourage him.

"See?" said Uncle Maurice. "A clever girl, like I said. Who knows what the goy thinks, but she says she likes to hear me talk and that's clever. And if she does, that's not only clever but wise. I'm just kidding. Look, don't you like chicken? Eat it. It isn't kosher."

"She doesn't mind if it's kosher," said Aunt Sarah. "She married a Jew, why should she mind? It isn't kosher."

"How do you know what she minds?" asked Uncle Maurice. "Are you an expert on Christians? And did she marry a Jew? Is this a Jew? He's no Jew, better to call him . . . Look, I'm kidding. Making a joke at my nephew's expense." My husband is a placid man, he drank his drink in silence, not even requiring the satisfaction of a private smile. Uncle Maurice went on at once. "Your husband isn't my only kin married out of the tribe. The other was my own blood brother. Born in Poland same as me, but three when he came, a good age to come. It broke my mama's heart when he married."

"Don't talk about that now," said Aunt Sarah. "They don't care, don't start talking about it." She gestured aimlessly in the air.

Uncle Maurice flicked his fingers to silence her. "My mama said kaddish for him. Do you what that is? Mourning, but it's the black of night. You think it was prejudice, but it wasn't. It was his age, twenty-one only and he would have made a fine rabbi. Who wants a rabbi with a Christian wife? With a doctor maybe it's different, maybe not. When the old people died we forgave him, our own flesh and blood, we wouldn't be prejudiced. He brings his family here once a month sometimes. Three beautiful children, blond as Norwegians. The wife is Norwegian. My God, my brother looks like a Norwegian these days, no one could accuse him of being a Jew. Smart kids, too, with the hands and with the head, a good combination. But are they Jews or Norwegians? My brother says who cares. Not me. And now my nephew does the same. What is happening to us?"

William leaned toward him and put his hand on the arm of the sofa. "I don't know why you're talking like this," he said, "but it isn't pleasant for us. You know that. Aren't we welcome?"

Uncle Maurice looked alarmed and puzzled. With an effort he smiled. "I'm making a joke only," he said. "Kidding. Sometimes I don't make too good a joke. I like to be good-natured. And you're my favorite nephew. Not like a son but the son of a man better than a brother. Your father was not only my brother-in-law, he was a fine man in his own right. Talk about Christians, now he was a man they liked. Stop being a Jew, they used to say to him. Be one of us. But if I forget you Oh Jerusalem, that was his motto. He's dead so I sent the wire myself, he would have said that. A hundred Christians walked behind him to his grave. And not debtors either. Friends. He'd give the shirt off his back, ten dollars if he had eleven. Nothing mean came from his lips. If only his sister was like that. But I made my bed and out of it came two fine sons. Both married now and none to shiksas, thank God. I beat him there."

I reached for a chunk of steak and ate it. It was a strange moment for me. I felt involved and yet irresponsible. I was sure that there was nothing I could do. Uncle Maurice leaned forward and cocked his head to look directly in my face.

"Now I've said too much and you're angry, little shiksa," he said. "You think I'm a bigot when I'm not. I don't care who my sons marry. Understand me. When Jews marry out, who is it to? Country girls and dyed blondes. For the money. I know. Not you, I know that. Don't take it personal. Why get angry? Be reasonable."

Aunt Sarah stood up. "Chicken sandwiches, everybody," she said. "Eat some chicken sandwiches." William and I reached for the sandwiches, our hands briefly touching. Abruptly Aunt Sarah sat back down, and when she spoke again, all pretense had left her voice, and it was hard and angry. "Be quiet, Maurice. You make it worse. Be quiet."

"That shows how much you know," said Uncle Maurice. "I'm not talking about our niece, I'm talking to her. If you had eyes you'd see we're friends already, the niece and me. She knows I kid her." He bobbed his head to encourage my answer. Chicken sandwiches saved me from speech and I merely smiled and nodded yes.

"You go out of your way to be insulting and ruin a pleasant visit," said Aunt Sarah. "I'm not surprised, I knew it. I said don't invite, it isn't necessary, but you insisted. All my life it's like that."

The quarrel was no longer easy and no longer amusing. I looked down at my lap and picked bread crumbs from my skirt and carefully placed them in an ashtray. Across from me William sat silently, his lips stiff, and I thought how much worse it was for him than for me. The undivorceable family, the burden of Uncle Maurice always on his back.

"You think it's all my fault," said Uncle Maurice. "Always to my wife it's my fault, and then she wonders I feel persecuted. Look. Listen to me. Where would my sons have found Christians? Who are they to know high-type Christians? My nephew the doctor, that's different. Merchants, what do they do, somebody comes in our little store looking for a bargain and six months credit? There's a line romance doesn't crawl over. Let's don't quarrel. I'm a fool, everybody knows it. Ask my wife, she'll tell you. Ask your husband, he remembers. Nobody pays any attention to me. I'm not a rabbi, I'm not even an elder, maybe I'm not a good Jew. If I offended, I'm sorry, I can't say more than sorry. I don't mean to talk like that, but there it is, out before I hear it in my brains. Your husband's father said to me, Maurice, if you would listen you wouldn't have such pain, you would see we accept you. So let your children be Norwegian. I don't care. I welcome them as my kin."

He paused a moment and as he paused I saw anger on his face and I felt once more that it was directed at me. "But do I hate my own people?" he asked. "If there's the choice to be scorned as a Jew or to scorn the Jew, I'll be scorned, by God. That doesn't scare me."

As quickly risen, his anger fell and he turned to William, and he seemed puzzled and beseeching. "There I go, I'm a loudmouth. Why can't I stop talking? It is a disease?"

"I always tell you," said Aunt Sarah, her voice hammering across the coffee table, a menacing hard voice, "you should listen once in a while. Avoid pain with silence. Hear nothing. Say nothing."

"Who taught you that besides me?" asked Uncle Maurice, turning on her. "William's father was a silent man and married a talkative woman, a good balance. And I talk and who do I get? I get a talkative woman too, a bad balance. Is that fair? What is fair? He was loved by the Christians as a man, and by the Jews too. He never turned his back on his people or his religion. And my Christian friends, who are they? The bookie, the barber, the wholesaler. And the Jews, they think I'm no good, a turn-coat. Why should they care for me? I'm not like him, I'm a loudmouth. My nephew brings his wife here and I want to please her, to make a friend for myself. A pretty girl. A shiksa. But I offend her. I offend my wife. I offend my nephew. Jews and Christians, it doesn't matter. I'm a loudmouth. I'm nothing."

Aunt Sarah had been trying to interrupt him and finally she did. "I tell you now," she said, in a warning charged overbearing voice, "be quiet now for good."

"Everybody be quiet," said William quietly, raising his hand in a slow silencing gesture. "This isn't good. You're hurting yourself. Please."

But neither one nor the other could be stopped. Aunt Sarah pulled herself forward on her chair and looked at her husband. Her emotions, like his, had their own irrevocable direction, and nothing William or I could do or say could stop the movement of her rage. We could only sit and endure.

"When we knew William and the girl were coming," she said, "I said don't talk about shiksas and Christians and goyim and mixed marriage. I'm no fool, I know how it goes with you after twenty-eight years. And you said you wouldn't. But you talk and talk, you can't not talk. You're a fool."

"A fool and a loudmouth," said Uncle Maurice with a startling shout of laughter. "A fool and a loudmouth, a Christian and a Jew all at once. That's a good one, a good joke. Which am I more of? Who knows? I saw the kind of world it was, a Christian world. Okay, a Christian in a Christian world, I said. That's what I said."

"Maurice, I say be quiet," said Aunt Sarah.

"Six churches on six Sundays," he said. "There I was, smelling of stuffed cabbage and sour cream. I was eighteen and they said you're welcome to be a Christian but they acted you're not welcome. So back I came, back to the Jews with my tail between my legs. You didn't know that, did you, William? You thought you were the only one wanted out."

"You're saying more than you mean," said William. "I don't

want out. Let's change the subject. We're here only a short time. Tell us about your sons, tell us about them."

"No," said Aunt Sarah, "he can't change the subject. He doesn't care about anything. He has to talk until he makes a fool of himself and me."

"Is the truth foolish?" asked Uncle Maurice in a reasoning questioning tone. "Is it foolish to teach the young? I'm telling this boy from my own experience. Is it foolish to say no to a grilled ham and cheese and yes to stuffed cabbage? Why should I turn my back for a mess of pottage? The hands were the hands of Esau but the voice was the voice of Jacob. So back I came to the Jews, gladly. And when my brother, my blood brother, married a shiksa I said I know what it's like, don't go. But he went and he never looked back at us. He says a Jew is what a man believes, how can he say that? A Jew is a Jew. But he looks like a Norwegian these days. How could he go so easy? I couldn't go but my kid brother could. The truth is you can't be one of them so why try. They bolt the door and say don't come. And we say who wants to come. And who does? Besides my brother."

"Nobody," said Aunt Sarah. "Why accuse William? Why talk about it?"

Uncle Maurice turned abruptly to me with a gesture of both hands, half apology, half condescension, mixed as all his gestures were. "Not that I scorn the religion," he said. "A man believes as he believes and no matter so long as he believes. Me, I'm a free thinker. The business of hogs is hogwash, I say. That's a joke. I don't eat shellfish because I don't like shellfish. It's dirty. But miracles, raising the dead, that won't swallow. I tried and it choked in my throat. I like you, you listen. Can't they say fine man and let it go at that? But who knows beyond the grave. There are so many of them. And here is one in our own place, married to our nephew the doctor. Taking the best of us, the learned man. Sitting there thinking her husband's uncle is a fool and a loudmouth. Don't cringe, nephew, you pay your call from duty and you don't have to see us anymore. Forget the family of your father. Now you have cousins on the other side. Tillers of the soil maybe. Smart with the hands, but with the head? Remember what happened to Heine. On his deathbed back he came. It's in your blood. Centuries of the peddle cart. M.D. doesn't mean a thing. Now you peddle pills is all, a middle man to sell prescriptions to society ladies with little aches. You should come back to us with the big aches. I could tell you aches."

William reached over and shook Uncle Maurice's knee. "I'm not going anywhere," he said. "I haven't turned my back, I've only gotten married. Look, could I ever look like a Norwegian? Stop hurting yourself. Stop trying to hurt us. We've done nothing."

But nothing could be saved. Aunt Sarah rose to her feet and stood over Uncle Maurice in a posture of threat and wrath. "So our nephew only has Christians for patients? He refuses Jews? You set out to ruin the visit of my brother's son and you ruin it. Why? You can't be quiet?" She turned to me in another rush of fury. "My brother said don't marry him, I know him from the old country when you were a baby, he's a loudmouth with an itch to be what he isn't. But I was a fool, I wouldn't listen."

Uncle Maurice stood up, indignant and defensive. He stared at her for a moment, how silently he stared. "That is not so," he said in a voice of quiet and control. "He loved me better than a brother. You sour life for me, don't sour that. He accepted me for me. He alone accepted me. Let them all say I am a loudmouth and a fool, he loved me better than a brother. Quiet, Maurice, he said, easy, Maurice. He said, Be what you can, nothing more, nothing less, it's good enough. He didn't scorn me. When I was eighteen and came back ashamed, all laughed but him and scorned me. Oh, Moishe, you forgot Jerusalem, they said, they who remembered only the ghetto. But he whose heart was Jerusalem said, Be what you can, nothing more, nothing less. Be Moses if you can, but if not be Maurice and don't blame yourself."

"Then why blame yourself?" asked William, so pained, so gentle. "He loved you better than a brother and accepted you. And we accept you. Don't blame yourself."

"So," said Uncle Maurice. He sat down again and looked at his necktie. "Your father, my brother-in-law, never turned his back once on his people. My own blood brother, he never looked over his shoulder after he walked away from the Jews. Was that hard? Be Maurice, is that easy? One son says I am not Jew enough. I should wear a skull cap and go to his fancy synagogue. The other son says I'm Jew too much, I should drop even Yom Kippur. So what do I do? What can I be? Just Maurice, neither more or less. And what is that? Is that an honor?"

He sat quite still, only his crossed leg bobbing to the echoed rhythm of his voice. When finally in the silence he lifted his head, he looked sick and foolish and shrewd. And we were ashamed to see him.

As if she had been waiting for just that moment, Aunt Sarah went over to him. She put her hand on his shoulder, and I thought that that first kind touch was the goal, the inevitable purpose of all her rage, repeated endlessly over twenty-eight years of embarrassment and quarrel.

"Look, you'd better go," she said to us. "He talks too much and then he's ashamed and then he's tired."

"Is he sick?" asked William, their nephew the doctor. "Can I do something?" But he knew, as I did, that we were hardly in it.

"Is tired sick?" asked Uncle Maurice. He laughed and looked from William to me and he seemed to be mustering strength for another attack of words. "You paid your call from duty. Next time come to visit. No chicken sandwiches, we'll have gefillte fish. We're Jews, nothing more, nothing less, and proud of it. Accept us or not, we don't care. I'm not prejudiced. Who am I to judge my nephew and his wife? Judge yourself, but who can do that? We see people looking at us is how we judge ourselves. You think I'm looking at you but I'm not. I look only at the son of my friend and I smile at you as he smiled at me. You didn't choose easy, William, it isn't easy to be William, but remember Jerusalem. There I go, talking too much. But I'm not going to cut out my tongue if nobody likes me talking. Not my wife, not my nephew, not the shiksa."

"Be quiet," said Aunt Sarah, so quiet and gentle it hardly sounded like her. "Say goodbye to them, but don't talk."

AUTHOR'S NOTE ON "OH JERUSALEM"

Mrs. Packer has kindly contributed this short essay:

> You ask if I would contribute a short note on my "conception of fiction or the directions in which I think short fiction is moving." That "or" is very important, representing not merely alternative but opposition. For, my conception is quite different from the direction I think fiction is moving in.
>
> Judging by short stories in serious publications and by the

hint of the future that surfaces in writing classes, I think short fiction late this afternoon and early tomorrow will fall into three different groups: the put-on, aestheticism, and celebration of the absurd. The categories are not airtight and many writers can be found in all three in part. And there are in each category fascinating writers, inventive, original, serious, and influential.

Although he is one who falls in several categories, John Barth is the master of the put-on. The wildness of his invention and the strength of his wit are marvelous. The put-on is based on disparity and exaggeration. There is disruption in the flow of images, rhythms, common sense chronology, and impact on the reader. Symbols are at once enticing and private. The put-on has fingers in history, psychology, myth. The reader senses the approach of ultimates, accompanied by the sound of loud laughter, including his own. The put-on is Joseph K. played by Stan Laurel, Huck Finn turning out to be *The Mysterious Stranger*, George Eliot laughing at Daniel Deronda. For me, put-on novels are good bed-time reading, because they are fresh and exciting and keep you awake until a respectable hour, but not beyond. One is not driven so deep into such books that he can't get out.

Aestheticism has two roots, the assertion of the preeminence of style and an insistence of the artistic consciousness directing the flow of images. Thus it sacrifices awareness of the done to the doer and seriousness of matter to fineness of manner. Consider Nabokov. His elegant language, his puns, jokes, his acerbity and scorn, his tricks of perception, indeed of identity, of injecting himself as artist into the body of the work (thereby, in my judgment, giving the lie to its seriousness and destroying its unity)—through our appreciation of these qualities we become intensely, concentratedly aware of Nabokov. He wrote the books. They did not "happen" as, say, Faulkner's novels seem simply to be. The spirit behind aestheticism seems more that of the poet exploring his consciousness and displaying his sensibilities than that of the fiction writer creating a moral universe.

And then there is the celebration of the absurd. I don't wish to denigrate this celebration for it seems especially attuned to our times. It is believed to have famous ancestors, but I think it is not so much the child of Hester Prynne and The Ancient Mariner as of *Miss Lonelyhearts* and S. J. Perelman, at least in its Black Comedy incarnation. The absurdists are concerned with the anti-hero, victim of the absurd universe. The human condition is unpleasant, inconsequential, worthless. Society is lies and unredeemable.

Manners interfere with the only good, which is raw experience or sensation. Morals are mere counters in the class struggle. Man is irrational, life unpredictable, and the only emotions worth going for are anger, hilarity, or self-pity. Although sometimes absurdism is expressed straight, more often it comes by way of bright wit, invention, unusual incident, strange characters, as it does with Jean Genet.

To me these three kinds of fiction represent a new romanticism. Anti-society, anti-tradition, anti-morals, and finally anti-fiction. Despite their present vigor and excitement, these three herald a decay of serious fiction.

How do we explain our immense longing to abandon ourselves to a mere book, sometimes undertaking a commitment of weeks of evenings, often ignoring our own lives? Surely no other art form makes such demands on our time, intensity, concentration, and self-forgetfulness all at once. Yet from childhood we have sought the vicarious experience that fiction provides. When we read, selves we repress or cannot acknowledge come alive. Dark dead corners of our beings are suddenly vibrant. We experience anguish without panic, infidelity without guilt, failure without remorse. We take chances, seek adventures, fulfill passions. Yet we have the serenity to contemplate the full weight and meaning of all that happens. And we are satisfied, deeply.

Human beings live at different levels of sophistication and imaginative need and capacity. For a four-year old, Babar suffices. At nine, Toad of Toad Hall is wonderful. And only a fine and serious writer can create that sensuous and moral world into which intelligent, perceptive readers will gladly go. Style, vivid and apt detail, deeply rendered point of view, the sense of human complexity are part of this world.

There is more. Man is an actor. Actions have consequences. Consequences are important. It is this sequence of notions that gives form as well as meaning to fiction. We read in order to experience an imaginative involvement with characters behaving toward man, God, and the Universe in determinative fateful ways. Without that involvement, the intellect may be stimulated, the funny bone tickled, appreciation and respect heightened, but emotion will not be engaged.

Reading a great writer is a journey to the limits of human sensitivity and stress and significance. We expect, not miraculously, to be the better for the journey, and not merely in the sense of raising our contribution to the beggar's cup (although that too). We expect to bring back with us a greater awareness of human possibility, including our own, and a recommitment to the excitement of being human.

Of course there is nothing more painful than to read a morally earnest writer who lacks style. To me style is the ability to establish tone and viewpoint by the way words are strung together as well as by the ideas presented. Some might claim there is no difference but obviously there are more ways than one to say "I skinned a cat." Style is the writer's way of nurturing relevance and exactness and surprise all at once in sentences and paragraphs and chapters. A fiction writer can get pretty far on style all by itself, but he cannot get all the way to greatness.

Consider *Our Lady of the Flowers*. Because of Genet's balanced, exact images, the surprise of his metaphors, the strangeness of his interests, his wit, his gladness, we are willing to take his peculiar journey with him. Smiling and appreciative, we await the murder by Our Lady, the execution of Our Lady. We appreciate Genet's perceptions, but our sympathies are not engaged. This is due in part to Genet's control over us by his tone of elegant amusement at his own imaginative longings, and in part to his basic indifference to our most deeply held moral concerns, such as the sanctity of the life even of a used up old man.

Compare that to our response to Raskolnikov, Nostromo, Joe Christmas, even Leonard Bast. Obviously, there is a difference in the writers' intentions. What I'm suggesting is that that difference is decisive in fiction. The put-on, aestheticism, and the celebration of the absurd can be nearly perfect of their kind, providing the reader with a sense of rightness of image, laughter, of admiration and pleasure, even of learning. But a truly great experience requires a combination of style, vicariousness and moral intensity and effect. Although I admire the accomplishments of Barth, Nabokov, Genet, and others, I have to admit that the fates of Giles, even Humbert Humbert, and Our Lady do not affect my emotions one way or the other. When I leave the books I'm not changed from what I was when I entered them. Of course, few are chosen to write truly great fiction, but I believe that all who are called ought to try.

Joyce Carol Oates

In the Region of Ice*

SISTER IRENE WAS A TALL, DEFT WOMAN in her early thirties. What one could see of her face made a striking impression—serious hard gray eyes, a long slender nose, a face waxen with thought. Seen at the right time, from the right angle, she was almost handsome; in her past teaching positions she had drawn a little upon the fact of her being young and brilliant and also a nun, but she was beginning to grow out of that.

This was a new university and an entirely new world. She had heard—of course it was true—that the Jesuit administration of this school had hired her at the last moment to save money and to head off the appointment of a man of dubious religious commitment. She had prayed for the necessary energy to get her through this first semester. She had no trouble with teaching itself; once she stood before a classroom she felt herself capable of anything. It was the world immediately outside the classroom that confused and alarmed

* Reprinted by permission of the author and of Blanche C. Gregory, Inc., Authors' Representatives. This story first appeared in *The Atlantic Monthly*. Copyright © 1966 by Joyce Carol Oates.

her, though she let none of this show—the cynicism of her colleagues, the indifference of many of the students, and above all, the looks she got that told her nothing much would be expected of her because she was a nun. This took energy, strength. At times she had the idea that she was on trial and that the excuses she made to herself about her discomfort were only the common excuses made by guilty people. But in front of a class she had no time to worry about herself or the conflicts in her mind. She became, once and for all, a figure existing only for the benefit of others, an instrument by which facts were communicated.

About two weeks after the semester began, Sister Irene noticed a new student in her class. He was slight and fair-haired, and his face was blank, but not blank by accident, blank on purpose, suppressed and restricted into a dumbness that looked hysterical. She was prepared for him before he raised his hand, and when she saw his arm jerk, as if he had at last lost control of it, she nodded to him without hesitation.

"Sister, how can this be reconciled with Shakespeare's vision in *Hamlet?* How can these opposing views be in the same mind?"

Students glanced at him, mildly surprised. He did not belong in the class, and this was mysterious, but his manner was urgent and blind.

"There is no need to reconcile opposing views," Sister Irene said, leaning forward against the podium. "In one play Shakespeare suggests one vision, in another play another; the plays are not simultaneous creations, and even if they were, we never demand a logical—"

"We must demand a logical consistency," the young man said. "The idea of education itself is predicated upon consistency, order, sanity—"

He had interrupted her, and she hardened her face against him— for his sake, not her own, since she did not really care. But he noticed nothing. "Please see me after class," she said.

After class the young man hurried up to her.

"Sister Irene, I hope you didn't mind my visiting today. I'd heard some things, interesting things," he said. He stared at her, and something in her face allowed him to smile. "I—could we talk in your office? Do you have the time?"

They walked down to her office. Sister Irene sat at her desk, and the young man sat facing her; for a moment they were self-conscious and silent.

"Well, I suppose you know—I'm a Jew," he said.

Sister Irene stared at him. "Yes?" she said.

"What am I doing at a Catholic university, huh?" He grinned. "That's what you want to know."

She made a vague movement of her hand to show that she had no thoughts on this, nothing at all, but he seemed not to catch it. He was sitting on the edge of the straight-backed chair. She saw that he was young but did not really look young. There were harsh lines on either side of his mouth, as if he had misused that youthful mouth somehow. His skin was almost as pale as hers, his eyes were dark and somehow not quite in focus. He looked at her and through her and around her, as his voice surrounded them both. His voice was a little shrill at times.

"Listen, I did the right thing today—visiting your class! God, what a lucky accident it was; some jerk mentioned you, said you were a good teacher—I thought, what a laugh! These people know about good teachers, here? But yes, listen, yes, I'm not kidding—you are good. I mean that."

Sister Irene frowned. "I don't quite understand what all this means."

He smiled and waved aside her formality, as if he knew better. "Listen, I got my B.A. at Columbia, then I came back here to this crappy city. I mean, I did it on purpose, I wanted to come back. I wanted to. I have my reasons for doing things. I'm on a three-thousand-dollar fellowship," he said, and waited for that to impress her. "You know, I could have gone almost anywhere with that fellowship, and I came back home here—my home's in the city—and enrolled here. This was last year. This is my second year. I'm working on a thesis, I mean I was, my master's thesis—but the hell with that. What I want to ask you is this: Can I enroll in your class, is it too late? We have to get special permission if we're late."

Sister Irene felt something nudging her, some uneasiness in him that was pleading with her not to be offended by his abrupt, familiar manner. He seemed to be promising another self, a better self, as if his fair, childish, almost cherubic face were doing tricks to distract her from what his words said.

"Are you in English studies?" she asked.

"I was in history. Listen," he said, and his mouth did something odd, drawing itself down into a smile that made the lines about it deepen like knives, "listen, they kicked me out."

He sat back, watching her. He crossed his legs. He took out a package of cigarettes and offered her one. Sister Irene shook her head, staring at his hands. They were small and stubby and might have belonged to a ten-year-old, and the nails were a strange near-violet color. It took him a while to extract a cigarette.

"Yeah, kicked me out. What do you think of that?"

"I don't understand."

"My master's thesis was coming along beautifully, and then this bastard—I mean, excuse me, this professor, I won't pollute your office with his name—he started making criticisms, he said some things were unacceptable, he—" The boy leaned forward and hunched his narrow shoulders in a parody of secrecy. "We had an argument. I told him some frank things, things only a broadminded person could hear about himself. That takes courage, right? He didn't have it! He kicked me out of the master's program, so now I'm coming into English. Literature is greater than history; European history is one big pile of garbage. Skyhigh. Filth and rotting corpses, right? Aristotle says that poetry is higher than history; he's right; in your class today I suddenly realized that this is my field, Shakespeare, only Shakespeare is—"

Sister Irene guessed that he was going to say that only Shakespeare was equal to him, and she caught the moment of recognition and hesitation, the half-raised arm, the keen, frowning forehead, the narrowed eyes; then he thought better of it and did not end the sentence. "The students in your class are mainly negligible, I can tell you that. You're new here, and I've been here a year—I would have finished my studies last year but my father got sick, he was hospitalized, I couldn't take exams and it was a mess—but I'll make it through English in one year or drop dead. I can do it, I can do anything. I'll take six courses at once—" He broke off, breathless. Sister Irene tried to smile. "All right then, it's settled? You'll let me in? Have I missed anything so far?"

He had no idea of the rudeness of his question. Sister Irene, feeling suddenly exhausted, said, "I'll give you a syllabus of the course."

"Fine! Wonderful!"

He got to his feet eagerly. He looked through the schedule, muttering to himself, making favorable noises. It struck Sister Irene that she was making a mistake to let him in. There were these moments when one had to make an intelligent decision . . . But she was sympathetic with him, yes. She was sympathetic with something about him.

She found out his name the next day: Allen Weinstein.

After this, she came to her Shakespeare class with a sense of excitement. It became clear to her at once that Weinstein was the most intelligent student in the class. Until he had enrolled, she had not understood what was lacking, a mind that could appreciate her own. Within a week his jagged, protean mind had alienated the other students, and though he sat in the center of the class, he seemed totally alone, encased by a miniature world of his own. When he spoke of the "frenetic humanism of the High Renaissance," Sister Irene dreaded the raised eyebrows and mocking smiles of the other students, who no longer bothered to look at Weinstein. She wanted to defend him, but she never did, because there was something rude and dismal about his knowledge; he used it like a weapon, talking passionately of Nietzsche and Goethe and Freud until Sister Irene would be forced to close discussion.

In meditation, alone, she often thought of him. When she tried to talk about him to a young nun, Sister Carlotta, everything sounded gross. "But no, he's an excellent student," she insisted. "I'm very grateful to have him in class. It's just that . . . he thinks ideas are real." Sister Carlotta, who loved literature also, had been forced to teach grade-school arithmetic for the last four years. That might have been why she said, a little sharply, "You don't think ideas are real?"

Sister Irene acquiesced with a smile, but of course she did not think so: only reality is real.

When Weinstein did not show up for class on the day the first paper was due, Sister Irene's heart sank, and the sensation was somehow a familiar one. She began her lecture and kept waiting for the door to open and for him to hurry noisily back to his seat, grinning an apology toward her—but nothing happened.

If she had been deceived by him, she made herself think angrily, it was as a teacher and not as a woman. He had promised her nothing.

Weinstein appeared the next day near the steps of the liberal arts building. She heard someone running behind her, a breathless exclamation "Sister Irene!" She turned and saw him, panting and grinning in embarrassment. He wore a dark-blue suit with a necktie, and he looked, despite his childish face, like a little old man; there was something oddly precarious and fragile about him. "Sister Irene, I owe you an apology, right?" He raised his eyebrows and smiled a sad, forlorn, yet irritatingly conspiratorial smile. "The first paper —not in on time, and I know what your rules are . . . You won't accept late papers, I know—that's good discipline, I'll do that when I teach, too. But, unavoidably, I was unable to come to school yesterday. There are many—many—" He gulped for breath, and Sister Irene had the startling sense of seeing the real Weinstein stare out at her, a terrified prisoner behind the confident voice. "There are many complications in family life. Perhaps you are unaware—I mean—"

She did not like him, but she felt this sympathy, something tugging and nagging at her the way her parents had competed for her love, so many years ago. They had been whining, weak people, and out of their wet need for affection, the girl she had been (her name was Yvonne) had emerged stronger than either of them, contemptuous of tears because she had seen so many. But Weinstein was different; he was not simply weak, perhaps he was not weak at all, but his strength was confused and hysterical. She felt her customary rigidity as a teacher begin to falter. "You may turn your paper in today, if you have it," she said, frowning.

Weinstein's mouth jerked into an incredulous grin. "Wonderful! Marvelous!" he said. "You are very understanding, Sister Irene, I must say. I must say . . . I didn't expect, really . . ." He was fumbling in a shabby old briefcase for the paper. Sister Irene waited. She was prepared for another of his excuses, certain that he did not have the paper, when he suddenly straightened up and handed her something. "Here! I took the liberty of writing thirty pages instead of just fifteen," he said. He was obviously quite excited; his cheeks were mottled pink and white. "You may disagree violently with my interpretation—I expect you to, in fact I'm counting on it—but let me warn you, I have the exact proof, precise, specific proof, right here in the play itself!" He was thumping at a book, his voice growing louder and shriller. Sister Irene, startled, wanted to put her hand over his mouth and soothe him.

"Look," he said breathlessly, "may I talk with you? I have a class now I hate, I loathe, I can't bear to sit through! Can I talk with you instead?"

Because she was nervous, she stared at the title page of the paper: "Erotic Melodies in *Romeo and Juliet*" by Allen Weinstein, Jr.

"All right?" he said. "Can we walk around here? Is it all right? I've been anxious to talk with you about some things you said in class."

She was reluctant, but he seemed not to notice. They walked slowly along the shaded campus paths. Weinstein did all the talking, of course, and Sister Irene recognized nothing in his cascade of words that she had mentioned in class. "The humanist must be committed to the totality of life," he said passionately. "This is the failing one finds everywhere in the academic world! I found it in New York and I found it here and I'm no ingénu, I don't go around with my mouth hanging open—I'm experienced, look, I've been to Europe, I've lived in Rome! I went everywhere in Europe except Germany, I don't talk about Germany . . . Sister Irene, think of the significant men in the last century, the men who've changed the world! Jews, right? Marx, Freud, Einstein! Not that I believe Marx, Marx is a madman . . . and Freud, no, my sympathies are with spiritual humanism. I believe that the Jewish race is the exclusive . . . the exclusive, what's the word, the exclusive means by which humanism will be extended . . . Humanism begins by excluding the Jew, and now," he said, with a high, surprised laugh, "the Jew will perfect it. After the Nazis, only the Jew is authorized to understand humanism, its limitations and its possibilities. So, I say that the humanist is committed to life in its totality and not just to his profession! The religious person is totally religious, he *is* his religion! What else? I recognize in you a humanist and a religious person—"

But he did not seem to be talking to her, or even looking at her. "Here, read this," he said. "I wrote it last night." It was a long free-verse poem, typed on a typewriter whose ribbon was worn out. "There's this trouble with my father, a wonderful man, a lovely man, but his health—his strength is fading, do you see? What must it be to him to see his son growing up? I mean, I'm a man now, he's getting old, weak, his health is bad—it's hell, right? I sympathize with him. I'd do anything for him, I'd cut open my veins, anything for a father—right? That's why I wasn't in school yesterday," he said, and his voice dropped for the last sentence, as if he had been dragged back to earth by a fact.

Sister Irene tried to read the poem, then pretended to read it. A jumble of words dealing with "life" and "death" and "darkness" and "love." "What do you think?" Weinstein said nervously, trying to read it over her shoulder and crowding against her.

"It's very . . . passionate," Sister Irene said.

This was the right comment; he took the poem back from her in silence, his face flushed with excitement. "Here, at this school, I have few people to talk with. I haven't shown anyone else that poem." He looked at her with his dark, intense eyes, and Sister Irene felt them focus upon her. She was terrified at what he was trying to do—he was trying to force her into a human relationship.

"Thank you for your paper," she said, turning away.

When he came the next day, ten minutes late, he was haughty and disdainful. He had nothing to say and sat with his arms folded. Sister Irene took back with her to the convent a feeling of betrayal and confusion. She had been hurt. It was absurd, and yet— She spent too much time thinking about him, as if he were somehow a kind of crystallization of her own loneliness; but she had no right to think so much of him. She did not want to think of him or of her loneliness. But Weinstein did so much more than think of his predicament, he embodied it, he acted it out, and that was perhaps why he facinated her. It was as if he were doing a dance for her, a dance of shame and agony and delight, and so long as he did it, she was safe. She felt embarrassment for him, but also anxiety; she wanted to protect him. When the dean of the graduate school questioned her about Weinstein's work, she insisted that he was an "excellent" student, though she knew the dean had not wanted to hear that.

She prayed for guidance, she spent hours on her devotions, she was closer to her vocation than she had been for some years. Life at the convent became tinged with unreality, a misty distortion that took its tone from the glowering skies of the city at night, identical smokestacks ranged against the clouds and giving to the sky the excrement of the populated and successful earth. This city was not her city, this world was not her world. She felt no pride in knowing this, it was a fact. The little convent was not like an island in the center of this noisy world, but rather a kind of hole or crevice the world did not bother with, something of no interest. The convent's rhythm of life had nothing to do with the world's rhythm, it did not violate or alarm it in any way. Sister Irene tried to draw together the fragments of her life and synthesize them somehow in her vocation as a nun: she was a nun, she was recognized as a nun and had given herself happily to that life, she had a name, a place, she had dedicated her superior intelligence to the Church, she worked without pay and without expecting gratitude, she had given up pride, she did not think of herself but only of her work and her vocation, she did not think of anything external to these, she saturated herself daily in the knowledge that she was involved in the mystery of Christianity. A daily terror attended this knowledge, however, for she sensed herself being drawn by that student, that Jewish boy, into a relationship she was not ready for. She wanted to cry out in fear that she was being forced into the role of a Christian, and what did that mean? What could her studies tell her? What could the other nuns tell her? She was alone, no one could help her, he was making her into a Christian, and to her that was a mystery, a thing of terror, something others slipped on the way they slipped on their clothes, casually and thoughtlessly, but to her a magnificent and terrifying wonder.

For days she carried Weinstein's paper, marked A, around with her; he did not come to class. One day she checked with the graduate officer and was told that Weinstein had called in to say his father was ill and he would not be able to attend classes for a while. "He's strange, I remember him," the secretary said. "He missed all his exams last spring and made a lot of trouble. He was in and out of here every day."

So there was no more of Weinstein for a while, and Sister Irene stopped expecting him to hurry into class. Then, one morning, she found a letter from him in her mailbox.

He had printed it in black ink, very carefully, as if he had not trusted handwriting. The return address was in bold letters that, like his voice, tried to grab onto her: Birchcrest Manor. Somewhere north of the city. "Dear Sister Irene," the block letters said, "I am doing well here and have time for reading and relaxing. The Manor is delightful. My doctor here is an excellent, intelligent man who has time for me unlike my former doctor. If you have time, you might drop in on my father, who worries about me too much, I think, and explain to him what my condition is. He doesn't seem to understand. I feel about this new life the way that boy, what's his name, in *Measure for Measure*, feels about the prospects of a different life; you remember what he says to his sister when she visits him in prision, how he is looking forward to an escape into another world. Perhaps you could *explain* this to my father and he would stop worrying." The letter ended with the father's name and address, in letters that were just a little too big. Sister Irene, walking slowly down the corridor as she read the letter, felt her eyes cloud over with tears. She was cold with fear, it was something she had never experienced before. She knew what Weinstein was trying to tell her, and the desperation of his attempt made it all the more pathetic; he did not deserve this, why did God allow him to suffer so?

She read through Claudio's speech to his sister, in *Measure for Measure:*

> Ay, but to die, and go we know not where;
> To lie in cold obstruction and to rot;
> This sensible warm motion to become
> A kneaded clod; and the delighted spirit
> To bathe in fiery floods, or to reside
> In thrilling region of thick-ribbèd ice,
> To be imprison'd in the viewless winds
> And blown with restless violence round about
> The pendent world; or to be worse than worst
> Of those that lawless and incertain thought
> Imagines howling! 'Tis too horrible!
> The weariest and most loathèd worldly life
> That age, ache, penury, and imprisonment
> Can lay on nature is a paradise
> To what we fear of death.

Sister Irene called the father's number that day. "Allen Weinstein residence, who may I say is calling?" a woman said, bored. "May I speak to Mr. Weinstein? It's urgent—about his son," Sister Irene said. There was a pause at the other end. "You want to talk to his mother, maybe?" the woman said. "His mother? Yes, his mother, then. Please. It's very important."

She talked with this strange, unsuspected woman, a disembodied voice that suggested absolutely no face, and insisted upon going over that afternoon. The woman was nervous, but Sister Irene, who was a university professor after all, knew enough to hide her own nervousness. She kept waiting for the woman to say, "Yes, Allen has mentioned you . . ." but nothing happened.

She persuaded Sister Carlotta to ride over with her. This urgency of hers was something they were all amazed by. They hadn't suspected that the set of her gray eyes could change to this blurred, distracted alarm, this sense of mission that seemed to have come to her from nowhere. Sister Irene drove across the city in the late afternoon traffic, with the high whining noises from residential streets where trees were being sawed down in pieces. She understood now the secret, sweet wildness that Christ must have felt, giving himself for man, dying for the billions of men who would never know of him and never understand the sacrifice. For the first time she approached the realization of that great act. In her troubled mind the city traffic was jumbled and yet oddly coherent, an image of the world that was always out of joint with what was happening in it, its inner history struggling with its external spectacle. This sacrifice of Christ's, so mysterious and legendary now, almost lost in time—it was that by which Christ transcended both God and man at one moment, more than man because of his fate to do what no other man could do, and more than God because no god could suffer as he did. She felt a flicker of something close to madness.

She drove nervously, uncertainly, afraid of missing the street and afraid of finding it too, for while one part of her rushed forward to confront these people who had betrayed their son, another part of her would have liked nothing so much as to be waiting as usual for the summons to dinner, safe in her room . . . When she found the street and turned onto it, she was in a state of breathless excitement. Here, lawns were bright green and marred with only a few leaves, magically clean, and the houses were enormous and pompous, a mixture of styles: ranch houses, colonial houses, French country houses, white-bricked wonders with curving glass and clumps of birch trees somehow encircled by white concrete. Sister Irene stared as if she had blundered into another world. This was a kind of heaven, and she was too shabby for it.

The Weinstein's house was the strangest one of all: it looked like a small Alpine lodge, with an inverted-V-shaped front entrance.

Sister Irene drove up the black-topped driveway and let the car slow to a stop; she told Sister Carlotta she would not be long.

At the door she was met by Weinstein's mother, a small nervous woman with hands like her son's. "Come in, come in," the woman said. She had once been beautiful, that was clear, but now in missing beauty she was not handsome or even attractive but looked ruined and perplexed, the misshapen swelling of her white-blond professionally set hair like a cap lifting up from her surprised face. "He'll be right in. Allen?" she called, "our visitor is here." They went into the living room. There was a grand piano at one end and an organ at the other. In between were scatterings of brilliant modern furniture, in conversational groups, and several puffed-up white rugs on the polished floor. Sister Irene could not stop shivering. "Professor, it's so strange, but let me say when the phone rang I had a feeling—I had a feeling," the woman said, with damp eyes. Sister Irene sat, and the woman hovered about her. "Should I call you Professor? We don't—you know—we don't understand the technicalities that go with—Allen, my son, wanted to go here to the Catholic school; I told my husband why not? Why fight? It's the thing these days, they do anything they want for knowledge. And he had to come home, you know. He couldn't take care of himself in New York, that was the beginning of the trouble— Should I call you Professor?"

"You can call me Sister Irene."

"Sister Irene?" the woman said, touching her throat in awe, as if something intimate and unexpected had happened.

Then Weinstein's father appeared, hurrying. He took long impatient strides. Sister Irene stared at him and in that instant doubted everything—he was in his fifties, a tall, sharply handsome man, heavy but not fat, holding his shoulders back with what looked like an effort, but holding them back just the same. He wore a dark suit, and his face was flushed, as if he had run a long distance.

"Now," he said, coming to Sister Irene and with a precise wave of his hand motioning his wife off, "now let's straighten this out. A lot of confusion over that kid, eh?" He pulled a chair over, scraping it across a rug and pulling one corner over, so that its brown underside was exposed. "I came home early just for this, Libby phoned me. Sister, you got a letter from him, right?"

The wife looked at Sister Irene over her husband's shoulder as if trying somehow to coach her, knowing that this man was so loud and impatient that no one could remember anything in his presence.

"A letter—yes—today—"

"He says what in it? You got the letter, eh? Can I see it?"

She gave it to him and wanted to explain, but he silenced her with a flick of his hand. He read through the letter so quickly that Sister Irene thought perhaps he was trying to impress her with his skill at reading. "So?" he said, raising his eyes, smiling, "so what is this? He's happy out there, he says. He doesn't communicate with us anymore, but he writes to you and says he's happy—what's that? I mean, what the hell is that?"

"But he isn't happy. He wants to come home," Sister Irene said. It was so important that she make him understand that she could not trust her voice; goaded by this man, it might suddenly turn shrill, as his son's did. "Someone must read their letters before they're mailed, so he tried to tell me something by making an allusion to—"

"What?"

"—an allusion to a play, so that I would know. He might be thinking of suicide, he must be very unhappy—"

She ran out of breath. Weinstein's mother begun to cry, but the father was shaking his head jerkily back and forth. "Forgive me, Sister, but it's a lot of crap, he needs the hospital, he needs help—right? It costs me fifty a day out there, and they've got the best place in the state, I figure it's worth it. He needs help, that kid, what do I care if he's unhappy? He's unbalanced!" he said angrily. "You want us to get him out again? We argued with the judge for two hours to get him in, an acquaintance of mine. Look, he can't control himself—he was smashing things here, he was hysterical, his room is like an animal was in it. You ever seen anybody hysterical? They need help, lady, and you do something about it fast! You do something! We made up our minds to do something and we did it! This letter—what the hell is the letter? He never talked like that to us!"

"But he means the opposite of what he says—"

"Then he *is* crazy! I'm the first to admit it." He was perspiring, and his face had darkened. "I've got no pride left, this late. He's a little bastard, you want to know? He calls me names, he's filthy, got a filthy mouth—that's being smart, huh? They give him a big scholarship for his filthy mouth? I went to college too, and I got out and knew something, and I for Christ's sake did something with it; my wife is an intelligent woman, a learned woman, would you guess she does book reviews for the little newspaper out here? Intelligent isn't crazy—crazy isn't intelligent—maybe for you at the school he writes nice papers and gets an A, but out here, around the house, he can't control himself, and we got him committed!"

"But—"

"We're fixing him up, don't worry about it!" He turned to his wife. "Libby, get out of here, I mean it. I'm sorry, but get out of here, you're making a fool of yourself, go stand in the kitchen or something, you and the goddamn maid can cry on each other's shoulders. That one in the kitchen is nuts too, they're all nuts. Sister," he said, his voice lowering, "I thank you immensely for coming out here. This is wonderful, your interest in my son. And I see he admires you—that letter there. But what about that letter? If he did want to get out, which I don't admit—he was willing to be committed, in the end he said OK himself—if he wanted out I wouldn't do it. Why? So what if he wants to come back? The next day he wants something else, what then? He's a sick kid, and I'm the first to admit it."

Sister Irene felt that sickness spread to her. She stood. The room was so big that it seemed it must be a public place; there had been nothing personal or private about their conversation. Weinstein's mother was standing by the fireplace, sobbing. The father jumped to his feet and wiped his forehead in a gesture that was meant to help Sister Irene on her way out. "God, what a day," he said, his eyes snatching at hers for understanding, "you know—one of those days all day long? Sister, I thank you a lot. A professor interested in him—he's a smart kid, eh? Yes, I thank you a lot. There should be more people in the world that care about others, like you. I mean that."

On the way back to the convent, the man's words returned to her, and she could not get control of them; she could not even feel anger. She had been pressed down, forced back, what could she do? Weinstein might have been watching her somehow from a barred window, and he surely would have understood. The strange idea she had had on the way over, something about understanding

Christ, came back to her now and sickened her. But the sickness was small. It could be contained.

About a month after her visit to his father, Weinstein himself showed up. He was dressed in a suit as before, even the necktie was the same. He came right into her office as if he had been pushed and could not stop.

"Sister," he said, and shook her hand. He must have seen fear in her because he smiled ironically. "Look, I'm released. I'm let out of the nut house. Can I sit down?"

He sat. Sister Irene was breathing quickly, as if in the presence of an enemy who does not know that he is an enemy.

"So, they finally let me out. I heard what you did. You talked with him, that was all I wanted. You're the only one who gave a damn. Because you're a humanist and a religious person, you respect . . . the individual. Listen," he said, whispering, "it was hell out there! Hell! Birchcrest Manor! All fixed up with fancy chairs and *Life* magazines lying around—and what do they do to you? They locked me up, they gave me shock treatments! Shock treatments, how do you like that, it's discredited by everybody now—they're crazy out there themselves, sadists—they locked me up, they gave me hypodermic shots, they didn't treat me like a human being! Do you know what that is," Weinstein demanded savagely, "not to be treated like a human being? They made me an animal—for fifty dollars a day! Dirty filthy swine! Now I'm an outpatient because I stopped swearing at them. I found somebody's bobby pin, and when I wanted to scream I pressed it under my fingernail, and it stopped me—the screaming went inside and not out—so they gave me good reports, those sick bastards, now I'm an outpatient and I can walk along the street and breathe in the same filthy exhaust from the buses like all you normal people! Christ," he said, and threw himself back against the chair.

Sister Irene stared at him. She wanted to take his hand, to make some gesture that would close the aching distance between them. "Mr. Weinstein—"

"Call me Allen!" he said sharply.

"I'm very sorry—I'm terribly sorry—"

"My own parents committed me, but of course they didn't know what it was like. It was hell," he said, thickly, "and there isn't any hell except what other people do to you. The psychiatrist out there, the main shrink, he hates Jews, too, some of us were positive of that, and he's got a bigger nose than I do, a real beak." He made a noise of disgust. "A dirty bastard, a sick, dirty, pathetic bastard— all of them— Anyway, I'm getting out of here, and I came to ask you a favor."

"What do you mean?"

"I'm getting out. I'm leaving. I'm going up to Canada and lose myself, I'll get a job, I'll forget everything. I'll kill myself maybe—what's the difference? Look, can you lend me some money?"

"Money?"

"Just a little! I have to get to the border, I'm going to take a bus."

"But I don't have any money—"

"No money?" He stared at her. "You mean—you don't have any? Sure you have some!"

She stared at him as if he had asked her to do something obscene. Everything was splotched and uncertain before her eyes. "You must . . . you must go back," she said, "you're making a—"

"I'll pay it back. Look, I'll pay it back, can you go to where you live or something and get it? I'm in a hurry. My friends are sons of bitches: one of them pretended he didn't see me yesterday—I stood right in the middle of the sidewalk and yelled at him, I called him some appropriate names! So he didn't see me, huh? You're the only one who understands me, you understand me like a poet, you—"

"I can't help you, I'm sorry—I—"

He looked to one side of her and then flashed his gaze back, as if he could not control it. He seemed to be trying to clear his vision. "You have the soul of a poet," he whispered, "you're the only one. Everybody else is rotten! Can't you lend me some money, ten dollars maybe? I have three thousand in the bank, and I can't touch it! They take everything away from me, they make me into an animal . . . You know I'm not an animal, don't you? Don't you?"

"Of course," Sister Irene whispered.

"You could get money. Help me. Give me your hand or something, touch me, help me—please—" He reached for her hand and she drew back. He stared at her and his face seemed about to crumble, like a child's. "I want something from you, but I don't know what—I want something!" he cried. "Something real! I want you to look at me like I was a human being, is that too much to ask? I have a brain, I'm alive, I'm suffering—what does that mean? Does that mean nothing? I want something real and not this phony Christian love garbage—it's all in the books, it isn't personal—I want something real—look—"

He tried to take her hand again, and this time she jerked away. She got to her feet. "Mr. Weinstein," she said, "please—"

"You! You—nun," he said scornfully, his mouth twisted into a mock grin. "You nun! There's nothing under that ugly outfit, right? And you're not particularly smart even though you think you are; my father has more brains in his foot than you—"

He got to his feet and kicked the chair.

"You bitch!" he cried.

She shrank back against her desk as if she thought he might hit her, but he only ran out of the office.

Weinstein: the name was to become disembodied from the figure, as time went on. The semester passed, the autumn drizzle turned into snow, Sister Irene rode to school in the morning and left in the afternoon, four days a week, anonymous in her black winter cloak, quiet and stunned. University teaching was an anonymous task, each day dissociated from the rest, with no necessary sense of unity among the teachers: they came and went separately and might for a year just miss a colleague who left his office five minutes before they arrived, and it did not matter.

She heard of Weinstein's death, his suicide by drowning, from the English department secretary, a handsome white-haired woman who kept a transistor radio on her desk. Sister Irene was not surprised; she had been thinking of him as dead for months. "They identified him by some special television way they have now," the secretary said. "They're shipping the body back. It was up in Quebec . . ."

Sister Irene could feel a part of herself drifting off, lured by the plains of white snow to the north, the quiet, the emptiness, the sweep of the Great Lakes up to the silence of Canada. But she called that part of herself back. She could only be one person in her lifetime. That was the ugly truth, she thought, that she could not really regret Weinstein's suffering and death; she had only one life and had already given it to someone else. He had come too late to her. Fifteen years ago, perhaps, but not now.

She was only one person, she thought, walking down the corridor in a dream. Was she safe in this single person, or was she trapped? She had only one identity. She could make only one choice. What she had done or hadn't done was the result of that choice, and how was she guilty? If she could have felt guilt, she thought, she might at least have been able to feel something.

Miss Oates has this to say about the story:

> The central idea for the story grew out of a reading of *Antigone*, in which tragedy is suggested as the commitment to a particular way of life or an essence; Antigone's tragedy is that she is herself, and not another. This struck me as perhaps the essence—simple though it is—of tragedy, and the sentimental who believe that all things are possible or at least should be attempted are unable to understand this. It is the very tragedy of existence—a universal dilemma.

Eudora Welty

Death of a Traveling Salesman*

R. J. BOWMAN, WHO FOR FOURTEEN YEARS HAD TRAVELED for a shoe company through Mississippi, drove his Ford along a rutted dirt path. It was a long day! The time did not seem to clear the noon hurdle and settle into soft afternoon. The sun, keeping its strength here even in winter, stayed at the top of the sky, and every time Bowman stuck his head out of the dusty car to stare up the road, it seemed to reach a long arm down and push against the top of his head, right through his hat—like the practical joke of an old drummer, long on the road. It made him feel all the more angry and helpless. He was feverish, and he was not quite sure of the way.

This was his first day back on the road after a long siege of influenza. He had had very high fever, and dreams, and had become weakened and pale, enough to tell the difference in the mirror, and he could not think clearly. . . . All afternoon, in the midst of his anger, and for no reason, he had thought of his dead grand-

---

* From A CURTAIN OF GREEN AND OTHER STORIES, copyright, 1941, by Eudora Welty. Reprinted by permission of Harcourt Brace Jovanovich, Inc.

mother. She had been a comfortable soul. Once more Bowman wished he could fall into the big feather bed that had been in her room. . . . Then he forgot her again.

This desolate hill country! And he seemed to be going the wrong way—it was as if he were going back, far back. There was not a house in sight. . . . There was no use wishing he were back in bed, though. By paying the hotel doctor his bill he had proved his recovery. He had not even been sorry when the pretty trained nurse said good-bye. He did not like illness, he distrusted it, as he distrusted the road without signposts. It angered him. He had given the nurse a really expensive bracelet, just because she was packing up her bag and leaving.

But now—what if in fourteen years on the road he had never been ill before and never had an accident? His record was broken, and he had even begun almost to question it. . . . He had gradually put up at better hotels, in the bigger towns, but weren't they all, eternally, stuffy in summer and drafty in winter? Women? He could only remember little rooms within little rooms, like a nest of Chinese paper boxes, and if he thought of one woman he saw the worn loneliness that the furniture of that room seemed built of. And he himself—he was a man who always wore rather wide-brimmed black hats, and in the wavy hotel mirrors had looked something like a bullfighter, as he paused for that inevitable instant on the landing, walking downstairs to supper. . . . He leaned out of the car again, and once more the sun pushed at his head.

Bowman had wanted to reach Beulah by dark, to go to bed and sleep off his fatigue. As he remembered, Beulah was fifty miles away from the last town, on a graveled road. This was only a cow trail. How had he ever come to such a place? One hand wiped the sweat from his face, and he drove on.

He had made the Beulah trip before. But he had never seen this hill or this petering-out path before—or that cloud, he thought shyly, looking up and then down quickly—any more than he had seen this day before. Why did he not admit he was simply lost and had been for miles? . . . He was not in the habit of asking the way of strangers, and these people never knew where the very roads they lived on went to; but then he had not even been close enough to anyone to call out. People standing in the fields now and then, or on top of the haystacks, had been too far away, looking like leaning sticks or weeds, turning a little at the solitary rattle of his car across their countryside, watching the pale sobered winter dust where it chunked out behind like big squashes down the road. The stares of these distant people had followed him solidly like a wall, impenetrable, behind which they turned back after he had passed.

The cloud floated there to one side like the bolster on his grandmother's bed. It went over a cabin on the edge of a hill, where two bare chinaberry trees clutched at the sky. He drove through a heap of dead oak leaves, his wheels stirring their weightless sides to make a silvery melancholy whistle as the car passed through their bed. No car had been along this way ahead of him. Then he saw that he was on the edge of a ravine that fell away, a red erosion, and that this was indeed the road's end.

He pulled the brake. But it did not hold, though he put all his strength into it. The car, tipped toward the edge, rolled a little. Without doubt, it was going over the bank.

He got out quietly, as though some mischief had been done him and he had his dignity to remember. He lifted his bag and sample case out, set them down, and stood back and watched the car roll over the edge. He heard something—not the crash he was listening for, but a slow, unuproarious crackle. Rather distastefully he went to look over, and he saw that his car had fallen into a tangle of immense grapevines as thick as his arm, which caught it and held it, rocked it like a grotesque child in a dark cradle, and then, as he watched, concerned somehow that he was not still inside it, released it gently to the ground.

He sighed.

Where am I? he wondered with a shock. Why didn't I do something? All his anger seemed to have drifted away from him. There was the house, back on the hill. He took a bag in each hand and with almost childlike willingness went toward it. But his breathing came with difficulty, and he had to stop to rest.

It was a shotgun house, two rooms and an open passage between, perched on the hill. The whole cabin slanted a little under the heavy heaped-up vine that covered the roof, light and green, as though forgotten from summer. A woman stood in the passage.

He stopped still. Then all of a sudden his heart began to behave strangely. Like a rocket set off, it began to leap and expand into uneven patterns of beats which showered into his brain, and he could not think. But in scattering and falling it made no noise. It shot up with great power, almost elation, and fell gently, like acrobats into nets. It began to pound profoundly, then waited irresponsibly, hitting in some sort of inward mockery first at his ribs, then against his eyes, then under his shoulder blades, and against the roof of his mouth when he tried to say, "Good afternoon, madam." But he could not hear his heart—it was as quiet as ashes falling. This was rather comforting; still, it was shocking to Bowman to feel his heart beating at all.

Stock-still in his confusion, he dropped his bags, which seemed to drift in slow bulks gracefully through the air and to cushion themselves on the gray prostrate grass near the doorstep.

As for the woman standing there, he saw at once that she was old. Since she could not possibly hear his heart, he ignored the pounding and now looked at her carefully, and yet in his distraction dreamily, with his mouth open.

She had been cleaning the lamp, and held it, half blackened, half clear, in front of her. He saw her with the dark passage behind her. She was a big woman with a weather-beaten but unwrinkled face; her lips were held tightly together, and her eyes looked with a curious dulled brightness into his. He looked at her shoes, which were like bundles. If it were summer she would be barefoot. . . . Bowman, who automatically judged a woman's age on sight, set her age at fifty. She wore a formless garment of some gray coarse material, rough-dried from a washing, from which her arms appeared pink and unexpectedly round. When she never said a word, and sustained her quiet pose of holding the lamp, he was convinced of the strength in her body.

"Good afternoon, madam," he said.

She stared on, whether at him or at the air around him he could not tell, but after a moment she lowered her eyes to show that she would listen to whatever he had to say.

"I wonder if you would be interested—" He tried once more. "An accident—my car . . ."

Her voice emerged low and remote, like a sound across a lake. "Sonny he ain't here."

"Sonny?"

"Sonny ain't here now."

Her son—a fellow able to bring my car up, he decided in blurred relief. He pointed down the hill. "My car's in the bottom of the ditch. I'll need help."

"Sonny ain't here, but he'll be here."

She was becoming clearer to him and her voice stronger, and Bowman saw that she was stupid.

He was hardly surprised at the deepening postponement and tedium of his journey. He took a breath, and heard his voice speaking over the silent blows of his heart. "I was sick. I am not strong yet. . . . May I come in?"

He stooped and laid his big black hat over the handle on his bag. It was a humble motion, almost a bow, that instantly struck him as absurd and betraying of all his weakness. He looked up at the woman, the wind blowing his hair. He might have continued for a long time in this unfamiliar attitude; he had never been a patient man, but when he was sick he had learned to sink submissively into the pillows, to wait for his medicine. He waited on the woman.

Then she, looking at him with blue eyes, turned and held open the door, and after a moment Bowman, as if convinced in his action, stood erect and followed her in.

Inside, the darkness of the house touched him like a professional hand, the doctor's. The woman set the half-cleaned lamp on a table in the center of the room and pointed, also like a professional person, a guide, to a chair with a yellow cowhide seat. She herself crouched on the hearth, drawing her knees up under the shapeless dress.

At first he felt hopefully secure. His heart was quieter. The room was enclosed in the gloom of yellow pine boards. He could see the other room, with the foot of an iron bed showing, across the passage. The bed had been made up with a red-and-yellow pieced quilt that looked like a map or a picture, a little like his grandmother's girlhood painting of Rome burning.

He had ached for coolness, but in this room it was cold. He stared at the hearth with dead coals lying on it and iron pots in the corners. The hearth and the smoked chimney were of the stone he had seen ribbing the hills, mostly slate. Why is there no fire? he wondered.

And it was so still. The silence of the fields seemed to enter and move familiarly through the house. The wind used the open hall. He felt that he was in a mysterious, quiet, cool danger. It was necessary to do what? . . . To talk.

"I have a nice line of women's low-priced shoes . . ." he said.

But the woman answered, "Sonny 'll be here. He's strong. Sonny 'll move your car."

"Where is he now?"

"Farms for Mr. Redmond."

Mr. Redmond. Mr. Redmond. That was someone he would never have to encounter, and he was glad. Somehow the name did not appeal to him. . . . In a flare of touchiness and anxiety, Bowman wished to avoid even mention of unknown men and their unknown farms.

"Do you two live here alone?" He was surprised to hear his old voice, chatty, confidential, inflected for selling shoes, asking a question like that—a thing he did not even want to know.

"Yes. We are alone."

He was surprised at the way she answered. She had taken a long time to say that. She had nodded her head in a deep way too. Had she wished to affect him with some sort of premonition? he wondered unhappily. Or was it only that she would not help him, after all, by talking with him? For he was not strong enough to receive the impact of unfamiliar things without a little talk to break their fall. He had lived a month in which nothing had happened except in his head and his body—an almost inaudible life of heartbeats and dreams that came back, a life of fever and privacy, a delicate life which had left him weak to the point of—what? Of begging. The pulse in his palm leapt like a trout in a brook.

He wondered over and over why the woman did not go ahead with cleaning the lamp. What prompted her to stay there across the room, silently bestowing her presence upon him? He saw that with her it was not a time for doing little tasks. Her face was grave; she was feeling how right she was. Perhaps it was only politeness. In docility he held his eyes stiffly wide; they fixed themselves on the woman's clasped hands as though she held the cord they were strung on.

Then, "Sonny's coming," she said.

He himself had not heard anything, but there came a man

passing the window and then plunging in at the door, with two hounds beside him. Sonny was a big enough man, with his belt slung low about his hips. He looked at least thirty. He had a hot, red face that was yet full of silence. He wore muddy blue pants and an old military coat stained and patched. World War? Bowman wondered. Great God, it was a Confederate coat. On the back of his light hair he had a wide filthy black hat which seemed to insult Bowman's own. He pushed down the dogs from his chest. He was strong, with dignity and heaviness in his way of moving. . . . There was the resemblance to his mother.

They stood side by side. . . . He must account again for his presence here.

"Sonny, this man, he had his car to run off over the prec'pice an' wants to know if you will git it out for him," the woman said after a few minutes.

Bowman could not even state his case.

Sonny's eyes lay upon him.

He knew he should offer explanations and show money—at least appear either penitent or authoritative. But all he could do was to shrug slightly.

Sonny brushed by him going to the window, followed by the eager dogs, and looked out. There was effort even in the way he was looking, as if he could throw his sight out like a rope. Without turning Bowman felt that his own eyes could have seen nothing: it was too far.

"Got me a mule out there an' got me a block an' tackle," said Sonny meaningfully. "I *could* catch me my mule an' git me my ropes, an' before long I'd git your car out the ravine."

He looked completely around the room, as if in meditation, his eyes roving in their own distance. Then he pressed his lips firmly and yet shyly together, and with the dogs ahead of him this time, he lowered his head and strode out. The hard earth sounded, cupping to his powerful way of walking—almost a stagger.

Mischievously, at the suggestion of those sounds, Bowman's heart leapt again. It seemed to walk about inside him.

"Sonny's goin' to do it," the woman said. She said it again, singing it almost, like a song. She was sitting in her place by the hearth.

Without looking out, he heard some shouts and the dogs barking and the pounding of hoofs in short runs on the hill. In a few minutes Sonny passed under the window with a rope, and there was a brown mule with quivering, shining, purple-looking ears. The mule actually looked in the window. Under its eyelashes it turned target-like eyes into his. Bowman averted his head and saw the woman looking serenely back at the mule, with only satisfaction in her face.

She sang a little more, under her breath. It occurred to him, and it seemed quite marvelous, that she was not really talking to him, but rather following the thing that came about with words that were unconscious and part of her looking.

So he said nothing, and this time when he did not reply he felt a curious and strong emotion, not fear, rise up in him.

This time, when his heart leapt, something—his soul—seemed to leap too, like a colt invited out of a pen. He stared at the woman while the frantic nimbleness of his feeling made his head sway. He could not move; there was nothing he could do, unless perhaps he might embrace this woman who sat there growing old and shapeless before him.

But he wanted to leap up, to say to her, I have been sick and I found out then, only then, how lonely I am. Is it too late? My heart puts up a struggle inside me, and you may have heard it, protesting against emptiness. . . . It should be full, he would rush on to tell her, thinking of his heart now as a deep lake, it should be holding love like other hearts. It should be flooded with love. There would be a warm spring day . . . Come and stand in my heart, whoever you are, and a whole river would cover your feet and rise higher and take your knees in whirlpools, and draw you down to itself, your whole body, your heart too.

But he moved a trembling hand across his eyes, and looked at the placid crouching woman across the room. She was still as a statue. He felt ashamed and exhausted by the thought that he might, in one more moment, have tried by simple words and embraces to communicate some strange thing—something which seemed always to have just escaped him . . .

Sunlight touched the furthest pot on the hearth. It was late afternoon. This time tomorrow he would be somewhere on a good graveled road, driving his car past things that happened to people, quicker than their happening. Seeing ahead to the next day, he was glad, and knew that this was no time to embrace an old woman.

He could feel in his pounding temples the readying of his blood for motion and for hurrying away.

"Sonny's hitched up your car by now," said the woman. "He'll git it out the ravine right shortly."

"Fine!" he cried with his customary enthusiasm.

Yet it seemed a long time that they waited. It began to get dark. Bowman was cramped in his chair. Any man should know enough to get up and walk around while he waited. There was something like guilt in such stillness and silence.

But instead of getting up, he listened. . . . His breathing restrained, his eyes powerless in the growing dark, he listened uneasily for a warning sound, forgetting in wariness what it would be. Before long he heard something—soft, continuous, insinuating.

"What's that noise?" he asked, his voice jumping into the dark. Then wildly he was afraid it would be his heart beating so plainly in the quiet room, and she would tell him so.

"You might hear the stream," she said grudgingly.

Her voice was closer. She was standing by the table. He wondered why she did not light the lamp. She stood there in the dark and did not light it.

Bowman would never speak to her now, for the time was past. I'll sleep in the dark, he thought, in his bewilderment pitying himself.

Heavily she moved on to the window. Her arm, vaguely white, rose straight from her full side and she pointed out into the darkness.

"That white speck's Sonny," she said, talking to herself.

He turned unwillingly and peered over her shoulder; he hesitated to rise and stand beside her. His eyes searched the dusky air. The white speck floated smoothly toward her finger, like a leaf on a river, growing whiter in the dark. It was as if she had shown him something secret, part of her life, but had offered no explanation. He looked away. He was moved almost to tears, feeling for no reason that she had made a silent declaration equivalent to his own. His hand waited upon his chest.

Then a step shook the house, and Sonny was in the room. Bowman felt how the woman left him there and went to the other man's side.

"I done got your car out, mister," said Sonny's voice in the dark.

"She's settin' a-waitin' in the road, turned to go back where she come from."

"Fine!" said Bowman, projecting his own voice to loudness. "I'm surely obliged—I could never have done it myself—I was sick. . . ."

"I could do it easy," said Sonny.

Bowman could feel them both waiting in the dark, and he could hear the dogs panting out in the yard, waiting to bark when he should go. He felt strangely helpless and resentful. Now that he could go, he longed to stay. From what was he being deprived? His chest was rudely shaken by the violence of his heart. These people cherished something here that he could not see, they withheld some ancient promise of food and warmth and light. Between them they had a conspiracy. He thought of the way she had moved away from him and gone to Sonny, she had flowed toward him. He was shaking with cold, he was tired, and it was not fair. Humbly and yet angrily he stuck his hand into his pocket.

"Of course I'm going to pay you for everything—"

"We don't take money for such," said Sonny's voice belligerently.

"I want to pay. But do something more . . . Let me stay— tonight. . . ." He took another step toward them. If only they could see him, they would know his sincerity, his real need! His voice went on, "I'm not very strong yet, I'm not able to walk far, even back to my car, maybe, I don't know—I don't know exactly where I am—"

He stopped. He felt as if he might burst into tears. What would they think of him!

Sonny came over and put his hands on him. Bowman felt them pass (they were professional too) across his chest, over his hips. He could feel Sonny's eyes upon him in the dark.

"You ain't no revenuer come sneakin' here, mister, ain't got no gun?"

To this end of nowhere! And yet *he* had come. He made a grave answer. "No."

"You can stay."

"Sonny," said the woman, "you'll have to borry fire."

"I'll go git it from Redmond's," said Sonny.

"What?" Bowman strained to hear their words to each other.

"Our fire, it's out, and Sonny's got to borry some, because it's dark an' cold," she said.

"But matches—I have matches—"

"We don't have no need for 'em," she said proudly. "Sonny's goin' after his own fire."

"I'm goin' to Redmond's," said Sonny with an air of importance, and he went out.

After they had waited a while, Bowman looked out the window and saw a light moving over the hill. It spread itself out like a little fan. It zig-zagged along the field, darting and swift, not like Sonny at all. . . . Soon, enough, Sonny staggered in, holding a burning stick behind him in tongs, fire flowing in his wake, blazing light into the corners of the room.

"We'll make a fire now," the woman said, taking the brand.

When that was done she lit the lamp. It showed its dark and light. The whole room turned golden-yellow like some sort of flower, and the walls smelled of it and seemed to tremble with the quiet rushing of the fire and the waving of the burning lampwick in its funnel of light.

The woman moved among the iron pots. With the tongs she dropped hot coals on top of the iron lids. They made a set of soft vibrations, like the sound of a bell far away.

She looked up and over at Bowman, but he could not answer. He was trembling. . . .

"Have a drink, mister?" Sonny asked. He had brought in a chair from the other room and sat astride it with his folded arms across the back. Now we are all visible to one another, Bowman thought, and cried, "Yes sir, you bet, thanks!"

"Come after me and do just what I do," said Sonny.

It was another excursion into the dark. They went through the hall, out to the back of the house, past a shed and a hooded well. They came to a wilderness of thicket.

"Down on your knees," said Sonny.

"What?" Sweat broke out on his forehead.

He understood when Sonny began to crawl through a sort of tunnel that the bushes made over the ground. He followed, startled in spite of himself when a twig or a thorn touched him gently without making a sound, clinging to him and finally letting him go.

Sonny stopped crawling and, crouched on his knees, began to dig with both his hands into the dirt. Bowman shyly struck matches and made a light. In a few minutes Sonny pulled up a jug. He poured out some of the whisky into a bottle from his coat pocket, and buried the jug again. "You never know who's liable to knock at your door," he said, and laughed. "Start back," he said, almost formally. "Ain't no need for us to drink outdoors, like hogs."

At the table by the fire, sitting opposite each other in their chairs, Sonny and Bowman took drinks out of the bottle, passing it across. The dogs slept; one of them was having a dream.

"This is good," said Bowman. "This is what I needed." It was just as though he were drinking the fire off the hearth.

"He makes it," said the woman with quiet pride.

She was pushing the coals off the pots, and the smells of corn bread and coffee circled the room. She set everything on the table before the men, with a bone-handled knife stuck into one of the potatoes, splitting out its golden fiber. Then she stood for a minute looking at them, tall and full above them where they sat. She leaned a little toward them.

"You all can eat now," she said, and suddenly smiled.

Bowman had just happened to be looking at her. He set his cup back on the table in unbelieving protest. A pain pressed at his eyes. He saw that she was not an old woman. She was young, still young. He could think of no number of years for her. She was the same age as Sonny, and she belonged to him. She stood with the deep dark corner of the room behind her, the shifting yellow light scattering over her head and her gray formless dress, trembling over her tall body when it bent over them in its sudden communication. She was young. Her teeth were shining and her eyes glowed. She turned and walked slowly and heavily out of the room, and he heard her sit down on the cot and then lie down. The pattern on the quilt moved.

"She's goin' to have a baby," said Sonny, popping a bite into his mouth.

Bowman could not speak. He was shocked with knowing what was really in this house. A marriage, a fruitful marriage. That simple thing. Anyone could have had that.

Somehow he felt unable to be indignant or protest, although some sort of joke had certainly been played upon him. There was nothing remote or mysterious here—only something private. The only secret was the ancient communication between two people. But the memory of the woman's waiting silently by the cold hearth, of the man's stubborn journey a mile away to get fire, and how they finally brought out their food and drink and filled the room proudly with all they had to show, was suddenly too clear and too enormous within him for response. . . .

"You ain't as hungry as you look," said Sonny.

The woman came out of the bedroom as soon as the men had finished, and ate her supper while her husband stared peacefully into the fire.

Then they put the dogs out, with the food that was left.

"I think I'd better sleep here by the fire, on the floor," said Bowman.

He felt that he had been cheated, and that he could afford now to be generous. Ill though he was, he was not going to ask them for their bed. He was through with asking favors in this house, now that he understood what was there.

"Sure, mister."

But he had not known yet how slowly he understood. They had not meant to give him their bed. After a little interval they both rose and looking at him gravely went into the other room.

He lay stretched by the fire until it grew low and dying. He watched every tongue of blaze lick out and vanish. "There will be special reduced prices on all footwear during the month of January," he found himself repeating quietly, and then he lay with his lips tight shut.

How many noises the night had! He heard the stream running, the fire dying, and he was sure now that he heard his heart beating too, the sound it made under his ribs. He heard breathing, round and deep, of the man and his wife in the room across the passage. And that was all. But emotion swelled patiently within him, and he wished that the child were his.

He must get back to where he had been before. He stood weakly before the red coals and put on his overcoat. It felt too heavy on his shoulders. As he started out he looked and saw that the woman had never got through with cleaning the lamp. On some impulse he put all the money from his billfold under its fluted glass base, almost ostentatiously.

Ashamed, shrugging a little, and then shivering, he took his bags and went out. The cold of the air seemed to lift him bodily. The moon was in the sky.

On the slope he began to run, he could not help it. Just as he reached the road, where his car seemed to sit in the moonlight like a boat, his heart began to give off tremendous explosions like a rifle, bang bang bang.

He sank in fright onto the road, his bags falling about him. He felt as if all this had happened before. He covered his heart with both hands to keep anyone from hearing the noise it made.

But nobody heard it.

V

"OH WHAT A LOVELY WAR..."

"To save this town, we had to destroy this town."
>American officer explaining how he felt his unit saved a Vietnamese town during the February 1968 Tiet offensive

If man does find the solution for world peace, it will be the most revolutionary reversal of his record we have ever known.
>George C. Marshall
>Biennial Report of the
>Chief of Staff, Sept. 1, 1945

Cry "Havoc," and let slip the dogs of war.
>Antony in
>SHAKESPEARE's *Julius Caesar*, III, i, 273

Looking at corpses is humiliating... We have the impression that the same fate which had stretched these bodies on the ground, nails us here to look at them... Because every war is a civil war, every man who falls resembles the one who survives and calls him to account.

>   **CESARE PAVESE**
>   *The House on the Hill*

... and there is no discharge in that war.
>   *Ecclesiastes 8:8*

This is the patent age of new inventions
    For killing bodies, and for saving souls,
All propagated with the best intentions.

>   **LORD BYRON**
>   *Don Juan*

Ambrose Bierce

Chickamauga

ONE SUNNY AUTUMN AFTERNOON a child strayed away from its rude home in a small field and entered a forest unobserved. It was happy in a new sense of freedom from control, happy in the opportunity of exploration and adventure; for this child's spirit, in bodies of its ancestors, had for thousands of years been trained to memorable feats of discovery and conquest—victories in battles whose critical moments were centuries, whose victors' camps were cities of hewn stone. From the cradle of its race it had conquered its way through two continents and passing a great sea had penetrated a third, there to be born to war and dominion as a heritage.

The child was a boy aged about six years, the son of a poor planter. In his younger manhood the father had been a soldier, had fought against naked savages and followed the flag of his country into the capital of a civilized race to the far South. In the peaceful life of a planter the warrior-fire survived; once kindled, it is never extinguished. The man loved military books and pictures and the boy had understood enough to make himself a wooden sword, though even the eye of his father would hardly have known it for what it was. This weapon he now bore bravely, as became the son of an heroic race, and pausing now and again in the sunny space of the forest assumed, with some exaggeration, the postures of aggression and defense that he had been taught by the engraver's art. Made reckless by the ease with which he overcame invisible foes attempting to stay his advance, he committed the common enough military error of pushing the pursuit to a dangerous extreme, until he found himself upon the margin of a wide but shallow brook, whose rapid waters barred his direct advance against the flying foe that had crossed with illogical ease. But the intrepid victor was not to be baffled; the spirit of the race which had passed the great sea burned unconquerable in that small breast and would not be denied. Finding a place where some bowlders in the bed of the stream lay but a step or a leap apart, he made his way across and fell again upon the rear-guard of his imaginary foe, putting all to the sword.

Now that the battle had been won, prudence required that he withdraw to his base of operations. Alas; like many a mightier conqueror, and like one, the mightiest, he could not

curb the lust for war,
Nor learn that tempted Fate will leave the loftiest star.

Advancing from the bank of the creek he suddenly found himself confronted with a new and more formidable enemy: in the path that he was following, sat, bolt upright, with ears erect and paws suspended before it, a rabbit! With a startled cry the child turned and fled, he knew not in what direction, calling with inarticulate cries for his mother, weeping, stumbling, his tender skin cruelly torn by brambles, his little heart beating hard with terror—breathless, blind with tears—lost in the forest! Then, for more than an hour, he wandered with erring feet through the tangled undergrowth, till at last, overcome by fatigue, he lay down in a narrow space between two rocks, within a few yards of the stream and still grasping his toy sword, no longer a weapon but a companion, sobbed himself to sleep. The wood birds sang merrily above his head; the squirrels, whisking their bravery of tail, ran barking from tree to tree, unconscious of the pity of it, and somewhere far away was a strange, muffled thunder, as if the partridges were drumming in celebration of nature's victory over the son of her immemorial enslavers. And back at the little plantation, where white men and black were hastily searching the fields and hedges in alarm, a mother's heart was breaking for her missing child.

Hours passed, and then the little sleeper rose to his feet. The chill of the evening was in his limbs, the fear of the gloom in his heart. But he had rested, and he no longer wept. With some blind instinct which impelled to action he struggled through the undergrowth about him and came to a more open ground—on his right the brook, to the left a gentle acclivity studded with infrequent trees; over all, the gathering gloom of twilight. A thin, ghostly mist rose along the water. It frightened and repelled him; instead of recrossing, in the direction whence he had come, he turned his back upon it, and went forward toward the dark inclosing wood. Suddenly he saw before him a strange moving object which he took to be some large animal—a dog, a pig—he could not name it; perhaps it was a bear. He had seen pictures of bears, but knew of nothing to their discredit and had vaguely wished to meet one. But something in form or movement of this object—something in the awkwardness of its approach—told him that it was not a bear, and curiosity was stayed by fear. He stood still and as it came slowly on gained courage every moment, for he saw that at least it had not the long, menacing ears of the rabbit. Possibly his impressionable mind was half conscious of something familiar in its shambling, awkward gait. Before it had approached near enough to resolve his doubts he saw that it was followed by another and another. To right and to left were many more; the whole open space about him was alive with them—all moving toward the brook.

They were men. They crept upon their hands and knees. They used their hands only, dragging their legs. They used their knees only, their arms hanging idle at their sides. They strove to rise to their feet, but fell prone in the attempt. They did nothing naturally, and nothing alike, save only to advance foot by foot in the same direction. Singly, in pairs and in little groups, they came on through the gloom, some halting now and again while others crept slowly past them, then resuming their movement. They came by dozens and by hundreds; as far on either hand as one could see in the deepening gloom they extended and the black wood behind them appeared to be inexhaustible. The very ground seemed in motion toward the creek. Occasionally one who had paused did not again go on, but lay motionless. He was dead. Some, pausing, made strange gestures with their hands, erected their arms and lowered them again, clasped their heads; spread their palms upward, as men are sometimes seen to do in public prayer.

Not all of this did the child note; it is what would have been noted by an elder observer; he saw little but that these were men, yet crept like babes. Being men, they were not terrible, though unfamiliarly clad. He moved among them freely, going from one to another and peering into their faces with childish curiosity. All their faces were singularly white and many were streaked and gouted with red. Something in this—something too, perhaps, in their grotesque attitudes and movements—reminded him of the painted clown whom he had seen last summer in the circus, and he laughed as he watched them. But on and ever on they crept, these maimed and bleeding men, as heedless as he of the dramatic contrast between his laughter and their own ghastly gravity. To him it was a merry spectacle. He had seen his father's negroes creep upon their hands and knees for his amusement—had ridden them so, "making believe" they were his horses. He now approached one of these crawling figures from behind and with an agile movement mounted it astride. The man sank upon his breast, recovered, flung the small boy fiercely to the ground as an unbroken colt might have done, then turned upon him a face that lacked a lower jaw—from the upper teeth to the throat was a great red gap fringed with hanging shreds of flesh and splinters of bone. The unnatural prominence of nose, the absence of chin, the fierce eyes, gave this man the appearance of a great bird of prey crimsoned in throat and breast by the blood of its quarry. The man rose to his knees, the child to his feet. The man shook his fist at the child; the child, terrified at last, ran to a tree near by, got upon the farther side of it and took a more serious view of the situation. And so the clumsy multitude dragged itself slowly and painfully along in hideous pantomime—moved forward down the slope like a swarm of great black beetles, with never a sound of going—in silence profound, absolute.

Instead of darkening, the haunted landscape began to brighten. Through the belt of trees beyond the brook shone a strange red light, the trunks and branches of the trees making a black lacework against it. It struck the creeping figures and gave them monstrous shadows, which caricatured their movements on the lit grass. It fell upon their faces, touching their whiteness with a ruddy tinge, accentuating the strains with which so many of them were freaked and maculated. It sparkled on buttons and bits of metal in their clothing. Instinctively the child turned toward the growing splendor and moved down the slope with his horrible companions; in a few moments had passed the foremost of the throng—not much of a feat, considering his advantages. He placed himself in the lead, his wooden sword still in hand, and solemnly directed the march, conforming his pace to theirs and occasionally turning as if to see that his forces did not straggle. Surely such a leader never before had such a following.

Scattered about upon the ground now slowly narrowing by the encroachment of this awful march to water, were certain articles to which, in the leader's mind, were coupled no significant associations; an occasional blanket, tightly rolled lengthwise, doubled and the ends bound together with a string; a heavy knapsack here, and there a broken rifle—such things, in short, as are found in the rear of retreating troops, the "spoor" of men flying from their hunters. Everywhere near the creek, which here had a margin of lowland, the earth was trodden into mud by the feet of men and horses. An observer of better experience in the use of his eyes would have noticed that these footprints pointed in both directions; the ground had been twice passed over—in advance and in retreat. A few hours before, these desperate, stricken men, with their more fortunate and now distant comrades, had penetrated the forest in thousands. Their successive battalions, breaking into swarms and re-forming in lines, had passed the child on every side—had almost trodden on him as he slept. The rustle and murmur of their march had not awakened him. Almost within a stone's throw of where he lay they had fought a battle; but all unheard by him were the roar of the musketry, the shock of the cannon, "the thunder of the captains and the shouting." He had slept through it all, grasping his little wooden sword with perhaps a tighter clutch in unconscious sympathy with his martial environment, but as heedless of the grandeur of the struggle as the dead who had died to make the glory.

The fire beyond the belt of woods on the farther side of the creek, reflected to earth from the canopy of its own smoke, was now suffusing the whole landscape. It transformed the sinuous line of mist to the vapor of gold. The water gleamed with dashes of red, and red, too, were many of the stones protruding above the surface. But that was blood; the less desperately wounded had stained them in crossing. On them, too, the child now crossed with eager steps; he was going to the fire. As he stood upon the farther bank he turned about to look at the companions of his march. The advance was arriving at the creek. The stronger had already drawn themselves to the brink and plunged their faces into the flood. Three or four who lay without motion appeared to have no heads. At this the child's eyes expanded with wonder; even his hospitable understanding could not accept a phenomenon implying such vitality as that. After slaking their thirst these men had not had the strength to back away from the water, nor to keep their heads above it. They were drowned. In rear of these, the open spaces of the forest showed the leader as many formless figures of his grim command as at first; but not nearly so many were in motion. He waved his cap for their encouragement and smilingly pointed with his weapon in the direction of the guiding light—a pillar of fire to this strange exodus.

Confident of the fidelity of his forces, he now entered the belt of woods, passed through it easily in the red illumination, climbed a fence, ran across a field, turning now and again to coquet with his responsive shadow, and so approached the blazing ruin of a dwelling. Desolation everywhere! In all the wide glare not a living thing was visible. He cared nothing for that; the spectacle pleased, and he danced with glee in imitation of the wavering flames. He ran about, collecting fuel, but every object that he found was too heavy for him to cast in from the distance to which the heat limited his approach. In despair he flung in his sword—a surrender to the superior forces of nature. His military career was at an end.

Shifting his position, his eyes fell upon some outbuildings which had an oddly familiar appearance, as if he had dreamed of them. He stood considering them with wonder, when suddenly the entire plantation, with its inclosing forest, seemed to turn as if on a pivot. His little world swung half around; the points of the compass were reversed. He recognized the blazing building as his own home!

For a moment he stood stupefied by the power of the revelation, then ran with stumbling feet, making a half-circuit of the ruin.

There, conspicuous in the light of the conflagration, lay the dead body of a woman—the white face turned upward, the hands thrown out and clutched full of grass, the clothing deranged, the long dark hair in tangles and full of clotted blood. The greater part of the forehead was torn away, and from the jagged hole the brain protruded, overflowing the temple, a frothy mass of gray, crowned with clusters of crimson bubbles—the work of a shell.

The child moved his little hands, making wild, uncertain gestures. He uttered a series of inarticulate and indescribable cries —something between the chattering of an ape and the gobbling of a turkey—a startling, soulless, unholy sound, the language of a devil. The child was a deaf mute.

Then he stood motionless, with quivering lips, looking down upon the wreck.

Harris Downey

The Hunters*

PRIVATE MEADOWS WAS LOST. He had no idea which way his outfit had gone, had ever intended to go.

They were moving into France from the north. Naturally, their progress would be to the south. But during their fighting from Cherbourg they had moved in all directions. He did not know how long it had been since they left Cherbourg—three weeks, four weeks. It was some long undeterminable stretch of time. Nor did he know how many miles they had come—forty, fifty, maybe two hundred. They had come through villages—slowly, ferreting snipers from the ruins that their own artillery made. Someone had named the names of the villages but he had not understood. He had asked the names again and again, feeling that he should establish something familiar in his memory, feeling that he might come to understand where he was going, what he was doing. But between question and answer, he would fall back into the torpor that his life had been since Cher-

* From STORIES FROM EPOCH (Cornell University Press, 1966). Reprinted by permission of the author.

bourg. The answer, like a fragment slanting a helmet, would strike his mind obliquely and deflect away into the noisy and flashing anonymity of war.

He had traversed plow-furrowed fields when silence, imminent with violence, weighted him down like a pack. He had traversed shell-pelleted fields when fear tangled his legs like a barricade. He had seen his enemy and his comrades sprawled grotesque and cold in the neutrality of death, as impersonal as the cows among them, angling stiff legs to the sky. He had thrown grenades at hidden men; and once, staring into wide stark eyes down the bead of his aim, he had sighed out his breath toward a union more intimate than love—and more treacherous than its denial. He had seen a dog, tethered at the gate, howl at the noise of destruction and die in terror; had seen bees swarm from their hives at the ground-shake of cannon and hang in the air, directionless. He had seen Frenchmen return to their villages to gesticulate the glory of victory and, sobering, to peer from behind a silly grin at the rubbish that had been their homes. But these things had not touched him. He had left himself somewhere, and the farther he walked the terrain of war, the farther he went from himself.

He heard the spasmodic eruptions of war. He listened to silence hissing like the quick fuse of a bomb. Yet, he felt nothing—unless it were weariness. He walked under the high fire of artillery as though it were a canopy against the rain. At first, he had been unhappy and afraid; and perhaps, in the static musing, in the constant but unapprehended memory that was himself, he was yet unhappy and afraid.

Casually walking, talking to his friends, or running, crawling, squirming on his belly, looking ahead for cover, he had followed his leaders from sector to sector. The sun had come up on his left, on his right, from behind him, had sheered through the odd geometry of fields and had slid down the high summer clouds behind him, in front of him—always in a new tangent to the hedgerow. Twelve times, twenty times. How many times had he seen the sun point a surprising direction that was the west?

That morning he had seen the sun come up in the direction they were to move. Lying against the massed roots, he had looked through an opening of the hedgerow over a pasture that ran a quarter of a mile to a wood.

There near the woods he saw a farmhouse with spindly trees growing around it like a fence. He lay still, watching the sun slip above the treetops. To the right of him lay Barr, a replacement who had been in the company only a week or so, a talkative fellow who somehow managed to hold his happiness and his identity about him. Beyond Barr lay Pederson, whose twin brother had been wounded in his first skirmish and sent back. To the left of him was Harrod, whom Private Meadows had been with since induction. And beyond Harrod was Walton, a slow-talking, card-playing soldier who had come in with Barr. These men were his friends; by virtue of their position in the squad, they were his friends.

All along the row men lay with their heads in their helmets. Soon, from somewhere behind him, an order would be given and everyone would begin to move. But he would not comprehend the order. Even when it was passed on to him and he in turn passed it on, he would not consider its meaning. He had given up trying to understand words—orders, directions, cautions. He moved and lived in a channel of sounds, but his mind took them in as involuntarily as his lungs breathed the air. It was his eyes that activated him. He watched his leaders and his comrades. He followed. He did what they did. He listened acutely and unendingly but never accepted the meaning of sound. Consciously, he heard only silence, that dead silence which makes one feel that he has gone deaf.

As he looked through the hedgerow at the sun, he began to hear the silence gather. Even the men behind him, the lieutenant, the sergeants, had become silent. He could feel the silence creep along the hedgerow, turning the heads of his comrades. The sun, having cleared the trees, seemed to stick in the silence. The silence grew heavy. He could feel it on his back pressing him against the earth. The grass in the field was still, as though the silence were barrier against the wind. The silence swelled, grew taut, then violently burst.

It was artillery from his own lines. The barrage was steady and strong. From beyond the woods the fire was returned, its shells falling short in the field. The cows in the field had lifted their heads and now stood as still as stone. Two horses from the farmyard thundered across the level terrain. A fox bounding from the woods reached the clearing and raced round in a circle.

Private Meadows pulled his head away from the opening of the hedgerow and leaned back against the embankment of roots. His unit began to move down the hedgerow. He followed, on his hands and knees, dragging the butt of his rifle.

When they came to the end of the row, they bounded into the woods at the south. There in the woods they dispersed and moved to the east. It was there in the woods that he got lost. He had followed the others for a time and then, of a sudden, he was alone. The artillery had stopped. It was the silence that called him to consciousness. He walked on, listening. He could hear nothing but the crackle of twigs under his feet. There was no firing even in the distance. And but for the noise he himself made, the woods were quiet—no wind in the trees, no birds even. He sat down, leaned against the trunk of a tree, crossed his piece over his thighs, his finger on the trigger, and waited. He waited for a sound.

He had expected that other men would come from the direction he had come. But somewhere, skirting the trees, he must have got out of the line of advance, for no men came.

The woods were eerie. It seemed that all the men had walked off into another world, leaving him alone. He didn't like the silence. He got up and began to walk, taking a direction half left to the one that brought him to his silent place. He came to a cart path. But he would not enter it. He stayed in the woods, keeping the path in sight, following it; it was angling him again to the left. He walked slowly, cautiously, wondering whether he were approaching the enemy line. The woods were thick and dark. Each tree was watching him, listening to the sounds he made. Each step was a deepening into fear. It was not the sort of fear he knew under fire. There he was scared, but this was a worse fear—unrelenting and conscious.

He hardly moved at all, putting one foot carefully before him and looking about, listening with all his body to the silence, before he brought the other foot forward. Then he stopped still, like a man yelled into a brace. He had heard a voice. His heartbeat pounded the silence. Then, directionless, whispered, he heard distinctly: "Hey." It was an American word, he guessed. But

German snipers used American words as traps. He started to walk on, and then a little louder this time: "Hey." The word spiraled through the silence like a worm in wood. He halted again. He was afraid to turn. He dared not lift his rifle. Whoever called had a bead on him. Tentatively he put a foot forward, took a step. "Hey." He was playing with him as a cat does a rat, teasing him before he put the bullet in his back or between his eyes, waiting for him to make some particular move—to run, or turn, or lift his rifle, or gaze up into the barrel tracing him.

His enemy was all around him, saw him at every angle. He stood motionless, as though immobility forestalled the shot. He felt the sweat burst on his forehead. He was weak. In his memory he reviewed the sound, trying to divine its direction; and the voice came again. While he was listening to the voice in his memory, it came again, confusing him: "Hey, there." It came from all sides of him, the voice of the forest itself. "Put down your gun." The command was clear and slow—behind him. He lowered his rifle to the ground, stepped backward, waited. "Turn aroun'." He turned slowly, holding his breath. He saw no one.

He watched the trunks of trees, expecting a head—and a gun— to slip round into the open. "Where you goin', bud?" At the foot of a tree to his left oblique, partly concealed under a bush, sat a man on his haunches, leaning forward on his rifle. It was an American: the helmet, the green jacket. "What'cha scared of, bud?" The man stretched a foot forward and rose clear of the brush.

Private Meadows stood still. Was it a joke? He rather expected others to appear from the forest—from out of the brush, from behind the trees; expected all his lost comrades to appear from the silence that had swallowed them. He wondered whether he had not been lost in meditation; whether, as he followed his comrades through the trees, he had not fallen into a fearful dream and was now emerging into reality as one of his friends shook his shoulder, urging him on. He had been hypnotized by his fear. He wanted to cry but was too much exhausted to cry. The man standing before him, touching his shoulder with a thick hairy hand, was strange. He and the man were alone. And the silence was real. "Come out of it, bud." But the man was not concerned. A grin stretched over his fat face like a painted mouth stretching over a tight balloon. He was enjoying the joke he had played. "What'cha doin' here, soldier?" The voice was as cold as authority.

"I got lost," Private Meadows said.

Then the voice was as hooligan as persecution: "That's misbehavior before the enemy. They'd hang you for that. That's desertion."

Private Meadows didn't know the ensign of the man before him. Nor did he attempt to surmise it. It would be whatever the manner suggested it to be. In the man's manner there was some kind of authority. So Private Meadows answered with the only defence he knew: "I was lost."

"Me too," the man said. "*I'm* lost."

The man pointed to the gun on the ground. Private Meadows picked it up. Then he looked at the man squarely. Vaguely in his mind were the questions: *Why did you make me put it down? Why did you scare me?* But he never uttered them. They hung wordless in his mind, expressed only as the straight, surprised, and momentary stare. Then they faded into his real being, that shadowy remote musing, progressively growing dark since Cherbourg—and inaccessible. He looked off, into the direction he had been walking. "What are we gonna do?" he asked.

The man walked forward. His answer was a command: "Take it easy—till we know what's up."

Private Meadows put his arm through the sling, settled his rifle behind his shoulder, and followed. He was over his fright now, the weakness gone from his knees. He was safe again in the guidance of the Army.

He saw the broad round shoulders before him humping the air like an elephant's flanks and the heavy field boots scraping through the brush, flushing the silence. The noise of their progress was to Private Meadows an easeful shelter, like a low roof on a rainy night. Then there was the burst of a cannon—the slamming of a door in the giant structure of war, shattering the silence of the endless chambers that, for a moment, Private Meadows had forgot.

"A eighty-eight," the man said. They had both stopped at the cannon burst, had looked at each other and then in the direction of the sound. The burst came again, then again, as they stood motionless, listening. Then came the sound of rifle fire, pelleting the continuing bursts of the cannon. "Well, now we know where we are." The man spoke softly, his head, poked forward on the thick neck, malling up and down—a mechanical ram impelled by words. "Let's go," he said. He changed the direction nearly full right. They came to a dirt road. "You been on that road?" he asked. Private Meadows shook his head. "Must be mined. Or we'd be using it," the man said. "Sump'n comin'." Down the road, winding out from the trees, came a cart. They drew back, settled themselves behind a bush, and waited. The cart came slowly by, going in the direction from which they had come. A man walked beside the horse and from time to time put his hand at the bridle. In the seat of the cart was a woman holding a baby. In the back, among some baggage, sat a child, leaning her head against a mattress.

After the cart was out of sight, the two soldiers went again to the edge of the road. "Guess it ain't mined," the big one said. His eyes, nearly obscured under the net-covered helmet, were two little mice peering from under a crib. His grin was the lifting of a rake, and the mice scurried back into their holes. "Let's go," he said. He jumped the ditch and ran across the road.

Mechanically Private Meadows followed him. "Ain't we gonna try to get back?" he asked.

The man turned sharply and looked at him distrustfully. "You don't wanna go now, do you?"

"I don't know," Private Meadows said.

"We getting back, see. But we takin' the long way roun'." Private Meadows shrugged his shoulders. He was tired. The man had stuck his great round face close to his and was staring into his eyes. Private Meadows held his face against the stare but wearily closed his eyes. Sleep covered him like a breaker. His body swayed. Then he shook his head and opened his eyes. "Come on," the man said.

They walked through the woods, keeping within sight of the road. The distant rifle fire was continuous. The artillery had begun again, and from time to time a great cannon jolted all the other sounds to silence. Though they were walking oblique from the firing, Private Meadows wondered whether, on the tangent of their direction, they might not be approaching the enemy's lines. But this wonder was fleeting like the recurrent sleep that blacked him out whenever he closed his eyes. Responsibility had gone the way of his fear; he was automaton again. He was following.

The man, who had been walking ahead, jumped to cover behind a tree, at the same time wagging a fat hand around his waist in signal to Private Meadows. Private Meadows was behind a tree almost as quickly as the man and then, peering around, he saw the cause of alarm. A German soldier was coming toward them. He was unhelmeted, a cap pulled low over his forehead. Slung over his shoulder and hanging at his waist was a leather case. "Hey," the big man called in the whispering voice. The German was startled by the sight of the man even before he heard the voice; for at the utterance he had already stopped, gazing first at the face and then at the rifle pointing from the fat round hip. "Hey," the man repeated—needlessly—for the German was standing frozen in the first attitude of shock.

Without turning his gaze from the German, the man called out to Private Meadows: "Is it clear?"

"Looks clear," Private Meadows said, shuttling his gaze among the trees.

The man approached the German until he stood within a few feet of him. "Search him," he said.

Private Meadows, holding his rifle at the waist, came beside the German, with his left hand felt the pockets of the uniform and, walking behind him, lifted the leather case from his shoulder.

"What's in it?" the man asked still gazing at the German, thrusting the muzzle of his gun forward. The German, who had stood listless, his hands dropping to his sides after Private Meadows lifted the case from his shoulder, stared at his victor, as though in the uncomprehended words there was a new terror. Then quickly, as though guessing the meaning, he lifted his hands shoulder high in surrender. "Higher, you sonofabitch." The man motioned with the muzzle of his gun. The German understood the motion and lifted his hands above his head. "What's in it?" This time the voice was different. The German understood that the words were not for him. He cupped his hands behind his head.

"It's money," Private Meadows said. He held a handful of the bills in front of his companion.

"Christ! Kraut money," the big man said.

"It's filled with it," Private Meadows said, sliding the money back into the case.

"Where'd you get that money, bud?" the man said. The German became rigid. The terror returned to his eyes, but, with it, there seemed to be another feeling—of impatience, perhaps of injustice. "Where'd you steal that money, Kraut?" And at the question there came into the German's face a sense of outrage. The big man saw it. "You bastard," he said. "Can't you speak English?"

"Nein," the German said quickly. And he shook his head, "Nein."

"Nein, nein!" The man mocked him. "You dumb bastard." He lifted the muzzle of his gun and twice thrust it forward in the direction from which the German had come. "Get goin'," he said. "Vamoos." The German was doubtful. He turned his body slowly but kept shuttling his gaze from the gun to the fat dark face above it. "Get the hell goin'." The German took a step tentatively, looked once at the fair-faced soldier who was adjusting the leather case at his waist. But in his eyes there was neither help nor corroboration—only indecision and doubt as great as his own. He started walking slowly away, his hands still cupped over his head. Then, just as he took the first step that was quicker and surer than the rest, the shot cracked through the woods. He fell forward on his face.

The big man lowered his rifle. Private Meadows, his mouth wide open, watched him open the bolt and push it forward again. He looked down at the ejected cartridge case, awesomely, as though it were a rabbit out of a hat, surprising and not quite convincing.

"Let's get the hell outa here," the man said. He walked quickly past Private Meadows.

Private Meadows looked again where the German had fallen. He saw an arm lifted, like a swimmer's in arrested motion. He saw it fall forward. He turned and followed his leader.

They came to a clearing, a series of fields surrounded by hedgerows and forming a rolling terrain.

"Better not go out there," the man said. Yet, if they followed through the woods, along the edge of the clearing, they would approach too directly the enemy line. "We gone far enough anyways." He listened to the distant crack of the rifles. He sat down and pulled his rifle over his fat legs crossed like a sawbuck. "Let's see that money." Private Meadows handed him the case and sat down beside him. The man dumped the contents on the ground. There was a tablet of forms printed in German. He tossed it away. "Musta' been a pay-sergeant. . . . Suppose he was payin' men out on the goddamned *firin'* line?" The money was taped in seven tight bundles. "That sonofabitch was makin' way with somethin', you can bet your hat on that." He studied the numerals on the bills. He divided the money into two stacks and handed one stack to Private Meadows. He held up the case. "Want it?" Private Meadows looked at the case and then into the lariat eyes hesitantly. He shook his head. The man tossed the case beside the forms.

They both sat looking at the money in their hands. "Suppose it's any good?"

"It's German," Private Meadows said.

"Yeah, I guess so . . . but francs are good. We gonna get paid in francs. If ever we get paid."

"Maybe when we get to Germany—" Private Meadows said.

"Not me. I ain't go'n *get* that far," the man said. "Not me. Je-e-esus! Not me." He spread out his thick legs before him. "Look at them goats!"

In the clearing there were three goats. They had come through a break in the hedgerow or had climbed up some unnoticeable ravine, for they had not been there when the men first looked out. They neither grazed nor moved. It seemed that they were listening to the sounds of the firing.

"I'll take the one on the left," the man said. "You take the one on the right. And I'll bet you my stack of tens against it." He chunked out a bundle of the little bills.

Private Meadows spread the bundles of money fan-fashion, selected a bundle, threw it out, then turned toward the man—his look bending under the helmet to ask: *Now what?*

"We'll have to fire together or they'll be to hell and gone. Yours on the right." The man caracoled his arm into the sling and was adjusting himself to fire from the sitting position. Then Private Meadows understood.

"I . . . I don't think—" But the man was in position. Private Meadows thrust his arms through his sling quickly.

"Are you ready?"

"Say, do you think—"

"Are you ready?"

Private Meadows jerked himself to the kneeling position and slid the gun-butt into his shoulder, his face tight against the stock. He squinted his eyes as he leveled the sight. "OK."

The man muzzled against his gun, and each of his commands was whispered in the respiration of a breath: "Ready—Aim—Fire."

The rifles cracked. The right goat fell, its front legs bending before it. The left goat sprang into the air, like a horse rearing, then rushed forward and crashed face first into the ground. The middle goat lifted his head as though sniffing the air but did not move from where it stood.

"Look at that dumb bastard," the man said. He humped his shoulders over his rifle. "I bet I get him first shot." He turned his head towards Private Meadows, his chin sliding along the gunstock. "OK?" he asked impatiently.

"I—" But the man was straining in a flesh-taut position, ready to fire. "OK," Private Meadows said.

The man took aim. The goat started walking forward, his nose still in the air. The man shifted his gun, aimed again, fired. The goat bleated once, turned, and ran. The man shot again. The goat fell, gave three long trembling bleats, and was silent.

"Well, it's yours," the man said. He leaned back, picked up the money, and threw it to Private Meadows. "That bastard." He crawled back against the tree, put his gun on the ground beside him, and pulled a package from his knapsack. "Got a ration?" he asked.

"I got some choc'late," Private Meadows said. He stood up, holding the money out from him as if he might throw it back to the man or fling it into the woods. He looked down at the notes in his hand—thoughtfully, as though trying to recall how they came to be there. Then he slipped them into his jacket pocket. He sat down again and took out his chocolate. He took a bite of the hard cube, lay back on the ground, and immediately fell asleep.

"Hey. Hey, bud." The man was pushing his boot into Private Meadows' side. "Get up. The artillery's stopped."

Private Meadows sat up. The firing had almost stopped. "We must'a taken the hill," he said.

"It's a town," the man said. "A village. We were after a village."

Private Meadows stood up. "You suppose we really took it?"

"Sounds like it," the man said. "We better get goin'. We better start findin' ourselves." He started walking down the edge of the clearing. The hulking form, moored to some narrow gaze, rode the slow steps heavily, in strenuous swells and sudden falls. Private Meadows followed. To their right, the sun was halfway down the sky.

They came in view of a farmhouse. It stood in the clearing about fifty yards away. "Looks deserted," the man said. They stood looking over the field at the small squat house. "We'll see," the man said. He lifted his rifle and fired. Then they waited but there was no sign of life from the house. "Can't tell if I even hit." He fired again. And as they stood waiting for whatever they expected might happen, an aeroplane loomed from the south. They ducked quickly into the woods and there from among the trees watched the plane. It was flying low and unsteadily. "Damned thing's fallin'," the man said. And as he spoke, they saw a figure drop from the plane—and then another. A parachute opened and then fell into the jolt of full bloom. The second opened, leapt up at the hinges of the air, jolted. Then a third. They had not seen the third drop from the plane but there it moved, in echelon, with the others.

"Brother!" the man said, lifting his rifle. "I'll take the one on the left again. Same bet."

Private Meadows stared as the man pivoted his gun on the floating figure and fired.

"Quick, you bastard," the man said, stepping closer to him, his mouth curling down from the utterance in anger. The impatient words were command.

Private Meadows shouldered his gun and, while still leveling the figure into his sight, fired. He saw a body twitch, the hands fall from the cords, the head lean back. As he lowered his gun across his chest, he drew his heels together and stood straight and stiff, gaping at what he had done.

"Same again on the middle one," the man said. He lifted his gun but his target was already falling beyond the roof of the house. "God damn," he said, dropping his gun from his shoulder. "He's outa sight 'cause you waited so long. What were you waitin' for?"

"You don't shoot men when they're parachutin'."

"My ass! You don't shoot *prisoners*, do you?"

"You sure they were Germans?" His voice was almost supplication.

"How do I know?" He started walking into the woods. "Let's get the hell away from here."

Private Meadows stood holding his gun over his chest, his hand on the bolt. He looked over the field. The two white chutes, now lying on the ground, were barely visible. He drew his bolt, ejecting the cartridge case, thrust the bolt forward again, and, yet holding the gun across his chest, followed the man into the woods.

"Suppose they were *Americans!*" he called out.

The man stopped, turned back—the accusing, distrustful look again in his eyes. "American, French, Kraut, whatever they are, they're fly boys, playin' games in the air and sleepin' in a bed at night." His helmet was almost touching Private Meadows' own. "Look, bud, you shoot first and *suppose* afterwards, or you'll get lead between your own eyes." He drew back a step. "Ain't you killed any before?"

Private Meadows remembered the terrified eyes staring into his own. He answered doubtfully, in the voice of conjecture: "But I knew who I was killin'."

The fat lips drew tight round a sibilant of contempt. Then, "Killin's killin'," he said. "How long you been in this push anyways?"

"Since Cherbourg."

The man looked him up and down. "It's a wonder you lasted this long."

Through woods, over the dirt road, and through woods again to the first fields. Down a hedgerow cautiously. Debris of the advance: cartridge belts, helmets, clips yet filled with bullets, a knit cap, a dog lying dead, a deck of cards scattered, and letters. The wounded and dead removed, but the signs of death in the wreckage. And then the main road, from which the night before they had deployed. Now an ambulance passing, now a jeep. A squad of soldiers, bearded, and fatuous with grime, shoveling dirt from an embankment to cover the carcass of a cow. Salvage of tanks and trucks. Trees broken and charred. A column of medics, walking with stooped weariness, into a side road. Trucks, filled with infantrymen, coming up from the rear. Then the village: "This town off limits for all military personnel." Really no village at all, only rubble: a tall mahogany armoire standing erect and unscratched among bricks and nameless jointures of wood like an exaggerated product in an advertisement; the horseshoe arches of four windows, like a backstage flat, signifying a church; the graveyard, a grotesquery of holes, stone, and up-turned coffins; and, sitting atop a fallen door, a yellow and white kitten washing an outstretched paw.

At the entrance of the village and even in the street beyond the off-limits sign, there were soldiers. They stood in groups, but they were quiet, looking over the ruins of the village or down the wreckage-strewn road they had traversed, staring vacantly at the interpreter talking to a group of five Nazi officers or at the Military Police helping a sergeant line up a lengthening formation of prisoners. The scene was almost still, like a rehearsal of a play where everyone waits for the director to reach a decision.

The two soldiers stopped by an off-limits sign and surveyed the scene. "I gotta find my company," the big man said. He went up to a group of soldiers. Private Meadows watched him a moment and then followed after. He saw one of the soldiers answering the big man's question, pointing away from the village. And before Private Meadows reached the group, the big man walked away. Private Meadows stopped, ready to lift his hand in farewell, but the man went lunging on without looking back—the heavy body, in its laboring gait, an enemy to the air it humped and to the ground it scuffed: the beast that walks alone, that—among all the animals of the forest and in the meeting of its kind—is yet alone, the stalker of secret places, the hunter. Private Meadows sensed the solitariness; but he thought it was the realization of his own loneliness that made him shudder.

He approached the group of soldiers and asked the whereabouts of his company. All the men looked at him blankly. And then one, interpreting the silence of the group, answered: "I don't know."

Private Meadows turned away. Beyond the formation of prisoners he saw some French civilians crossing the street. A fat woman, carrying a hamper, walked down the side of the formation, a little white dog following her, scurrying from one side to the other to sniff at the boots of the prisoners or at something in the rubble.

He was alone again. He was lost.

At home he had often had a dream of being late for school. The scenes of the dream were always different, but the dream was always the same. An unsuccessful effort to get to school: the determination, the hurry; running down the street, then caught in some void where time passed and he stood still; or still discovering himself at a strange corner, not knowing the direction, not knowing how he came to be there. The remembrance of the dream was fleeting but the familiar hopeless feeling of it remained. He felt that no one here would know his company, that his company would be in a distant place maneuvering through some different duty. He had left his company that very same morning after sunrise and only now was the sun beginning to set. But his calculation gave him no assurance. He felt that he had been separated from his comrades for a campaign of time. And this—this feeling—was his real knowledge.

He went from soldier to soldier, from group to group, asking the position of his company— his question automatic and hopeless, but persistent like a sick man's fancy. And when a soldier answered *Yes* and named the directions, his mind was filled with only the realization of the soldier's knowing, so that he had to ask again.

His company was bivouacked less than a mile from the village. It was still twilight when he walked among his platoon.

"Meadows! Man, I thought you'd found your number." It was Barr. He was sitting on the ground, leaning against the wood fence. He touched the ground beside him in invitation for Meadows to sit.

"What happened to you?" Harrod, too, was leaning against the fence. He was smoking a cigarette. His face was black with grease and dirt.

"Guess I must'a got lost," Private Meadows said. He leaned his gun against the fence, dropping his helmet to the ground, and sat down.

Without looking around, Barr stretched his hand to his left and said: "They got Pederson." Private Meadows looked up at him. "And Walton was shot in the hip but he'll get all right, lucky dog." He put his feet out before him, crossed them at the ankles, said wearily: "We 'bout all would have got it if it wasn't for those bombers. Zoom. Bang. And not another eighty-eight booped after that."

"Those *what?*" Private Meadows asked.

"The bombers. The lucky dogs. Sleeping in England tonight."

"I got lost." Private Meadows said.

Harrod and Barr both looked at him.

"Well, you're home now, chum," Barr said. "Good ole Easy Company. Gonna have hot stuff tonight—out'a mess kit. And a sleep, I-hope-I-hope-I-hope, here against a soft warm fence."

"Wish they'd hurry with chow," Harrod said. "If I close my eyes, I'll never make it. . . . How much longer they gonna keep us in the line anyhow?"

"Couple of more days, I guess," Barr said. His tone was now flat as if he had no interest in what he said.

"I wonder if I'll live that long," Harrod said. There was nothing in his voice; it sounded like a routine speculation, as if he wondered whether he would be in town long enough to send his clothes to the laundry.

It was almost dark.

Private Meadows was bent forward, his arms lying against his thighs, his eyes pressed against his wrists. Barr noticed that each hand clutched a stack of notes and, as he started to ask what they were, he heard the sobbing. It simpered like a fuse and then burst. The shoulders shook convulsively. "What the hell, kid?" Barr sidled close to him and put his hand on his arm.

Harrod looked over at him, then flipped away the dead cigarette that he had been absently holding between his fingers. A whistle blew.

"Snap out of it, kid," Barr said, rising. "It's time for chow." He stepped back and picked up his mess kit. Then he and Harrod stood on each side of Private Meadows and waited.

AUTHOR'S NOTE ON "THE HUNTERS"

"The Hunters" was one of my first published stories. It won the O. Henry Memorial Prize in 1951 and in that same year was reprinted in The Best American Short Stories.

I was a long time in the Air Corps during World War II. I was in the European Theater mostly and kept long duty hours. I had no time to write anything. I couldn't even keep a journal but I did keep now-and-then notes; they at last filled a small satchel.

Of the notes I made from The Stars and Stripes, from Intelligence reports, and from observation, here are those that I recall using in "The Hunters": the wanton killing of the German paymaster, the innocent or spiteful killing of the parachuting American airmen by American ground soldiers, the distributing of the kraut money, the hysteria of domestic and wild animals, and, being Infantry-trained from back before that war, I was knowledgeable of artillery fire and all that.

Isaac Rosenfeld

The Brigadier*

WE HAVE BEEN FIGHTING THE ENEMY a very long time. So long that I, who entered the war a foot soldier, have had time to receive more than the usual number of decorations and promotions and to become a brigadier, attached to staff headquarters. I forget how many times I have been wounded and the names of all the battles and campaigns in which I have participated. The greater number of them, however, are not to be forgotten: Striplitz, Bougaumères, Trèle, Bzelokhorets, Kovinitsa, Laud Ingaume, El Khabhar, Woozi-Fassam, and so on. I am the oldest man in our field office, though not in the brigade itself. Lately, the newcomers have not been rising from the ranks, but from the Academy. They are young men who have not proved themselves in any way; some have not even fought.

I am settled into my work, which for many years, I am pleased to say, has been of an absorbing nature. It is difficult to recall the

* From ALPHA AND OMEGA by Isaac Rosenfeld. Copyright 1947 by Isaac Rosenfeld. Reprinted by permission of The Viking Press, Inc. and MacGibbon & Kee, Ltd.

time when I fretted with impatience to return to what I considered my natural life as a citizen. I am happy that I am no longer impatient. I have developed, instead, a great eagerness—an eagerness, however, which is thoroughly disciplined and in every way related to our military enterprise. I do not hesitate to call our enterprise the most glorious and far-reaching that has ever been undertaken.

Far-reaching is not quite the word—though it is only in an unofficial capacity that I admit as much. Let me say that it is not the word for me to use. As a matter, simply, of objective fact, what we are engaged in is, of course, that—I mean far-reaching—and much else besides. But for myself it is not enough, and the work I do must be otherwise defined. I have been studying the ends of our warfare while pursuing them; I have tried to make them a part of myself. I should not want it to be said that the Objective is one thing, and the brigadier's effort in its behalf is quite another, not related to it as the word one and the number one are related. My work is the war itself.

The office in which I do my work was once a schoolhouse; it stands in what used to be enemy country. A section of blackboard, cracked down the middle, is still affixed to the wall near my desk and on it you can read a lesson in the enemy's language, written by one of his children; when the chalk began to fade, I had it carefully restored and covered with a coat of shellac. I can read the enemy's hand—which is sometimes difficult even for scholars, as the script is spidery and irregular and varies not only with the dialect but with the very temperament of the writer. The broken lines read: ". . . of the cat and the dog? What will she . . ."; here the first line ends, broken off at the jagged edge of the board. "We," runs the second line, "know that the . . . [several words are obliterated] while the bird was singing. . . ." The third and last line: ". . . is what we all love. It makes us very happy." I like to imagine, although I know this is nothing but a child's exercise, that these broken lines, could I only complete them, would tell me more about the enemy than all the work of our specialists combined. As for my subordinates, I have led them to believe that these scraps of writing have something to do with logistics—which is all they care about.

The benches, the charts, the books and other blackboards of the schoolhouse have long since been removed. The rooms are now occupied by sturdy desks of our own design, developed during the war, and the walls are lined with filing cabinets and hung with maps of the region. The sides of the house have been reinforced against blast with sandbags, and the windows have been covered with intersecting strips of wire and tape which, when the sun is right, cast patterns of shadow upon our papers. If there were nothing else to do, it would be a pleasure to trace some of these patterns. The glass—these are the enemy's original panes—is very bright and clear. The enemy is known for the quality of his glass works. A strange people.

Our office is a relay station among the various fronts. The position of the fronts has grown so complicated through the years, that I never attempt to give our location with reference to the lines of battle. We are well in the center of one circle of fighting, on the periphery of a second, and connected by a long tangent with a third. From time to time our position appears enveloped, and we pack our papers, dismantle our immobile equipment, and prepare to retreat. Subsequent intelligence, however, informs us that the first reports, owing to the complexity of the warfare, were erroneous in many respects and that, far from being encircled, our position may be described as part of an arc thrown round the enemy's flank. The lines of battle, the longer I study them, seem to me more and more like the arms of many embracing bodies.

It is our general purpose, but not my specific task, to supply logistical information to headquarters in the front and in the rear. We are one of a number of stations that co-ordinate the numerous reports both of the enemy's movements and of our own, and relay these back and forth. These reports never fail to conflict with one another, and no matter how well trained our spies, pilots, observers, and scouts may be, we must keep a large staff working round the clock to prevent mistakes, repetitions, and inconsistencies from appearing in our dispatches. Even so we have blundered many times, and our only consolation, and at the same time the reason that reprimands from headquarters have not been more severe, is the fact that the enemy must work under the same disadvantages. Very often a report so complicated and contradictory that it seems impossible to submit, is nevertheless a true picture of the fighting. You can see what we are up against. And then there are the many spontaneous breakdowns of routine for which no one is to blame, the impatience of my superiors which is always interfering with the work, the orders handed down from above, countermanding orders that have already been carried out, and so many other difficulties that are part of the day's normal detail. To make matters worse a training class for scouts is held in the basement of our schoolhouse and we often hear them laughing or crying out in pain as they tumble about on the mats. I have been trying to get this class removed, thus far without success.

My own work developed as a subsidiary of the main logistical operation. My superiors are not yet convinced of the importance of my task (I have been at it for eleven years!), but some of them are interested, and all my equals and subordinates support me in it, so I am not required to give up my investigations. I work in a semiofficial capacity, filling in and sending out my own reports and as much corroborative material as I can lay my hands on—all this in addition to my regular duties. I am kept very busy indeed, seldom working less than sixteen hours at a stretch. I sometimes think, sitting as I do in an old schoolhouse, that I am both schoolmaster and pupil: a teacher to those who are beneath me in rank and an idiot child to my superiors.

I work on the enemy proper. I am trying to discover what he is, what motivates him, what his nature is. And if you say, as so many of my superiors do, that this is known, I reply that I am attacking his very essence. This is not known. In spite of the many long years that we have been at war with him, and the periods of time, in the past, when we lived at his side in restless peace, we know nothing of him that is really worth knowing and that must be known. I myself am convinced that victory will be impossible until we gain this knowledge—and it is precisely to this knowledge that I am devoting my life.

What do we know? The enemy is darker than we, and shorter in stature. His language, as I have indicated, has nothing in common with our own; his religion is an obscenity to all of us who have not made a specialty of studying it. Well then, as I say, he is shorter and darker, two positive facts. His language, though it would be too much trouble to go into it here, is of such and such a kind—a third fact—and his religion is this, that and the other thing, which gives us still another fact. So much we know. Still, what is he?

I have gone many times to the camps and hospitals in the rear to interview the prisoners we have taken. It teaches me nothing, but I nevertheless make my regular visits, and just the other week I returned from one of our hospitals. There was the usual sight in the wards; I am hardened to it. (And yet, almost as if to test myself, I try to recall what I have seen. Am I absolutely hardened?) There were the lightly wounded, their personalities not distorted by pain, and the natural qualities of these men could be observed: their churlishness, stupidity, sullenness, or good nature. They are much like our own soldiers, especially in their boredom. I spoke with them, I took my usual sampling—so many boys (as with our own troops, eleven-year-olds are not uncommon), so many youths, so many of the middle-aged, so many old men, old campaigners. The usual questions, the usual answers—home, parents, occupation, the government, women, disease, God, the purpose of the war, of life, of history, etc. There is nothing to be learned here that we don't already know. Then the wards of the severely wounded— the amputations, the blinded, the infected. The stench is the same as our own stench (the hospital orderlies deny this, maintaining that the enemy's is worse!). The ones with fever have fever, though their skins and eyes show it differently from ours. The delirious rave, the chilled shiver, the poisoned vomit and groan. There are outcries, the usual hysteria, weeping, coughing, and hemorrhage. One lies in a coma; the stump of his leg is gangrenous, it is too late, he cannot be saved. Another soldier has nearly every bone in his body broken: he has both his thighs in traction, a broken back, a broken arm, his skull wound in bandages. Can he be said to suffer either more or less than one of our own men in similar circumstances, or in any way differently from him? I attend an operation—it is the same thing over and over again. The mental casualties in their guarded ward are no different from ours. Some in straightjackets, strapped to their beds, some screaming, some colorless, lifeless, forever immobile. Here and there a dead body, not yet removed. I lift the sheet; the face is already puffed up. The shock of it is gone, and I can no longer remember what it actually used to be like. I poke a finger into a puffy cheek, leaving a depression which takes a long time to fill up again. It is the same death as our own.

I go to the hospitals, though I learn nothing there, and I go to the prison camps, also in vain. Once I had myself incarcerated, disguised as an enemy soldier. I slept with the men in their barracks, ate with them, studied them, was soon infested with the same lice. I was involved in a plan to escape, of which I informed our guards. No one saw through my disguise, and I, in turn, failed to see through the undisguised men and learned nothing. In fact, the few weeks I spent in prison camp were extremely discouraging, for if the gap between the enemy and ourselves is so small that I can pose, undetected, as one of his men, why is it that I can't cross over to him?

I have even suspected my project of a subtle treason. By "cross over to him," I mean of course, "cross the gulf that separates us from knowledge of his true nature." Now I know where I stand in this regard and it no longer troubles me; but at one time I feared that the second expression really meant nothing more than the first and I thought surely that my whole ambition was only to desert to the enemy. Perhaps he fascinated me in the precise sense of attraction, drawing me, through my desire to know, closer and closer to his side. My conscience drove me to my superior, Major General Box. He believes in my project and follows my reports with interest. The General reassured me; it is his opinion that we are all drawn to the enemy, particularly in such a long war, and that the enemy is drawn to us. In certain respects we even begin to resemble each other. But this is only natural, and has nothing to do with my project, which, far from being treason, remains the most important of the war.

I was reassured, but was soon taken with a fresh disquietude. A suggestion that the general had made, without meaning to do so, set me on a new course of activity. The general had said that in certain respects we come to resemble the enemy. What are these respects? Perhaps the knowledge that I was seeking really lay in myself? The resemblance to the enemy might have grown so strong in my case, that it was my own nature I would have to know in order to know his. I took a leave from the service, the only one I have had in the entire campaign, and spent a month in one of the enemy's mountain villages that had been captured by our troops. I lived away from the men, attended only by goats which forage high up among the rocks in this region. I had a hut to myself, and all the mountains necessary to a great introspection. But I learned nothing, nothing that I did not already know.

It was when I returned to active service that I began the most desperate work that I have as yet undertaken. I selected a group of twenty prisoners, all young, sturdy, healthy men. I lived with them until I grew to know them well; some were like my own sons, and one in particular, a peasant boy named Reri, I will say that I loved. I spent long hours out of doors with my companions, joined them in races and various sports, their own as well as ours. We went on long camping and fishing trips about the country, and I developed so great a trust in them that I even provided them with firearms and let them hunt with me. Evenings, when we were not camping under the open sky, we entertained ourselves in my lodge, drinking, playing cards or chess, listening to music, or holding the most intimate conversations—conversations and confidences that verged on love. We became very intimate; there has never been a group of men whom I have known or loved so well, never a youth as my Reri for whom I have had such a close and tender feeling. It was above all with Reri that I carried on my desperate yet gentle work; I strove to know him as completely as one man can ever hope to know another, and something in his response to me, perhaps an intuitive comprehension of my motive, promised that my effort would be rewarded. He was a handsome boy, taller than the average among the enemy, and fairer in color and complexion. Certainly one such as he could be known, a face as open as his could not long conceal the secrets of the inner nature. Often when I was not with him I would picture his face to myself, trusting that a chance moment of insight might reveal him, and therefore his whole people, to me. And I studied his image, sketching him and taking many photographs while he sat patiently before me. (I have kept these sketches and photographs, and look at them from time to time as I once looked at the living Reri. His image still saddens and perplexes me.) So, with all my companions, I engaged in an unceasing search after friendship and understanding, hoping that love would teach me what I was determined to know.

But my ultimate means were not to be gentle, and when I failed again I had to resort, with great reluctance, in shame and disgust, to the final means I had selected to attain my objective. As I had been their friend and lover and father, their teacher in the ways of our people and their pupil in the ways of theirs, so, at last, I became their torturer, hoping now to break them down and force them to yield what they had not been able to give freely. One day

I ordered them whipped, the next, beaten; all of them, including Reri. I stood by, directing their tortures and noting their surprise, their hatred of me, their screams and their pleas for mercy. I could not help feeling that I had betrayed them; but my guilt only excited me the more and made me inflict always greater agony and humiliation upon them. It must have been guilt that was responsible for my extreme excitement, in the grip of which, while supervising the tortures, I would feel an overwhelming hatred of the enemy, and become convinced that my hatred had brought me so much farther than love, to the very brink of knowledge. When my companions died, I trained, in much the same manner, a new group, in which I included some of the enemy's women. The experiment was repeated. This time I did not spare myself, but submitted in their company to some of the same tortures, as if there might still be lurking in me an essential particle of their enemy's nature which was itself either capable of yielding the truth, or of preventing me from finding it. The experiment failed again. Again I learned nothing, nothing at all.

I still go to the wards and the camps, and from time to time I still conduct tortures. I have devised many other means of coping with my problem, some of them not yet tested. Over the years, I have grown hardened to failure: I more or less expect it now as an essential element of my work. But though I am hardened and toughened and experienced, I find that my work grows more and more difficult. Because of my interest in prisoners, new duties have been assigned to me. Recently negotiations for the exchange of prisoners broke down between the enemy and ourselves, and their number keeps piling up, as ours does in their camps; it is now my duty to arrange for their transportation to the interior. And then there are still the many administrative details of my department, to which I must somehow find time to attend; there are still the hazards and ever greater complications of our old war, which we have not yet won, and which, I have become absolutely certain, we will never win unless I succeed in my task. To know the enemy! It is the whole purpose and nature of our war, its ultimate meaning, its glory and its greatness. Already I have succeeded in my own character, for I have become my task in my whole being. Nothing comes between me and the work I do. I have triumphed in my character and in my person, but I must still triumph over the enemy. Sometimes I see his armies standing before me, clearly revealed in their dark, powerful mass, and I rush out of the schoolhouse, out of our office, and I feel that in a moment, but one moment more, I will know the truth. And when I hear our gunfire from the front that winds around us in all directions, I know that if my faith is only great enough, the knowledge will come to me and I will win.

Isaac Babel

Crossing Into Poland*

THE COMMANDER OF THE VI DIVISION REPORTED: Novograd-Volynsk was taken at dawn today. The Staff had left Krapivno, and our baggage train was spread out in a noisy rearguard over the highroad from Brest to Warsaw built by Nicholas I upon the bones of peasants.

Fields flowered around us, crimson with poppies; a noontide breeze played in the yellowing rye; on the horizon virginal buckwheat rose like the wall of a distant monastery. The Volyn's peaceful stream moved away from us in sinuous curves and was lost in the pearly haze of the birch groves; crawling between flowery slopes, it wound weary arms through a wilderness of hops. The orange sun rolled down the sky like a lopped-off head, and mild light glowed from the cloud gorges. The standards of the sunset flew above our heads. Into the cool of evening dropped the smell of yesterday's blood, of slaughtered horses. The blackened Zbruch

* Reprinted by permission of S. G. Phillips, Inc. from THE COLLECTED SHORT STORIES OF ISAAC BABEL. Copyright © 1929 by S. G. Phillips, Inc.

roared, twisting itself into foamy knots at the falls. The bridges were down, and we waded across the river. On the waves rested a majestic moon. The horses were in to the cruppers, and the noisy torrent gurgled among hundreds of horses' legs. Somebody sank, loudly defaming the Mother of God. The river was dotted with the square black patches of the wagons, and was full of confused sounds, of whistling and singing, that rose above the gleaming hollows, the serpentine trails of the moon.

Far on in the night we reached Novograd. In the house where I was billeted I found a pregnant woman and two red-haired, scraggy-necked Jews. A third, huddled to the wall with his head covered up, was already asleep. In the room I was given I discovered turned-out wardrobes, scraps of women's fur coats on the floor, human filth, fragments of the occult crockery the Jews use only once a year, at Passover.

"Clear this up," I said to the woman. "What a filthy way to live!" The two Jews rose from their places and, hopping on their felt soles, cleared the mess from the floor. They skipped about noiselessly, monkey-fashion, like Japs in a circus act, their necks swelling and twisting. They put down for me a feather bed that had been disemboweled, and I lay down by the wall next to the third Jew, the one who was asleep. Faint-hearted poverty closed in over my couch.

Silence overcame all. Only the moon, clasping in her blue hands her round, bright, carefree face, wandered like a vagrant outside the window.

I kneaded my numbed legs and, lying on the ripped-open mattress, fell asleep. And in my sleep the Commander of the VI Division appeared to me; he was pursuing the Brigade Commander on a heavy stallion, fired at him twice between the eyes. The bullets pierced the Brigade Commander's head, and both his eyes dropped to the ground. "Why did you turn back the Brigade?" shouted Savitsky, the Divisional Commander, to the wounded man —and here I woke up, for the pregnant woman was groping over my face with her fingers.

"Good sir," she said, "you're calling out in your sleep and you're tossing to and fro. I'll make you a bed in another corner, for you're pushing my father about."

She raised her thin legs and rounded belly from the floor and removed the blanket from the sleeper. Lying on his back was an old man, a dead old man. His throat had been torn out and his face cleft in two, in his beard blue blood was clotted like a lump of lead.

"Good sir," said the Jewess, shaking up the feather bed, "the Poles cut his throat, and he begging them: 'Kill me in the yard so that my daughter shan't see me die.' But they did as suited them. He passed away in this room, thinking of me. —And now I should wish to know," cried the woman with sudden and terrible violence, "I should wish to know where in the whole world you could find another father like my father?"

Luigi Pirandello

War*

THE PASSENGERS WHO HAD LEFT ROME by the night express had had to stop until dawn at the small station of Fabriano in order to continue their journey by the small old-fashioned local joining the main line with Sulmona.

At dawn, in a stuffy and smoky second-class carriage in which five people had already spent the night, a bulky woman in deep mourning was hoisted in—almost like a shapeless bundle. Behind her—puffing and moaning, followed her husband—a tiny man, thin and weakly, his face death-white, his eyes small and bright and looking shy and uneasy.

Having at last taken a seat he politely thanked the passengers who had helped his wife and who had made room for her; then he turned round to the woman trying to pull down the collar of her coat and politely inquired:

---

* From the book THE MEDALS AND OTHER STORIES by Luigi Pirandello. Copyright, 1939, renewal, ©, 1967 by E. P. Dutton & Co., Inc. Reprinted by permission of the publishers.

"Are you all right, dear?"

The wife, instead of answering, pulled up her collar again to her eyes, so as to hide her face.

"Nasty world," muttered the husband with a sad smile.

And he felt it his duty to explain to his traveling companions that the poor woman was to be pitied for the war was taking away from her her only son, a boy of twenty to whom both had devoted their entire life, even breaking up their home at Sulmona to follow him to Rome, where he had to go as a student, then allowing him to volunteer for war with an assurance, however, that at least for six months he would not be sent to the front and now, all of a sudden, receiving a wire saying that he was due to leave in three days' time and asking them to go and see him off.

The woman under the big coat was twisting and wriggling, at times growling like a wild animal, feeling certain that all those explanations would not have aroused even a shadow of sympathy from those people who—most likely—were in the same plight as herself. One of them, who had been listening with particular attention, said:

"You should thank God that your son is only leaving now for the front. Mine has been sent there the first day of the war. He has already come back twice wounded and been sent back again to the front."

"What about me? I have two sons and three nephews at the front," said another passenger.

"Maybe, but in our case it is our *only* son," ventured the husband.

"What difference can it make? You may spoil your only son with excessive attentions, but you cannot love him more than you would all your other children if you had any. Paternal love is not like bread that can be broken into pieces and split amongst the children in equal shares. A father gives *all* his love to each one of his children without discrimination, whether it be one or ten, and if I am suffering now for my two sons, I am not suffering half for each of them but double . . ."

"True . . . true . . ." sighed the embarrassed husband, "but suppose (of course we all hope it will never be your case) a father has two sons at the front and he loses one of them, there is still one left to console him . . . while . . ."

"Yes," answered the other, getting cross, "a son left to console him but also a son left for whom he must survive, while in the case of the father of an only son if the son dies the father can die too and put an end to his distress. Which of the two positions is the worse? Don't you see how my case would be worse than yours?"

"Nonsense," interrupted another traveler, a fat, red-faced man with bloodshot eyes of the palest gray.

He was panting. From his bulging eyes seemed to spurt inner violence of an uncontrolled vitality which his weakened body could hardly contain.

"Nonsense," he repeated, trying to cover his mouth with his hand so as to hide the two missing front teeth. "Nonsense. Do we give life to our children for our own benefit?"

The other travelers stared at him in distress. The one who had had his son at the front since the first day of the war sighed: "You are right. Our children do not belong to us, they belong to the Country. . . ."

"Bosh," retorted the fat traveler. "Do we think of the Country when we give life to our children? Our sons are born because . . . well, because they must be born and when they come to life they take our own life with them. This is the truth. We belong to them but they never belong to us. And when they reach twenty they are exactly what we were at their age. We too had a father and mother, but there were so many other things as well . . . girls, cigarettes, illusions, new ties . . . and the Country, of course, whose call we would have answered—when we were twenty—even if father and mother had said no. Now, at our age, the love of our Country is still great, of course, but stronger than it is the love for our children. Is there any one of us here who wouldn't gladly take his son's place at the front if he could?"

There was a silence all round, everybody nodding as to approve.

"Why then," continued the fat man, "shouldn't we consider the feelings of our children when they are twenty? Isn't it natural that at their age they should consider the love for their Country (I am speaking of decent boys, of course) even greater than the love for us? Isn't it natural that it should be so, as after all they must look upon us as upon old boys who cannot move any more and must stay at home? If Country exists, if Country is a natural necessity, like bread, of which each of us must eat in order not to die of hunger, somebody must go to defend it. And our sons go, when they are twenty, and they don't want tears, because if they die, they die inflamed and happy (I am speaking, of course, of decent boys). Now, if one dies young and happy, without having the ugly sides of life, the boredom of it, the pettiness, the bitterness of disillusion . . . what more can we ask for him? Everyone should stop crying; everyone should laugh, as I do . . . or at least thank God—as I do —because my son, before dying, sent me a message saying that he was dying satisfied at having ended his life in the best way he could have wished. That is why, as you see, I do not even wear mourning. . . ."

He shook his light fawn coat as to show it; his livid lip over his missing teeth was trembling, his eyes were watery and motionless, and soon after he ended with a shrill laugh which might well have been a sob.

"Quite so . . . quite so . . ." agreed the others.

The woman who, bundled in a corner under her coat, had been sitting and listening had—for the last three months—tried to find in the words of her husband and her friends something to console her in her deep sorrow, something that might show her how a mother should resign herself to send her son not even to death but to a probable danger of life. Yet not a word had she found amongst the many which had been said . . . and her grief had been greater in seeing that nobody—as she thought—could share her feelings.

But now the words of the traveler amazed and almost stunned her. She suddenly realized that it wasn't the others who were wrong and could not understand her but herself who could not rise up to the same height of those fathers and mothers willing to resign themselves, without crying, not only to the departure of their sons but even to their death.

She lifted her head, she bent over from her corner trying to listen with great attention to the details which the fat man was giving to his companions about the way his son had fallen as a hero, for his King and his Country, happy and without regrets. It seemed to her that she had stumbled into a world she had never dreamt of, a world so far unknown to her and she was so pleased to hear everyone joining in congratulating that brave father who could so stoically speak of his child's death.

Then suddenly, just as if she had heard nothing of what had been said and almost as if waking up from a dream, she turned to the old man, asking him:

"Then . . . is your son really dead?"

Everybody stared at her. The old man, too, turned to look at her, fixing his great, bulging, horribly watery light gray eyes, deep in her face. For some little time he tried to answer, but words failed him. He looked and looked at her, almost as if only then—at that silly, incongruous question—he had suddenly realized at last that his son was really dead—gone for ever—for ever. His face contracted, became horribly distorted, then he snatched in haste a handkerchief from his pocket and, to the amazement of everyone, broke into harrowing, heart-rending, uncontrollable sobs.

VI

ARE ALL MEN BROTHERS?

Am I my brother's keeper?

        CAIN, Genesis 4:9

The question is not whether we will be extremists but what kind of extremist we will be. Will we be extremists for hate or will we be extremists for love? Will we be extremists for the preservation of injustice—or will we be extremists for the cause of justice?

        MARTIN LUTHER KING
Memphis, Tennessee, April 3, 1968

We hold these truths to be self-evident, that all men are created equal, that they are endowed by their Creator with certain inalienable Rights, . . .

        The Declaration of Independence

I think of the nestling fallen into the deep grass,
The turtle gasping in the dusty rubble of the highway,
The paralytic stunned in the tub, and the water rising,—
All things innocent, hapless, forsaken.

              THEODORE ROETHKE
           "The Meadow Mouse"

I was angry with my friend
I told my wrath, my wrath did end,
I was angry with my foe
I told it not, my wrath did grow.

              WILLIAM BLAKE
            "A Poison Tree"

"Nigger lover . . ."

"Let's get Whitey . . ."

The pure products of America go crazy—

           WILLIAM CARLOS WILLIAMS
           "To Elsie"

Flannery O'Connor

Revelation*

THE DOCTOR'S WAITING ROOM, which was very small, was almost full when the Turpins entered and Mrs. Turpin, who was very large, made it look even smaller by her presence. She stood looming at the the head of the magazine table set in the center of it, a living demonstration that the room was inadequate and ridiculous. Her little bright black eyes took in all the patients as she sized up the seating situation. There was one vacant chair and a place on the sofa occupied by a blond child in a dirty blue romper who should have been told to move over and make room for the lady. He was five or six, but Mrs. Turpin saw at once that no one was going to tell him to move over. He was slumped down in the seat, his arms idle at his sides and his eyes idle in his head; his nose ran unchecked.

Mrs. Turpin put a firm hand on Claud's shoulder and said in a

* Reprinted with the permission of Farrar, Straus & Giroux, Inc. from EVERYTHING THAT RISES MUST CONVERGE by Flannery O'Connor, copyright © 1964, 1965 by the Estate of Mary Flannery O'Connor.

voice that included anyone who wanted to listen, "Claud, you sit in that chair there," and gave him a push down into the vacant one. Claud was florid and bald and sturdy, somewhat shorter than Mrs. Turpin, but he sat down as if he were accustomed to doing what she told him to.

Mrs. Turpin remained standing. The only man in the room besides Claud was a lean stringy old fellow with a rusty hand spread out on each knee, whose eyes were closed as if he were asleep or dead or pretending to be so as not to get up and offer her his seat. Her gaze settled agreeably on a well-dressed grey-haired lady whose eyes met hers and whose expression said: if that child belonged to me, he would have some manners and move over—there's plenty of room there for you and him too.

Claud looked up with a sigh and made as if to rise.

"Sit down," Mrs. Turpin said. "You know you're not supposed to stand on that leg. He has an ulcer on his leg," she explained.

Claud lifted his foot onto the magazine table and rolled his trouser leg up to reveal a purple swelling on a plump marble-white calf.

"My!" the pleasant lady said. "How did you do that?"

"A cow kicked him," Mrs. Turpin said.

"Goodness!" said the lady.

Claud rolled his trouser leg down.

"Maybe the little boy would move over," the lady suggested, but the child did not stir.

"Somebody will be leaving in a minute," Mrs. Turpin said. She could not understand why a doctor—with as much money as they made charging five dollars a day to just stick their head in the hospital door and look at you—couldn't afford a decent-sized waiting room. This one was hardly bigger than a garage. The table was cluttered with limp-looking magazines and at one end of it there was a big green glass ash tray full of cigaret butts and cotton wads with little blood spots on them. If she had had anything to do with the running of the place, that would have been emptied every so often. There were no chairs against the wall at the head of the room. It had a rectangular-shaped panel in it that permitted a view of the office where the nurse came and went and the secretary listened to the radio. A plastic fern in a gold pot sat in the opening and trailed its fronds down almost to the floor. The radio was softly playing gospel music.

Just then the inner door opened and a nurse with the highest stack of yellow hair Mrs. Turpin had ever seen put her face in the crack and called for the next patient. The woman sitting beside Claud grasped the two arms of her chair and hoisted herself up; she pulled her dress free from her legs and lumbered through the door where the nurse had disappeared.

Mrs. Turpin eased into the vacant chair, which held her tight as a corset. "I wish I could reduce," she said, and rolled her eyes and gave a comic sigh.

"Oh, *you* aren't fat," the stylish lady said.

"Ooooo I am too," Mrs. Turpin said. "Claud he eats all he wants to and never weighs over one hundred and seventy-five pounds, but me I just look at something good to eat and I gain some weight," and her stomach and shoulders shook with laughter. "You can eat all you want to, can't you, Claud?" she asked, turning to him.

Claud only grinned.

"Well, as long as you have such a good disposition," the stylish lady said, "I don't think it makes a bit of difference what size you are. You just can't beat a good disposition."

Next to her was a fat girl of eighteen or nineteen, scowling into a thick blue book which Mrs. Turpin saw was entitled *Human Development*. The girl raised her head and directed her scowl at Mrs. Turpin as if she did not like her looks. She appeared annoyed that anyone should speak while she tried to read. The poor girl's face was blue with acne and Mrs. Turpin thought how pitiful it was to have a face like that at that age. She gave the girl a friendly smile but the girl only scowled the harder. Mrs. Turpin herself was fat but she had always had good skin, and, though she was forty-seven years old, there was not a wrinkle in her face except around her eyes from laughing too much.

Next to the ugly girl was the child, still in exactly the same position, and next to him was a thin leathery old woman in a cotton print dress. She and Claud had three sacks of chicken feed in their pump house that was in the same print. She had seen from the first that the child belonged with the old woman. She could tell by the way they sat—kind of vacant and white-trashy, as if they would sit there until Doomsday if nobody called and told them to get up. And at right angles but next to the well-dressed pleasant lady was a lank-faced woman who was certainly the child's mother. She had on a yellow sweat shirt and wine-colored slacks, both gritty-looking, and the rims of her lips were stained with snuff. Her dirty yellow hair was tied behind with a little piece of red paper ribbon. Worse than niggers any day, Mrs. Turpin thought.

The gospel hymn playing was, "When I looked up and He looked down," and Mrs. Turpin, who knew it, supplied the last line mentally, "And wona these days I know I'll we-eara crown."

Without appearing to, Mrs. Turpin always noticed people's feet. The well-dressed lady had on red and grey suede shoes to match her dress. Mrs. Turpin had on her good black patent leather pumps. The ugly girl had on Girl Scout shoes and heavy socks. The old woman had on tennis shoes and the white-trashy mother had on what appeared to be bedroom slippers, black straw with gold braid threaded through them—exactly what you would have expected her to have on.

Sometimes at night when she couldn't go to sleep, Mrs. Turpin would occupy herself with the question of who she would have chosen to be if she couldn't have been herself. If Jesus had said to her before he made her, "There's only two places available for you. You can either be a nigger or white-trash," what would she have said? "Please, Jesus, please," she would have said, "just let me wait until there's another place available," and he would have said, "No, you have to go right now and I have only those two places so make up your mind." She would have wiggled and squirmed and begged and pleaded but it would have been no use and finally she would have said, "All right, make me a nigger then—but that don't mean a trashy one." And he would have made her a neat clean respectable negro woman, herself but black.

Next to the child's mother was a red-headed youngish woman, reading one of the magazines and working on a piece of chewing gum, hell for leather, as Claud would say. Mrs. Turpin could not see the woman's feet. She was not white-trash, just common. Sometimes Mrs. Turpin occupied herself at night naming the classes of people. On the bottom of the heap were most colored people, not the kind she would have been if she had been one, but most of them; then next to them—not above, just away from—were the white-trash; then above them were the home-owners, and above them the home-and-land owners, to which she and Claud belonged. Above she and Claud were people with a lot of money and much bigger houses and much more land. But here the complexity of it would begin to bear in on her, for some of the people with a lot of money were common and ought to be below she and Claud and some of the people who had good blood had lost their money and had to rent and then there were colored people who owned their homes and land as well. There was a colored dentist in town who had two red Lincolns and a swimming pool and a farm with registered white-face cattle on it. Usually by the time she had fallen asleep all the classes of people were moiling and roiling around in her head, and she would dream they were all crammed in together in a box car, being ridden off to be put in a gas oven.

"That's a beautiful clock," she said and nodded to her right. It was a big wall clock, the face encased in a brass sunburst.

"Yes, it's very pretty," the stylish lady said agreeably. "And right on the dot too," she added, glancing at her watch.

The ugly girl beside her cast an eye upward at the clock, smirked, then looked directly at Mrs. Turpin and smirked again. Then she returned her eyes to her book. She was obviously the lady's daughter because, although they didn't look anything alike as to disposition, they both had the same shape of face and the same blue eyes. On the lady they sparkled pleasantly but in the girl's seared face they appeared alternately to smolder and to blaze.

What if Jesus had said, "All right, you can be white-trash or a nigger or ugly"!

Mrs. Turpin felt an awful pity for the girl, though she thought it was one thing to be ugly and another to act ugly.

The woman with the snuff-stained lips turned around in her chair and looked up at the clock. Then she turned back and appeared to look a little to the side of Mrs. Turpin. There was a cast in one of her eyes. "You want to know wher you can get you one of themther clocks?" she asked in a loud voice.

"No, I already have a nice clock," Mrs. Turpin said. Once somebody like her got a leg in the conversation, she would be all over it.

"You can get you one with green stamps," the woman said. "That's most likely wher he got hisn. Save you up enough, you can get you most anythang. I got me some joo'ry."

Ought to have got you a wash rag and some soap, Mrs. Turpin thought.

"I get contour sheets with mine," the pleasant lady said.

The daughter slammed her book shut. She looked straight in front of her, directly through Mrs. Turpin and on through the yellow curtain and the plate glass window which made the wall behind her. The girl's eyes seemed lit all of a sudden with a peculiar light, an unnatural light like night road signs give. Mrs. Turpin turned her head to see if there was anything going on outside that she should see, but she could not see anything. Figures passing cast only a pale shadow through the curtain. There was no reason the girl should single her out for her ugly looks.

"Miss Finley," the nurse said, cracking the door. The gum-chewing woman got up and passed in front of her and Claud and went into the office. She had on red high-heeled shoes.

Directly across the table, the ugly girl's eyes were fixed on Mrs. Turpin as if she had some very special reason for disliking her.

"This is wonderful weather, isn't it?" the girl's mother said.

"It's good weather for cotton if you can get the niggers to pick it," Mrs. Turpin said, "but niggers don't want to pick cotton any more. You can't get the white folks to pick it and now you can't get the niggers—because they got to be right up there with the white folks."

"They gonna *try* anyways," the white-trash woman said, leaning forward.

"Do you have one of those cotton-picking machines?" the pleasant lady asked.

"No," Mrs. Turpin said, "they leave half the cotton in the field. We don't have much cotton anyway. If you want to make it farming now, you have to have a little of everything. We got a couple of acres of cotton and a few hogs and chickens and just enough white-face that Claud can look after them himself."

"One thang I don't want," the white-trash woman said, wiping her mouth with the back of her hand. "Hogs. Nasty stinking things, a-gruntin and a-rootin all over the place."

Mrs. Turpin gave her the merest edge of her attention. "Our hogs are not dirty and they don't stink," she said. "They're cleaner than some children I've seen. Their feet never touch the ground. We have a pig-parlor—that's where you raise them on concrete," she explained to the pleasant lady, "and Claud scoots them down with the hose every afternoon and washes off the floor." Cleaner by far than that child right there, she thought. Poor nasty little thing. He had not moved except to put the thumb of his dirty hand into his mouth.

The woman turned her face away from Mrs. Turpin. "I know I wouldn't scoot down no hog with no hose," she said to the wall.

You wouldn't have no hog to scoot down, Mrs. Turpin said to herself.

"A-gruntin and a-rootin and a-groanin," the woman muttered.

"We got a little of everything," Mrs. Turpin said to the pleasant lady. "It's no use in having more than you can handle yourself with help like it is. We found enough niggers to pick our cotton this year but Claud he has to go after them and take them home again in the evening. They can't walk that half a mile. No they can't. I tell you," she said and laughed merrily, "I sure am tired of buttering up niggers, but you got to love em if you want em to work for you. When they come in the morning, I run out and I say, 'Hi yawl this morning?' and when Claud drives them off to the field I just wave to beat the band and they just wave back." And she waved her hand rapidly to illustrate.

"Like you read out of the same book," the lady said, showing she understood perfectly.

"Child, yes," Mrs. Turpin said. "And when they come in from the field, I run out with a bucket of icewater. That's the way it's going to be from now on," she said. "You may as well face it."

"One thang I know," the white-trash woman said. "Two thangs I ain't going to do: love no niggers or scoot down no hog with no hose." And she let out a bark of contempt.

The look that Mrs. Turpin and the pleasant lady exchanged indicated they both understood that you had to *have* certain things before you could *know* certain things. But every time Mrs. Turpin exchanged a look with the lady, she was aware that the ugly girl's peculiar eyes were still on her, and she had trouble bringing her attention back to the conversation.

"When you got something," she said, "you got to look after it." And when you ain't got a thing but breath and britches, she added to herself, you can afford to come to town every morning and just sit on the Court House coping and spit.

A grotesque revolving shadow passed across the curtain behind her and was thrown palely on the opposite wall. Then a bicycle clattered down against the outside of the building. The door opened and a colored boy glided in with a tray from the drug store. It had two large red and white paper cups on it with tops on them. He was a tall, very black boy in discolored white pants and a green nylon shirt. He was chewing gum slowly, as if to music. He set the tray down in the office opening next to the fern and stuck his head through to look for the secretary. She was not in there. He rested his arms on the ledge and waited, his narrow bottom stuck out, swaying slowly to the left and right. He raised a hand over his head and scratched the base of his skull.

"You see that button there, boy?" Mrs. Turpin said. "You can punch that and she'll come. She's probably in the back somewhere."

"Is thas right?" the boy said agreeably, as if he had never seen the button before. He leaned to the right and put his finger on it. "She sometime out," he said and twisted around to face his audience, his elbows behind him on the counter. The nurse appeared and he twisted back again. She handed him a dollar and he rooted in his pocket and made the change and counted it out to her. She gave him fifteen cents for a tip and he went out with the empty tray. The heavy door swung to slowly and closed at length with the sound of suction. For a moment no one spoke.

"They ought to send all them niggers back to Africa," the white-trash woman said. "That's wher they come from in the first place."

"Oh, I couldn't do without my good colored friends," the pleasant lady said.

"There's a heap of things worse than a nigger," Mrs. Turpin agreed. "It's all kinds of them just like it's all kinds of us."

"Yes, and it takes all kinds to make the world go round," the lady said in her musical voice.

As she said it, the raw-complexioned girl snapped her teeth together. Her lower lip turned downwards and inside out, revealing the pale pink inside of her mouth. After a second it rolled back up. It was the ugliest face Mrs. Turpin had ever seen anyone make and for a moment she was certain that the girl had made it at her. She was looking at her as if she had known and disliked her all her life—all of Mrs. Turpin's life, it seemed too, not just all the girl's life. Why, girl, I don't even know you, Mrs. Turpin said silently.

She forced her attention back to the discussion. "It wouldn't be practical to send them back to Africa," she said. "They wouldn't want to go. They got it too good here."

"Wouldn't be what they wanted—if I had anythang to do with it," the woman said.

"It wouldn't be a way in the world you could get all the niggers back over there," Mrs. Turpin said. "They'd be hiding out and lying down and turning sick on you and wailing and hollering and raring and pitching. It wouldn't be a way in the world to get them over there."

"They got over here," the trashy woman said. "Get back like they got over."

"It wasn't so many of them then," Mrs. Turpin explained.

The woman looked at Mrs. Turpin as if here was an idiot indeed but Mrs. Turpin was not bothered by the look, considering where it came from.

"Nooo," she said, "they're going to stay here where they can go to New York and marry white folks and improve their color. That's what they all want to do, every one of them, improve their color."

"You know what comes of that, don't you?" Claud asked.

"No, Claud, what?" Mrs. Turpin said.

Claud's eyes twinkled. "White-faced niggers," he said with never a smile.

Everybody in the office laughed except the white-trash and the ugly girl. The girl gripped the book in her lap with white fingers. The trashy woman looked around her from face to face as if she thought they were all idiots. The old woman in the feed sack dress continued to gaze expressionless across the floor at the high-top shoes of the man opposite her, the one who had been pretending to be asleep when the Turpins came in. He was laughing heartily, his hands still spread out on his knees. The child had fallen to the side and was lying now almost face down in the old woman's lap.

While they recovered from their laughter, the nasal chorus on the radio kept the room from silence.

> "You go to blank blank
> And I'll go to mine
> But we'll all blank along
> To-geth-ther,
>
> And all along the blank
> We'll hep eachother out
> Smile-ling in any kind of
> Weath-ther!"

Mrs. Turpin didn't catch every word but she caught enough to agree with the spirit of the song and it turned her thoughts sober. To help anybody out that needed it was her philosophy of life. She never spared herself when she found somebody in need, whether they were white or black, trash or decent. And of all she had to be thankful for, she was most thankful that this was so. If Jesus had said, "You can be high society and have all the money you want and be thin and svelte-like, but you can't be a good woman with it," she would have had to say, "Well don't make me that then. Make me a good woman and it don't matter what else, how fat or how ugly or how poor!" Her heart rose. He had not made her a nigger or white-trash or ugly! He had made her herself and given her a little of everything. Jesus, thank you! she said. Thank you thank you thank you! Whenever she counted her blessings she felt as buoyant as if she weighed one hundred and twenty-five pounds instead of one hundred and eighty.

"What's wrong with your little boy?" the pleasant lady asked the white-trashy woman.

"He has a ulcer," the woman said proudly. "He ain't give me a minute's peace since he was born. Him and her are just alike," she said, nodding at the old woman, who was running her leathery fingers through the child's pale hair. "Look like I can't get nothing down them two but Co' Cola and candy."

That's all you try to get down em, Mrs. Turpin said to herself. Too lazy to light the fire. There was nothing you could tell her about people like them that she didn't know already. And it was not just that they didn't have anything. Because if you gave them everything, in two weeks it would all be broken or filthy or they would have chopped it up for lightwood. She knew all this from her own experience. Help them you must, but help them you couldn't.

All at once the ugly girl turned her lips inside out again. Her eyes were fixed like two drills on Mrs. Turpin. This time there was no mistaking that there was something urgent behind them.

Girl, Mrs. Turpin exclaimed silently, I haven't done a thing to you! The girl might be confusing her with somebody else. There was no need to sit by and let herself be intimidated. "You must be in college," she said boldly, looking directly at the girl. "I see you reading a book there."

The girl continued to stare and pointedly did not answer.

Her mother blushed at this rudeness. "The lady asked you a question, Mary Grace," she said under her breath.

"I have ears," Mary Grace said.

The poor mother blushed again. "Mary Grace goes to Wellesley College," she explained. She twisted one of the buttons on her dress. "In Massachusetts," she added with a grimace. "And in the summer she just keeps right on studying. Just reads all the time, a real book worm. She's done real well at Wellesley; she's taking English and Math and History and Psychology and Social Studies," she rattled on, "and I think it's too much. I think she ought to get out and have fun."

The girl looked as if she would like to hurl them all through the plate glass window.

"Way up north," Mrs. Turpin murmured and thought, well, it hasn't done much for her manners.

"I'd almost rather to have him sick," the white-trash woman said, wrenching the attention back to herself. "He's so mean when he ain't. Look like some children just take natural to meanness. It's some gets bad when they get sick but he was the opposite. Took sick and turned good. He don't give me no trouble now. It's me waitin to see the doctor," she said.

If I was going to send anybody back to Africa, Mrs. Turpin thought, it would be your kind, woman. "Yes, indeed," she said aloud, but looking up at the ceiling, "it's a heap of things worse than a nigger." And dirtier than a hog, she added to herself.

"I think people with bad dispositions are more to be pitied than anyone on earth," the pleasant lady said in a voice that was decidedly thin.

"I thank the Lord he has blessed me with a good one," Mrs. Turpin said. "The day has never dawned that I couldn't find something to laugh at."

"Not since she married me anyways," Claud said with a comical straight face.

Everybody laughed except the girl and the white-trash.

Mrs. Turpin's stomach shook. "He's such a caution," she said, "that I can't help but laugh at him."

The girl made a loud ugly noise through her teeth.

Her mother's mouth grew thin and tight. "I think the worst

thing in the world," she said, "is an ungrateful person. To have everything and not appreciate it. I know a girl," she said, "who has parents who would give her anything, a little brother who loves her dearly, who is getting a good education, who wears the best clothes, but who can never say a kind word to anyone, who never smiles, who just criticises and complains all day long."

"Is she too old to paddle?" Claud asked.

The girl's face was almost purple.

"Yes," the lady said, "I'm afraid there's nothing to do but leave her to her folly. Some day she'll wake up and it'll be too late."

"It never hurt anyone to smile," Mrs. Turpin said. "It just makes you feel better all over."

"Of course," the lady said sadly, "but there are just some people you can't tell anything to. They can't take criticism."

"If it's one thing I am," Mrs. Turpin said with feeling, "it's grateful. When I think who all I could have been besides myself and what all I got, a little of everything, and a good disposition besides, I just feel like shouting, 'Thank you, Jesus, for making everything the way it is!' It could have been different!" For one thing, somebody else could have got Claud. At the thought of this, she was flooded with gratitude and a terrible pang of joy ran through her. "Oh thank you, Jesus, thank you!" she cried aloud.

The book struck her directly over her left eye. It struck almost at the same instant that she realized the girl was about to hurl it. Before she could utter a sound, the raw face came crashing across the table toward her, howling. The girl's fingers sank like clamps into the soft flesh of her neck. She heard the mother cry out and Claud shout, "Whoa!" There was an instant when she was certain that she was about to be in an earthquake.

All at once her visions narrowed and she saw everything as if it were happening in a small room far away, or as if she were looking at it through the wrong end of a telescope, Claud's face crumpled and fell out of sight. The nurse ran in, then out, then in again. Then the gangling figure of the doctor rushed out of the inner door. Magazines flew this way and that as the table turned over. The girl fell with a thud and Mrs. Turpin's vision suddenly reversed itself and she saw everything large instead of small. The eyes of the white-trashy woman were staring hugely at the floor. There the girl, held down on one side by the nurse and on the other by her mother, was wrenching and turning in their grasp. The doctor was kneeling astride her, trying to hold her arm down. He managed after a second to sink a long needle into it.

Mrs. Turpin felt entirely hollow except for her heart which swung from side to side as if it were agitated in a great empty drum of flesh.

"Somebody that's not busy call for the ambulance," the doctor said in the off-hand voice young doctors adopt for terrible occasions.

Mrs. Turpin could not have moved a finger. The old man who had been sitting next to her slipped nimbly into the office and made the call, for the secretary still seemed to be gone.

"Claud!" Mrs. Turpin called.

He was not in his chair. She knew she must jump up and find him but she felt like some one trying to catch a train in a dream, when everything moves in slow motion and the faster you try to run the slower you go.

"Here I am," a suffocated voice very unlike Claud's, said.

He was doubled up in the corner on the floor, pale as paper, holding his leg. She wanted to get up and go to him but she could not move. Instead, her gaze was drawn slowly downward to the churning face on the floor, which she could see over the doctor's shoulder.

The girl's eyes stopped rolling and focussed on her. They seemed a much lighter blue than before, as if a door that had been tightly closed behind them was now open to admit light and air.

Mrs. Turpin's head cleared and her power of motion returned. She leaned forward until she was looking directly into the fierce brilliant eyes. There was no doubt in her mind that the girl did know her, knew her in some intense and personal way, beyond time and place and condition. "What you got to say to me?" she asked hoarsely and held her breath, waiting, as for a revelation.

The girl raised her head. Her gaze locked with Mrs. Turpin's. "Go back to hell where you came from, you old wart hog," she whispered. Her voice was low but clear. Her eyes burned for a moment as if she saw with pleasure that her message had struck its target.

Mrs. Turpin sank back in her chair.

After a moment the girl's eyes closed and she turned her head wearily to the side.

The doctor rose and handed the nurse the empty syringe. He

leaned over and put both hands for a moment on the mother's shoulders, which were shaking. She was sitting on the floor, her lips pressed together, holding Mary Grace's hand in her lap. The girl's fingers were gripped like a baby's around her thumb. "Go on to the hospital," he said. "I'll call and make the arrangements."

"Now let's see that neck," he said in a jovial voice to Mrs. Turpin. He began to inspect her neck with his first two fingers. Two little moon-shaped lines like pink fish bones were indented over her windpipe. There was the beginning of an angry red swelling above her eye. His fingers passed over this also.

"Lea' me be," she said thickly and shook him off. "See about Claud. She kicked him."

"I'll see about him in a minute," he said and felt her pulse. He was a thin grey-haired young man, given to pleasantries. "Go home and have yourself a vacation the rest of the day," he said and patted her on the shoulder.

Quit your pattin me, Mrs. Turpin growled to herself.

"And put an ice pack over that eye," he said. Then he went and squatted down beside Claud and looked at his leg. After a moment he pulled him up and Claud limped after him into the office.

Until the ambulance came, the only sounds in the room were the tremulous moans of the girl's mother, who continued to sit on the floor. The white-trash woman did not take her eyes off the girl. Mrs. Turpin looked straight ahead at nothing. Presently the ambulance drew up, a long dark shadow, behind the curtain. The attendants came in and set the stretcher down beside the girl and lifted her expertly onto it and carried her out. The nurse helped the mother gather up her things. The shadow of the ambulance moved silently away and the nurse came back in the office.

"That ther girl is going to be a lunatic, ain't she?" the white-trash woman asked the nurse, but the nurse kept on to the back and never answered her.

"Yes, she's going to be a lunatic," the white-trash woman said to the rest of them.

"Po' critter," the old woman murmured. The child's face was still in her lap. His eyes looked idly out over her knees. He had not moved during the disturbance except to draw one leg up under him.

"I thank Gawd," the white-trash woman said fervently, "I ain't a lunatic."

Claud came limping out and the Turpins went home.

As their pick-up truck turned into their own dirt road and made the crest of the hill, Mrs. Turpin gripped the window ledge and looked out suspiciously. The land sloped gracefully down through a field dotted with lavender weeds and at the start of the rise their small yellow frame house, with its little flower beds spread out around it like a fancy apron, sat primly in its accustomed place between two giant hickory trees. She would not have been startled to see a burnt wound between two blackened chimneys.

Neither of them felt like eating so they put on their house clothes and lowered the shade in the bedroom and lay down, Claud with his leg on a pillow and herself with a damp washcloth over her eye. The instant she was flat on her back, the image of a razor-backed hog with warts on its face and horns coming out behind its ears snorted into her head. She moaned, a low quiet moan.

"I am not," she said tearfully, "a wart hog. From hell." But the denial had no force. The girl's eyes and her words, even the tone of her voice, low but clear, directed only to her, brooked no repudiation. She had been singled out for the message, though there was trash in the room to whom it might justly have been applied. The full force of this fact struck her only now. There was a woman there who was neglecting her own child but she had been overlooked. The message had been given to Ruby Turpin, a respectable, hard-working, church-going woman. The tears dried. Her eyes began to burn instead with wrath.

She rose on her elbow and the washcloth fell into her hand. Claud was lying on his back, snoring. She wanted to tell him what the girl had said. At the same time, she did not wish to put the image of herself as a wart hog from hell into his mind.

"Hey, Claud," she muttered and pushed his shoulder.

Claud opened one pale baby blue eye.

She looked into it warily. He did not think about anything. He just went his way.

"Wha, whasit?" he said and closed the eye again.

"Nothing," she said. "Does your leg pain you?"

"Hurts like hell," Claud said.

"It'll quit terreckly," she said and lay back down. In a moment

Claud was snoring again. For the rest of the afternoon they lay there. Claud slept. She scowled at the ceiling. Occasionally she raised her fist and made a small stabbing motion over her chest as if she were defending her innocence to invisible guests who were like the comforters of Job, reasonable-seeming but wrong.

About five-thirty Claud stirred. "Got to go after those niggers," he sighed, not moving.

She was looking straight up as if there were unintelligible handwriting on the ceiling. The protuberance over her eye had turned a greenish-blue. "Listen here," she said.

"What?"

"Kiss me."

Claud leaned over and kissed her loudly on the mouth. He pinched her side and their hands interlocked. Her expression of ferocious concentration did not change. Claud got up, groaning and growling, and limped off. She continued to study the ceiling.

She did not get up until she heard the pick-up truck coming back with the negroes. Then she rose and thrust her feet in her brown oxfords, which she did not bother to lace, and stumped out onto the back porch and got her red plastic bucket. She emptied a tray of ice cubes into it and filled it half full of water and went out into the back yard. Every afternoon after Claud brought the hands in, one of the boys helped him put out hay and the rest waited in the back of the truck until he was ready to take them home. The truck was parked in the shade under one of the hickory trees.

"Hi-yawl this evening?" Mrs. Turpin asked grimly, appearing with the bucket and the dipper. There were three women and a boy in the truck.

"Us doin nicely," the oldest woman said. "Hi you doin?" and her gaze struck immediately on the dark lump on Mrs. Turpin's forehead. "You done fell down, ain't you?" she asked in a solicitous voice. The old woman was dark and almost toothless. She had on an old felt hat of Claud's set back on her head. The other two women were younger and lighter and they both had new bright green sun hats. One of them had hers on her head; the other had taken hers off and the boy was grinning beneath it.

Mrs. Turpin set the bucket down on the floor of the truck. "Yawl hep yourselves," she said. She looked around to make sure

Claud had gone. "No. I didn't fall down," she said, folding her arms. "It was something worse than that."

"Ain't nothing bad happen to you!" the old woman said. She said it as if they all knew that Mrs. Turpin was protected in some special way by Divine Providence. "You just had you a little fall."

"We were in town at the doctor's office for where the cow kicked Mr. Turpin," Mrs. Turpin said in a flat tone that indicated they could leave off their foolishness. "And there was this girl there. A big fat girl with her face all broke out. I could look at that girl and tell she was peculiar but I couldn't tell how. And me and her mama were just talking and going along and all of a sudden WHAM! She throws this big book she was reading at me and . . ."

"Naw!" the old woman cried out.

"And then she jumps over the table and commences to choke me."

"Naw!" they all exclaimed, "naw!"

"Hi come she do that?" the old woman asked. "What ail her?"

Mrs. Turpin only glared in front of her.

"Somethin ail her," the old woman said.

"They carried her off in an ambulance," Mrs. Turpin continued, "but before she went she was rolling on the floor and they were trying to hold her down to give her a shot and she said something to me." She paused. "You know what she said to me?"

"What she say?" they asked.

"She said," Mrs. Turpin began, and stopped, her face very dark and heavy. The sun was getting whiter and whiter, blanching the sky overhead so that the leaves of the hickory tree were black in the face of it. She could not bring forth the words. "Something real ugly," she muttered.

"She sho shouldn't said nothin ugly to you," the old woman said. "You so sweet. You the sweetest lady I know."

"She pretty too," the one with the hat on said.

"And stout," the other one said. "I never knowed no sweeter white lady."

"That's the truth befo' Jesus," the old woman said. "Amen! You des as sweet and pretty as you can be."

Mrs. Turpin knew just exactly how much negro flattery was worth and it added to her rage. "She said," she began again and finished this time with a fierce rush of breath, "that I was an old wart hog from hell."

There was an astounded silence.

"Where she at!" the youngest woman cried in a piercing voice. "Lemme see her. I'll kill her!"

"I'll kill her with you!" the other one cried.

"She b'long in the sylum," the old woman said emphatically. "You the sweetest white lady I know."

"She pretty too," the other two said. "Stout as she can be and sweet. Jesus satisfied with her!"

"Deed he is," the old woman declared.

Idiots! Mrs. Turpin growled to herself. You could never say anything intelligent to a nigger. You could talk at them but not with them. "Yawl ain't drunk your water," she said shortly. "Leave the bucket in the truck when you're finished with it. I got more to do than just stand around and pass the time of day," and she moved off and into the house.

She stood for a moment in the middle of the kitchen. The dark protuberance over her eye looked like a miniature tornado cloud which might any moment sweep across the horizon of her brow. Her lower lip protruded dangerously. She squared her massive shoulders. Then she marched into the front of the house and out the side door and started down the road to the pig parlor. She had the look of a woman going single-handed, weaponless, into battle.

The sun was a deep yellow now like a harvest moon and was riding westward very fast over the far tree line as if it meant to reach the hogs before she did. The road was rutted and she kicked several good-sized stones out of her path as she strode along. The pig parlor was on a little knoll at the end of a lane that ran off from the side of the barn. It was a square of concrete as large as a small room, with a board fence about four feet high around it. The concrete floor sloped slightly so that the hog wash could drain off into a trench where it was carried to the field for fertilizer. Claud was standing on the outside, on the edge of the concrete, hanging onto the top board, hosing down the floor inside. The hose was connected to the faucet of a water trough nearby.

Mrs. Turpin climbed up beside him and glowered down at the hogs inside. There were seven long-snouted bristly shoats in it— tan with liver-colored spots—and an old sow a few weeks off from farrowing. She was lying on her side grunting. The shoats were running about shaking themselves like idiot children, their little slit pig eyes searching the floor for anything left. She had read that pigs were the most intelligent animal. She doubted it. They were supposed to be smarter than dogs. There had even been a pig astronaut. He had performed his assignment perfectly but died of a heart attack afterwards because they left him in his electric suit, sitting upright throughout his examination when naturally a hog should be on all fours.

A-gruntin and a-rootin and a-groanin.

"Gimme that hose," she said, yanking it away from Claud. "Go on and carry them niggers home and then get off that leg."

"You look like you might have swallowed a mad dog," Claud observed, but he got down and limped off. He paid no attention to her humors.

Until he was out of earshot, Mrs. Turpin stood on the side of the pen, holding the hose and pointing the stream of water at the hind quarters of any shoat that looked as if it might try to lie down. When he had had time to get over the hill, she turned her head slightly and wrathful eyes scanned the path. He was nowhere in sight. She turned back again and seemed to gather herself up. Her shoulders rose and she drew in her breath.

"What do you send me a message like that for?" she said in a low fierce voice, barely above a whisper but with the force of a shout in its concentrated fury. "How am I a hog and me both? How am I saved and from hell too?" Her free fist was knotted and with the other she gripped the hose, blindly pointing the stream of water in and out of the eye of the old sow whose outraged squeal she did not hear.

The pig parlor commanded a view of the back pasture where their twenty beef cows were gathered around the hay-bales Claud and the boy had put out. The freshly cut pasture sloped down to the highway. Across it was their cotton field and beyond that a dark green dusty wood which they owned as well. The sun was behind the wood, very red, looking over the paling of trees like a farmer inspecting his own hogs.

"Why me?" she rumbled. "It's no trash around here, black or white, that I haven't given to. And break my back to the bone every day working. And do for the church."

She appeared to be the right size woman to command the arena before her. "How am I a hog?" she demanded. "Exactly how am I like them?" and she jabbed the stream of water at the shoats. "There was plenty of trash there. It didn't have to be me.

"If you like trash better, go get yourself some trash then," she railed. "You could have made me trash. Or a nigger. If trash is what you wanted why didn't you make me trash?" She shook her fist with the hose in it and a watery snake appeared momentarily in the air. "I could quit working and take it easy and be filthy," she growled. "Lounge about the sidewalks all day drinking root beer. Dip snuff and spit in every puddle and have it all over my face. I could be nasty.

"Or you could have made me a nigger. It's too late for me to be a nigger," she said with deep sarcasm, "but I could act like one. Lay down in the middle of the road and stop traffic. Roll on the ground."

In the deepening light everything was taking on a mysterious hue. The pasture was growing a peculiar glassy green and the streak of highway had turned lavender. She braced herself for a final assault and this time her voice rolled out over the pasture. "Go on," she yelled, "call me a hog! Call me a hog again. From hell. Call me a wart hog from hell. Put the bottom rail on top. There'll still be a top and bottom!"

A garbled echo returned to her.

A final surge of fury shook her and she roared, "Who do you think you are?"

The color of everything, field and crimson sky, burned for a moment with a transparent intensity. The question carried over the pasture and across the highway and the cotton field and returned to her clearly like an answer from beyond the wood.

She opened her mouth but no sound came out of it.

A tiny truck, Claud's, appeared on the highway, heading rapidly out of sight. Its gears scraped thinly. It looked like a child's toy. At any moment a bigger truck might smash into it and scatter Claud's and the niggers' brains all over the road.

Mrs. Turpin stood there, her gaze fixed on the highway, all her muscles rigid, until in five or six minutes the truck reappeared, returning. She waited until it had had time to turn into their own road. Then like a monumental statue coming to life, she bent her head slowly and gazed, as if through the very heart of mystery, down into the pig parlor at the hogs. They had settled all in one corner around the old sow who was grunting softly. A red glow suffused them. They appeared to pant with a secret life.

Until the sun slipped finally behind the tree line, Mrs. Turpin remained there with her gaze bent to them as if she were absorbing some abysmal life-giving knowledge. At last she lifted her head. There was only a purple streak in the sky, cutting through a field of crimson and leading, like an extension of the highway, into the descending dusk. She raised her hands from the side of the pen in a gesture hieratic and profound. A visionary light settled in her eyes. She saw the streak as a vast swinging bridge extending upward from the earth through a field of living fire. Upon it a vast horde of souls were rumbling toward heaven. There were whole companies of white-trash, clean for the first time in their lives, and bands of black niggers in white robes, and battalions of freaks and lunatics shouting and clapping and leaping like frogs. And bringing up the end of the procession was a tribe of people whom she recognized at once as those who, like herself and Claud, had always had a little of everything and the God-given wit to use it right. She leaned forward to observe them closer. They were marching behind the others with great dignity, accountable as they had always been for good order and common sense and respectable behavior. They alone were on key. Yet she could see by their shocked and altered faces that even their virtues were being burned away. She lowered her hands and gripped the rail of the hog pen, her eyes small but fixed unblinkingly on what lay ahead. In a moment the vision faded but she remained where she was, immobile.

At length she got down and turned off the faucet and made her slow way on the darkening path to the house. In the woods around her the invisible cricket choruses had struck up, but what she heard were the voices of the souls climbing upward into the starry field and shouting hallelujah.

Philip Roth

Defender of the Faith*

IN MAY OF 1945, only a few weeks after the fighting had ended in Europe, I was rotated back to the States, where I spent the remainder of the war with a training company at Camp Crowder, Missouri. Along with the rest of the Ninth Army, I had been racing across Germany so swiftly during the late winter and spring that when I boarded the plane, I couldn't believe its destination lay to the west. My mind might inform me otherwise, but there was an inertia of the spirit that told me we were flying to a new front, where we would disembark and continue our push eastward—eastward until we'd circled the globe, marching through villages along whose twisting, cobbled streets crowds of the enemy would watch us take possession of what, up till then, they'd considered their own. I had changed enough in two years not to mind the trembling of the old people, the crying of the very young, the uncertainty and fear in the eyes of the once arrogant. I had been fortunate enough to develop an infantryman's heart, which, like his feet, at first aches

---

* GOODBYE COLUMBUS. Copyright © 1959 by Philip Roth. Reprinted by permission of the publisher, Houghton Mifflin Company.

and swells but finally grows horny enough for him to travel the weirdest paths without feeling a thing.

Captain Paul Barrett was my C.O. in Camp Crowder. The day I reported for duty, he came out of his office to shake my hand. He was short, gruff, and fiery, and—indoors or out—he wore his polished helmet liner pulled down to his little eyes. In Europe, he had received a battlefield commission and a serious chest wound, and he'd been returned to the States only a few months before. He spoke easily to me, and at the evening formation he introduced me to the troops. "Gentlemen," he said, "Sergeant Thurston, as you know, is no longer with this company. Your new first sergeant is Sergeant Nathan Marx, here. He is a veteran of the European theater, and consequently will expect to find a company of soldiers here, and not a company of *boys*."

I sat up late in the orderly room that evening, trying half-heartedly to solve the riddle of duty rosters, personnel forms, and morning reports. The Charge of Quarters slept with his mouth open on a mattress on the floor. A trainee stood reading the next day's duty roster, which was posted on the bulletin board just inside the screen door. It was a warm evening, and I could hear radios playing dance music over in the barracks. The trainee, who had been staring at me whenever he thought I wouldn't notice, finally took a step in my direction.

"Hey, Sarge—we having a G.I. party tomorrow night?" he asked. A G.I. party is a barracks cleaning.

"You usually have them on Friday nights?" I asked him.

"Yes," he said, and then he added, mysteriously, "that's the whole thing."

"Then you'll have a G.I. party."

He turned away, and I heard him mumbling. His shoulders were moving, and I wondered if he was crying.

"What's your name, soldier?" I asked.

He turned, not crying at all. Instead, his green-speckled eyes, long and narrow, flashed like fish in the sun. He walked over to me and sat on the edge of my desk. He reached out a hand. "Sheldon," he said.

"Stand on your feet, Sheldon."

Getting off the desk, he said, "Sheldon Grossbart." He smiled at the familiarity into which he'd led me.

"You against cleaning the barracks Friday night, Grossbart?"

I said. "Maybe we shouldn't have G.I. parties. Maybe we should get a maid." My tone startled me. I felt I sounded like every top sergeant I had ever known.

"No, Sergeant." He grew serious, but with a seriousness that seemed to be only the stifling of a smile. "It's just—G.I. parties on Friday night, of all nights."

He slipped up onto the corner of the desk again—not quite sitting, but not quite standing, either. He looked at me with those speckled eyes flashing, and then made a gesture with his hand. It was very slight—no more than a movement back and forth of the wrist—and yet it managed to exclude from our affairs everything else in the orderly room, to make the two of us the center of the world. It seemed, in fact, to exclude everything even about the two of us except our hearts.

"Sergeant Thurston was one thing," he whispered, glancing at the sleeping C.Q., "but we thought that with you here things might be a little different."

"We?"

"The Jewish personnel."

"Why?" I asked, harshly. "What's on your mind?" Whether I was still angry at the "Sheldon" business, or now at something else, I hadn't time to tell, but clearly I was angry.

"We thought you—Marx, you know, like Karl Marx. The Marx Brothers. Those guys are all—M-a-r-x. Isn't that how *you* spell it, Sergeant?"

"M-a-r-x."

"Fishbein said—" He stopped. "What I mean to say, Sergeant—" His face and neck were red, and his mouth moved but no words came out. In a moment, he raised himself to attention, gazing down at me. It was as though he had suddenly decided he could expect no more sympathy from me than from Thurston, the reason being that I was of Thurston's faith, and not his. The young man had managed to confuse himself as to what my faith really was, but I felt no desire to straighten him out. Very simply, I didn't like him.

When I did nothing but return his gaze, he spoke, in an altered tone. "You see, Sergeant," he explained to me, "Friday nights, Jews are supposed to go to services."

"Did Sergeant Thurston tell you you couldn't go to them when there was a G.I. party?"

"No."

"Did he say you had to stay and scrub the floors?"

"No, Sergeant."

"Did the Captain say you had to stay and scrub the floors?"

"That isn't it, Sergeant. It's the other guys in the barracks." He leaned toward me. "They think we're goofing off. But we're not. That's when Jews go to services, Friday night. We have to."

"Then go."

"But the other guys make accusations. They have no right."

"That's not the Army's problem, Grossbart. It's a personal problem you'll have to work out yourself."

"But it's un*fair*."

I got up to leave. "There's nothing I can do about it," I said.

Grossbart stiffened and stood in front of me. "But this is a matter of *religion*, sir."

"Sergeant," I said.

"I mean 'Sergeant,'" he said, almost snarling.

"Look, go see the chaplain. You want to see Captain Barrett, I'll arrange an appointment."

"No, no. I don't want to make trouble, Sergeant. That's the first thing they throw up to you. I just want my rights!"

"Damn it, Grossbart, stop whining. You have your rights. You can stay and scrub floors or you can go to shul—"

The smile swam in again. Spittle gleamed at the corners of his mouth. "You mean church, Sergeant."

"I mean shul, Grossbart!"

I walked past him and went outside. Near me, I heard the scrunching of a guard's boots on gravel. Beyond the lighted windows of the barracks, young men in T shirts and fatigue pants were sitting on their bunks, polishing their rifles. Suddenly there was a light rustling behind me. I turned and saw Grossbart's dark frame fleeing back to the barracks, racing to tell his Jewish friends that they were right—that, like Karl and Harpo, I was one of them.

The next morning, while chatting with Captain Barrett, I recounted the incident of the previous evening. Somehow, in the telling, it must have seemed to the Captain that I was not so much explaining Grossbart's position as defending it. "Marx, I'd fight side by side with a nigger if the fella proved to me he was a man. I pride myself," he said, looking out the window, "that I've got an open mind. Consequently, Sergeant, nobody gets special treatment here, for the good *or* the bad. All a man's got to do is prove himself. A man fires well on the range, I give him a weekend pass. He scores high in P.T., he gets a weekend pass. He *earns* it." He turned from the window and pointed a finger at me. "You're a Jewish fella, am I right, Marx?"

"Yes, sir."

"And I admire you. I admire you because of the ribbons on your chest. I judge a man by what he shows me on the field of battle, Sergeant. It's what he's got *here*," he said, and then, though I expected he would point to his heart, he jerked a thumb toward the buttons straining to hold his blouse across his belly. "Guts," he said.

"O.K., sir. I only wanted to pass on to you how the men felt."

"Mr. Marx, you're going to be old before your time if you worry about how the men feel. Leave that stuff to the chaplain—that's his business, not yours. Let's us train these fellas to shoot straight. If the Jewish personnel feels the other men are accusing them of goldbricking—well, I just don't know. Seems awful funny that suddenly the Lord is calling so loud in Private Grossman's ear he's just got to run to church."

"Synagogue," I said.

"Synagogue is right, Sergeant. I'll write that down for handy reference. Thank you for stopping by."

That evening, a few minutes before the company gathered outside the orderly room for the chow formation, I called the C.Q., Corporal Robert LaHill, in to see me. LaHill was a dark, burly fellow whose hair curled out of his clothes wherever it could. He had a glaze in his eyes that made one think of caves and dinosaurs. "LaHill," I said, "when you take the formation, remind the men that they're free to attend church services *whenever* they are held, provided they report to the orderly room before they leave the area."

LaHill scratched his wrist, but gave no indication that he'd heard or understood.

"LaHill," I said, "*church.* You remember? Church, priest, Mass, confession."

He curled one lip into a kind of smile; I took it for a signal that for a second he had flickered back up into the human race.

"Jewish personnel who want to attend services this evening are to fall out in front of the orderly room at 1900," I said. Then, as an afterthought, I added, "By order of Captain Barrett."

A little while later, as the day's last light—softer than any I had seen that year—began to drop over Camp Crowder, I heard LaHill's thick, inflectionless voice outside my window: "Give me your ears, troopers. Toppie says for me to tell you that at 1900 hours all Jewish personnel is to fall out in front, here, if they want to attend the Jewish Mass."

At seven o'clock, I looked out the orderly-room window and saw three soldiers in starched khakis standing on the dusty quadrangle. They looked at their watches and fidgeted while they whispered back and forth. It was getting dimmer, and, alone on the otherwise deserted field, they looked tiny. When I opened the door, I heard the noises of the G.I. party coming from the surrounding barracks—bunks being pushed to the walls, faucets pounding water into buckets, brooms whisking at the wooden floors, cleaning the dirt away for Saturday's inspection. Big puffs of cloth moved round and round on the windowpanes. I walked outside, and the moment my foot hit the ground I thought I heard Grossbart call to the others, "'Ten-*hut!*" Or maybe, when they all three jumped to attention, I imagined I heard the command.

Grossbart stepped forward. "Thank you, sir," he said.

"'Sergeant,' Grossbart," I reminded him. "You call officers 'sir.' I'm not an officer. You've been in the Army three weeks—you know that."

He turned his palms out at his sides to indicate that, in truth, he and I lived beyond convention. "Thank you, anyway," he said.

"Yes," a tall boy behind him said. "Thanks a lot."

And the third boy whispered, "Thank you," but his mouth barely fluttered, so that he did not alter by more than a lip's movement his posture of attention.

"For what?" I asked.

Grossbart snorted happily. "For the announcement. The Corporal's announcement. It helped. It made it—"

"Fancier." The tall boy finished Grossbart's sentence.

Grossbart smiled. "He means formal, sir. Public," he said to me. "Now it won't seem as though we're just taking off—goldbricking because the work has begun."

"It was by order of Captain Barrett," I said.

"Aaah, but you pull a little weight," Grossbart said. "So we thank you." Then he turned to his companions. "Sergeant Marx, I want you to meet Larry Fishbein."

The tall boy stepped forward and extended his hand. I shook it. "You from New York?" he asked.

"Yes."

"Me, too." He had a cadaverous face that collapsed inward from his cheekbone to his jaw, and when he smiled—as he did at the news of our communal attachment—revealed a mouthful of bad teeth. He was blinking his eyes a good deal, as though he were fighting back tears. "What borough?" he asked.

I turned to Grossbart. "It's five after seven. What time are services?"

"Shul," he said, smiling, "is in ten minutes. I want you to meet Mickey Halpern. This is Nathan Marx, our sergeant."

The third boy hopped forward. "Private Michael Halpern." He saluted.

"Salute officers, Halpern," I said. The boy dropped his hand, and, on its way down, in his nervousness, checked to see if his shirt pockets were buttoned.

"Shall I march them over, sir?" Grossbart asked. "Or are you coming along?"

From behind Grossbart, Fishbein piped up. "Afterward, they're having refreshments. A ladies' auxiliary from St. Louis, the rabbi told us last week."

"The chaplain," Halpern whispered.

"You're welcome to come along," Grossbart said.

To avoid his plea, I looked away, and saw, in the windows of the barracks, a cloud of faces staring out at the four of us. "Hurry along, Grossbart," I said.

"O.K., then," he said. He turned to the others. "Double time, *march!*"

They started off, but ten feet away Grossbart spun around and, running backward, called to me, "Good *shabbus*, sir!" And then the three of them were swallowed into the alien Missouri dusk.

Even after they had disappeared over the parade ground, whose green was now a deep blue, I could hear Grossbart singing the double-time cadence, and as it grew dimmer and dimmer, it suddenly touched a deep memory—as did the slant of the light—and I was remembering the shrill sounds of a Bronx playground where, years ago, beside the Grand Concourse, I had played on long spring evenings such as this. It was a pleasant memory for a young man so far from peace and home, and it brought so many recollections with it that I began to grow exceedingly tender about myself. In fact, I indulged myself in a reverie so strong that I felt as though a hand were reaching down inside me. It had to reach so very far to touch me! It had to reach past those days in the forests of Belgium, and past the dying I'd refused to weep over; past the nights in German farmhouses whose books we'd burned to warm us; past endless stretches when I had shut off all softness I might feel for my fellows, and had managed even to deny myself the posture of a conqueror—the swagger that I, as a Jew, might well have worn as my boots whacked against the rubble of Wesel, Münster, and Braunschweig.

But now one night noise, one rumor of home and time past, and memory plunged down through all I had anesthetized, and came to what I suddenly remembered was myself. So it was not altogether curious that, in search of more of me, I found myself following Grossbart's tracks to Chapel No. 3, where the Jewish services were being held.

I took a seat in the last row, which was empty. Two rows in front of me sat Grossbart, Fishbein, and Halpern, holding little white Dixie cups. Each row of seats was raised higher than the one in front of it, and I could see clearly what was going on. Fishbein was pouring the contents of his cup into Grossbart's, and Grossbart looked mirthful as the liquid made a purple arc between Fishbein's hand and his. In the glaring yellow light, I saw the chaplain standing on the platform at the front; he was chanting the first line of the responsive reading. Grossbart's prayer book remained closed on his lap; he was swishing the cup around. Only Halpern responded to the chant by praying. The fingers of his right hand were spread wide across the cover of his open book. His cap was pulled down low onto his brow, which made it round, like a yarmulke. From time to time, Grossbart wet his lips at the cup's edge; Fishbein, his long yellow face a dying light bulb, looked from here to there, craning forward to catch sight of the faces down the row, then of those in front of him, then behind. He saw me, and his eyelids beat a tattoo. His elbow slid into Grossbart's side, his neck inclined toward his friend, he whispered something, and then, when the congregation next responded to the chant, Grossbart's voice was among the others. Fishbein looked into his book now, too; his lips, however, didn't move.

Finally, it was time to drink the wine. The chaplain smiled down at them as Grossbart swigged his in one long gulp, Halpern sipped, meditating, and Fishbein faked devotion with an empty cup. "As I look down amongst the congregation"—the chaplain grinned at the word—"this night, I see many new faces, and I want to welcome you to Friday-night services here at Camp Crowder. I am Major Leo Ben Ezra, your chaplain." Though an American, the chaplain spoke deliberately—syllable by syllable, almost—as though to communicate, above all, with the lip readers in his audience. "I have only a few words to say before we adjourn to the refreshment room, where the kind ladies of the Temple Sinai, St. Louis, Missouri, have a nice setting for you."

Applause and whistling broke out. After another momentary grin, the chaplain raised his hands, palms out, his eyes flicking upward a moment, as if to remind the troops where they were and Who Else might be in attendance. In the sudden silence that followed, I thought I heard Grossbart cackle, "Let the goyim clean the floors!" Were those the words? I wasn't sure, but Fishbein, grinning, nudged Halpern. Halpern looked dumbly at him, then went back to his prayer book, which had been occupying him all through the rabbi's talk. One hand tugged at the black kinky hair that stuck out under his cap. His lips moved.

The rabbi continued. "It is about the food that I want to speak to you for a moment. I know, I know, I know," he intoned, wearily, "how in the mouths of most of you the *trafe* food tastes like ashes. I know how you gag, some of you, and how your parents suffer to think of their children eating foods unclean and offensive to the palate. What can I tell you? I can only say, close your eyes and swallow as best you can. Eat what you must to live, and throw away the rest. I wish I could help more. For those of you who find this impossible, may I ask that you try and try, but then come to see me in private. If your revulsion is so great, we will have to seek aid from those higher up."

A round of chatter rose and subsided. Then everyone sang "Ain Kelohainu"; after all those years, I discovered I still knew the

words. Then, suddenly, the service over, Grossbart was upon me.
"Higher up? He means the General?"
"Hey, Shelly," Fishbein said, "he means God." He smacked his face and looked at Halpern. "How high can you go!"
"Sh-h-h!" Grossbart said. "What do you think, Sergeant?"
"I don't know," I said. "You better ask the chaplain."
"I'm going to. I'm making an appointment to see him in private. So is Mickey."
Halpern shook his head. "No, no, Sheldon—"
"You have rights, Mickey," Grossbart said. "They can't push us around."
"It's O.K.," said Halpern. "It bothers my mother, not me."
Grossbart looked at me. "Yesterday he threw up. From the hash. It was all ham and God knows what else."
"I have a cold—that was why," Halpern said. He pushed his yarmulke back into a cap.
"What about you, Fishbein?" I asked. "You kosher, too?"
He flushed. "A little. But I'll let it ride. I have a very strong stomach, and I don't eat a lot anyway." I continued to look at him, and he held up his wrist to reinforce what he'd just said; his watch strap was tightened to the last hole, and he pointed that out to me.
"But services are important to you?" I asked him.
He looked at Grossbart. "Sure, sir."
" 'Sergeant.' "
"Not so much at home," said Grossbart, stepping between us, "but away from home it gives one a sense of his Jewishness."
"We have to stick together," Fishbein said.
I started to walk toward the door; Halpern stepped back to make way for me.
"That's what happened in Germany," Grossbart was saying, loud enough for me to hear. "They didn't stick together. They let themselves get pushed around."
I turned. "Look, Grossbart. This is the Army, not summer camp."
He smiled. "So?"
Halpern tried to sneak off, but Grossbart held his arm.
"Grossbart, how old are you?" I asked.
"Nineteen."

"And you?" I said to Fishbein.

"The same. The same month, even."

"And what about him?" I pointed to Halpern, who had by now made it safely to the door.

"Eighteen," Grossbart whispered. "But like he can't tie his shoes or brush his teeth himself. I feel sorry for him."

"I feel sorry for all of us, Grossbart," I said, "but just act like a man. Just don't overdo it."

"Overdo what, sir?"

"The 'sir' business, for one thing. Don't overdo that," I said.

I left him standing there. I passed by Halpern, but he did not look at me. Then I was outside, but, behind, I heard Grossbart call, "Hey, Mickey, my *leben,* come on back. Refreshments!"

"*Leben!*" My grandmother's word for me!

One morning a week later, while I was working at my desk, Captain Barrett shouted for me to come into his office. When I entered, he had his helmet liner squashed down so far on his head that I couldn't even see his eyes. He was on the phone, and when he spoke to me, he cupped one hand over the mouthpiece. "Who the hell is Grossbart?"

"Third platoon, Captain," I said. "A trainee."

"What's all this stink about food? His mother called a goddam congressman about the food." He uncovered the mouthpiece and slid his helmet up until I could see his bottom eyelashes. "Yes, sir," he said into the phone. "Yes, sir. I'm still here, sir. I'm asking Marx, here, right now—"

He covered the mouthpiece again and turned his head back toward me. "Lightfoot Harry's on the phone," he said, between his teeth. "This congressman calls General Lyman, who calls Colonel Sousa, who calls the Major, who calls me. They're just dying to stick this thing on me. Whatsa matter?" He shook the phone at me. "I don't feed the troops? What the hell is this?"

"Sir, Grossbart is strange—" Barrett greeted that with a mockingly indulgent smile. I altered my approach. "Captain, he's a very orthodox Jew, and so he's only allowed to eat certain foods."

"He throws up, the congressman said. Every time he eats something, his mother says, he throws up!"

"He's accustomed to observing the dietary laws, Captain."

"So why's his old lady have to call the White House?"

"Jewish parents, sir—they're apt to be more protective than you expect. I mean, Jews have a very close family life. A boy goes away from home, sometimes the mother is liable to get very upset. Probably the boy mentioned something in a letter, and his mother misinterpreted."

"I'd like to punch him one right in the mouth," the Captain said. "There's a goddam war on, and he wants a silver platter!"

"I don't think the boy's to blame, sir. I'm sure we can straighten it out by just asking him. Jewish parents worry—"

"*All* parents worry, for Christ's sake. But they don't get on their high horse and start pulling strings—"

I interrupted, my voice higher, tighter than before. "The home life, Captain, is very important—but you're right, it may sometimes get out of hand. It's a very wonderful thing, Captain, but because it's so close, this kind of thing . . ."

He didn't listen any longer to my attempt to present both myself and Lightfoot Harry with an explanation for the letter. He turned back to the phone. "Sir?" he said. "Sir—Marx, here, tells me Jews have a tendency to be pushy. He says he thinks we can settle it right here in the company. . . . Yes, sir. . . . I *will* call back, sir, soon as I can." He hung up. "Where are the men, Sergeant?"

"On the range."

With a whack on the top of his helmet, he crushed it down over his eyes again, and charged out of his chair. "We're going for a ride," he said.

The Captain drove, and I sat beside him. It was a hot spring day, and under my newly starched fatigues I felt as though my armpits were melting down onto my sides and chest. The roads were dry, and by the time we reached the firing range, my teeth felt gritty with dust, though my mouth had been shut the whole trip. The Captain slammed the brakes on and told me to get the hell out and find Grossbart.

I found him on his belly, firing wildly at the five-hundred-feet target. Waiting their turns behind him were Halpern and Fishbein. Fishbein, wearing a pair of steel-rimmed G.I. glasses I hadn't seen on him before, had the appearance of an old peddler who would gladly have sold you his rifle and the cartridges that were slung all over him. I stood back by the ammo boxes waiting for Grossbart to finish spraying the distant targets. Fishbein straggled back to stand near me.

"Hello, Sergeant Marx," he said.

"How are you?" I mumbled.

"Fine, thank you. Sheldon's really a good shot."

"I didn't notice."

"I'm not so good, but I think I'm getting the hang of it now. Sergeant, I don't mean to, you know, ask what I shouldn't—" The boy stopped. He was trying to speak intimately, but the noise of the shooting forced him to shout at me.

"What is it?" I asked. Down the range, I saw Captain Barrett standing up in the jeep, scanning the line for me and Grossbart.

"My parents keep asking and asking where we're going," Fishbein said. "Everybody says the Pacific. I don't care, but my parents—If I could relieve their minds, I think I could concentrate more on my shooting."

"I don't know where, Fishbein. Try to concentrate anyway."

"Sheldon says you might be able to find out."

"I don't know a thing, Fishbein. You just take it easy, and don't let Sheldon—"

"*I'm* taking it easy, Sergeant. It's at home—"

Grossbart had finished on the line, and was dusting his fatigues with one hand. I called to him. "Grossbart, the Captain wants to see you."

He came toward us. His eyes blazed and twinkled. "Hi!"

"Don't point that goddam rifle!" I said.

"I wouldn't shoot you, Sarge." He gave me a smile as wide as a pumpkin, and turned the barrel aside.

"Damn you, Grossbart, this is no joke! Follow me."

I walked ahead of him, and had the awful suspicion that, behind me, Grossbart was *marching*, his rifle on his shoulder, as though he were a one-man detachment. At the jeep, he gave the Captain a rifle salute. "Private Sheldon Grossbart, sir."

"At ease, Grossman." The Captain sat down, slid over into the empty seat, and, crooking a finger, invited Grossbart closer.

"Bart, sir. Sheldon Gross*bart*. It's a common error." Grossbart nodded at me; *I* understood, he indicated. I looked away just as the mess truck pulled up to the range, disgorging a half-dozen K.P.s with rolled-up sleeves. The mess sergeant screamed at them while they set up the chow-line equipment.

"Grossbart, your mama wrote some congressman that we don't feed you right. Do you know that?" the Captain said.

"It was my father, sir. He wrote to Representative Franconi that my religion forbids me to eat certain foods."

"What religion is that, Grossbart?"

"Jewish."

"'Jewish, *sir*,'" I said to Grossbart.

"Excuse me, sir. Jewish, sir."

"What have you been living on?" the Captain asked. "You've been in the Army a month already. You don't look to me like you're falling to pieces."

"I eat because I have to, sir. But Sergeant Marx will testify to the fact that I don't eat one mouthful more than I need to in order to survive."

"Is that so, Marx?" Barrett asked.

"I've never seen Grossbart eat, sir," I said.

"But you heard the rabbi," Grossbart said. "He told us what to do, and I listened."

The Captain looked at me. "Well, Marx?"

"I still don't know what he eats and doesn't eat, sir."

Grossbart raised his arms to plead with me, and it looked for a moment as though he were going to hand me his weapon to hold. "But, Sergeant—"

"Look, Grossbart, just answer the Captain's questions," I said sharply.

Barrett smiled at me, and I resented it. "All right, Grossbart," he said. "What is it you want? The little piece of paper? You want out?"

"No, sir. Only to be allowed to live as a Jew. And for the others, too."

"What others?"

"Fishbein, sir, and Halpern."

"They don't like the way we serve, either?"

"Halpern throws up, sir. I've seen it."

"I thought *you* throw up."

"Just once, sir. I didn't know the sausage was sausage."

"We'll give menus, Grossbart. We'll show training films about the food, so you can identify when we're trying to poison you."

Grossbart did not answer. The men had been organized into two long chow lines. At the tail end of one, I spotted Fishbein—

or, rather, his glasses spotted me. They winked sunlight back at me. Halpern stood next to him, patting the inside of his collar with a khaki handkerchief. They moved with the line as it began to edge up toward the food. The mess sergeant was still screaming at the K.P.s. For a moment, I was actually terrified by the thought that somehow the mess sergeant was going to become involved in Grossbart's problem.

"Marx," the Captain said, "you're a Jewish fella—am I right?"

I played straight man. "Yes, sir."

"How long you been in the Army? Tell this boy."

"Three years and two months."

"A year in combat, Grossbart. Twelve goddam months in combat all through Europe. I admire this man." The Captain snapped a wrist against my chest. "Do you hear him peeping about the food? Do you? I want an answer, Grossbart. Yes or no."

"No, sir."

"And why not? He's a Jewish fella."

"Some things are more important to some Jews than other things to other Jews."

Barrett blew up. "Look, Grossbart. Marx, here, is a good man—a goddam hero. When you were in high school, Sergeant Marx was killing Germans. Who does more for the Jews—you, by throwing up over a lousy piece of sausage, a piece of first-cut meat, or Marx, by killing those Nazi bastards? If I was a Jew, Grossbart, I'd kiss this man's feet. He's a goddam hero, and *he* eats what we give him. Why do you have to cause trouble is what I want to know! What is it you're buckin' for—a discharge?"

"No, sir."

"I'm talking to a wall! Sergeant, get him out of my way." Barrett swung himself back into the driver's seat. "I'm going to see the chaplain." The engine roared, the jeep spun around in a whirl of dust, and the Captain was headed back to camp.

For a moment, Grossbart and I stood side by side, watching the jeep. Then he looked at me and said, "I don't want to start trouble. That's the first thing they toss up to us."

When he spoke, I saw that his teeth were white and straight, and the sight of them suddenly made me understand that Grossbart actually did have parents—that once upon a time someone had taken little Sheldon to the dentist. He was their son. Despite all the talk about his parents, it was hard to believe in Grossbart as a child, an heir—as related by blood to anyone, mother, father, or, above all, to me. This realization led me to another.

"What does your father do, Grossbart?" I asked as we started to walk back toward the chow line.

"He's a tailor."

"An American?"

"Now, yes. A son in the Army," he said, jokingly.

"And your mother?" I asked.

He winked. "A *ballabusta*. She practically sleeps with a dustcloth in her hand."

"She's also an immigrant?"

"All she talks is Yiddish, still."

"And your father, too?"

"A little English. 'Clean,' 'Press,' 'Take the pants in.' That's the extent of it. But they're good to me."

"Then, Grossbart—" I reached out and stopped him. He turned toward me, and when our eyes met, his seemed to jump back, to shiver in their sockets. "Grossbart—you were the one who wrote that letter, weren't you?"

It took only a second or two for his eyes to flash happy again. "Yes." He walked on, and I kept pace. "It's what my father *would* have written if he had known how. It was his name, though. *He* signed it. He even mailed it. I sent it home. For the New York postmark."

I was astonished, and he saw it. With complete seriousness, he thrust his right arm in front of me. "Blood is blood, Sergeant," he said, pinching the blue vein in his wrist.

"What the hell *are* you trying to do, Grossbart?" I asked. "I've seen you eat. Do you know that? I told the Captain I don't know what you eat, but I've seen you eat like a hound at chow."

"We work hard, Sergeant. We're in training. For a furnace to work, you've got to feed it coal."

"Why did you say in the letter that you threw up all the time?"

"I was really talking about Mickey there. I was talking *for* him. He would never write, Sergeant, though I pleaded with him. He'll waste away to nothing if I don't help. Sergeant, I used my name—my father's name—but it's Mickey, and Fishbein, too, I'm watching out for."

"You're a regular Messiah, aren't you?"

We were at the chow line now.

"That's a good one, Sergeant," he said, smiling. "But who knows? Who can tell? Maybe you're the Messiah—a little bit. What Mickey says is the Messiah is a collective idea. He went to Yeshiva, Mickey, for a while. He says *together* we're the Messiah. Me a little bit, you a little bit. You should hear that kid talk, Sergeant, when he gets going."

"Me a little bit, you a little bit," I said. "You'd like to believe that, wouldn't you, Grossbart? That would make everything so clean for you."

"It doesn't seem too bad a thing to believe, Sergeant. It only means we should all *give* a little, is all."

I walked off to eat my rations with the other noncoms.

Two days later, a letter addressed to Captain Barrett passed over my desk. It had come through the chain of command—from the office of Congressman Franconi, where it had been received, to General Lyman, to Colonel Sousa, to Major Lamont, now to Captain Barrett. I read it over twice. It was dated May 14, the day Barrett had spoken with Grossbart on the rifle range.

> Dear Congressman:
>
> First let me thank you for your interest in behalf of my son, Private Sheldon Grossbart. Fortunately, I was able to speak with Sheldon on the phone the other night, and I think I've been able to solve our problem. He is, as I mentioned in my last letter, a very religious boy, and it was only with the greatest difficulty that I could persuade him that the religious thing to do—what God Himself would want Sheldon to do—would be to suffer the pangs of religious remorse for the good of his country and all mankind. It took some doing, Congressman, but finally he saw the light. In fact, what he said (and I wrote down the words on a scratch pad so as never to forget), what he said was "I guess you're right, Dad. So many millions of my fellow-Jews gave up their lives to the enemy, the least I can do is live for a while minus a bit of my heritage so as to help end this struggle and regain for all the children of God dignity and humanity." That, Congressman, would make any father proud.
>
> By the way, Sheldon wanted me to know—and to pass on to you—the name of a soldier who helped him reach this decision: SERGEANT NATHAN MARX. Sergeant Marx is a combat vet-

eran who is Sheldon's first sergeant. This man has helped Sheldon over some of the first hurdles he's had to face in the Army, and is in part responsible for Sheldon's changing his mind about the dietary laws. I know Sheldon would appreciate any recognition Marx could receive.

Thank you and good luck. I look forward to seeing your name on the next election ballot.

Respectfully,
Samuel E. Grossbart

Attached to the Grossbart communiqué was another, addressed to General Marshall Lyman, the post commander, and signed by Representative Charles E. Franconi, of the House of Representatives. The communiqué informed General Lyman that Sergeant Nathan Marx was a credit to the U.S. Army and the Jewish people.

What was Grossbart's motive in recanting? Did he feel he'd gone too far? Was the letter a strategic retreat—a crafty attempt to strengthen what he considered our alliance? Or had he actually changed his mind, via an imaginary dialogue between Grossbart père and Grossbart fils? I was puzzled, but only for a few days— that is, only until I realized that, whatever his reasons, he had actually decided to disappear from my life; he was going to allow himself to become just another trainee. I saw him at inspection, but he never winked; at chow formations, but he never flashed me a sign. On Sundays, with the other trainees, he would sit around watching the noncoms' softball team, for which I pitched, but not once did he speak an unnecessary word to me. Fishbein and Halpern retreated, too—at Grossbart's command, I was sure. Apparently he had seen that wisdom lay in turning back before he plunged over into the ugliness of privilege undeserved. Our separation allowed me to forgive him our past encounters, and, finally, to admire him for his good sense.

Meanwhile, free of Grossbart, I grew used to my job and my administrative tasks. I stepped on a scale one day, and discovered I had truly become a noncombatant; I had gained seven pounds. I found patience to get past the first three pages of a book. I thought about the future more and more, and wrote letters to girls I'd known before the war. I even got a few answers. I sent away to Columbia for a Law School catalogue. I continued to follow the war in the Pacific, but it was not my war. I thought I could see the end, and sometimes, at night, I dreamed that I was walking on the streets of Manhattan—Broadway, Third Avenue, 116th Street, where I had lived the three years I attended Columbia. I curled myself around these dreams and I began to be happy.

And then, one Saturday, when everybody was away and I was alone in the orderly room reading a month-old copy of the *Sporting News,* Grossbart reappeared.

"You a baseball fan, Sergeant?"

I looked up. "How are you?"

"Fine," Grossbart said. "They're making a soldier out of me."

"How are Fishbein and Halpern?"

"Coming along," he said. "We've got no training this afternoon. They're at the movies."

"How come you're not with them?"

"I wanted to come over and say hello."

He smiled—a shy, regular-guy smile, as though he and I well knew that our friendship drew its sustenance from unexpected visits, remembered birthdays, and borrowed lawnmowers. At first it offended me, and then the feeling was swallowed by the general uneasiness I felt at the thought that everyone on the post was locked away in a dark movie theater and I was here alone with Grossbart. I folded up my paper.

"Sergeant," he said, "I'd like to ask a favor. It is a favor, and I'm making no bones about it."

He stopped, allowing me to refuse him a hearing—which, of course, forced me into a courtesy I did not intend. "Go ahead."

"Well, actually it's two favors."

I said nothing.

"The first one's about these rumors. Everybody says we're going to the Pacific."

"As I told your friend Fishbein, I don't know," I said. "You'll just have to wait to find out. Like everybody else."

"You think there's a chance of any of us going East?"

"Germany?" I said. "Maybe."

"I meant New York."

"I don't think so, Grossbart. Offhand."

"Thanks for the information, Sergeant," he said.

"It's not information, Grossbart. Just what I surmise."

"It certainly would be good to be near home. My parents—you

know." He took a step toward the door and then turned back. "Oh, the other thing. May I ask the other?"

"What is it?"

"The other thing is—I've got relatives in St. Louis, and they say they'll give me a whole Passover dinner if I can get down there. God, Sergeant, that'd mean an awful lot to me."

I stood up. "No passes during basic, Grossbart."

"But we're off from now till Monday morning, Sergeant. I could leave the post and no one would even know."

"I'd know. You'd know."

"But that's all. Just the two of us. Last night, I called my aunt, and you should have heard her. 'Come—come,' she said. 'I got gefilte fish, *chrain*—the works!' Just a day, Sergeant. I'd take the blame if anything happened."

"The Captain isn't here to sign a pass."

"You could sign."

"Look, Grossbart—"

"Sergeant, for two months, practically, I've been eating *trafe* till I want to die."

"I thought you'd made up your mind to live with it. To be minus a little bit of heritage."

He pointed a finger at me. "You!" he said. "That wasn't for you to read."

"I read it. So what?"

"That letter was addressed to a congressman."

"Grossbart, don't feed me any baloney. You *wanted* me to read it."

"Why are you persecuting me, Sergeant?"

"Are you kidding!"

"I've run into this before," he said, "but never from my own!"

"Get out of here, Grossbart! Get the hell out of my sight!"

He did not move. "Ashamed, that's what you are," he said. "So you take it out on the rest of us. They say Hitler himself was half a Jew. Hearing you, I wouldn't doubt it."

"What are you trying to do with me, Grossbart?" I asked him. "What are you after? You want me to give you special privileges, to change the food, to find out about your orders, to give you weekend passes."

"You even talk like a goy!" Grossbart shook his fist. "Is this just a weekend pass I'm asking for? Is a Seder sacred, or not?"

Seder! It suddenly occurred to me that Passover had been celebrated weeks before. I said so.

"That's right," he replied. "Who says no? A month ago—and I was in the field eating hash! And now all I ask is a simple favor. A Jewish boy I thought would understand. My aunt's willing to go out of her way—to make a Seder a month later. . . ." He turned to go, mumbling.

"Come back here!" I called. He stopped and looked at me. "Grossbart, why can't you be like the rest? Why do you have to stick out like a sore thumb?"

"Because I'm a Jew, Sergeant. I *am* different. Better, maybe not. But different."

"This is a war, Grossbart. For the time being *be* the same."

"I refuse."

"What?"

"I refuse. I can't stop being me, that's all there is to it." Tears came to his eyes. "It's a hard thing to be a Jew. But now I understand what Mickey says—it's a harder thing to stay one." He raised a hand sadly toward me. "Look at *you*."

"Stop crying!"

"Stop this, stop that, stop the other thing! *You* stop, Sergeant. Stop closing your heart to your own!" And, wiping his face with his sleeve, he ran out the door. "The least we can do for one another—the least . . ."

An hour later, looking out of the window, I saw Grossbart headed across the field. He wore a pair of starched khakis and carried a little leather ditty bag. I went out into the heat of the day. It was quiet; not a soul was in sight except, over by the mess hall, four K.P.s sitting around a pan, sloped forward from their waists, gabbing and peeling potatoes in the sun.

"Grossbart!" I called.

He looked toward me and continued walking.

"Grossbart, get over here!"

He turned and came across the field. Finally, he stood before me.

"Where are you going?" I asked.

"St. Louis. I don't care."

"You'll get caught without a pass."

"So I'll get caught without a pass."

"You'll go to the stockade."

"I'm *in* the stockade." He made an about-face and headed off. I let him go only a step or two. "Come back here," I said, and he followed me into the office, where I typed out a pass and signed the Captain's name, and my own initials after it.

He took the pass and then, a moment later, reached out and grabbed my hand. "Sergeant, you don't know how much this means to me."

"O.K.," I said. "Don't get in any trouble."

"I wish I could show you how much this means to me."

"Don't do me any favors. Don't write any more congressmen for citations."

He smiled. "You're right. I won't. But let me do something."

"Bring me a piece of that gefilte fish. Just get out of here."

"I will!" he said. "With a slice of carrot and a little horseradish. I won't forget."

"All right. Just show your pass at the gate. And don't tell *anybody*."

"I won't. It's a month late, but a good Yom Tov to you."

"Good Yom Tov, Grossbart," I said.

"You're a good Jew, Sergeant. You like to think you have a hard heart, but underneath you're a fine, decent man. I mean that."

Those last three words touched me more than any words from Grossbart's mouth had the right to. "All right, Grossbart," I said. "Now call me 'sir,' and get the hell out of here."

He ran out the door and was gone. I felt very pleased with myself; it was a great relief to stop fighting Grossbart, and it had cost me nothing. Barrett would never find out, and if he did, I could manage to invent some excuse. For a while, I sat at my desk, comfortable in my decision. Then the screen door flew back and Grossbart burst in again. "Sergeant!" he said. Behind him I saw Fishbein and Halpern, both in starched khakis, both carrying ditty bags like Grossbart's.

"Sergeant, I caught Mickey and Larry coming out of the movies. I almost missed them."

"Grossbart—did I say tell no one?" I said.

"But my aunt said I could bring friends. That I should, in fact."

"*I'm* the Sergeant, Grossbart—not your aunt!"

Grossbart looked at me in disbelief. He pulled Halpern up by his sleeve. "Mickey, tell the Sergeant what this would mean to you."

Halpern looked at me and, shrugging, said, "A lot."

Fishbein stepped forward without prompting. "This would mean a great deal to me and my parents, Sergeant Marx."

"No!" I shouted.

Grossbart was shaking his head. "Sergeant, I could see you denying me, but how you can deny Mickey, a Yeshiva boy—that's beyond me."

"I'm not denying Mickey anything," I said. "You just pushed a little too hard, Grossbart. *You* denied him."

"I'll give him my pass, then," Grossbart said. "I'll give him my aunt's address and a little note. At least let him go."

In a second, he had crammed the pass into Halpern's pants pocket. Halpern looked at me, and so did Fishbein. Grossbart was at the door, pushing it open. "Mickey, bring me a piece of gefilte fish, at least," he said, and then he was outside again.

The three of us looked at one another, and then I said, "Halpern, hand that pass over."

He took it from his pocket and gave it to me. Fishbein had now moved to the doorway, where he lingered. He stood there for a moment with his mouth slightly open, and then he pointed to himself. "And me?" he asked.

His utter ridiculousness exhausted me. I slumped down in my seat and felt pulses knocking at the back of my eyes. "Fishbein," I said, "you understand I'm not trying to deny you anything, don't you? If it was my Army, I'd serve gefilte fish in the mess hall. I'd sell *kugel* in the PX, honest to God."

Halpern smiled.

"You understand, don't you, Halpern?"

"Yes, Sergeant."

"And you, Fishbein? I don't want enemies. I'm just like you—I want to serve my time and go home. I miss the same things you miss."

"Then, Sergeant," Fishbein said, "why don't you come, too?"

"Where?"

"To St. Louis. To Shelly's aunt. We'll have a regular Seder. Play hide-the-matzoh." He gave me a broad, black-toothed smile.

I saw Grossbart again, on the other side of the screen.
"Pst!" He waved a piece of paper. "Mickey, here's the address.
Tell her I couldn't get away."

Halpern did not move. He looked at me, and I saw the shrug moving up his arms into his shoulders again. I took the cover off my typewriter and made out passes for him and Fishbein. "Go," I said. "The three of you."

I thought Halpern was going to kiss my hand.

That afternoon, in a bar in Joplin, I drank beer and listened with half an ear to the Cardinal game. I tried to look squarely at what I'd become involved in, and began to wonder if perhaps the struggle with Grossbart wasn't as much my fault as his. What was I that I had to *muster* generous feelings? Who was I to have been feeling so grudging, so tight-hearted? After all, I wasn't being asked to move the world. Had I a right, then, or a reason, to clamp down on Grossbart, when that meant clamping down on Halpern, too? And Fishbein—that ugly, agreeable soul? Out of the many recollections of my childhood that had tumbled over me these past few days I heard my grandmother's voice: "What are you making a *tsimmes?*" It was what she would ask my mother when, say, I had cut myself while doing something I shouldn't have done, and her daughter was busy bawling me out. I needed a hug and a kiss, and my mother would moralize. But my grandmother knew—mercy overrides justice. I should have known it, too. Who was Nathan Marx to be such a penny pincher with kindness? Surely, I thought, the Messiah himself—if He should ever come—won't niggle over nickels and dimes. God willing, he'll hug and kiss.

The next day, while I was playing softball over on the parade ground, I decided to ask Bob Wright, who was noncom in charge of Classification and Assignment, where he thought our trainees would be sent when their cycle ended, in two weeks. I asked casually, between innings, and he said, "They're pushing them all into the Pacific. Shulman cut the orders on your boys the other day."

The news shocked me, as though I were the father of Halpern, Fishbein, and Grossbart.

That night, I was just sliding into sleep when someone tapped on my door. "Who is it?" I asked.

"Sheldon."

He opened the door and came in. For a moment, I felt his presence without being able to see him. "How was it?" I asked.

He popped into sight in the near-darkness before me. "Great, Sergeant." Then he was sitting on the edge of the bed. I sat up.

"How about you?" he asked. "Have a nice weekend?"

"Yes."

"The others went to sleep." He took a deep, paternal breath. We sat silent for a while, and a homey feeling invaded my ugly little cubicle; the door was locked, the cat was out, the children were safely in bed.

"Sergeant, can I tell you something? Personal?"

I did not answer, and he seemed to know why. "Not about me. About Mickey. Sergeant, I never felt for anybody like I feel for him. Last night I heard Mickey in the bed next to me. He was crying so, it could have broken your heart. Real sobs."

"I'm sorry to hear that."

"I had to talk to him to stop him. He held my hand, Sergeant—he wouldn't let it go. He was almost hysterical. He kept saying if he only knew where we were going. Even if he knew it *was* the Pacific, that would be better than nothing. Just to know."

Long ago, someone had taught Grossbart the sad rule that only lies can get the truth. Not that I couldn't believe in the fact of Halpern's crying; his eyes *always* seemed red-rimmed. But, fact or not, it became a lie when Grossbart uttered it. He was entirely strategic. But then—it came with the force of indictment—so was I! There are strategies of aggression, but there are strategies of retreat as well. And so, recognizing that I myself had not been without craft and guile, I told him what I knew. "It is the Pacific."

He let out a small gasp, which was not a lie. "I'll tell him. I wish it was otherwise."

"So do I."

He jumped on my words. "You mean you think you could do something? A change, maybe?"

"No, I couldn't do a thing."

"Don't you know anybody over at C. and A.?"

"Grossbart, there's nothing I can do," I said. "If your orders are for the Pacific, then it's the Pacific."

"But Mickey—"

"Mickey, you, me—everybody, Grossbart. There's nothing to be done. Maybe the war'll end before you go. Pray for a miracle."

"But—"

"Good night, Grossbart." I settled back, and was relieved to feel the springs unbend as Grossbart rose to leave. I could see him clearly now; his jaw had dropped, and he looked like a dazed prize-fighter. I noticed for the first time a little paper bag in his hand.

"Grossbart." I smiled. "My gift?"

"Oh, yes, Sergeant. Here—from all of us." He handed me the bag. "It's egg roll."

"Egg roll?" I accepted the bag and felt a damp grease spot on the bottom. I opened it, sure that Grossbart was joking.

"We thought you'd probably like it. You know—Chinese egg roll. We thought you'd probably have a taste for—"

"Your aunt served egg roll?"

"She wasn't home."

"Grossbart, she invited you. You told me she invited you and your friends."

"I know," he said. "I just reread the letter. *Next* week."

I got out of bed and walked to the window. "Grossbart," I said. But I was not calling to him.

"What?"

"What are you, Grossbart? Honest to God, what are you?"

I think it was the first time I'd asked him a question for which he didn't have an immediate answer.

"How can you do this to people?" I went on.

"Sergeant, the day away did us all a world of good. Fishbein, you should see him, he *loves* Chinese food."

"But the Seder," I said.

"We took second best, Sergeant."

Rage came charging at me. I didn't sidestep. "Grossbart, you're a liar!" I said. "You're a schemer and a crook. You've got no respect for anything. Nothing at all. Not for me, for the truth—not even for poor Halpern! You use us all—"

"Sergeant, Sergeant, I feel for Mickey. Honest to God, I do. I *love* Mickey. I try—"

"You try! You feel!" I lurched toward him and grabbed his shirt front. I shook him furiously. "Grossbart, get out! Get out and stay the hell away from me. Because if I see you, I'll make your life miserable. *You understand that?*"

"Yes."

I let him free, and when he walked from the room, I wanted to spit on the floor where he had stood. I couldn't stop the fury. It engulfed me, owned me, till it seemed I could only rid myself of it with tears or an act of violence. I snatched from the bed the bag Grossbart had given me and, with all my strength, threw it out the window. And the next morning, as the men policed the area around the barracks, I heard a great cry go up from one of the trainees, who had been anticipating only his morning handful of cigarette butts and candy wrappers. "Egg roll!" he shouted. "Holy Christ, Chinese goddam egg roll!"

A week later, when I read the orders that had come down from C. and A., I couldn't believe my eyes. Every single trainee was to be shipped to Camp Stoneman, California, and from there to the Pacific—every trainee but one. Private Sheldon Grossbart. He was to be sent to Fort Monmouth, New Jersey. I read the mimeographed sheet several times. Dee, Farrell, Fishbein, Fuselli, Fylypowycz, Glinicki, Gromke, Gucwa, Halpern, Hardy, Helebrandt, right down to Anton Zygadlo—all were to be headed West before the month was out. All except Grossbart. He had pulled a string, and I wasn't it.

I lifted the phone and called C. and A.

The voice on the other end said smartly, "Corporal Shulman, sir."

"Let me speak to Sergeant Wright."

"Who is this calling, sir?"

"Sergeant Marx."

And, to my surprise, the voice said, "*Oh!*" Then, "Just a minute, Sergeant."

Shulman's "*Oh!*" stayed with me while I waited for Wright to come to the phone. Why "*Oh!*"? Who was Shulman? And then, so simply, I knew I'd discovered the string that Grossbart had pulled. In fact, I could hear Grossbart the day he'd discovered Shulman in the PX, or in the bowling alley, or maybe even at services. "Glad to meet you. Where you from? Bronx? Me, too. Do you know So-and-So? And So-and-So? Me, too! You work at C. and A.? Really? Hey, how's chances of getting East? Could you do something? Change something? Swindle, cheat, lie? We gotta help each other, you know. If the Jews in Germany . . ."

Bob Wright answered the phone. "How are you, Nate? How's the pitching arm?"

"Good. Bob, I wonder if you could do me a favor." I heard clearly my own words, and they so reminded me of Grossbart that I dropped more easily than I could have imagined into what I had planned. "This may sound crazy, Bob, but I got a kid here on orders to Monmouth who wants them changed. He had a brother killed in Europe, and he's hot to go to the Pacific. Says he'd feel like a coward if he wound up Stateside. I don't know, Bob—can anything be done? Put somebody else in the Monmouth slot?"

"Who?" he asked cagily.

"Anybody. First guy in the alphabet. I don't care. The kid just asked if something could be done."

"What's his name?"

"Grossbart, Sheldon."

Wright didn't answer.

"Yeah," I said. "He's a Jewish kid, so he thought I could help him out. You know."

"I guess I can do something," he finally said. "The Major hasn't been around here for weeks. Temporary duty to the golf course. I'll try, Nate, that's all I can say."

"I'd appreciate it, Bob. See you Sunday." And I hung up, perspiring.

The following day, the corrected orders appeared: Fishbein, Fuselli, Fylypowycz, Glinicki, Gromke, Grossbart, Gucwa, Halpern, Hardy . . . Lucky Private Harley Alton was to go to Fort Monmouth, New Jersey, where, for some reason or other, they wanted an enlisted man with infantry training.

After chow that night, I stopped back at the orderly room to straighten out the guard-duty roster. Grossbart was waiting for me. He spoke first.

"You son of a bitch!"

I sat down at my desk, and while he glared at me, I began to make the necessary alterations in the duty roster.

"What do you have against me?" he cried. "Against my family? Would it kill you for me to be near my father, God knows how many months he has left to him?"

"Why so?"

"His heart," Grossbart said. "He hasn't had enough troubles

in a lifetime, you've got to add to them. I curse the day I ever met you, Marx! Shulman told me what happened over there. There's no limit to your anti-Semitism, is there? The damage you've done here isn't enough. You have to make a special phone call! You really want me dead!"

I made the last few notations in the duty roster and got up to leave. "Good night, Grossbart."

"You owe me an explanation!" He stood in my path.

"Sheldon, you're the one who owes explanations."

He scowled. "To *you?*"

"To me, I think so—yes. Mostly to Fishbein and Halpern."

"That's right, twist things around. I owe nobody nothing, I've done all I could do for them. Now I think I've got the right to watch out for myself."

"For each other we have to learn to watch out, Sheldon. You told me yourself."

"You call this watching out for me—what you did?"

"No. For all of us."

I pushed him aside and started for the door. I heard his furious breathing behind me, and it sounded like steam rushing from an engine of terrible strength.

"*You'll* be all right," I said from the door. And, I thought, so would Fishbein and Halpern be all right, even in the Pacific, if only Grossbart continued to see—in the obsequiousness of the one, the soft spirituality of the other—some profit for himself.

I stood outside the orderly room, and I heard Grossbart weeping behind me. Over in the barracks, in the lighted windows, I could see the boys in their T shirts sitting on their bunks talking about their orders, as they'd been doing for the past two days. With a kind of quiet nervousness, they polished shoes, shined belt buckles, squared away underwear, trying as best they could to accept their fate. Behind me, Grossbart swallowed hard, accepting his. And then, resisting with all my will an impulse to turn and seek pardon for my vindictiveness, I accepted my own.

Albert Camus

The Guest*

THE SCHOOLMASTER WAS WATCHING the two men climb toward him. One was on horseback, the other on foot. They had not yet tackled the abrupt rise leading to the schoolhouse built on the hillside. They were toiling onward, making slow progress in the snow, among the stones, on the vast expanse of the high, deserted plateau. From time to time the horse stumbled. Without hearing anything yet, he could see the breath issuing from the horse's nostrils. One of the men, at least, knew the region. They were following the trail although it had disappeared days ago under a layer of dirty white snow. The schoolmaster calculated that it would take them half an hour to get onto the hill. It was cold; he went back into the school to get a sweater.

He crossed the empty, frigid classroom. On the blackboard the four rivers of France, drawn with four different colored chalks,

* From EXILE AND THE KINGDOM, by Albert Camus, trans. by Justin O'Brien. Copyright © 1957, 1958 by Alfred A. Knopf, Inc. Reprinted by permission of the publisher.

had been flowing toward their estuaries for the past three days. Snow had suddenly fallen in mid-October after eight months of drought without the transition of rain, and the twenty pupils, more or less, who lived in the villages scattered over the plateau had stopped coming. With fair weather they would return. Daru now heated only the single room that was his lodging, adjoining the classroom and giving also onto the plateau to the east. Like the class windows, his window looked to the south too. On that side the school was a few kilometers from the point where the plateau began to slope toward the south. In clear weather could be seen the purple mass of the mountain range where the gap opened onto the desert.

Somewhat warmed, Daru returned to the window from which he had first seen the two men. They were no longer visible. Hence they must have tackled the rise. The sky was not so dark, for the snow had stopped falling during the night. The morning had opened with a dirty light which had scarcely become brighter as the ceiling of clouds lifted. At two in the afternoon it seemed as if the day were merely beginning. But still this was better than those three days when the thick snow was falling amidst unbroken darkness with little gusts of wind that rattled the double door of the classroom. Then Daru had spent long hours in his room, leaving it only to go to the shed and feed the chickens or get some coal. Fortunately the delivery truck from Tadjid, the nearest village to the north, had brought his supplies two days before the blizzard. It would return in forty-eight hours.

Besides, he had enough to resist a siege, for the little room was cluttered with bags of wheat that the administration left as a stock to distribute to those of his pupils whose families had suffered from the drought. Actually they had all been victims because they were all poor. Every day Daru would distribute a ration to the children. They had missed it, he knew, during these bad days. Possibly one of the fathers or big brothers would come this afternoon and he could supply them with grain. It was just a matter of carrying them over to the next harvest. Now shiploads of wheat were arriving from France and the worst was over. But it would be hard to forget that poverty, that army of ragged ghosts wandering in the sunlight, the plateaus burned to a cinder month after month, the earth shriveled up little by little, literally scorched, every stone bursting into dust under one's foot. The sheep had died then by thousands and even a few men, here and there, sometimes without anyone's knowing.

In contrast with such poverty, he who lived almost like a monk in his remote schoolhouse, nonetheless satisfied with the little he had and with the rough life, had felt like a lord with his whitewashed walls, his narrow couch, his unpainted shelves, his well, and his weekly provision of water and food. And suddenly this snow, without warning, without the foretaste of rain. This is the way the region was, cruel to live in, even without men—who didn't help matters either. But Daru had been born here. Everywhere else, he felt exiled.

He stepped out onto the terrace in front of the schoolhouse. The two men were now halfway up the slope. He recognized the horseman as Balducci, the old gendarme he had known for a long time. Balducci was holding on the end of a rope an Arab who was walking behind him with hands bound and head lowered. The gendarme waved a greeting to which Daru did not reply, lost as he was in contemplation of the Arab dressed in a faded blue jellaba, his feet in sandals but covered with socks of heavy raw wool, his head surmounted by a narrow, short *chèche*. They were approaching. Balducci was holding back his horse in order not to hurt the Arab, and the group was advancing slowly.

Within earshot, Balducci shouted: "One hour to do the three kilometers from El Ameur!" Daru did not answer. Short and square in his thick sweater, he watched them climb. Not once had the Arab raised his head. "Hello," said Daru when they got up onto the terrace. "Come in and warm up." Balducci painfully got down from his horse without letting go the rope. From under his bristling mustache he smiled at the schoolmaster. His little dark eyes, deepset under a tanned forhead, and his mouth surrounded with wrinkles made him look attentive and studious. Daru took the bridle, led the horse to the shed, and came back to the two men, who were now waiting for him in the school. He led them into his room. "I am going to heat up the classroom," he said. "We'll be more comfortable there." When he entered the room again, Balducci was on the couch. He had undone the rope tying him to the Arab, who had squatted near the stove. His hands still bound, the *chèche* pushed back on his head, he was looking toward the window. At first Daru noticed only his huge lips, fat, smooth, almost Negroid; yet his nose was straight, his eyes were dark and full of fever. The *chèche* revealed an obstinate forehead and, under the weathered skin now rather discolored by the cold, the whole face had a restless and rebellious look that struck Daru when the Arab, turning his face toward him, looked him straight in the eyes. "Go into the other room," said the schoolmaster, "and I'll make you some mint tea." "Thanks," Balducci said. "What a chore! How I long for retirement." And addressing his prisoner in Arabic: "Come on, you." The Arab got up and, slowly, holding his bound wrists in front of him, went into the classroom.

With the tea, Daru brought a chair. But Balducci was already enthroned on the nearest pupil's desk and the Arab had squatted against the teacher's platform facing the stove, which stood between the desk and the window. When he held out the glass of tea to the prisoner, Daru hesitated at the sight of his bound hands. "He might perhaps be untied." "Sure," said Balducci. "That was for the trip." He started to get to his feet. But Daru, setting the glass on the floor, had knelt beside the Arab. Without saying anything, the Arab watched him with his feverish eyes. Once his hands were free, he rubbed his swollen wrists against each other, took the glass of tea, and sucked up the burning liquid in swift little sips.

"Good," said Daru. "And where are you headed?"

Balducci withdrew his mustache from the tea. "Here, son."

"Odd pupils! And you're spending the night?"

"No. I'm going back to El Ameur. And you will deliver this fellow to Tinguit. He is expected at police headquarters."

Balducci was looking at Daru with a friendly little smile.

"What's this story?" asked the schoolmaster. "Are you pulling my leg?"

"No, son. Those are the orders."

"The orders? I'm not . . ." Daru hesitated, not wanting to hurt the old Corsican. "I mean, that's not my job."

"What! What's the meaning of that? In wartime people do all kinds of jobs."

"Then I'll wait for the declaration of war!"

Balducci nodded.

"O.K. But the orders exist and they concern you too. Things are brewing, it appears. There is talk of a forthcoming revolt. We are mobilized, in a way."

Daru still had his obstinate look.

"Listen, son," Balducci said. "I like you and you must understand. There's only a dozen of us at El Ameur to patrol throughout the whole territory of a small department and I must get back in a hurry. I was told to hand this guy over to you and return without delay. He couldn't be kept there. His village was beginning to stir; they wanted to take him back. You must take him to Tinguit tomorrow before the day is over. Twenty kilometers shouldn't faze a husky fellow like you. After that, all will be over. You'll come back to your pupils and your comfortable life."

Behind the wall the horse could be heard snorting and pawing the earth. Daru was looking out the window. Decidedly, the weather was clearing and the light was increasing over the snowy plateau. When all the snow was melted, the sun would take over again and once more would burn the fields of stone. For days, still, the unchanging sky would shed its dry light on the solitary expanse where nothing had any connection with man.

"After all," he said, turning around toward Balducci, "what did he do?" And, before the gendarme had opened his mouth, he asked: "Does he speak French?"

"No, not a word. We had been looking for him for a month, but they were hiding him. He killed his cousin."

"Is he against us?"

"I don't think so. But you can never be sure."

"Why did he kill?"

"A family squabble, I think. One owed the other grain, it seems. It's not at all clear. In short, he killed his cousin with a billhook. You know, like a sheep, *kreezk!*"

Balducci made the gesture of drawing a blade across his throat and the Arab, his attention attracted, watched him with a sort of anxiety. Daru felt a sudden wrath against the man, against all men with their rotten spite, their tireless hates, their blood lust.

But the kettle was singing on the stove. He served Balducci more tea, hesitated, then served the Arab again, who, a second time, drank avidly. His raised arms made the jellaba fall open and the schoolmaster saw his thin, muscular chest.

"Thanks, kid," Balducci said. "And now, I'm off."

He got up and went toward the Arab, taking a small rope from his pocket.

"What are you doing?" Daru asked dryly.

Balducci, disconcerted, showed him the rope.

"Don't bother."

The old gendarme hesitated. "It's up to you. Of course, you are armed?"

"I have my shotgun."

"Where?"

"In the trunk."

"You ought to have it near your bed."

"Why? I have nothing to fear."

"You're crazy, son. If there's an uprising, no one is safe, we're all in the same boat."

"I'll defend myself. I'll have time to see them coming."

Balducci began to laugh, then suddenly the mustache covered the white teeth.

"You'll have time? O.K. That's just what I was saying. You have always been a little cracked. That's why I like you, my son was like that."

At the same time he took out his revolver and put it on the desk.

"Keep it; I don't need two weapons from here to El Ameur."

The revolver shone against the black paint of the table. When the gendarme turned toward him, the schoolmaster caught the smell of leather and horseflesh.

"Listen, Balducci," Daru said suddenly, "every bit of this disgusts me, and first of all your fellow here. But I won't hand him over. Fight, yes, if I have to. But not that."

The old gendarme stood in front of him and looked at him severely.

"You're being a fool," he said slowly. "I don't like it either. You don't get used to putting a rope on a man even after years of it, and you're even ashamed—yes, ashamed. But you can't let them have their way."

"I won't hand him over," Daru said again.

"It's an order, son, and I repeat it."

"That's right. Repeat to them what I've said to you: I won't hand him over."

Balducci made a visible effort to reflect. He looked at the Arab and at Daru. At last he decided.

"No, I won't tell them anything. If you want to drop us, go ahead; I'll not denounce you. I have an order to deliver the prisoner and I'm doing so. And now you'll just sign this paper for me."

"There's no need. I'll not deny that you left him with me."

"Don't be mean with me. I know you'll tell the truth. You're from hereabouts and you are a man. But you must sign, that's the rule."

Daru opened his drawer, took out a little square bottle of purple ink, the red wooden penholder with the "sergeant-major" pen he used for making models of penmanship, and signed. The gendarme carefully folded the paper and put it into his wallet. Then he moved toward the door.

"I'll see you off," Daru said.

"No," said Balducci. "There's no use being polite. You insulted me."

He looked at the Arab, motionless in the same spot, sniffed peevishly, and turned away toward the door. "Good-by, son," he said. The door shut behind him. Balducci appeared suddenly outside the window and then disappeared. His footsteps were muffled by the snow. The horse stirred on the other side of the wall and several chickens fluttered in fright. A moment later Balducci reappeared outside the window leading the horse by the bridle. He walked toward the little rise without turning around and disappeared from sight with the horse following him. A big stone could be heard bouncing down. Daru walked back toward the prisoner, who, without stirring, never took his eyes off him. "Wait," the schoolmaster said in Arabic and went toward the bedroom. As he was going through the door, he had a second thought, went to the desk, took the revolver, and stuck it in his pocket. Then, without looking back, he went into his room.

For some time he lay on his couch watching the sky gradually close over, listening to the silence. It was this silence that had seemed painful to him during the first days here, after the war. He had requested a post in the little town at the base of the foothills separating the upper plateaus from the desert. There, rocky walls, green and black to the north, pink and lavender to the south, marked the frontier of eternal summer. He had been named to a post farther north, on the plateau itself. In the beginning, the solitude and the silence had been hard for him on these wastelands peopled only by stones. Occasionally, furrows suggested cultivation, but they had been dug to uncover a certain kind of stone good for building. The only plowing here was to harvest rocks. Elsewhere a thin layer of soil accumulated in the hollows would be scraped out to enrich paltry village gardens. This is the way it was: bare rock covered three quarters of the region. Towns sprang up, flourished, then disappeared; men came by, loved one another or fought bitterly, then died. No one in this desert, neither he nor his guest, mattered. And yet, outside this desert neither of them, Daru knew, could have really lived.

When he got up, no noise came from the classroom. He was amazed at the unmixed joy he derived from the mere thought that the Arab might have fled and that he would be alone with no decision to make. But the prisoner was there. He had merely stretched out between the stove and the desk. With eyes open, he was staring at the ceiling. In that position, his thick lips were particularly noticeable, giving him a pouting look. "Come," said Daru. The Arab got up and followed him. In the bedroom, the schoolmaster pointed to a chair near the table under the window. The Arab sat down without taking his eyes off Daru.

"Are you hungry?"

"Yes," the prisoner said.

Daru set the table for two. He took flour and oil, shaped a cake in a frying-pan, and lighted the little stove that functioned on bottled gas. While the cake was cooking, he went out to the shed to get cheese, eggs, dates, and condensed milk. When the cake was done he set it on the window sill to cool, heated some condensed milk diluted with water, and beat up the eggs into an omelette. In one of his motions he knocked against the revolver stuck in his right pocket. He set the bowl down, went into the classrom, and put the revolver in his desk drawer. When he came back to the room, night was falling. He put on the light and served the Arab. "Eat," he said. The Arab took a piece of the cake, lifted it eagerly to his mouth, and stopped short.

"And you?" he asked.

"After you. I'll eat too."

The thick lips opened slightly. The Arab hesitated, then bit into the cake determinedly.

The meal over, the Arab looked at the schoolmaster. "Are you the judge?"

"No, I'm simply keeping you until tomorrow."

"Why do you eat with me?"

"I'm hungry."

The Arab fell silent. Daru got up and went out. He brought back a folding bed from the shed, set it up between the table and the stove, perpendicular to his own bed. From a large suitcase which, upright in a corner, served as a shelf for papers, he took two blankets and arranged them on the camp bed. Then he stopped, felt useless, and sat down on his bed. There was nothing more to do or to get ready. He had to look at this man. He looked at him, therefore, trying to imagine his face bursting with rage. He couldn't do so. He could see nothing but the dark yet shining eyes and the animal mouth.

"Why did you kill him?" he asked in a voice whose hostile tone surprised him.

The Arab looked away.

"He ran away. I ran after him."

He raised his eyes to Daru again and they were full of a sort of woeful interrogation. "Now what will they do to me?"

"Are you afraid?"

He stiffened, turning his eyes away.

"Are you sorry?"

The Arab stared at him openmouthed. Obviously he did not understand. Daru's annoyance was growing. At the same time he felt awkward and self-conscious with his big body wedged between the two beds.

"Lie down there," he said impatiently. "That's your bed."

The Arab didn't move. He called to Daru:

"Tell me!"

The schoolmaster looked at him.

"Is the gendarme coming back tomorrow?"

"I don't know."

"Are you coming with us?"

"I don't know. Why?"

The prisoner got up and stretched out on top of the blankets, his feet toward the window. The light from the electric bulb shone straight into his eyes and he closed them at once.

"Why?" Daru repeated, standing beside the bed.

The Arab opened his eyes under the blinding light and looked at him, trying not to blink.

"Come with us," he said.

In the middle of the night, Daru was still not asleep. He had gone to bed after undressing completely; he generally slept naked. But when he suddenly realized that he had nothing on, he hesitated. He felt vulnerable and the temptation came to him to put his clothes back on. Then he shrugged his shoulders; after all, he wasn't a child and, if need be, he could break his adversary in two.

From his bed he could observe him, lying on his back, still motionless with his eyes closed under the harsh light. When Daru turned out the light, the darkness seemed to coagulate all of a sudden. Little by little, the night came back to life in the window where the starless sky was stirring gently. The schoolmaster soon made out the body lying at his feet. The Arab still did not move, but his eyes seemed open. A faint wind was prowling around the schoolhouse. Perhaps it would drive away the clouds and the sun would reappear.

During the night the wind increased. The hens fluttered a little and then were silent. The Arab turned over on his side with his back to Daru, who thought he heard him moan. Then he listened for his guest's breathing, become heavier and more regular. He listened to that breath so close to him and mused without being able to go to sleep. In this room where he had been sleeping alone for a year, this presence bothered him. But it bothered him also by imposing on him a sort of brotherhood he knew well but refused to accept in the present circumstances. Men who share the same rooms, soldiers or prisoners, develop a strange alliance as if, having cast off their armor with their clothing, they fraternized every evening, over and above their differences, in the ancient community of dream and fatigue. But Daru shook himself; he didn't like such musings, and it was essential to sleep.

A little later, however, when the Arab stirred slightly, the schoolmaster was still not asleep. When the prisoner made a second move, he stiffened, on the alert. The Arab was lifting himself slowly on his arms with almost the motion of a sleepwalker. Seated upright in bed, he waited motionless without turning his head toward Daru, as if he were listening attentively. Daru did not stir; it had just occurred to him that the revolver was still in the drawer of his desk. It was better to act at once. Yet he continued to observe the prisoner, who, with the same slithery motion, put his feet on the ground, waited again, then began to stand up slowly. Daru was about to call out to him when the Arab began to walk, in a quite natural but extraordinarily silent way. He was heading toward the door at the end of the room that opened into the shed. He lifted the latch with precaution and went out, pushing the door behind him but without shutting it. Daru had not stirred. "He is running away," he merely thought. "Good riddance!" Yet he listened attentively. The hens were not fluttering; the guest must be on the plateau. A faint sound of water reached him, and he didn't know what it was until the Arab again stood framed in the doorway, closed the door carefully, and came back to bed without a sound. Then Daru turned his back on him and fell asleep. Still later he seemed, from the depths of his sleep, to hear furtive steps around the schoolhouse. "I'm dreaming! I'm dreaming!" he repeated to himself. And he went on sleeping.

When he awoke, the sky was clear; the loose window let in a cold, pure air. The Arab was asleep, hunched up under the blankets now, his mouth open, utterly relaxed. But when Daru shook him, he started dreadfully, staring at Daru with wild eyes as if he had never seen him and such a frightened expression that the schoolmaster stepped back. "Don't be afraid. It's me. You must eat." The Arab nodded his head and said yes. Calm had returned to his face, but his expression was vacant and listless.

The coffee was ready. They drank it seated together on the folding bed as they munched their pieces of the cake. Then Daru led the Arab under the shed and showed him the faucet where he washed. He went back into the room, folded the blankets and the bed, made his own bed and put the room in order. Then he went through the classroom and out onto the terrace. The sun was already rising in the blue sky; a soft, bright light was bathing the deserted plateau. On the ridge the snow was melting in spots. The stones were about to reappear. Crouched on the edge of the plateau, the schoolmaster looked at the deserted expanse. He thought of Balducci. He had hurt him, for he had sent him off in a way as if he didn't want to be associated with him. He could still hear the gendarme's farewell and, without knowing why, he felt strangely empty and vulnerable. At that moment, from the other side of the schoolhouse, the prisoner coughed. Daru listened to him almost despite himself and then, furious, threw a pebble that whistled through the air before sinking into the snow. That man's stupid crime revolted him, but to hand him over was contrary to honor. Merely thinking of it made him smart with humiliation. And he cursed at one and the same time his own people who had sent him this Arab and the Arab too who had dared to kill and not managed to get away. Daru got up, walked in a circle on the terrace, waited motionless, and then went back into the schoolhouse.

The Arab, leaning over the cement floor of the shed, was washing his teeth with two fingers. Daru looked at him and said:

"Come." He went back into the room ahead of the prisoner. He slipped a hunting-jacket on over his sweater and put on walking-shoes. Standing, he waited until the Arab had put on his *chèche* and sandals. They went into the classroom and the schoolmaster pointed to the exit, saying: "Go ahead." The fellow didn't budge. "I'm coming," said Daru. The Arab went out. Daru went back into the room and made a package of pieces of rusk, dates, and sugar. In the classroom, before going out, he hesitated a second in front of his desk, then crossed the threshold and locked the door. "That's the way," he said. He started toward the east, followed by the prisoner. But, a short distance from the schoolhouse, he thought he heard a slight sound behind them. He retraced his steps and examined the surroundings of the house; there was no one there. The Arab watched him without seeming to understand. "Come on," said Daru.

They walked for an hour and rested beside a sharp peak of limestone. The snow was melting faster and faster and the sun was drinking up the puddles at once, rapidly cleaning the plateau, which gradually dried and vibrated like the air itself. When they resumed walking, the ground rang under their feet. From time to time a bird rent the space in front of them with a joyful cry. Daru breathed in deeply the fresh morning light. He felt a sort of rapture before the vast familiar expanse, now almost entirely yellow under its dome of blue sky. They walked an hour more, descending toward the south. They reached a level height made up of crumbly rocks. From there on, the plateau sloped down, eastward, toward a low plain where there were a few spindly trees and, to the south, toward outcroppings of rock that gave the landscape a chaotic look.

Daru surveyed the two directions. There was nothing but the sky on the horizon. Not a man could be seen. He turned toward the Arab, who was looking at him blankly. Daru held out the package to him. "Take it," he said. "There are dates, bread, and sugar. You can hold out for two days. Here are a thousand francs too." The Arab took the package and the money but kept his full hands at chest level as if he didn't know what to do with what was being given him. "Now look," the schoolmaster said as he pointed in the direction of the east, "there's the way to Tinguit. You have a two-hour walk. At Tinguit you'll find the administration and the police. They are expecting you." The Arab looked toward the east, still holding the package and the money against his chest. Daru took his elbow and turned him rather roughly toward the south. At the foot of the height on which they stood could be seen a faint path. "That's the trail across the plateau. In a day's walk from here you'll find pasturelands and the first nomads. They'll take you in and shelter you according to their law." The Arab had now turned toward Daru and a sort of panic was visible in his expression. "Listen," he said. Daru shook his head: "No, be quiet. Now I'm leaving you." He turned his back on him, took two long steps in the direction of the school, looked hesitantly at the motionless Arab, and started off again. For a few minutes he heard nothing but his own step resounding on the cold ground and did not turn his head. A moment later, however, he turned around. The Arab was still there on the edge of the hill, his arms hanging now, and he was looking at the schoolmaster. Daru felt something rise in his throat. But he swore with impatience, waved vaguely, and started off again. He had already gone some distance when he again stopped and looked. There was no longer anyone on the hill.

Daru hesitated. The sun was now rather high in the sky and was beginning to beat down on his head. The schoolmaster retraced his steps, at first somewhat uncertainly, then with decision. When he reached the little hill, he was bathed in sweat. He climbed it as fast as he could and stopped, out of breath, at the top. The rock-fields to the south stood out sharply against the blue sky, but on the plain to the east a steamy heat was already rising. And in that slight haze, Daru, with heavy heart, made out the Arab walking slowly on the road to prison.

A little later, standing before the window of the classroom, the schoolmaster was watching the clear light bathing the whole surface of the plateau, but he hardly saw it. Behind him on the blackboard, among the winding French rivers, sprawled the clumsily chalked-up words he had just read: "You handed over our brother. You will pay for this." Daru looked at the sky, the plateau, and, beyond, the invisible lands stretching all the way to the sea. In this vast landscape he had loved so much, he was alone.

Doris Lessing

The Black Madonna*

THERE ARE SOME COUNTRIES in which the arts, let alone Art, cannot be said to flourish. Why this should be so it is hard to say, although of course we all have our theories about it. For sometimes it is the most barren soil that sends up gardens of those flowers which we all agree are the crown and justification of life, and it is this fact which makes it hard to say, finally, why the soil of Zambesia should produce such reluctant plants.

Zambesia is a tough, sunburnt, virile, positive country contemptuous of subtleties and sensibility: yet there have been States with these qualities which have produced art, though perhaps with the left hand. Zambesia is, to put it mildly, unsympathetic to those ideas so long taken for granted in other parts of the world, to do with liberty, fraternity and the rest. Yet there are those, and some of the finest souls among them, who maintain that art is impossible without a minority whose leisure is guaranteed by a hard-working

* Copyright © 1951, 1953, 1954, 1957, 1958, 1962, 1963, 1964, 1965 by Doris Lessing. Reprinted by permission of Simon & Schuster, Inc.

majority. And whatever Zambesia's comfortable minority may lack, it is not leisure.

Zambesia—but enough; out of respect for ourselves and for scientific accuracy, we should refrain from jumping to conclusions. Particularly when one remembers the almost wistful respect Zambesians show when an artist does appear in their midst.

Consider, for instance, the case of Michele.

He came out of the internment camp at the time when Italy was made a sort of honorary ally, during the Second World War. It was a time of strain for the authorities, because it is one thing to be responsible for thousands of prisoners of war whom one must treat according to certain recognized standards; it is another to be faced, and from one day to the next, with these same thousands transformed by some international legerdemain into comrades in arms. Some of the thousands stayed where they were in the camps; they were fed and housed there at least. Others went as farm labourers, though not many; for while the farmers were as always short of labour, they did not know how to handle farm labourers who were also white men: such a phenomenon had never happened in Zambesia before. Some did odd jobs around the towns, keeping a sharp eye out for the trade unions, who would neither admit them as members nor agree to their working.

Hard, hard, the lot of these men, but fortunately not for long, for soon the war ended and they were able to go home.

Hard, too, the lot of the authorities, as has been pointed out; and for that reason they were doubly willing to take what advantages they could from the situation; and that Michele was such an advantage there could be no doubt.

His talents were first discovered when he was still a prisoner of war. A church was built in the camp, and Michele decorated its interior. It became a show-place, that little tin-roofed church in the prisoners' camp, with its whitewashed walls covered all over with frescoes depicting swarthy peasants gathering grapes for the vintage, beautiful Italian girls dancing, plump dark-eyed children. Amid crowded scenes of Italian life, appeared the Virgin and her Child, smiling and beneficent, happy to move familiarly among her people.

Culture-loving ladies who had bribed the authorities to be taken inside the camp would say, "Poor thing, how homesick he must be." And they would beg to be allowed to leave half a crown for the artist. Some were indignant. He was a prisoner, after all, captured in the very act of fighting against justice and democracy, and what right had he to protest?—for they felt these paintings as a sort of protest. What was there in Italy that we did not have right here in Westonville, which was the capital and hub of Zambesia? Were there not sunshine and mountains and fat babies and pretty girls here? Did we not grow—if not grapes, at least lemons and oranges and flowers in plenty?

People were upset—the desperation of nostalgia came from the painted white walls of that simple church, and affected everyone according to his temperament.

But when Michele was free, his talent was remembered. He was spoken of as "that Italian artist." As a matter of fact, he was a bricklayer. And the virtues of those frescoes might very well have been exaggerated. It is possible they would have been overlooked altogether in a country where picture-covered walls were more common.

When one of the visiting ladies came rushing out to the camp in her own car, to ask him to paint her children, he said he was not qualified to do so. But at last he agreed. He took a room in the town and made some nice likenesses of the children. Then he painted the children of a great number of the first lady's friends. He charged ten shillings a time. Then one of the ladies wanted a portrait of herself. He asked ten pounds for it; it had taken him a month to do. She was annoyed, but paid.

And Michele went off to his room with a friend and stayed there drinking red wine from the Cape and talking about home. While the money lasted he could not be persuaded to do any more portraits.

There was a good deal of talk among the ladies about the dignity of labour, a subject in which they were well versed; and one felt they might almost go so far as to compare a white man with a kaffir, who did not understand the dignity of labour either.

He was felt to lack gratitude. One of the ladies tracked him down, found him lying on a camp-bed under a tree with a bottle of wine, and spoke to him severely about the barbarity of Mussolini and the fecklessness of the Italian temperament. Then she demanded that he should instantly paint a picture of herself in her new evening dress. He refused, and she went home very angry.

It happened that she was the wife of one of our most important citizens, a General or something of that kind, who was at that time engaged in planning a military tattoo or show for the benefit of the civilian population. The whole of Westonville had been discussing this show for weeks. We were all bored to extinction by dances, fancy-dress balls, fairs, lotteries and other charitable entertainments. It is not too much to say that while some were dying for freedom, others were dancing for it. There comes a limit to everything. Though, of course, when the end of the war actually came and the thousands of troops stationed in the country had to go home—in short, when enjoying ourselves would no longer be a duty, many were heard to exclaim that life would never be the same again.

In the meantime, the Tattoo would make a nice change for us all. The military gentlemen responsible for the idea did not think of it in these terms. They thought to improve morale by giving us some idea of what war was really like. Headlines in the newspaper were not enough. And in order to bring it all home to us, they planned to destroy a village by shell-fire before our very eyes.

First, the village had to be built.

It appears that the General and his subordinates stood around in the red dust of the parade-ground under a burning sun for the whole of one day, surrounded by building materials, while hordes of African labourers ran around with boards and nails, trying to make something that looked like a village. It became evident that they would have to build a proper village in order to destroy it; and this would cost more than was allowed for the whole entertainment. The General went home in a bad temper, and his wife said what they needed was an artist, they needed Michele. This was not because she wanted to do Michele a good turn; she could not endure the thought of him lying around singing while there was work to be done. She refused to undertake any delicate diplomatic missions when her husband said he would be damned if he would ask favours of any little Wop. She solved the problem for him in her own way: a certain Captain Stocker was sent out to fetch him.

The Captain found him on the same camp-bed under the same tree, in rolled-up trousers, and an uncollared shirt; unshaven, mildly drunk, with a bottle of wine standing beside him on the earth. He was singing an air so wild, so sad, that the Captain was uneasy. He stood at ten paces from the disreputable fellow and felt the indignities of his position. A year ago, this man had been a mortal enemy to be shot at sight. Six months ago, he had been an enemy prisoner. Now he lay with his knees up, in an untidy shirt that had certainly once been military. For the Captain, the situation crystallised in a desire that Michele should salute him.

"Piselli!" he said sharply.

Michele turned his head and looked at the Captain from the horizontal. "Good morning," he said affably.

"You are wanted," said the Captain.

"Who?" said Michele. He sat up, a fattish, olive-skinned little man. His eyes were resentful.

"The authorities."

"The war is over?"

The Captain, who was already stiff and shiny enough in his laundered khaki, jerked his head back frowning, chin out. He was a large man, blond, and wherever his flesh showed, it was brick-red. His eyes were small and blue and angry. His red hands, covered all over with fine yellow bristles, clenched by his side. Then he saw the disappointment in Michele's eyes, and the hands unclenched. "No it is not over," he said. "Your assistance is required."

"For the war?"

"For the war effort. I take it you are interested in defeating the Germans?"

Michele looked at the Captain. The little dark-eyed artisan looked at the great blond officer with his cold blue eyes, his narrow mouth, his hands like bristle-covered steaks. He looked and said: "I am very interested in the end of the war."

"*Well?*" said the Captain between his teeth.

"The pay?" said Michele.

"You will be paid."

Michele stood up. He lifted the bottle against the sun, then took a gulp. He rinsed his mouth out with wine and spat. Then he poured what was left on to the red earth, where it made a bubbling purple stain.

"I am ready," he said. He went with the Captain to the waiting lorry, where he climbed in beside the driver's seat and not, as the Captain had expected, into the back of the lorry. When they had arrived at the parade-ground the officers had left a message that the Captain would be personally responsible for Michele and for the village. Also for the hundred or so labourers who were sitting around on the grass verges waiting for orders.

The Captain explained what was wanted. Michele nodded. Then he waved his hand at the Africans. "I do not want these," he said.

"You will do it yourself—a village?"

"Yes."

"With no help?"

Michele smiled for the first time. "I will do it."

The Captain hesitated. He disapproved on principle of white men doing heavy manual labour. He said: "I will keep six to do the heavy work."

Michele shrugged; and the Captain went over and dismissed all but six of the Africans. He came back with them to Michele.

"It is hot," said Michele.

"Very," said the Captain. They were standing in the middle of the parade-ground. Around its edge trees, grass, gulfs of shadow. Here, nothing but reddish dust, drifting and lifting in a low hot breeze.

"I am thirsty," said Michele. He grinned. The Captain felt his stiff lips loosen unwillingly in reply. The two pairs of eyes met. It was a moment of understanding. For the Captain, the little Italian had suddenly become human. "I will arrange it," he said, and went off down-town. By the time he had explained the position to the right people, filled in forms and made arrangements, it was late afternoon. He returned to the parade-ground with a case of Cape brandy, to find Michele and the six black men seated together under a tree. Michele was singing an Italian song to them, and they were harmonizing with him. The sight affected the Captain like an attack of nausea. He came up, and the Africans stood to attention. Michele continued to sit.

"You said you would do the work yourself?"

"Yes, I said so."

The Captain then dismissed the Africans. They departed, with friendly looks towards Michele, who waved at them. The Captain was beef-red with anger. "You have not started yet?"

"How long have I?"

"Three weeks."

"Then there is plenty of time," said Michele, looking at the bottle of brandy in the Captain's hand. In the other were two glasses. "It is evening," he pointed out. The Captain stood frowning for a moment. Then he sat down on the grass, and poured out two brandies.

"Ciao," said Michele.

"Cheers," said the Captain. Three weeks, he was thinking. Three weeks with this damned little Itie! He drained his glass and refilled it, and set it in the grass. The grass was cool and soft. A tree was flowering somewhere close—hot waves of perfume came on the breeze.

"It is nice here," said Michele. "We will have a good time together. Even in a war, there are times of happiness. And of friendship. I drink to the end of the war."

Next day, the Captain did not arrive at the parade-ground until after lunch. He found Michele under the trees with a bottle. Sheets of ceiling board had been erected at one end of the parade-ground in such a way that they formed two walls and a part of a third, and a slant of steep roof supported on struts.

"What's that?" said the Captain, furious.

"The church," said Michele.

"Wha-at?"

"You will see. Later. It is very hot." He looked at the brandy bottle that lay on its side on the ground. The Captain went to the lorry and returned with the case of brandy. They drank. Time passed. It was a long time since the Captain had sat on grass under a tree. It was a long time, for that matter, since he had drunk so much. He always drank a great deal, but it was regulated to the times and seasons. He was a disciplined man. Here, sitting on the grass beside this little man whom he still could not help thinking of as an enemy, it was not that he let his self-discipline go, but that he felt himself to be something different: he was temporarily set outside his normal behaviour. Michele did not count. He listened to Michele talking about Italy, and it seemed to him he was listening to a savage speaking: as if he heard tales from the mythical South Sea islands where a man like himself might very well go just once in his life. He found himself saying he would like to make a trip to Italy after the war. Actually, he was attracted only by the

North and by Northern people. He had visited Germany, under Hitler, and though it was not the time to say so, had found it very satisfactory. Then Michele sang him some Italian songs. He sang Michele some English songs. Then Michele took out photographs of his wife and children, who lived in a village in the mountains of North Italy. He asked the Captain if he were married. The Captain never spoke about his private affairs.

He had spent all his life in one or other of the African colonies as a policeman, magistrate, native commissioner, or in some other useful capacity. When the war started, military life came easily to him. But he hated city life, and had his own reasons for wishing the war over. Mostly, he had been in bush-stations with one or two other white men, or by himself, far from the rigours of civilisation. He had relations with native women; and from time to time visited the city where his wife lived with her parents and the children. He was always tormented by the idea that she was unfaithful to him. Recently he had even appointed a private detective to watch her; he was convinced the detective was inefficient. Army friends coming from L―― where his wife was, spoke of her at parties, enjoying herself. When the war ended, she would not find it so easy to have a good time. And why did he not simply live with her and be done with it? The fact was, he could not. And his long exile to remote bush-stations was because he needed the excuse not to. He could not bear to think of his wife for too long; she was that part of his life he had never been able, so to speak, to bring to heel.

Yet he spoke of her now to Michele, and of his favourite bush-wife, Nadya. He told Michele the story of his life, until he realized that the shadows from the trees they sat under had stretched right across the parade-ground to the grandstand. He got unsteadily to his feet, and said: "There is work to be done. You are being paid to work."

"I will show you my church when the light goes."

The sun dropped, darkness fell, and Michele made the Captain drive his lorry on to the parade-ground a couple of hundred yards away and switch on his lights. Instantly, a white church sprang up from the shapes and shadows of the bits of board.

"Tomorrow, some houses," said Michele cheerfully.

At the end of a week, the space at the end of the parade-ground had crazy gawky constructions of lath and board over it, that looked in the sunlight like nothing on this earth. Privately, it upset the Captain; it was like a nightmare that these skeleton-like shapes should be able to persuade him, with the illusions of light and dark, that they were a village. At night, the Captain drove up his lorry, switched on the lights, and there it was, the village, solid and real against a background of full green trees. Then, in the morning sunlight, there was nothing there, just bits of board stuck in the sand.

"It is finished," said Michele.

"You were engaged for three weeks," said the Captain. He did not want it to end, this holiday from himself.

Michele shrugged. "The army is rich," he said. Now, to avoid curious eyes, they sat inside the shade of the church, with the case of brandy between them. The Captain talked, talked endlessly, about his wife, about women. He could not stop talking.

Michele listened. Once he said: "When I go home—when I go home—I shall open my arms . . ." He opened them, wide. He closed his eyes. Tears ran down his cheeks. "I shall take my wife in my arms, and I shall ask nothing, nothing. I do not care. It is enough to be together. That is what the war has taught me. It is enough, it is enough. I shall ask no questions and I shall be happy."

The Captain stared before him, suffering. He thought how he dreaded his wife. She was a scornful creature, gray and hard, who laughed at him. She had been laughing at him ever since they married. Since the war, she had taken to calling him names like Little Hitler, and Storm-trooper. "Go ahead, my little Hitler," she had cried last time they met. "Go ahead, my Storm-trooper. If you want to waste your money on private detectives, go ahead. But don't think I don't know what *you* do when you're in the bush. I don't care what you do, but remember that I know it . . ."

The Captain remembered her saying it. And there sat Michele on his packing-case, saying: "It's a pleasure for the rich, my friend, detectives and the law. Even jealousy is a pleasure I don't want any more. Ah, my friend, to be together with my wife again, and the children, that is all I ask of life. That and wine and food and singing in the evenings." And the tears wetted his cheeks and splashed on to his shirt.

That a man should cry, good lord! thought the Captain. And without shame! He seized the bottle and drank.

Three days before the great occasion, some high-ranking officers came strolling through the dust, and found Michele and the Captain sitting together on the packing-case, singing. The Captain's shirt was open down the front, and there were stains on it.

The Captain stood to attention with the bottle in his hand, and Michele stood to attention too, out of sympathy with his friend. Then the officers drew the Captain aside—they were all cronies of his—and said, what the hell did he think he was doing? And why wasn't the village finished?

Then they went away.

"Tell them it is finished," said Michele. "Tell them I want to go."

"No," said the Captain, "no. Michele, what would you do if your wife . . ."

"This world is a good place. We should be happy—that is all."

"Michele . . ."

"I want to go. There is nothing to do. They paid me yesterday."

"Sit down, Michele. Three more days, and then it's finished."

"Then I shall paint the inside of the church as I painted the one in the camp."

The Captain laid himself down on some boards and went to sleep. When he woke, Michele was surrounded by the pots of paint he had used on the outside of the village. Just in front of the Captain was a picture of a black girl. She was young and plump. She wore a patterned blue dress and her shoulders came soft and bare out of it. On her back was a baby slung in a band of red stuff. Her face was turned towards the Captain and she was smiling.

"That's Nadya," said the Captain. "Nadya . . ." He groaned loudly. He looked at the black child and shut his eyes. He opened them, and mother and child were still there. Michele was very carefully drawing thin yellow circles around the heads of the black girl and her child.

"Good God," said the Captain, "you can't do that."

"Why not?"

"You can't have a black Madonna."

"She was a peasant. This is a peasant. Black peasant Madonna for black country."

"This is a German village," said the Captain.

"This is my Madonna," said Michele angrily. "Your German village and my Madonna. I paint this picture as an offering to the Madonna. She is pleased—I feel it."

The Captain lay down again. He was feeling ill. He went back to sleep. When he woke for the second time it was dark. Michele had brought in a flaring paraffin lamp, and by its light was working on the long wall. A bottle of brandy stood beside him. He painted until long after midnight, and the Captain lay on his side and watched, as passive as a man suffering a dream. Then they both went to sleep on the boards. The whole of the next day Michele stood painting black Madonnas, black saints, black angels. Outside, troops were practising in the sunlight, bands were blaring and motorcyclists roared up and down. But Michele painted on, drunk and oblivious. The Captain lay on his back, drinking and muttering about his wife. Then he would say "Nadya, Nadya," and burst into sobs.

Towards nightfall the troops went away. The officers came back, and the Captain went off with them to show how the village sprang into being when the great lights at the end of the parade-ground were switched on. They all looked at the village in silence. They switched the lights off, and there were only the tall angular boards leaning like gravestones in the moonlight. On went the lights—and there was the village. They were silent, as if suspicious. Like the Captain, they seemed to feel it was not right. Uncanny it certainly was, but *that* was not it. Unfair—that was the word. It was cheating. And profoundly disturbing.

"Clever chap, that Italian of yours," said the General.

The Captain, who had been woodenly correct until this moment, suddenly came rocking up to the General, and steadied himself by laying his hand on the august shoulder. "Bloody Wops," he said. "Bloody kaffirs. Bloody . . . Tell you what, though, there's one Itie that's some good. Yes, there is. I'm telling you. He's a friend of mine, actually."

The General looked at him. Then he nodded at his underlings. The Captain was taken away for disciplinary purposes. It was decided, however, that he must be ill, nothing else could account for such behaviour. He was put to bed in his own room with a nurse to watch him.

He woke twenty-four hours later, sober for the first time in weeks. He slowly remembered what had happened. Then he sprang out of bed and rushed into his clothes. The nurse was just in time to see him run down the path and leap into his lorry.

He drove at top speed to the parade-ground, which was flooded with light in such a way that the village did not exist. Everything was in full swing. The cars were three deep around the square, with people on the running-boards and even the roofs. The grandstand was packed. Women dressed up as gipsies, country girls, Elizabethan court dames, and so on, wandered about with trays of ginger beer and sausage-rolls and programmes at five shillings each in aid of the war effort. On the square, troops deployed, obsolete machine-guns were being dragged up and down, bands played, and motorcyclists roared through flames.

As the Captain parked the lorry, all this activity ceased, and the lights went out. The Captain began running around the outside of the square to reach the place where the guns were hidden in a mess of net and branches. He was sobbing with the effort. He was a big man, and unused to exercise, and sodden with brandy. He had only one idea in his mind—to stop the guns firing, to stop them at all costs.

Luckily, there seemed to be a hitch. The lights were still out. The unearthly graveyard at the end of the square glittered white in the moonlight. Then the lights briefly switched on, and the village sprang into existence for just long enough to show large red crosses all over a white building beside the church. Then moonlight flooded everything again, and the crosses vanished. "Oh, the bloody fool!" sobbed the Captain, running, running as if for his life. He was no longer trying to reach the guns. He was cutting across a corner of the square direct to the church. He could hear some officers cursing behind him: "Who put those red crosses there? Who? We can't fire on the Red Cross."

The Captain reached the church as the searchlights burst on. Inside, Michele was kneeling on the earth looking at his first Madonna. "They are going to kill my Madonna," he said miserably.

"Come away, Michele, come away."

"They're going to . . ."

The Captain grabbed his arm and pulled. Michele wrenched himself free and grabbed a saw. He began hacking at the ceiling board. There was a dead silence outside. They heard a voice booming through the loudspeakers: "The village that is about to be shelled is an English village, not as represented on the programme, a German village. Repeat, the village that is about to be shelled is . . ."

Michele had cut through two sides of a square around the Madonna.

"Michele," sobbed the Captain, *"get out of here."*

Michele dropped the saw, took hold of the raw edges of the board and tugged. As he did so, the church began to quiver and lean. An irregular patch of board ripped out and Michele staggered back into the Captain's arms. There was a roar. The church seemed to dissolve around them into flame. Then they were running away from it, the Captain holding Michele tight by the arm. "Get down," he shouted suddenly, and threw Michele to the earth. He flung himself down beside him. Looking from under the crook of his arm, he heard the explosion, saw a great pillar of smoke and flame, and the village disintegrated in a flying mass of debris. Michele was on his knees gazing at his Madonna in the light from the flames. She was unrecognizable, blotted out with dust. He looked horrible, quite white, and a trickle of blood soaked from his hair down one cheek.

"They shelled my Madonna," he said.

"Oh, damn it, you can paint another one," said the Captain. His own voice seemed to him strange, like a dream voice. He was certainly crazy, as mad as Michele himself . . . He got up, pulled Michele to his feet, and marched him towards the edge of the field. There they were met by the ambulance people. Michele was taken off to hospital, and the Captain was sent back to bed.

A week passed. The Captain was in a darkened room. That he was having some kind of a breakdown was clear, and two nurses stood guard over him. Sometimes he lay quiet. Sometimes he muttered to himself. Sometimes he sang in a thick clumsy voice bits out of opera, fragments from Italian songs, and—over and over again—"There's a Long Long Trail." He was not thinking of anything at all. He shied away from the thought of Michele as if it were dangerous. When, therefore, a cheerful female voice announced that a friend had come to cheer him up, and it would do him good to have some company, and he saw a white bandage moving towards him in the gloom, he turned sharp over on to his side, face to the wall.

"Go away," he said. "Go away, Michele."

"I have come to see you," said Michele. "I have brought you a present."

The Captain slowly turned over. There was Michele, a cheerful ghost in the dark room. "You fool," he said. "You messed everything up. What did you paint those crosses for?"

"It was a hospital," said Michele. "In a village there is a hospital, and on the hospital the Red Cross, the beautiful Red Cross—no?"

"I was nearly court-martialled."

"It was my fault," said Michele. "I was drunk."

"I was responsible."

"How could you be responsible when I did it? But it is all over. Are you better?"

"Well, I suppose those crosses saved your life."

"I did not think," said Michele. "I was remembering the kindness of the Red Cross people when we were prisoners."

"Oh shut up, shut up, shut up."

"I have brought you a present."

The Captain peered through the dark. Michele was holding up a picture. It was of a native woman with a baby on her back smiling sideways out of the frame.

Michele said: "You did not like the haloes. So this time, no haloes. For the Captain—no Madonna." He laughed. "You like it? It is for you. I painted it for you."

"God damn you!" said the Captain.

"You do not like it?" said Michele, very hurt.

The Captain closed his eyes. "What are you going to do next?" he asked tiredly.

Michele laughed again. "Mrs. Pannerhurst, the lady of the General, she wants me to paint her picture in her white dress. So I paint it."

"You should be proud to."

"Silly bitch. She thinks I am good. They know nothing—savages. Barbarians. Not you, Captain, you are my friend. But these people they know nothing."

The Captain lay quiet. Fury was gathering in him. He thought of the General's wife. He disliked her, but he had known her well enough.

"These people," said Michele. "They do not know a good

picture from a bad picture. I paint, I paint, this way, that way. There is the picture—I look at it and laugh inside myself." Michele laughed out loud. "They say, he is a Michelangelo, this one, and try to cheat me out of my price. Michele—Michelangelo—that is a joke, no?"

The Captain said nothing.

"But for you I painted this picture to remind you of our good times with the village. You are my friend. I will always remember you."

The Captain turned his eyes sideways in his head and stared at the black girl. Her smile at him was half innocence, half malice.

"Get out," he said suddenly.

Michele came closer and bent to see the Captain's face. "You wish me to go?" He sounded unhappy. "You saved my life. I was a fool that night. But I was thinking of my offering to the Madonna —I was a fool, I say it myself. I was drunk, we are fools when we are drunk."

"Get out of here," said the Captain again.

For a moment the white bandage remained motionless. Then it swept downwards in a bow.

Michele turned towards the door.

"And take that bloody picture with you."

Silence. Then, in the dim light, the Captain saw Michele reach out for the picture, his white head bowed in profound obeisance. He straightened himself and stood to attention, holding the picture with one hand, and keeping the other stiff down his side. Then he saluted the Captain.

"Yes, *sir*," he said, and he turned and went out of the door with the picture.

The Captain lay still. He felt—what did he feel? There was a pain under his ribs. It hurt to breathe. He realized he was unhappy. Yes, a terrible unhappiness was filling him, slowly, slowly. He was unhappy because Michele had gone. Nothing had ever hurt the Captain in all his life as much as that mocking *Yes, sir*. Nothing. He turned his face to the wall and wept. But silently. Not a sound escaped him, for the fear the nurses might hear.

Doris Lessing, responding to questions put to her about the "germ" of the tale, and the way she would like it "read," comments:

There was no single "germ" of this tale. In Rhodesia during the war, Italian prisoners-of-war ceased, overnight, to be enemies, became friends. I knew some. The colour-bar did not come easily to them: they liked Africans as people, unlike most Rhodesians. I knew a couple who painted portraits, for pocket-money: they had no illusions about their talent.

To say how I'd like it read is to attack, probably, how literature is "taught." No one should read anything at all, unless he wants to, needs to. If there is an attraction between reader and story, or novel, then the reader should ignore critics, reviewers, teachers, and tutors and—read the story, in a communication between himself and it. People don't read like this any longer: or very few of them. They are taught to look about for what other people have said about what they read.

VII

WHAT CAN A MAN BELIEVE IN?

> What is a man,
> If his chief good and market of his time
> Be but to sleep and feed? A beast no more . . .
>
> Hamlet in
> SHAKESPEARE's *Hamlet,* IV, iv, 33–34

> I'm getting older—my hair's getting gray, and yet how little I know, how little! All the same, I think I do know one thing which is not only true but also most important. I'm certain of it. Oh, if only I could convince you that there's not going to be any happiness for us and our generation, that there mustn't be and won't be . . . we must work and work. Happiness, well, that's for those who come after us, our remote descendants.
>
> Vershinin in
> ANTON CHEKHOV's
> *The Three Sisters*

> Truth may perhaps come to the price of a pearl, that showeth best by day; but it will not rise to the price of a diamond, that showeth best in varied lights.
>
> FRANCIS BACON
> "Of Truth"

Astride of a grave and a difficult birth. Down in the hole, lingeringly the grave-digger puts on the forceps. We have time to grow old. The air is full of our cries. . . . But habit is a great deadener.

>Vladimir in
>SAMUEL BECKETT'S
>*Waiting for Godot*

I stand for the reform of municipal morals and the plain ten commandments. New worlds for old. Union of all, jew, moslem, and gentile. Three acres and a cow for all children of nature. Saloon motor hearses. Compulsory manual labor for all. All parks open to the public day and night. Electric dishscrubbers. Tuberculosis, lunacy, war and mendicancy must now cease. General amnesty, weekly carnival, with masked license, bonuses for all, esperanto the universal brotherhood. No more patriotism of barspongers and dropsical imposters. Free money, free love, and a free lay church in a free lay state.

>Leopold Bloom in
>JAMES JOYCE'S *Ulysses*

Jordon Pecile

A Piece of Polenta*

JUST BEFORE LEAVING ITALY at the end of a year on a Fulbright grant, I visited my father's family in a country village in the province of Udine. Except for a certain curiosity to see my father's birthplace, I had little desire to make the difficult journey from Florence. I had already postponed it twice during the year, following other Fulbright students to Cortina for the Christmas holidays and to Sicily for spring vacation instead. Only the knowledge that my father, were he alive, would be disappointed if I failed to visit his family when I was so near made me decide to go. In the end, the obligation which I felt to take the trip made it seem like a reluctant pilgrimage, reminding me of the ritual of carrying a basket of flowers with my mother to my father's grave in Wilkes-Barre every year on All Souls' Day.

I waited until the end of my courses at the university because with each additional month in Italy I gained a better grasp of the

* From STORIES FROM EPOCH, Baxter Hathaway, ed. (Cornell University Press, 1966). Reprinted by permission of Jordan Pecile.

language, and I didn't want to fumble awkwardly for words before my father's family. In that part of northeastern Italy, between Treviso and Gorizia, an ancient Latin dialect called Friulano is spoken. I had heard this dialect often as a child, when my father and his Friulian friends gathered around the wine bottle under our grapevine. Their coarse voices as they shouted about their work in the coal mines and about the old country drew me away from my games to watch and ridicule as they got drunk and fell asleep in the late afternoons under our arbor.

That arbor, leaning against the back porch and the kitchen windows, was my father's strongest tie to his boyhood home. He was proud of the twisting, dark vines which each year yielded the first bunches of ripe grapes in the neighborhood. Every October he would patiently try to teach me the art of making wine from the small, sour grapes. Pretending he needed my help to turn the wooden press, he would ask me to stay home from school to watch him; but I hated his damp, spidery wine cellar and the empty barrels smelling of ferment. Ashamed of my father's alien ways, I stubbornly resisted all his attempts to teach me to make wine or to speak Friulano.

Remembering how difficult it had always been to understand my father, I knew it would be necessary to speak at least a good grammatical Italian, if not Friulano, when I visited his brothers. By the end of a year of study which started slowly at the University for Foreigners in Perugia, I finally felt that I was fluent enough to carry on simple conversations with the family, and wrote them the date of my visit which had been so long delayed.

Since my father's village was only fourteen kilometers from the capital of the province, I felt sure that my uncles would be at the station in Udine to meet me when I arrived, and on the train I wondered if they still looked enough like my father to be recognized easily. Attilio and Tarcesio, the two brothers who had remained in Italy after my father emigrated, were both older than he. Through the years, they had written him several short letters, after such events as the death of his mother or the birth of another child. To every letter my father replied immediately with packages of clothing and generous gifts of money. Once, shortly after the war, he sent them a large family photograph. My brothers and I, elaborately groomed in bow ties and white shoes, were grouped around my father in the photographer's studio, against the pastel backdrop of a garden with a sprinkling fountain and swaying ferns. In order to be seen from behind her husband and three tall sons, my mother, tiny and buxom, had to stand on a box. In the photograph she looked massive, towering over our heads, but my father was pleased and the portrait was mailed.

In return, we received from Italy one of those sepia-tinted photographs which are printed like postcards, showing my father's two brothers standing together self-consciously in the center, each surrounded by his small family. Before Uncle Attilio, mustachioed and husky, sat a dark and fearless looking woman dressed in black; this was Aunt Firma, my father had explained, the handsome sister-in-law who was as strong as a rock and ruler of both households. In front of Uncle Tarcesio, an emaciated man with deep circles under his eyes, sat a frail woman clutching at a bulky, netted shawl; this was poor Aunt Clelia. There were only three children in the picture, two boys aged fourteen and ten, and a six-year-old girl. The older son, as tall and dark as I, was wearing a tweed sport coat which had once belonged to me. He was named Americo because he was born shortly after my father reached the United States, and the family hoped my father might send for him someday. A younger boy, Rino, stood stiffly at attention next to Americo; he was wearing my long-outgrown corduroy suit with knickers. Standing beside Aunt Clelia was the girl, Celesta, wide-eyed with wonder, dressed for her First Communion with a crown of flowers and a long veil over her thick, black hair. Rosary beads were entwined around her clasped, gloved hands, and white paper roses were strewn at her feet.

One son was missing from the postcard sent from Udine after the war. He was the oldest son, my father explained, and Nazi soldiers had taken him one day from his work in the wheat fields as a laborer for their salt mines; he never was located after that.

For years my father had hoped to return someday to see his brothers and his family home, but always there were more urgent uses for the small savings he could accumulate. When at one time he had saved almost enough for the round trip, my mother insisted that the money be used for my college education, and he postponed his visit without argument. Three years later he died, and the last of the letters from Italy was a painfully written response to my cable describing his death. My uncles expressed their own long-nurtured hope that they might have seen their brother once more; but since God had denied them this, they hoped that I, his first son, would be able to visit the family in his place.

It was dusk when the local from Mestre finally arrived in Udine, and I was tired from the long day's traveling and apprehensive about meeting my uncles. I had little taste for the emotional scene which was bound to take place in public on the station platform, so I delayed descending until the other passengers disappeared. Only a few got off, and the narrow platform was soon deserted as the train continued on to Trieste. Standing alone in the shadows, I wondered if my letter had been received, or if they weren't able to meet me after all. I started to carry my suitcase into the second-class waiting room when I remembered that in Italy it cost five lire for visitors to enter onto the boarding platforms, and no doubt my uncles would be waiting by the stiles. Turning, I carried my luggage down the stairs and through an underpass, following the *Uscita* signs to the station lobby.

Opposite the exit I saw them huddled together, eagerly scanning the faces of everyone passing through the gates from the trains. I should have known them in any place; they were wearing the same dark suits of the postcard photograph, and though different from my father in height and weight, had the same high forehead with its fine fringe of light hair, the same deep-set blue eyes and wrinkled, leathery skin stretched tightly across sallow cheeks. I felt them searching my face for some sign of recognition on my part, then looking at each other for reassurance before they rushed forward shouting, "Giordano!"

They grabbed me in a strong and tearful embrace. "*Che miracolo!*" they kept repeating. "What a miracle, to see poor Gildo's son at last!" I was given the demonstratively affectionate welcome which is so common in Italian stations and which I had nervously anticipated aboard the train. People passing through the lobby considerately gave wide berth to our family reunion, barely glancing at my emotional uncles who were alternately hugging and standing off to admire their nephew from America.

Embarrassed, I was relieved when at last Uncle Attilio picked up my suitcase and led me out of the lobby and across the street to a waiting car. "This is the taxi of Fagagna," he said, and proudly introduced me to the grinning, coarse old driver as "Gildo's boy, from the United States."

"Pontebabba, Guido," the driver said, thrusting out his hand. "Does he speak Friulano?" he asked my uncles.

"Why should he?" Uncle Tarcesio answered. "He speaks Italian better than we do, and he writes it too, don't you, Giordano?"

"Never mind, I speak American very good," Guido said in English, not listening. "I live in the States for ten years, in Pennsylvania," he informed me carefully.

"That's where he earned all the money to buy his taxi," Uncle Attilio commented, beckoning for me to sit in the little Fiat while he lifted my suitcase in the trunk.

"Yes, but at what a price!" said the driver, speaking rapidly in Italian again. "I caught this asthma in the coal mines in your country and came back to Fagagna a ruined man. Here, not even the doctors know what I have, although they charge me all they can get and won't admit anything. Your good father died from it, and so will I someday. I used to work next to your father for a long time," he said over his shoulder to me as he switched on the ignition, "until I got this asthma and decided to come home. Two thousand dollars I saved in America before I returned to Fagagna to buy my own piece of land and this car!"

"And now he thinks he's a Cavalier!" scoffed my uncle.

Uncle Tarcesio got in the car and interrupted the two old men. "Let's have an *aperitivo* together before we go back to Fagagna," he said. "We could go across the street to Cappo Rosso's."

"No," his brother said. "We must go back as we promised; they're waiting for us and Firma will have supper ready."

"What a shame, to come all the way to Udine and not celebrate an occasion such as this without even a glass of beer," Uncle Tarcesio said. "*Pazienza*, Giordano! We'll celebrate when we get home, and again tomorrow when we go around to all the houses in Fagagna to introduce you to the neighbors who are waiting to see you, especially those who have relatives in America. I hope you are as good a wine drinker as your poor father because we will have to drink to your health many times." He settled back then, smiling in anticipation.

Crowded into the narrow back seat with an uncle on each side, I watched the driver maneuver his car noisily across the piazza, honking the horn as if he were sounding ruffles and flourishes for some visiting hero. He swerved around the corners of winding side streets and soon entered the stream of bicycle traffic on the country roads. Lowering my head to look through the windshield, I saw in the distance, across the vine-clad plains of Friuli, the snow-capped Alpine foothills. Against the hazy blueness of this ridge, slender campaniles and tall, black cypresses stood in sharp silhouettes. In a cloud of dust we sped past whitewashed cottages with shuttered windows, occasionally passing the stone and tile country houses of the gentry. From quiet pasture lands, the road led upward, lined with mulberry orchards and long rows of grapevines. Women wrapped in black kerchiefs walked along the chalky road, and the boys in corduroy shorts and wooden shoes carried cans of milk hung from poles slung across their shoulders. Lights were being turned on in modern roadside canteens, and on each tiny farm there was a flurry of activity around the barn. The entire spring countryside, divided into innumerable square fields, looked as carefully landscaped and tended as the City Park in Wilkes-Barre, and an evening calm seemed to have settled over this small part of the world. I began to wonder, briefly, why I had hesitated so long before coming here.

When we finally entered the empty main piazza of Fagagna, it was too dark to see the village clearly. Uncle Attilio leaned across me and said, *"Ci siamo,* Giordano!" The little Fiat passed under an arch and jolted to a stop in a courtyard enclosed by an aged, stuccoed dwelling. Uncle Tarcesio called out to a little group gathered in the dim light of an open door. There was no movement; the family remained clustered together, waiting.

"Americo," called Uncle Attilio, "come and meet your cousin! Rino, take his suitcase. Hurry, for we are hungry!"

From the group emerged a tall broad-shouldered young man with a wide grin across his face. "Welcome, cousin," he said and threw his arms around me.

"Holy Mary, he arrived safely," cried an Aunt; then suddenly they surrounded me and kissed me, one by one, on both cheeks, to the immense enjoyment of my uncles, who moved aside to pay the driver.

"Come, don't eat him up! Take him inside, into the light so you can see him," laughed Uncle Attilio, and amid shouts of *"Ben venuto!*" I was ushered into a fragrant kitchen, where Uncle Attilio proudly presented the rest of the family. Americo was brought forward first for these formal introductions, since he was the oldest son and would be my special guide during the visit. He knew all the girls in the village and promised that I'd meet them after eleven o'clock Mass on Sunday. Because we were almost equal in height, both dark and about the same age, the women were quick to find a familial resemblance. My cousin, however, was more robust than I, and his right hand, when he extended it, was almost twice the size of mine, and his grip was twice as powerful.

Rino, Uncle Attilio's younger son, was introduced next; he was a stocky, bashful boy, who had just come in from the fields and was still wearing his cap and heavy work clothes. "*Ciao*, Giordano," he said in a deep voice, shaking hands and grinning self-consciously.

Then my uncle brought forward the women, first presenting his good wife Firma, who was afraid of nothing and did a man's work everyday. Behind her, brimming with excitement, was Aunt Clelia, who had been sickly ever since the Nazis had stolen her son. She was painfully frail and even on so warm a night was wrapped in a short, heavy shawl. Aunt Clelia put an arm round her daughter Celesta and gently pushed her forward, a pale, thin girl who curtsied with a shy smile.

Without further ceremony, Aunt Firma took charge. "*S'accomodi, Signore,*" she said. "The polenta is almost ready and supper will be on the table shortly, because I know you must be starving after such a long trip." She moved toward a massive wood-stove set in a brick alcove which must have been a fireplace at one time. The top was crowded with frying pans and kettles and a battered black coffeepot. Aunt Firma opened one of the stove lids and set a copper bucket down into the red hole. Aunt Clelia, hovering nervously behind her like a lady in waiting, handed her a short wooden pole, and she started stirring vigorously in circular motions.

"Go on," Aunt Firma said to her son. "Take him to wash up, and you, Rino, can carry his valise upstairs. Quickly!" she admonished, "The polenta will be ready any time now!"

I followed Americo into a small pantry which appeared to be all that separated the kitchen from the stable. Through a partly open door I caught a glimpse of several cows and heard their restless noises as they moved about in their stalls. The pantry was as cool and sweet-smelling as the kitchen, in spite of the animals next door. Pots of basil stood on the window sill and bunches of garlic and dried herbs hung from beams overhead, filling the small space with their combined aromas. Tall baskets of onions and a small barrel of black olives stood against the wall. I washed my hands and face at a high sink by ladling cold well water from buckets which stood, brimful, on a shelf next to the cement sink.

When we returned to the kitchen my uncles and Rino were sitting at a wooden table covered with oilcloth and set with heavy white dishes. Uncle Attilio at the head of the table indicated that I should sit on the bench at his left, my back against the whitewashed wall. Americo sat down next to me and filled my glass with wine. The uncles wanted to talk about my father, whom they called *"povero Gildo,"* making a heavy sign of the cross and bowing their heads everytime they mentioned his name. In detail they described the Mass for the Dead which they had requested in the Church of Fagagna after receiving my cable, naming, with some disagreement, all the people who had attended the Mass and all those who had sent flowers.

They had wanted so much to see my father again, but now they were happy enough to see his son, whom they had never even in their imaginations expected to meet. "Truly," said Aunt Firma, continuing to stir the polenta with her wooden stick, her sleeves rolled up to the elbows, "your mother must be a fine, big woman to have such a tall son." No one would believe that my mother was not the outsized woman she seemed, standing on a box behind my father in the family photograph. To decide the point, their leather album was brought out, wrapped in layers of newspaper, and I had to go over the names of my brothers and tell what each was doing now. They were eager to hear about our life in America; my father had always been so vague in his letters, they said, although of course they knew he was very successful and must have been very happy. I told them about his job as boss over six miners (*Che bravo!*), about the modern house he finally bought for us (*Che ricchezza!*), and then about his death from miner's asthma (*Che peccato!*).

We had no difficulty understanding each other; the family spoke a Venetian-accented Italian to me, lapsing into Friulano only to clarify certain meanings to one another. Americo was the arbiter in this, since he had gone to school longer and knew Italian better than any of the others.

"The polenta is ready," announced Aunt Firma finally, red-faced as she turned from the stove, carrying the heavy copper bucket to the center of the table and overturning it onto a well-scrubbed board covered with a clean cloth. A hissing cloud of steam escaped as the thick, bubbling cornmeal mixture slid down the sides of the bucket and lay quivering on the cloth in the cool air. Rising, Uncle Attilio took a silk thread from his wife and started to slice the drying cornmeal cake neatly in squares. It was a ritual I had seen my father perform at home on rare occasions like his birthday, when my mother let him make a polenta. For a moment the sight of my uncle neatly cutting the polenta with a piece of thread, and the steamy smell of the cornmeal, like Proust's tea-soaked morsel of madeleine, brought back a sudden rush of memories of our Wilkes-Barre kitchen, bright with enamel and stainless steel, and I remembered painfully how awkward my father had always felt around his own home, and how ashamed I was of his strange, alien habits.

Then for the first time I realized how lonely my father had always been and how successfully his growling had hidden his feelings from us. Neither his American-born wife nor his sons could offer companionship for him. But there was no need to wonder why he had left home to take his chances in another country. I looked down at the bare, trampled dirt floor of the kitchen and then at my cousin Americo leaning forward with his elbows on the table, watching his father cut the polenta, and I thought that there, but for my father's courage and the grace of God, would I be also.

When the polenta was cut and pieces were passed around, Aunt Clelia served deep bowls of black-bean soup which was thick and hot and had a pungent taste. To cool his soup, Uncle Attilio poured in some wine and passed the bottle to me, motioning for me to do likewise.

"We eat the polenta with our fingers, *Signore*," Aunt Clelia said, "but if you want to use a fork, go ahead. Do not be ashamed to eat as you like and as much as you want."

"No, no," I said quickly, and picked up the polenta with my hands and dipped it in the soup.

The bean soup was followed by platters of homemade salami and *prosciutto*, thinly sliced, and bowls of a regional white cheese which we ate with more polenta and ripe tomatoes in oil and oregano. The wine bottle was passed around until it was emptied, and then Uncle Tarcesio disappeared to fill it up again. There was little conversation during the meal; everyone was concentrating on his food, and I sensed that they were all trying to eat as noiselessly as possible, in deference to the stranger at their table. When finally Aunt Clelia served strong coffee in small cups, I was so dazed by the food and wine that I was almost asleep.

The climax of the meal came after the dishes were cleared away, when Aunt Firma, followed by Aunt Clelia, carried in a long, flat cake which was placed ceremoniously in the center of the table. The cake was a baroque creation ornate with scrolls and flowers in white and pink icings and smelling sweetly of rum. Across the top, in elaborate script, were the words, "*Ben venuto,* Giordano."

Not to be outdone by his wife, Uncle Attilio went outside to some inexhaustible wine cellar, returning with another bottle, corked and covered with dust, saved for just such a celebration. It was a bottle of *Piccolit,* the sweet dessert wine of Friuli, he said, filling small glasses on a tray.

When we had all been served with cake and wine, Uncle Attilio slowly lighted his pipe and rose from his seat at the head of the table. "*Salute,* Giordano," he said, lifting his glass toward me. "I never expected to see you in this house, and I still can't believe that you came all the way from America and are taking your father's place at our table! When your father left here almost thirty years ago, he was as old as you are now. How our mother cried that day! I wanted your father to wait until after Americo was born, but Firma herself urged him to go while he had the chance. Now we are glad that he went, and very proud that you came so far to visit us."

Amidst cheers and applause, Uncle Attilio sat down and the family lifted their glasses and drank. Then I too got up, with my head already spinning from the wine and the food, and began another toast while Uncle Tarcesio hastily refilled the empty wine glasses. Unsteadily and rather rhetorically, I said something about my father always hoping to return to die in the house where he was born. It must have been harder for him to leave this house than any of us would ever realize, I told them, for he never found anything in America to take its place. Some plants transplanted grow stronger, I said, while others whose roots are torn in the movement might grow poorly for a while, but will wither and die before their time. A matter of roots. Then I thought I had better sit down, for I was getting too maudlin. Was it the wine, I wondered, or was it for oratorical effect that I chose those words, simply to show off my fluent Italian? Sober, I could handle words, but now the soft Italian phrases were managing me, and their effect on the family supper was devastating. Aunt Clelia made a swift sign of the cross and kissed her hand toward heaven. Twisting the corners of her apron, Aunt Firma bowed her head, nodding, "*E vero, é vero!*" Sudden tears appeared in my uncles' eyes, and I felt I had better finish and sit down.

No cheers and no applause greeted my speech. Under the cloud of emotion, we drained our glasses of wine and then the aunts and Celesta started to clear the table.

The stairway to the bedrooms was outside, so Americo lighted a candle and led the way, pointing to the outhouse as we climbed the steps and telling me I had better go since it got very cold during the night. I took the candle and walked across the courtyard to the convenience, which was a narrow wooden shelter perched at the edge of one of the slopes descending gently behind the house and carefully cultivated with vines crawling along low trellises.

Later, I undressed by candlelight in the cold bedroom, clean and bare except for a huge double bed with a chest as its foot and a china pitcher and basin on an iron stand in one corner. Over the bed was a picture of the Madonna pointing to her bleeding heart, and the dried palms of some past Easter were draped around the black frame. My suitcase had been opened and placed on the chest.

"Put your shoes outside the door and Rino will polish them for you in the morning," Americo said, "and if you will fold your clothes and leave them by the door, my mother will take them early in the morning and press them for you before you wake up."

I placed my clothes on top of his by the door, then climbed into bed. Americo blew out the candle. In the darkness, he lifted himself on an elbow and whispered, "I hope to reach the United States someday soon, Giordano. All my life I have been waiting to go to your country. My parents wish it as well; they have always wanted me to follow your father and live in America. But it's hard to get into the States now. After the War I registered with the American consulate in Genoa for a visa under the emigration quota, and I have been waiting ever since because the quota for my category is always full.

"Here life is hard, Giordano," my cousin continued. "There is nothing to look forward to except continuing to work in the half-profits fields which my father and Rino cultivate. I want to go to America and make enough to help my father buy some land for himself before he is too old. All my papers are ready; I need only the visa. I know that there are many jobs for Italians in America. I'd like to live in your house."

I waited for him to continue, but he had stopped talking. I lay in the high, hard bed looking out through the unshuttered window at the sky. I heard the steps creak as my uncle and his wife passed our door on their way to bed. A door was slammed on the other side of the house, where Uncle Tarcesio slept with his family. From down below came the occasional rustling sounds of the cows next to the kitchen. In the darkness, I wondered how it must have been for my father, night after night, dreaming the same things Americo had just described. Then I sensed how he must have felt in America, not victorious as his brothers thought, but so defeated he couldn't even complain.

Finally, I got up. I walked across the cold, unpainted floor to the window and looked down into the courtyard enclosed by the ancient, crumbling house. In the moonlight, I could see the shape of an empty wine barrel rolled against the wall. Now, when it was no longer possible, I wanted to go back and sit with my father under his grapevine and talk with him in his language; I wanted to help him make wine and tell him that I had seen his family home and understood his foreign ways.

Turning from the window, I walked noiselessly back to bed. "Stay," I said. "Stay here, Americo." But my cousin was already asleep.

Jordon Pecile wrote the following comment on his story in response to the editors' request:

"A Piece of Polenta" was written on board ship coming home from Italy; it was thrift season and steerage was crowded with glassy-eyed emigrants and returning Italian-Americans—greenhorns, they used to be called. I started with the urge to say something, articulate for them, make some kind of noise, but I soon found that my notes were severely limited by what I knew, by my own limited experience. Maybe most of us start this way and hope to draw general truth out of personal experience, but I think now that in slipping into thinly veiled autobiographical narrative I escaped—or avoided—most of the real problems of writing fiction. In this sense, however, my struggle with the narrative materials of "Polenta" was never so much to give them form as to discover their meaning. The materials suggested their own form, the form of a journey at once forward in time and backward to the source; I had to figure out why the journey had troubled me so, why I should want to trouble anyone else with it, and how it might be made to represent the common experience of all those forlorn faces lining the rails around me.

Soon after I finished the piece (I'm not sure it qualifies for the generic term of story), I tried it out, in my innocence, on the *New Yorker*. It was returned with a letter by one of their lady-editors saying that they had liked it well-enough, and they believed it all right ("the terms are all true"), but that the piece failed for them because "it does not extend the reader's experience." The criticism has rankled through these years, because if the lady was right I had indeed failed, for she had touched on the genesis and the goal of my work. At any rate, it has never been possible for me to judge the accuracy of her criticism and what I should like to do is pass it on and submit it to the ultimate test of the present reader.

Anton Chekhov

Rothschild's Fiddle*

THE TOWN WAS A LITTLE ONE, worse than a village, and it was inhabited by scarcely any but old people who died with an infrequency that was really annoying. In the hospital and in the prison fortress very few coffins were needed. In fact business was bad. If Yakov Ivanov had been an undertaker in the chief town of the province he would certainly have had a house of his own, and people would have addressed him as Yakov Matveyitch; here in this wretched little town people called him simply Yakov; his nickname in the street was for some reason Bronze, and he lived in a poor way like a humble peasant, in a little old hut in which there was only one room, and in this room he and Marfa, the stove, a double bed, the coffins, his bench, and all their belongings were crowded together.

Yakov made good, solid coffins. For peasants and working peo-

* Reprinted with permission of The Macmillan Company from THE CHORUS GIRL AND OTHER STORIES by Anton Chekhov, translated by Constance Garnett. Copyright 1920 by The Macmillan Company, renewed 1948 by David Garnett.

ple he made them to fit himself, and this was never unsuccessful, for there were none taller and stronger than he, even in the prison, though he was seventy. For gentry and for women he made them to measure, and used an iron foot-rule for the purpose. He was very unwilling to take orders for children's coffins, and made them straight off without measurements, contemptuously, and when he was paid for the work he always said:

"I must confess I don't like trumpery jobs."

Apart from his trade, playing the fiddle brought him in a small income.

The Jews' orchestra conducted by Moisey Ilyitch Shahkes, the tinsmith, who took more than half their receipts for himself, played as a rule at weddings in the town. As Yakov played very well on the fiddle, especially Russian songs, Shahkes sometimes invited him to join the orchestra at a fee of half a rouble a day, in addition to tips from the visitors. When Bronze sat in the orchestra first of all his face became crimson and perspiring; it was hot, there was a suffocating smell of garlic, the fiddle squeaked, the double bass wheezed close to his right ear, while the flute wailed at his left, played by a gaunt, red-haired Jew who had a perfect network of red and blue veins all over his face, and who bore the name of the famous millionaire Rothschild. And this accursed Jew contrived to play even the liveliest things plaintively. For no apparent reason Yakov little by little became possessed by hatred and contempt for the Jews, and especially for Rothschild; he began to pick quarrels with him, rail at him in unseemly language and once even tried to strike him, and Rothschild was offended and said, looking at him ferociously:

"If it were not that I respect you for your talent, I would have sent you flying out of the window."

Then he began to weep. And because of this Yakov was not often asked to play in the orchestra; he was only sent for in case of extreme necessity in the absence of one of the Jews.

Yakov was never in a good temper, as he was continually having to put up with terrible losses. For instance, it was a sin to work on Sundays or Saints' days, and Monday was an unlucky day, so that in the course of the year there were some two hundred days on which, whether he liked it or not, he had to sit with his hands folded. And only think, what a loss that meant. If anyone in the town had a wedding without music, or if Shahkes did not send for Yakov, that was a loss, too. The superintendent of the prison was ill for two years and was wasting away, and Yakov was impatiently waiting for him to die, but the superintendent went away to the chief town of the province to be doctored, and there took and died. There's a loss for you, ten roubles at least, as there would have been an expensive coffin to make, lined with brocade. The thought of his losses haunted Yakov, especially at night; he laid his fiddle on the bed beside him, and when all sorts of nonsensical ideas came into his mind he touched a string; the fiddle gave out a sound in the darkness, and he felt better.

On the sixth of May of the previous year Marfa had suddenly been taken ill. The old woman's breathing was laboured, she drank a great deal of water, and she staggered as she walked, yet she lighted the stove in the morning and even went herself to get water. Towards evening she lay down. Yakov played his fiddle all day; when it was quite dark he took the book in which he used every day to put down his losses, and, feeling dull, he began adding up the total for the year. It came to more than a thousand roubles. This so agitated him that he flung the reckoning beads down, and trampled them under his feet. Then he picked up the reckoning beads, and again spent a long time clicking with them and heaving deep, strained sighs. His face was crimson and wet with perspiration. He thought that if he had put that lost thousand roubles in the bank, the interest for a year would have been at least forty roubles, so that forty roubles was a loss too. In fact, wherever one turned there were losses and nothing else.

"Yakov!" Marfa called unexpectedly. "I am dying."

He looked round at his wife. Her face was rosy with fever, unusually bright and joyful-looking. Bronze, accustomed to seeing her face always pale, timid, and unhappy-looking, was bewildered. It looked as if she really were dying and were glad that she was going away for ever from that hut, from the coffins, and from Yakov. . . . And she gazed at the ceiling and moved her lips, and her expression was one of happiness, as though she saw death as her deliverer and were whispering with him.

It was daybreak; from the windows one could see the flush of dawn. Looking at the old woman, Yakov for some reason reflected that he had not once in his life been affectionate to her, had had no feeling for her, had never once thought to buy her a kerchief, or to bring her home some dainty from a wedding, but had done nothing but shout at her, scold her for his losses, shake his fists at her; it is true he had never actually beaten her, but he had frightened her, and at such times she had always been numb with terror. Why, he had forbidden her to drink tea because they spent too much without that, and she drank only hot water. And he understood why she had such a strange, joyful face now, and he was overcome with dread.

As soon as it was morning he borrowed a horse from a neighbour and took Marfa to the hospital. There were not many patients there, and so he had not long to wait, only three hours. To his great satisfaction the patients were not being received by the doctor, who was himself ill, but by the assistant, Maxim Nikolaitch, an old man of whom everyone in the town used to say that, though he drank and was quarrelsome, he knew more than the doctor.

"I wish you good-day," said Yakov, leading his old woman into the consulting room. "You must excuse us, Maxim Nikolaitch, we are always troubling you with our trumpery affairs. Here you see my better half is ailing, the partner of my life, as they say, excuse the expression. . . ."

Knitting his grizzled brows and stroking his whiskers the assistant began to examine the old woman, and she sat on a stool, a wasted, bent figure with a sharp nose and open mouth, looking like a bird that wants to drink.

"H——m . . . Ah! . . ." the assistant said slowly, and he heaved a sigh. "Influenza and possibly fever. There's typhus in the town now. Well, the old woman has lived her life, thank God. . . . How old is she?"

"She'll be seventy in another year, Maxim Nikolaitch."

"Well, the old woman has lived her life, it's time to say goodbye."

"You are quite right in what you say, of course, Maxim Nikolaitch," said Yakov, smiling from politeness, "and we thank you feelingly for your kindness, but allow me to say every insect wants to live."

"To be sure," said the assistant, in a tone which suggested that it depended upon him whether the woman lived or died. "Well, then, my good fellow, put a cold compress on her head, and give her these powders twice a day, and so good-bye. Bonjour."

From the expression of his face Yakov saw that it was a bad

case, and that no sort of powders would be any help; it was clear to him that Marfa would die very soon, if not to-day, to-morrow. He nudged the assistant's elbow, winked at him, and said in a low voice:

"If you would just cup her, Maxim Nikolaitch."

"I have no time, I have no time, my good fellow. Take your old woman and go in God's name. Good-bye."

"Be so gracious," Yakov besought him. "You know yourself that if, let us say, it were her stomach or her inside that were bad, then powders or drops, but you see she had got a chill! In a chill the first thing is to let blood, Maxim Nikolaitch."

But the assistant had already sent for the next patient, and a peasant woman came into the consulting room with a boy.

"Go along, go along," he said to Yakov, frowning. "It's no use to——"

"In that case put on leeches, anyway! Make us pray for you for ever."

The assistant flew into a rage and shouted:

"You speak to me again! You blockhead. . . ."

Yakov flew into a rage too, and he turned crimson all over, but he did not utter a word. He took Marfa on his arm and led her out of the room. Only when they were sitting in the cart he looked morosely and ironically at the hospital, and said:

"A nice set of artists they have settled here! No fear, but he would have cupped a rich man, but even a leech he grudges to the poor. The Herods!"

When they got home and went into the hut, Marfa stood for ten minutes holding on to the stove. It seemed to her that if she were to lie down Yakov would talk to her about his losses, and scold her for lying down and not wanting to work. Yakov looked at her drearily and thought that to-morrow was St. John the Divine's, and next day St. Nikolay the Wonder-worker's, and the day after that was Sunday, and then Monday, an unlucky day. For four days he would not be able to work, and most likely Marfa would die on one of those days; so he would have to make the coffin to-day. He picked up his iron rule, went up to the old woman and took her measure. Then she lay down, and he crossed himself and began making the coffin.

When the coffin was finished Bronze put on his spectacles and wrote in his book: "Marfa Ivanov's coffin, two roubles, forty kopecks."

And he heaved a sigh. The old woman lay all the time silent with her eyes closed. But in the evening, when it got dark, she suddenly called the old man.

"Do you remember, Yakov," she asked, looking at him joyfully. "Do you remember fifty years ago God gave us a little baby with flaxen hair? We used always to be sitting by the river then, singing songs . . . under the willows," and laughing bitterly, she added: "The baby girl died."

Yakov racked his memory, but could not remember the baby or the willows.

"It's your fancy," he said.

The priest arrived; he administered the sacrament and extreme unction. Then Marfa began muttering something unintelligible, and towards morning she died. Old women, neighbours, washed her, dressed her, and laid her in the coffin. To avoid paying the sacristan, Yakov read the psalms over the body himself, and they got nothing out of him for the grave, as the grave-digger was a crony of his. Four peasants carried the coffin to the graveyard, not for money, but from respect. The coffin was followed by old women, beggars, and a couple of crazy saints, and the people who met it crossed themselves piously. . . . And Yakov was very much pleased that it was so creditable, so decorous, and so cheap, and no offence to anyone. As he took his last leave of Marfa he touched the coffin and thought: "A good piece of work!"

But as he was going back from the cemetery he was overcome by acute depression. He didn't feel quite well: his breathing was laboured and feverish, his legs felt weak, and he had a craving for drink. And thoughts of all sorts forced themselves on his mind. He remembered again that all his life he had never felt for Marfa, had never been affectionate to her. The fifty-two years they had lived in the same hut had dragged on a long, long time, but it had somehow happened that in all that time he had never once thought of her, had paid no attention to her, as though she had been a cat or a dog. And yet, every day, she had lighted the stove, had cooked and baked, had gone for the water, had chopped the wood, had slept with him in the same bed, and when he came home drunk from the weddings always reverently hung his fiddle on the wall and put him to bed, and all this in silence, with a timid, anxious expression.

Rothschild, smiling and bowing, came to meet Yakov.

"I was looking for you, uncle," he said. "Moisey Ilyitch sends you his greetings and bids you come to him at once."

Yakov felt in no mood for this. He wanted to cry.

"Leave me alone," he said, and walked on.

"How can you," Rothschild said, fluttered, running on in front. "Moisey Ilyitch will be offended! He bade you come at once!"

Yakov was revolted at the Jew's gasping for breath and blinking, and having so many red freckles on his face. And it was disgusting to look at his green coat with black patches on it, and all his fragile, refined figure.

"Why are you pestering me, garlic?" shouted Yakov. "Don't persist!"

The Jew got angry and shouted too:

"Not so noisy, please, or I'll send you flying over the fence!"

"Get out of my sight!" roared Yakov, and rushed at him with his fists. "One can't live for you scabby Jews!"

Rothschild, half dead with terror, crouched down and waved his hands over his head, as though to ward off a blow; then he leapt up and ran away as fast as his legs could carry him: as he ran he gave little skips and kept clasping his hands, and Yakov could see how his long thin spine wriggled. Some boys, delighted at the incident, ran after him shouting "Jew! Jew!" Some dogs joined in the chase barking. Someone burst into a roar of laughter, then gave a whistle; the dogs barked with even more noise and unanimity. Then a dog must have bitten Rothschild, as a desperate, sickly scream was heard.

Yakov went for a walk on the grazing ground, then wandered on at random in the outskirts of the town, while the street boys shouted:

"Here's Bronze! Here's Bronze!"

He came to the river, where the curlews floated in the air uttering shrill cries and the ducks quacked. The sun was blazing hot, and there was a glitter from the water, so that it hurt the eyes to look at it. Yakov walked by a path along the bank and saw a plump, rosy-cheeked lady come out of the bathing-shed, and thought about her: "Ugh! you otter!"

Not far from the bathing-shed boys were catching crayfish with bits of meat; seeing him, they began shouting spitefully, "Bronze!

Bronze!" And then he saw an old spreading willow-tree with a big hollow in it, and a crow's nest on it. . . . And suddenly there rose up vividly in Yakov's memory a baby with flaxen hair, and the willow-tree Marfa had spoken of. Why, that is it, the same willow-tree—green, still, and sorrowful. . . . How old it has grown, poor thing!

He sat down under it and began to recall the past. On the other bank, where now there was the water meadow, in those days there stood a big birch-wood, and yonder on the bare hillside that could be seen on the horizon an old, old pine forest used to be a bluish patch in the distance. Big boats used to sail on the river. But now it was all smooth and unruffled, and on the other bank there stood now only one birch-tree, youthful and slender like a young lady, and there was nothing on the river but ducks and geese, and it didn't look as though there had ever been boats on it. It seemed as though even the geese were fewer than of old. Yakov shut his eyes, and in his imagination huge flocks of white geese soared, meeting one another.

He wondered how it had happened that for the last forty or fifty years of his life he had never once been to the river, or if he had been by it he had not paid attention to it. Why, it was a decent sized river, not a trumpery one; he might have gone in for fishing and sold the fish to merchants, officials, and the bar-keeper at the station, and then have put money in the bank; he might have sailed in a boat from one house to another, playing the fiddle, and people of all classes would have paid to hear him; he might have tried getting big boats afloat again—that would be better than making coffins; he might have bred geese, killed them and sent them in the winter to Moscow. Why, the feathers alone would very likely mount up to ten roubles in the year. But he had wasted his time, he had done nothing of this. What losses! Ah! What losses! And if he had gone in for all those things at once—catching fish and playing the fiddle, and running boats and killing geese—what a fortune he would have made! But nothing of this had happened, even in his dreams; life had passed uselessly without any pleasure, had been wasted for nothing, not even a pinch of snuff; there was nothing left in front, and if one looked back—there was nothing there but losses, and such terrible ones, it made one cold all over. And why was it a man could not live so as to avoid these losses and misfortunes? One wondered why they had cut down the birch copse and the pine forest. Why was he walking with no reason on the grazing ground? Why do people always do what isn't needful? Why had Yakov all his life scolded, bellowed, shaken his fists, ill-treated his wife, and, one might ask, what necessity was there for him to frighten and insult the Jew that day? Why did people in general hinder each other from living? What losses were due to it! what terrible losses! If it were not for hatred and malice people would get immense benefit from one another.

In the evening and the night he had visions of the baby, of the willow, of fish, of slaughtered geese, and Marfa looking in profile like a bird that wants to drink, and the pale, pitiful face of Rothschild, and faces moved down from all sides and muttered of losses. He tossed from side to side, and got out of bed five times to play the fiddle.

In the morning he got up with an effort and went to the hospital. The same Maxim Nikolaitch told him to put a cold compress on his head, and gave him some powders, and from his tone and expression of face Yakov realized that it was a bad case and that no powders would be any use. As he went home afterwards, he reflected that death would be nothing but a benefit; he would not have to eat or drink, or pay taxes or offend people, and, as a man lies in his grave not for one year but for hundreds and thousands, if one reckoned it up the gain would be enormous. A man's life meant loss: death meant gain. This reflection was, of course, a just one, but yet it was bitter and mortifying; why was the order of the world so strange, that life, which is given to man only once, passes away without benefit?

He was not sorry to die, but at home, as soon as he saw his fiddle, it sent a pang to his heart and he felt sorry. He could not take the fiddle with him to the grave, and now it would be left forlorn, and the same thing would happen to it as to the birch copse and the pine forest. Everything in this world was wasted and would be wasted! Yakov went out of the hut and sat in the doorway, pressing the fiddle to his bosom. Thinking of his wasted, profitless life, he began to play, he did not know what, but it was plaintive and touching, and tears trickled down his cheeks. And the harder he thought, the more mournfully the fiddle wailed.

The latch clicked once and again, and Rothschild appeared at the gate. He walked across half the yard boldly, but seeing Yakov he stopped short, and seemed to shrink together, and probably from terror, began making signs with his hands as though he wanted to show on his fingers what o'clock it was.

"Come along, it's all right," said Yakov in a friendly tone, and he beckoned him to come up. "Come along!"

Looking at him mistrustfully and apprehensively, Rothschild began to advance, and stopped seven feet off.

"Be so good as not to beat me," he said, ducking. "Moisey Ilyitch has sent me again. 'Don't be afraid,' he said; 'go to Yakov again and tell him,' he said, 'we can't get on without him.' There is a wedding on Wednesday. . . . Ye—es! Mr. Shapovalov is marrying his daughter to a good man. . . . And it will be a grand wedding, oo-oo!" added the Jew, screwing up one eye.

"I can't come," said Yakov, breathing hard. "I'm ill, brother."

And he began playing again, and the tears gushed from his eyes on to the fiddle. Rothschild listened attentively, standing sideways to him and folding his arms on his chest. The scared and perplexed expression on his face, little by little, changed to a look of woe and suffering; he rolled his eyes as though he were experiencing an agonizing ecstasy, and articulated, "Vachhh!" and tears slowly ran down his cheeks and trickled on his greenish coat.

And Yakov lay in bed all the rest of the day grieving. In the evening, when the priest confessing him asked, Did he remember any special sin he had committed? straining his failing memory he thought again of Marfa's unhappy face, and the despairing shriek of the Jew when the dog bit him, and said, hardly audibly, "Give the fiddle to Rothschild."

"Very well," answered the priest.

And now everyone in the town asks where Rothschild got such a fine fiddle. Did he buy it or steal it? Or perhaps it had come to him as a pledge. He gave up the flute long ago, and now plays nothing but the fiddle. As plaintive sounds flow now from his bow, as came once from his flute, but when he tries to repeat what Yakov played, sitting in the doorway, the effect is something so sad and sorrowful that his audience weep, and he himself rolls his eyes and articulates "Vachhh! . . ." And this new air was so much liked in the town that the merchants and officials used to be continually sending for Rothschild and making him play it over and over again a dozen times.

Ryunosuke Akutagawa

In a Grove*

THE TESTIMONY OF A WOODCUTTER QUESTIONED BY A HIGH POLICE COMMISSIONER

YES, SIR. Certainly, it was I who found the body. This morning, as usual, I went to cut my daily quota of cedars, when I found the body in a grove in a hollow in the mountains. The exact location? About 150 meters off the Yamashina stage road. It's an out-of-the-way grove of bamboo and cedars.

The body was lying flat on its back dressed in a bluish silk kimono and a wrinkled head-dress of the Kyoto style. A single sword-stroke had pierced the breast. The fallen bamboo-blades around it were stained with bloody blossoms. No, the blood was no longer running. The wound had dried up, I believe. And also, a gad-fly was stuck fast there, hardly noticing my footsteps.

You ask me if I saw a sword or any such thing?

---

* From RASHOMON AND OTHER STORIES, by Ryunosuke Akutagawa. By permission of Liveright, Publishers, N.Y. Copyright 1952 by Liveright Publishing Corp.

No, nothing, sir. I found only a rope at the root of a cedar near by. And . . . well, in addition to a rope, I found a comb. That was all. Apparently he must have made a battle of it before he was murdered, because the grass and fallen bamboo-blades had been trampled down all around.

"A horse was near by?"

No, sir. It's hard enough for a man to enter, let alone a horse.

THE TESTIMONY OF A TRAVELING BUDDHIST PRIEST QUESTIONED BY A HIGH POLICE COMMISSIONER

The time? Certainly, it was about noon yesterday, sir. The unfortunate man was on the road from Sekiyama to Yamashina. He was walking toward Sekiyama with a woman accompanying him on horseback, who I have since learned was his wife. A scarf hanging from her head hid her face from view. All I saw was the color of her clothes, a lilac-colored suit. Her horse was a sorrel with a fine mane. The lady's height? Oh, about four feet five inches. Since I am a Buddhist priest, I took little notice about her details. Well, the man was armed with a sword as well as a bow and arrows. And I remember that he carried some twenty odd arrows in his quiver.

Little did I expect that he would meet such a fate. Truly human life is as evanescent as the morning dew or a flash of lightning. My words are inadequate to express my sympathy for him.

THE TESTIMONY OF A POLICEMAN QUESTIONED BY A HIGH POLICE COMMISSIONER

The man that I arrested? He is a notorious brigand called Tajomaru. When I arrested him, he had fallen off his horse. He was groaning on the bridge at Awataguchi. The time? It was in the early hours of last night. For the record, I might say that the other day I tried to arrest him, but unfortunately he escaped. He was wearing a dark blue silk kimono and a large plain sword. And, as you see, he got a bow and arrows somewhere. You say that this bow and these arrows look like the ones owned by the dead man? Then Tajomaru must be the murderer. The bow wound with leather strips, the black lacquered quiver, the seventeen arrows with hawk feathers—these were all in his possession I believe. Yes, sir, the horse is, as you say, a sorrel with a fine mane. A little beyond the stone bridge I found the horse grazing by the roadside, with his long rein dangling. Surely there is some providence in his having been thrown by the horse.

Of all the robbers prowling around Kyoto, this Tajomaru has given the most grief to the women in town. Last autumn a wife who came to the mountain back of the Pindora of the Toribe Temple, presumably to pay a visit, was murdered, along with a girl. It has been suspected that it was his doing. If this criminal murdered the man, you cannot tell what he may have done with the man's wife. May it please your honor to look into this problem as well.

THE TESTIMONY OF AN OLD WOMAN QUESTIONED BY A HIGH POLICE COMMISSIONER

Yes, sir, that corpse is the man who married my daughter. He does not come from Kyoto. He was a samurai in the town of Kokufu in the province of Wakasa. His name was Kanazawa no Takehiko, and his age was twenty-six. He was of a gentle disposition, so I am sure he did nothing to provoke the anger of others.

My daughter? Her name is Masago, and her age is nineteen. She is a spirited, fun-loving girl, but I am sure she has never known any man except Takehiko. She has a small, oval, dark-complected face with a mole at the corner of her left eye.

Yesterday Takehiko left for Wakasa with my daughter. What bad luck it is that things should have come to such a sad end! What has become of my daughter? I am resigned to giving up my son-in-law as lost, but the fate of my daughter worries me sick. For heaven's sake leave no stone unturned to find her. I hate that robber Tajomaru, or whatever his name is. Not only my son-in-law, but my daughter . . . (Her later words were drowned in tears.)

TAJOMARU'S CONFESSION

I killed him, but not her. Where's she gone? I can't tell. Oh, wait a minute. No torture can make me confess what I don't know. Now things have come to such a head, I won't keep anything from you.

Yesterday a little past noon I met that couple. Just then a puff of wind blew, and raised her hanging scarf, so that I caught a glimpse of her face. Instantly it was again covered from my view. That may have been one reason; she looked like a Bodhisattva. At that moment I made up my mind to capture her even if I had to kill her man.

Why? To me killing isn't a matter of such great consequence as you might think. When a woman is captured, her man has to be killed anyway. In killing, I use the sword I wear at my side. Am I the only one who kills people? You, you don't use your swords. You kill people with your power, with your money. Sometimes you kill them on the pretext of working for their good. It's true they don't bleed. They are in the best of health, but all the same you've killed them. It's hard to say who is a greater sinner, you or me. (An ironical smile.)

But it would be good if I could capture a woman without killing her man. So, I made up my mind to capture her, and do my best not to kill him. But it's out of the question on the Yamashina stage road. So I managed to lure the couple into the mountains.

It was quite easy. I became their traveling companion, and I told them there was an old mound in the mountain over there, and that I had dug it open and found many mirrors and swords. I went on to tell them I'd buried the things in a grove behind the mountain, and that I'd like to sell them at a low price to anyone who would care to have them. Then . . . you see, isn't greed terrible? He was beginning to be moved by my talk before he knew it. In less than half an hour they were driving their horse toward the mountain with me.

When he came in front of the grove, I told them that the treasures were buried in it, and I asked them to come and see. The man had no objection—he was blinded by greed. The woman said she would wait on horseback. It was natural for her to say so, at the sight of a thick grove. To tell you the truth, my plan worked just as I wished, so I went into the grove with him, leaving her behind alone.

The grove is only bamboo for some distance. About fifty yards ahead there's a rather open clump of cedars. It was a convenient spot for my purpose. Pushing my way through the grove, I told him a plausible lie that the treasures were buried under the cedars. When I told him this, he pushed his laborious way toward the slender cedar visible through the grove. After a while the bamboo thinned out, and we came to where a number of cedars grew in a row. As soon as we got there, I seized him from behind. Because he was a trained, sword-bearing warrior, he was quite strong, but he was taken by surprise, so there was no help for him. I soon tied him up to the root of a cedar. Where did I get a rope? Thank heaven, being a robber, I had a rope with me, since I might have to scale a wall at any moment. Of course it was easy to stop him from calling out by gagging his mouth with fallen bamboo leaves.

When I disposed of him, I went to his woman and asked her to come and see him, because he seemed to have been suddenly taken sick. It's needless to say that this plan also worked well. The woman, her sedge hat off, came into the depths of the grove, where I led her by the hand. The instant she caught sight of her husband, she drew a small sword. I've never seen a woman of such violent temper. If I'd been off guard, I'd have got a thrust in my side. I dodged, but she kept on slashing at me. She might have wounded me deeply or killed me. But I'm Tajomaru. I managed to strike down her small sword without drawing my own. The most spirited woman is defenseless without a weapon. At last I could satisfy my desire for her without taking her husband's life.

Yes, . . . without taking his life. I had no wish to kill him. I was about to run away from the grove, leaving the woman behind in tears, when she frantically clung to my arm. In broken fragments of words, she asked that either her husband or I die. She said it was more trying than death to have her shame known to two men. She gasped out that she wanted to be the wife of whichever survived. Then a furious desire to kill him seized me. (Gloomy excitement.)

Telling you in this way, no doubt I seem a crueler man than you. But that's because you didn't see her face. Especially her burning eyes at that moment. As I saw her eye to eye, I wanted to make her my wife even if I were to be struck by lightning. I wanted to make her my wife . . . this single desire filled my mind. This was not only lust, as you might think. At that time if I'd had no other desire than lust, I'd surely not have minded knocking her down and running away. Then I wouldn't have stained my sword with his blood. But the moment I gazed at her face in the dark grove, I decided not to leave there without killing him.

But I didn't like to resort to unfair means to kill him. I untied him and told him to cross swords with me. (The rope that was found at the root of the cedar is the rope I dropped at the time.) Furious with anger, he drew his thick sword. And quick as thought, he sprang at me ferociously, without speaking a word. I needn't tell you how our fight turned out. The twenty-third stroke . . . please remember this. I'm impressed with this fact still. Nobody under the sun has ever clashed swords with me twenty strokes. (A cheerful smile.)

When he fell, I turned toward her, lowering my blood-stained sword. But to my great astonishment she was gone. I wondered to where she had run away. I looked for her in the clump of cedars. I listened, but heard only a groaning sound from the throat of the dying man.

As soon as we started to cross swords, she may have run away through the grove to call for help. When I thought of that, I decided it was a matter of life and death to me. So, robbing him of his sword, and bow and arrows, I ran out to the mountain road. There I found her horse still grazing quietly. It would be a mere waste of words to tell you the later details, but before I entered town I had already parted with the sword. That's all my confession. I know that my head will be hung in chains anyway, so put me down for the maximum penalty. (A defiant attitude.)

THE CONFESSION OF A WOMAN WHO HAS COME TO THE *SHIMIZU* TEMPLE

That man in the blue silk kimono, after forcing me to yield to him, laughed mockingly as he looked at my bound husband. How horrified my husband must have been! But no matter how hard he struggled in agony, the rope cut into him all the more tightly. In spite of myself I ran stumblingly toward his side. Or rather I tried to run toward him, but the man instantly knocked me down. Just at that moment I saw an indescribable light in my husband's eyes. Something beyond expression . . . his eyes make me shudder even now. That instantaneous look of my husband, who couldn't speak a word, told me all his heart. The flash in his eyes was neither anger nor sorrow . . . only a cold light, a look of loathing. More struck by the look in his eyes than by the blow of the thief, I called out in spite of myself and fell unconscious.

In the course of time I came to, and found that the man in blue silk was gone. I saw only my husband still bound to the root of the cedar. I raised myself from the bamboo-blades with difficulty, and looked into his face; but the expression in his eyes was just the same as before.

Beneath the cold contempt in his eyes, there was hatred. Shame, grief, and anger . . . I don't know how to express my heart at that time. Reeling to my feet, I went up to my husband.

"Takehiko," I said to him, "since things have come to this pass, I cannot live with you. I'm determined to die, . . . but you must die, too. You saw my shame. I can't leave you alive as you are."

This was all I could say. Still he went on gazing at me with loathing and contempt. My heart breaking, I looked for his sword. It must have been taken by the robber. Neither his sword nor his bow and arrows were to be seen in the grove. But fortunately my small sword was lying at my feet. Raising it over head, once more I said, "Now give me your life. I'll follow you right away."

When he heard these words, he moved his lips with difficulty. Since his mouth was stuffed with leaves, of course his voice could not be heard at all. But at a glance I understood his words. Despising me, his look said only, "Kill me." Neither conscious nor unconscious, I stabbed the small sword through the lilac-colored kimono into his breast.

Again at this time I must have fainted. By the time I managed to look up, he had already breathed his last—still in bonds. A streak of sinking sunlight streamed through the clump of cedars and bamboos, and shone on his pale face. Gulping down my sobs, I untied the rope from his dead body. And . . . and what has become of me since I have no more strength to tell you. Anyway I hadn't the strength to die. I stabbed my own throat with the small sword, I threw myself into a pond at the foot of the mountain, and I tried to kill myself in many ways. Unable to end my life, I am still living in dishonor. (A lonely smile.) Worthless as I am, I must have been forsaken even by the most merciful Kwannon. I killed my own husband. I was violated by the robber. Whatever can I do? Whatever can I . . . I . . . (Gradually, violent sobbing.)

THE STORY OF THE MURDERED MAN, AS TOLD THROUGH A MEDIUM

After violating my wife, the robber, sitting there, began to speak comforting words to her. Of course I couldn't speak. My whole body was tied fast to the root of a cedar. But meanwhile I winked at her many times, as much as to say, "Don't believe the robber." I wanted to convey some such meaning to her. But my wife, sitting dejectedly on the bamboo leaves, was looking hard at her lap. To all appearance, she was listening to his words. I was agonized by jealousy. In the meantime the robber went on with his clever talk, from one subject to another. The robber finally made his bold, brazen proposal. "Once your virtue is stained, you won't get along well with your husband, so won't you be my wife instead? It's my love for you that made me be violent toward you."

While the criminal talked, my wife raised her face as if in a trance. She had never looked so beautiful as at that moment. What did my beautiful wife say in answer to him while I was sitting bound there? I am lost in space, but I have never thought of her answer without burning with anger and jealousy. Truly she said, . . . "Then take me away with you wherever you go."

This is not the whole of her sin. If that were all, I would not be tormented so much in the dark. When she was going out of the grove as if in a dream, her hand in the robber's, she suddenly turned pale, and pointed at me tied to the root of the cedar, and said, "Kill him! I cannot marry you as long as he lives." "Kill him!" she cried many times, as if she had gone crazy. Even now these words threaten to blow me headlong into the bottomless abyss of darkness. Has such a hateful thing come out of a human mouth ever before? Have such cursed words ever struck a human ear, even once? Even once such as . . . (A sudden cry of scorn.) At these words the robber himself turned pale. "Kill him," she cried, clinging to his arms. Looking hard at her, he answered neither yes nor no. . . . but hardly had I thought about his answer before she had been knocked down into the bamboo leaves. (Again a cry of scorn.) Quietly folding his arms, he looked at me and said,

"What will you do with her? Kill her or save her? You have only to nod. Kill her?" For these words alone I would like to pardon his crime.

While I hesitated, she shrieked and ran into the depths of the grove. The robber instantly snatched at her, but he failed even to grasp her sleeve.

After she ran away, he took up my sword, and my bow and arrows. With a single stroke he cut one of my bonds. I remember his mumbling, "My fate is next." Then he disappeared from the grove. All was silent after that. No, I heard someone crying. Untying the rest of my bonds, I listened carefully, and I noticed that it was my own crying. (Long silence.)

I raised my exhausted body from the root of the cedar. In front of me there was shining the small sword which my wife had dropped. I took it up and stabbed it into my breast. A bloody lump rose to my mouth, but I didn't feel any pain. When my breast grew cold, everything was as silent as the dead in their graves. What profound silence! Not a single bird-note was heard in the sky over this grave in the hollow of the mountains. Only a lonely light lingered on the cedars and mountain. By and by the light gradually grew fainter, till the cedars and bamboo were lost to view. Lying there, I was enveloped in deep silence.

Then someone crept up to me. I tried to see who it was. But darkness had already been gathering round me. Someone . . . that someone drew the small sword softly out of my breast in its invisible hand. At the same time once more blood flowed into my mouth. And once and for all I sank down into the darkness of space.

Heinrich Böll

Murke's Collected Silences[*]

EVERY MORNING, after entering Broadcasting House, Murke performed an existential exercise. Here in this building the elevator was the kind known as a paternoster—open cages carried on a conveyor belt, like beads on a rosary, moving slowly and continuously from bottom to top, across the top of the elevator shaft, down to the bottom again, so that passengers could step on and off at any floor. Murke would jump onto the paternoster but, instead of getting off at the second floor, where his office was, he would let himself be carried on up, past the third, fourth, fifth floors, and he was seized with panic every time the cage rose above the level of the fifth floor and ground its way up into the empty space where oily chains, greasy rods and groaning machinery pulled and pushed the elevator from an upward into a downward direction, and Murke would stare in terror at the bare brick walls, and sigh with relief as the elevator passed through the lock, dropped into place, and began its slow

[*] From 18 STORIES by Heinrich Böll. Copyright © 1966 by Heinrich Böll. Translated by Leila Vennewitz. Used with permission of McGraw-Hill Book Co.

descent, past the fifth, fourth, third floors. Murke knew his fears were unfounded: obviously nothing would ever happen, nothing could ever happen, and even if it did it could be nothing worse than finding himself up there at the top when the elevator stopped moving and being shut in for an hour or two at the most. He was never without a book in his pocket, and cigarettes; yet as long as the building had been standing, for three years, the elevator had never once failed. On certain days it was inspected, days when Murke had to forego those four and a half seconds of panic, and on these days he was irritable and restless, like people who had gone without breakfast. He needed this panic, the way other people need their coffee, their oatmeal or their fruit juice.

So when he stepped off the elevator at the second floor, the home of the Cultural Department, he felt light-hearted and relaxed, as light-hearted and relaxed as anyone who loves and understands his work. He would unlock the door to his office, walk slowly over to his armchair, sit down and light a cigarette. He was always first on the job. He was young, intelligent, and had a pleasant manner, and even his arrogance, which occasionally flashed out for a moment—even that was forgiven him since it was known he had majored in psychology and graduated *cum laude*.

For two days now, Murke had been obliged to go without his panic-breakfast: unusual circumstances had required him to get to Broadcasting House at eight A.M., dash off to a studio and begin work right away, for he had been told by the Director of Broadcasting to go over the two talks on The Nature of Art which the great Bur-Malottke had taped and to cut them according to Bur-Malottke's instructions. Bur-Malottke, who had converted to Catholicism during the religious fervor of 1945, had suddenly, "overnight," as he put it, "felt religious qualms," he had "suddenly felt he might be blamed for contributing to the religious overtones in radio," and he had decided to omit God, Who occurred frequently in both his half-hour talks on The Nature of Art, and replaced Him with a formula more in keeping with the mental outlook which he had professed before 1945. Bur-Malottke had suggested to the producer that the word God be replaced by the formula "that higher Being Whom we revere," but he had refused to retape the talks, requesting instead that God be cut out of the tapes and replaced by "that higher Being Whom we revere." Bur-Malottke was a friend of the Director, but this friendship was not the reason for the Director's willingness to oblige him: Bur-Malottke was a man one simply did not contradict. He was the author of numerous books of a belletristic-philosophical-religious and art-historical nature, he was on the editorial staff of three periodicals and two newspapers, and closely connected with the largest publishing house. He had agreed to come to Broadcasting House for fifteen minutes on Wednesday and tape the words "that higher Being Whom we revere" as often as God was mentioned in his talks: the rest was up to the technical experts.

It had not been easy for the Director to find someone whom he could ask to do the job; he thought of Murke, but the suddenness with which he thought of Murke made him suspicious—he was a dynamic, robust individual—so he spent five minutes going over the problem in his mind, considered Schwendling, Humkoke, Miss Broldin, but he ended up with Murke. The Director did not like Murke; he had, of course, taken him on as soon as his name had been put forward, the way a zoo director, whose real love is the rabbits and the deer, naturally accepts wild animals too for the simple reason that a zoo must contain wild animals—but what the Director really loved was rabbits and deer, and for him Murke was an intellectual wild animal. In the end his dynamic personality triumphed, and he instructed Murke to cut Bur-Malottke's talks. The talks were to be given on Thursday and Friday, and Bur-Malottke's misgivings had come to him on Sunday night—one might just as well commit suicide as contradict Bur-Malottke, and the Director was much too dynamic to think of suicide.

So Murke spent Monday afternoon and Tuesday morning listening three times to the two half-hour talks on The Nature of Art; he had cut out God, and in the short breaks which he took, during which he silently smoked a cigarette with the technician, reflected on the dynamic personality of the Director and the inferior Being Whom Bur-Malottke revered. He had never read a line of Bur-Malottke, never heard one of his talks before. Monday night he had dreamed of a staircase as tall and steep as the Eiffel Tower, and he had climbed it but soon noticed that the stairs were slippery with soap, and the Director stood down below and called out: "Go on, Murke, go on . . . show us what you can do—go on!" Tuesday night the dream had been similar: he had been at a fairground, strolled casually over to the roller coaster, paid his thirty pfennigs to a man whose face seemed familiar, and as he got on the roller coaster he saw that it was at least ten miles long, he knew there was no going back, and realized that the man who had taken his thirty pfennigs had been the Director. Both mornings after these dreams he had not needed the harmless panic-breakfast up there in the empty space above the paternoster.

Now it was Wednesday. He was smiling as he entered the building, got into the paternoster, let himself be carried up as far as the sixth floor—four and a half seconds of panic, the grinding of the chains, the bare brick walls—he rode down as far as the fourth floor, got out and walked toward the studio where he had an appointment with Bur-Malottke. It was two minutes to ten as he sat down in his green chair, waved to the technician and lit his cigarette. His breathing was quiet, he took a piece of paper out of his breast pocket and glanced at the clock: Bur-Malottke was always on time, at least he had a reputation for being punctual; and as the second hand completed the sixtieth minute of the tenth hour, the minute hand slipped onto the twelve, the hour hand onto the ten, the door opened, and in walked Bur-Malottke. Murke got up, and with a pleasant smile walked over to Bur-Malottke and introduced himself. Bur-Malottke shook hands, smiled and said: "Well, let's get started!" Murke picked up the sheet of paper from the table, put his cigarette between his lips, and, reading from the list, said to Bur-Malottke:

"In the two talks, God occurs precisely twenty-seven times—so I must ask you to repeat twenty-seven times the words we are to splice. We would appreciate it if we might ask you to repeat them thirty-five times, so as to have a certain reserve when it comes to splicing."

"Granted," said Bur-Malottke with a smile, and sat down.

"There is one difficulty, however," said Murke: "where God occurs in the genitive, such as 'God's will,' 'God's love,' 'God's purpose,' He must be replaced by the noun in question followed by the words 'of that higher Being Whom we revere.' I must ask you, therefore, to repeat the words 'the will' twice, 'the love' twice, and 'the purpose' three times, followed each time by 'of that higher

Being Whom we revere,' giving us a total of seven genitives. Then there is one spot where you use the vocative and say 'O God'— here I suggest you substitute 'O Thou higher Being Whom we revere.' Everywhere else only the nominative case applies."

It was clear that Bur-Malottke had not thought of these complications; he began to sweat, the grammatical transposition bothered him. Murke went on: "In all," he said, in his pleasant, friendly manner, "the twenty-seven sentences will require one minute and twenty seconds radio time, whereas the twenty-seven times 'God' occurs require only twenty seconds. In other words, in order to take care of your alterations we shall have to cut half a minute from each talk."

Bur-Malottke sweated more heavily than ever; inwardly he cursed his sudden misgivings and asked: "I suppose you've already done the cutting, have you?"

"Yes, I have," said Murke, pulling a flat metal box out of his pocket; he opened it and held it out to Bur-Malottke: it contained some darkish sound-tape scraps, and Murke said softly: "God twenty-seven times, spoken by you. Would you care to have them?"

"No I would not," said Bur-Malottke, furious. "I'll speak to the Director about the two half-minutes. What comes after my talks in the program?"

"Tomorrow," said Murke, "your talk is followed by the regular program Neighborly News, edited by Grehm."

"Damn," said Bur-Malottke, "it's no use asking Grehm for a favor."

"And the day after tomorrow," said Murke, "your talk is followed by Let's Go Dancing."

"Oh God, that's Huglieme," groaned Bur-Malottke, "never yet has Light Entertainment given way to Culture by as much as a fifth of a minute."

"No," said Murke, "it never has, at least—" and his youthful face took on an expression of irreproachable modesty—"at least not since I've been working here."

"Very well," said Bur-Malottke and glanced at the clock, "we'll be through here in ten minutes, I take it, and then I'll have a word with the Director about that minute. Let's go. Can you leave me your list?"

"Of course," said Murke, "I know the figures by heart."

The technician put down his newspaper as Murke entered the little glass booth. The technician was smiling. On Monday and Tuesday, during the six hours they listened to Bur-Malottke's talks and did their cutting, Murke and the technician had not exchanged a single personal word; now and again they exchanged glances, and when they stopped for a breather the technician had passed his cigarettes to Murke and the next day Murke passed his to the technician, and now when Murke saw the technician smiling he thought: If there is such a thing as friendship in this world, then this man is my friend. He laid the metal box with the snippets from Bur-Malottke's talk on the table and said quietly: "Here we go." He plugged into the studio and said into the microphone: "I'm sure we can dispense with the run-through, Professor. We might as well start right away—would you please begin with the nominatives?"

Bur-Malottke nodded, Murke switched off his own microphone, pressed the button which turned on the green light in the studio and heard Bur-Malottke's solemn, carefully articulated voice intoning: "That higher Being Whom we revere—that higher Being . . ."

Bur-Malottke pursed his lips toward the muzzle of the mike as if he wanted to kiss it, sweat ran down his face, and through the glass Murke observed with cold detachment the agony that Bur-Malottke was going through; then he suddenly switched Bur-Malottke off, stopped the moving tape that was recording Bur-Malottke's words, and feasted his eyes on the spectacle of Bur-Malottke behind the glass, soundless, like a fat, handsome fish. He switched on his microphone and his voice came quietly into the studio: "I'm sorry, but our tape was defective, and I must ask you to begin again at the beginning with the nominatives." Bur-Malottke swore, but his curses were silent ones which only he could hear, for Murke had disconnected him and did not switch him on again until he had begun to say "that higher Being . . ." Murke was too young, considered himself too civilized, to approve of the word hate. But here, behind the glass pane, while Bur-Malottke repeated his genitives, he suddenly knew the meaning of hatred: he hated this great fat, handsome creature, whose books—two million three hundred and fifty thousand copies of them—lay around in libraries, bookstores, bookshelves and bookcases, and not for one second did he dream of suppressing this hatred. When Bur-Malottke had repeated two genitives, Murke switched on his own mike and said quietly: "Excuse me for interrupting you: the nominatives were excellent, so was the first genitive, but would you mind doing the second genitive again? Rather gentler in tone, rather more relaxed —I'll play it back to you." And although Bur-Malottke shook his head violently he signaled to the technician to play back the tape in the studio. They saw Bur-Malottke give a start, sweat more profusely than ever, then hold his hands over his ears until the tape came to an end. He said something, swore, but Murke and the technician could not hear him; they had disconnected him. Coldly Murke waited until he could read from Bur-Malottke's lips that he had begun again with the higher Being, he turned on the mike and the tape, and Bur-Malottke continued with the genitives.

When he was through, he screwed up Murke's list into a ball, rose from his chair, drenched in sweat and fuming, and made for the door; but Murke's quiet, pleasant young voice called him back. Murke said: "But Professor, you've forgotten the vocative." Bur-Malottke looked at him, his eyes blazing with hate, and said into the mike: "O Thou higher Being Whom we revere!"

As he turned to leave, Murke's voice called him back once more. Murke said: "I'm sorry, Professor, but, spoken like that, the words are useless."

"For God's sake," whispered the technician, "watch it!" Bur-Malottke was standing stock-still by the door, his back to the glass booth, as if transfixed by Murke's voice.

Something had happened to him which had never happened to him before: he was helpless, and this young voice, so pleasant, so remarkably intelligent, tortured him as nothing had ever tortured him before. Murke went on:

"I can, of course, paste it into the talk the way it is, but I must point out to you, Professor, that it will have the wrong effect."

Bur-Malottke turned, walked back to the microphone, and said in low and solemn tones:

"O Thou higher Being Whom we revere."

Without turning to look at Murke, he left the studio. It was exactly quarter past ten, and in the doorway he collided with a young, pretty woman carrying some sheet music. The girl, a vivacious redhead, walked briskly to the microphone, adjusted it, and moved the table to one side so she could stand directly in front of the mike.

In the booth Murke chatted for half a minute with Huglieme, who was in charge of Light Entertainment. Pointing to the metal container, Huglieme said: "Do you still need that?" And Murke said, "Yes, I do." In the studio the redhead was singing, "Take my lips, just as they are, they're so lovely." Huglieme switched on his microphone and said quietly: "D'you mind keeping your trap shut for another twenty seconds, I'm not quite ready." The girl laughed, made a face, and said: "O.K., pansy dear." Murke said to the technician: "I'll be back at eleven; we can cut it up then and splice it all together."

"Will we have to hear it through again after that?" asked the technician. "No," said Murke, "I wouldn't listen to it again for a million marks."

The technician nodded, inserted the tape for the red-haired singer, and Murke left.

He put a cigarette between his lips, did not light it, and walked along the rear corridor toward the second paternoster, the one on the south side leading down to the coffee shop. The rugs, the corridors, the furniture and the pictures, everything irritated him. The rugs were impressive, the corridors were impressive, the furniture was impressive, and the pictures were in excellent taste, but he suddenly felt a desire to take the sentimental picture of the Sacred Heart which his mother had sent him and see it somewhere here on the wall. He stopped, looked round, listened, took the picture from his pocket and stuck it between the wallpaper and the frame of the door to the Assistant Drama Producer's office. The tawdry little print was highly colored, and beneath the picture of the Sacred Heart were the words: *I prayed for you at St. James' Church.*

Murke continued along the corridor, got into the paternoster, and was carried down. On this side of the building the Schrumsnot ashtrays, which had won a Good Design Award, had already been installed. They hung next to the illuminated red figures indicating the floor: a red four, a Schrumsnot ashtray, a red three, a Schrumsnot ashtray, a red two, a Schrumsnot ashtray. They were handsome ashtrays, scallop-shaped, made of beaten copper, the beaten copper base an exotic marine plant, nodular seaweed—and each ashtray had cost two hundred and fifty-eight marks and seventy-seven pfennigs. They were so handsome that Murke could never bring himself to soil them with cigarette ash, let alone anything as sordid as a butt. Other smokers all seemed to have had the same feeling —empty packs, butts and ash littered the floor under the handsome ashtrays: apparently no one had the courage to use them as ashtrays; they were copper, burnished, forever empty.

Murke saw the fifth ashtray next to the illuminated red zero rising toward him, the air was getting warmer, there was a smell of food. Murke jumped off and stumbled into the coffee shop. Three free-lance colleagues were sitting at a table in the corner. The table was covered with used plates, cups, and saucers.

The three men were the joint authors of a radio series, *The Lung, A Human Organ;* they had collected their fee together, breakfasted together, were having a drink together, and were now throwing dice for the expense voucher. One of them, Wendrich, Murke knew well, but just then Wendrich shouted: "Art!"—"art," he shouted again, "art, art!" and Murke felt a spasm, like the frog when Galvani discovered electricity. The last two days Murke had heard the word *art* too often, from Bur-Malottke's lips; it occurred exactly one hundred and thirty-four times in the two talks; and he had heard the talks three times, which meant he had heard the word *art* four hundred and two times, too often to feel any desire to discuss it. He squeezed past the counter toward a booth in the far corner and was relieved to find it empty. He sat down, lit his cigarette, and when Wulla, the waitress, came, he said: "Apple juice, please," and was glad when Wulla went off again at once. He closed his eyes tight, but found himself listening willy-nilly to the conversation of the free-lance writers over in the corner, who seemed to be having a heated argument about art; each time one of them shouted "art" Murke winced. It's like being whipped, he thought.

As she brought him the apple juice Wulla looked at him in concern. She was tall and strongly built, but not fat, she had a healthy, cheerful face, and as she poured the apple juice from the jug into the glass she said: "You ought to take a vacation, sir, and quit smoking."

She used to call herself Wilfriede-Ulla, but later, for the sake of simplicity, she combined the names into Wulla. She especially admired the people from the Cultural Department.

"Lay off, will you?" said Murke, "please!"

"And you ought to take some nice ordinary girl to the movies one night," said Wulla.

"I'll do that this evening," said Murke, "I promise you."

"It doesn't have to be one of those dolls," said Wulla, "Just some nice, quiet, ordinary girl, with a kind heart. There are still some of those around."

"Yes," said Murke, "I know they're still around, as a matter of fact I know one." Well, that's fine then, thought Wulla, and went over to the free lances, one of whom had ordered three drinks and three coffees. Poor fellows, thought Wulla, art will be the death of them yet. She had a soft spot for the free lances and was always trying to persuade them to economize. The minute they have any money, she thought, they blow it; she went up to the counter and, shaking her head, passed on the order for the three drinks and the three coffees.

Murke drank some of the apple juice, stubbed out his cigarette in the ashtray, and thought with apprehension of the hours from eleven to one when he had to cut up Bur-Malottke's sentences and paste them into the right places in the talks. At two o'clock the Director wanted both talks played back to him in his studio. Murke thought about soap, about staircases, steep stairs and roller coasters, he thought about the dynamic personality of the Director, he thought about Bur-Malottke, and was startled by the sight of Schwendling coming into the coffee shop.

Schwendling had on a shirt of large red and black checks and made a beeline for the booth where Murke was hiding. Schwendling was humming the tune which was very popular just then: "Take my lips, just as they are, they're so lovely. . . ." He stopped short when he saw Murke, and said: "Hullo, you here? I thought you were busy carving up that crap of Bur-Malottke's."

"I'm going back at eleven," said Murke.

"Wulla, let's have some beer," shouted Schwendling over to the counter, "a pint. Well," he said to Murke, "you deserve extra time off for that, it must be a filthy job. The old man told me all about it."

Murke said nothing, and Schwendling went on:

"Have you heard the latest about Muckwitz?"

Murke, not interested, first shook his head, then for politeness' sake asked: "What's he been up to?"

Wulla brought the beer, Schwendling swallowed some, paused for effect, and announced: "Muckwitz is doing a feature about the Steppes."

Murke laughed and said: "What's Fenn doing?"

"Fenn," said Schwendling, "Fenn's doing a feature about the Tundra."

"And Weggucht?"

"Weggucht is doing a feature about me, and after that I'm going to do a feature about him, you know the old saying: You feature me, I'll feature you. . . . ."

Just then one of the free lances jumped up and shouted across the room: "Art—art—that's the only thing that matters!"

Murke ducked, like a soldier when he hears the mortars being fired from the enemy trenches. He swallowed another mouthful of apple juice and winced again when a voice over the loudspeaker said: "Mr. Murke is wanted in Studio Thirteen—Mr. Murke is wanted in Studio Thirteen." He looked at his watch, it was only half-past ten, but the voice went on relentlessly: "Mr. Murke is wanted in Studio Thirteen—Mr. Murke is wanted in Studio Thirteen." The loudspeaker hung above the counter, immediately below the motto the Director had had painted on the wall: *Discipline Above All*.

"Well," said Schwendling, "that's it, you'd better go."

"Yes," said Murke, "that's it."

He got up, put money for the apple juice on the table, pressed past the free lances' table, got into the paternoster outside and was carried up once more past the five Schrumsnot ashtrays. He saw his Sacred Heart picture still sticking in the Assistant Producer's doorframe and thought:

"Thank God, now there's at least one corny picture in this place."

He opened the door of the studio booth, saw the technician sitting alone and relaxed in front of three cardboard boxes, and asked wearily: "What's up?"

"They were ready sooner than expected, and we've got an extra half hour in hand," said the technician. "I thought you'd be glad of the extra time."

"I certainly am," said Murke, "I've got an appointment at one. Let's get on with it then. What's the idea of the boxes?"

"Well," said the technician, "for each grammatical case I've got one box—the nominatives in the first, the genitives in the second, and in that one—" he pointed to the little box on the right with the words "Pure Chocolate" on it, and said: "In that one I have the two vocatives, the good one in the right-hand corner, the bad one in the left."

"That's terrific," said Murke, "so you've already cut up the crap."

"That's right," said the technician, "and if you've made a note of the order in which the cases have to be spliced it won't take us more than an hour. Did you write it down?"

"Yes, I did," said Murke. He pulled a piece of paper from his pocket with the numbers 1 to 27; each number was followed by a grammatical case.

Murke sat down, held out his cigarette pack to the technician; they both smoked while the technician laid the cut tapes with Bur-Malottke's talks on the roll.

"In the first cut," said Murke, "we have to stick in a nominative."

The technician put his hand into the first box, picked up one of the snippets and stuck it into the space.

"Next comes a genitive," said Murke.

They worked swiftly, and Murke was relieved that it all went so fast.

"Now," he said, "comes the vocative; we'll take the bad one, of course."

The technician laughed and stuck Bur-Malottke's bad vocative into the tape.

"Next," he said, "next!" "Genitive," said Murke.

The Director conscientiously read every listener's letter. The one he was reading at this particular moment went as follows:

> Dear Radio,
> I am sure you can have no more faithful listener than myself. I am an old woman, a little old lady of seventy-seven, and I have been listening to you every day for thirty years. I have never been sparing with my praise. Perhaps you remember my letter about the program: "The Seven Souls of Kaweida the Cow." It was a lovely program—but now I have to be angry with you! The way the canine soul is being neglected in radio is gradually becoming a disgrace. And you call that humanism. I am sure Hitler had his bad points: if one is to believe all one hears, he was a dreadful man, but one thing he did have: a real affection for dogs, and he did a lot for them. When are dogs going to come into their own again in German radio? The way you tried to do it in the program "Like Cat and Dog" is certainly not the right one:

it was an insult to every canine soul. If my little Lohengrin could only talk, he'd tell you! And the way he barked, poor darling, all through your terrible program, it almost made me die of shame. I pay my two marks a month like any other listener and stand on my rights and demand to know: When are dogs going to come into their own again in German radio?

With kind regards—in spite of my being so cross with you,

Sincerely yours,
Jadwiga Herchen (retired)

P.S. In case none of those cynics of yours who run your programs should be capable of doing justice to the canine soul, I suggest you make use of my modest attempts, which are enclosed herewith. I do not wish to accept any fee. You may send it direct to the S.P.C.A. Enclosed: 35 manuscripts.

Yours,
J.H.

The Director sighed. He looked for the scripts, but his secretary had evidently filed them away. The Director filled his pipe, lit it, ran his tongue over his dynamic lips, lifted the receiver and asked to be put through to Krochy. Krochy had a tiny office with a tiny desk, although in the best of taste, upstairs in Culture and was in charge of a section as narrow as his desk: Animals in the World of Culture.

"Krochy speaking," he said diffidently into the telephone.

"Say, Krochy," said the Director, "when was the last time we had a program about dogs?"

"Dogs, sir?" said Krochy. "I don't believe we ever have, at least not since I've been here."

"And how long have you been here, Krochy?" And upstairs in his office Krochy trembled, because the Director's voice was so gentle; he knew it boded no good when that voice became gentle.

"I've been here ten years now, sir," said Krochy.

"It's a disgrace," said the Director, "that you've never had a program about dogs; after all, that's your department. What was the title of your last program?"

"The title of my last program was—" stammered Krochy.

"You don't have to repeat every sentence," said the Director, "we're not in the army."

"Owls in the Ruins," said Krochy timidly.

"Within the next three weeks," said the Director, gentle again now, "I would like to hear a program about the canine soul."

"Certainly, sir," said Krochy; he heard the click as the Director put down the receiver, sighed deeply and said: "Oh God!"

The Director picked up the next listener's letter.

At this moment Bur-Malottke entered the room. He was always at liberty to enter unannounced, and he made frequent use of this liberty. He was still sweating as he sank wearily into a chair opposite the Director and said:

"Well, good morning."

"Good morning," said the Director, pushing the listener's letter aside. "What can I do for you?"

"Could you give me one minute?"

"Bur-Malottke," said the Director, with a generous, dynamic gesture, "does not have to ask me for one minute; hours, days, are at your disposal."

"No," said Bur-Malottke, "I don't mean an ordinary minute, I mean one minute of radio time. Due to the changes my talk has become one minute longer."

The Director grew serious, like a satrap distributing provinces. "I hope," he said, sourly, "it's not a political minute."

"No," said Bur-Malottke, "It's half a minute of Neighborly News and half a minute of Light Entertainment."

"Thank God for that," said the Director. "I've got a credit of seventy-nine seconds with Light Entertainment and eighty-three seconds with Neighborly News. I'll be glad to let someone like Bur-Malottke have one minute."

"I am overcome," said Bur-Malottke.

"Is there anything else I can do for you?" asked the Director.

"I would appreciate it," said Bur-Malottke, "if we could gradually start correcting all the tapes I have made since 1945. One day," he said—he passed his hand over his forehead and gazed wistfully at the genuine Kokoschka above the Director's desk—"one day I shall—" he faltered, for the news he was about to break to the Director was too painful for posterity "—one day I shall—die," and he paused again, giving the Director a chance to look gravely shocked and raise his hand in protest, "and I cannot bear the thought that after my death tapes may be run off on which I say things I no longer believe in. Particularly in some of my political utterances, during the fervor of 1945, I let myself be persuaded to make statements which today fill me with serious misgivings and which I can only account for on the basis of that spirit of youthfulness which has always distinguished my work. My written works are already in process of being corrected, and I would like to ask you to give me the opportunity of correcting my spoken works as well."

The Director was silent, he cleared his throat slightly, and little shining beads of sweat appeared on his forehead: it occurred to him that Bur-Malottke had spoken for at least an hour every month since 1945, and he made a swift calculation while Bur-Malottke went on talking: twelve times ten hours meant one hundred and twenty hours of spoken Bur-Malottke.

"Pedantry," Bur-Malottke was saying, "is something that only impure spirits regard as unworthy of genius; we know, of course"— and the Director felt flattered to be ranked by the We among the pure spirits—"that the true geniuses, the great geniuses, were pedants. Himmelsheim once had a whole printed edition of his *Seelon* rebound at his own expense because he felt that three or four sentences in the central portion of the work were no longer appropriate. The idea that some of my talks might be broadcast which no longer correspond to my convictions when I depart this earthly life—I find such an idea intolerable. How do you propose we go about it?"

The beads of sweat on the Director's forehead had become larger. "First of all," he said in a subdued voice, "an exact list would have to be made of all your broadcast talks, and then we would have to check in the archives to see if all the tapes were still there."

"I should hope," said Bur-Malottke, "that none of the tapes has been erased without notifying me. I have not been notified, therefore no tapes have been erased."

"I will see to everything," said the Director.

"Please do," said Bur-Malottke curtly, and rose from his chair. "Good-by."

"Good-by," said the Director, as he accompanied Bur-Malottke to the door.

The free lances in the coffee shop had decided to order lunch. They had had some more drinks, they were still talking about art, their conversation was quieter now but no less intense. They all jumped to their feet when Wanderburn suddenly came in. Wanderburn was a tall, despondent-looking writer with dark hair, an attractive face somewhat etched by the stigma of fame. On this particular morning he had not shaved, which made him look even more attractive. He walked over to the table where the three free lances were sitting, sank exhausted into a chair and said: "For God's sake, give me a drink. I always have the feeling in this building that I'm dying of thirst."

They passed him a drink, a glass that was still standing on the table, and the remains of a bottle of soda water. Wanderburn swallowed the drink, put down his glass, looked at each of the three men in turn, and said: "I must warn you about the radio business, about this pile of junk—this immaculate, shiny, slippery pile of junk. I'm warning you. It'll destroy us all." His warning was sincere and impressed the three young men very much; but the three young men did not know that Wanderburn had just come from the accounting department where he had picked up a nice fat fee for a quick job of editing the Book of Job.

"They cut us," said Wanderburn, "they consume our substance, splice us together again, and it'll be more than any of us can stand."

He finished the soda water, put the glass down on the table and, his coat flapping despondently about him, strode to the door.

On the dot of noon Murke finished the splicing. They had just stuck in the last snippet, a genitive, when Murke got up. He already had his hand on the doorknob when the technician said: "I wish I could afford a sensitive and expensive conscience like that. What'll we do with the box?" He pointed to the flat tin lying on the shelf next to the cardboard boxes containing the new tapes.

"Just leave it there," said Murke.

"What for?"

"We might need it again."

"D'you think he might get pangs of conscience all over again?"

"He might," said Murke, "we'd better wait and see. So long."

He walked to the front paternoster, rode down to the second floor, and for the first time that day entered his office. His secretary had gone to lunch; Murke's boss, Humkoke, was sitting by the phone reading a book. He smiled at Murke, got up and said: "Well, I see you survived. Is this your book? Did you put it on the desk?"

He held it out for Murke to read the title, and Murke said: "Yes, that's mine." The book had a jacket of green, gray and orange and was called "Batley's Lyrics of the Gutter"; it was about a young English writer a hundred years ago who had drawn up a catalogue of London slang.

"It's a marvelous book," said Murke.

"Yes," said Humkoke, "it is marvelous, but you never learn."

Murke eyed him questioningly.

"You never learn that one doesn't leave marvelous books lying around when Wanderburn is liable to turn up, and Wanderburn is always liable to turn up. He saw it at once, of course, opened it, read it for five minutes, and what's the result?"

Murke said nothing.

"The result," said Humkoke, "is two hour-long broadcasts by Wanderburn on 'Lyrics of the Gutter.' One day this fellow will do a feature about his own grandmother, and the worst of it is that one of his grandmothers was one of mine too. Please, Murke, try and remember: never leave marvelous books around when Wanderburn is liable to turn up, and, I repeat, he's always liable to turn up. That's all, you can go now, you've got the afternoon off, and I'm sure you've earned it. Is the stuff ready? Did you hear it through again?"

"It's all done," said Murke, "but I can't hear the talks through again, I simply can't."

" 'I simply can't' is a very childish thing to say," said Humkoke.

"If I have to hear the word Art one more time today I shall become hysterical," said Murke.

"You already are," said Humkoke, "and I must say you've every reason to be. Three hours of Bur-Malottke, that's too much for anybody, even the toughest of us, and you're not even tough." He threw the book on the table, took a step toward Murke and said: "When I was your age I once had to cut three minutes out of a four-hour speech of Hitler's, and I had to listen to the speech three times before I was considered worthy of suggesting which three minutes should be cut. When I began listening to the tape for the first time I was still a Nazi, but by the time I had heard the speech for the third time I wasn't a Nazi any more; it was a drastic cure, a terrible one, but very effective."

"You forget," said Murke quietly, "that I had already been cured of Bur-Malottke before I had to listen to his tapes."

"You really are a vicious beast!" said Humkoke with a laugh. "That'll do for now, the Director is going to hear it through again at two. Just see that you're available in case anything goes wrong."

"I'll be at home from two to three," said Murke.

"One more thing," said Humkoke, pulling out a yellow biscuit tin from a shelf next to Murke's desk, "what's this scrap you've got here?"

Murke colored. "It's—" he stammered, "I collect a certain kind of left-overs."

"What kind of left-overs?" asked Humkoke.

"Silences," said Murke, "I collect silences."

Humkoke raised his eyebrows, and Murke went on: "When I have to cut tapes, in the places where the speakers sometimes pause for a moment—or sigh, or take a breath, or there is absolute silence — I don't throw that away, I collect it. Incidentally, there wasn't a single second of silence in Bur-Malottke's tapes."

Humkoke laughed: "Of course not, he would never be silent. And what do you do with the scrap?"

"I splice it together and play back the tape when I'm at home in the evening. There's not much yet, I only have three minutes so far—but then people aren't silent very often."

"You know, don't you, that it's against regulations to take home sections of tape?"

"Even silences?" asked Murke.

Humkoke laughed and said: "For God's sake, get out!"

And Murke left.

When the Director entered his studio a few minutes after two, the Bur-Malottke tape had just been turned on:

> . . . and wherever, however, why ever, and whenever we begin to discuss the Nature of Art, we must first look to that higher Being Whom we revere, we must bow in awe before that higher Being Whom we revere, and we must accept Art as a gift from that higher Being Whom we revere. Art. . . .

No, thought the Director, I really can't ask anyone to listen to Bur-Malottke for a hundred and twenty hours. No, he thought, there are some things one simply cannot do, things I wouldn't want to wish even on Murke. He returned to his office and switched on the loudspeaker just in time to hear Bur-Malottke say: "O Thou higher Being Whom we revere. . . ." No, thought the Director, no, no.

Murke lay on his chesterfield at home smoking. Next to him on a chair was a cup of tea, and Murke was gazing at the white ceiling of the room. Sitting at his desk was a very pretty blonde who was staring out of the window at the street. Between Murke and the girl, on a low coffee table, stood a tape recorder, recording. Not a word was spoken, not a sound was made. The girl was pretty and silent enough for a photographer's model.

"I can't stand it," said the girl suddenly, "I can't stand it, it's inhuman, what you want me to do. There are some men who expect a girl to do immoral things, but it seems to me that what you are asking me to do is even more immoral than the things other men expect a girl to do."

Murke sighed. "Oh hell," he said, "Rina dear, now I've got to cut all that out; do be sensible, be a good girl and put just five more minutes' silence on the tape."

"Put silence," said the girl, with what thirty years ago would have been called a pout. "Put silence, that's another of your inventions. I wouldn't mind putting words onto a tape—but putting silence. . . ."

Murke had got up and switched off the tape recorder. "Oh Rina," he said, "if you only knew how precious your silence is to me. In the evening, when I'm tired, when I'm sitting here alone, I play back your silence. Do be a dear and put just three more minutes' silence on the tape for me and save me the cutting; you know how I feel about cutting." "Oh all right," said the girl, "but give me a cigarette at least."

Murke smiled, gave her a cigarette and said: "This way I have your silence in the original and on tape, that's terrific." He switched the tape on again, and they sat facing one another in silence till the telephone rang. Murke got up, shrugged helplessly, and lifted the receiver.

"Well," said Humkoke, "the tapes ran off smoothly, the boss couldn't find a thing wrong with them. . . . You can go to the movies now. And think about snow."

"What snow?" asked Murke, looking out onto the street, which lay basking in brilliant summer sunshine.

"Come on now," said Humkoke, "you know we have to start thinking about the winter programs. I need songs about snow, stories about snow—we can't fool around for the rest of our lives with Schubert and Stifter. No one seems to have any idea how badly we need snow songs and snow stories. Just imagine if we have a long hard winter with lots of snow and freezing temperatures: where are we going to get our snow programs from? Try and think of something snowy."

"All right," said Murke, "I'll try and think of something." Humkoke had hung up.

"Come along," he said to the girl, "we can go to the movies."

"May I speak again now?" said the girl.

"Yes," said Murke, "speak!"

It was just at this time that the Assistant Drama Producer had finished listening again to the one-act play scheduled for that evening. He liked it, only the ending did not satisfy him. He was sitting in the glass booth in Studio Thirteen next to the technician, chewing a match and studying the script.

> (*Sound-effects of a large empty church*)
> ATHEIST: (*in a loud clear voice*) Who will remember me when I have become the prey of worms?
> (*Silence*)
> ATHEIST: (*his voice a shade louder*) Who will wait for me when I have turned into dust?
> (*Silence*)
> ATHEIST: (*louder still*) And who will remember me when I have turned into leaves?
> (*Silence*)

There were twelve such questions called out by the atheist into the church, and each question was followed by—? Silence.

The Assistant Producer removed the chewed match from his lips, replaced it with a fresh one and looked at the technician, a question in his eyes.

"Yes," said the technician, "if you ask me: I think there's a bit too much silence in it."

"That's what I thought," said the Assistant Producer; "the author thinks so too and he's given me leave to change it. There should just be a voice saying: "God"—but it ought to be a voice without church sound-effects, it would have to be spoken somehow in a different acoustical environment. Have you any idea where I can get hold of a voice like that at this hour?"

The technician smiled, picked up the metal container which was still lying on the shelf. "Here you are," he said, "here's a voice saying 'God' without any sound-effects."

The Assistant Producer was so surprised he almost swallowed the match, choked a little and got it up into the front of his mouth again. "It's quite all right," the technician said with a smile, "we had to cut it out of a talk, twenty-seven times."

"I don't need it that often, just twelve times," said the Assistant Producer.

"It's a simple matter, of course," said the technician, "to cut out the silence and stick in God twelve times—if you'll take the responsibility."

"You're a godsend," said the Assistant Producer, "and I'll be responsible. Come on, let's get started." He gazed happily at the tiny, lusterless tape snippets in Murke's tin box. "You really are a godsend," he said, "come on, let's go!"

The technician smiled, for he was looking forward to being able to present Murke with the snippets of silence: it was a lot of silence, altogether nearly a minute; it was more silence than he had ever been able to give Murke, and he liked the young man.

"O.K.," he said with a smile, "here we go."

The Assistant Producer put his hand in his jacket pocket, took out a pack of cigarettes; in doing so he touched a crumpled piece of paper, he smoothed it out and passed it to the technician: "Funny, isn't it, the corny stuff you can come across in this place? I found this stuck in my door."

The technician took the picture, looked at it, and said: "Yes, it's funny," and he read out the words under the picture:

I prayed for you at St. James' Church.

VIII

HOW MUCH CAN A MAN PAY?

And worse I may be yet: the worst is not
So long as we can say "this is the worst."
>   Edgar in
>   SHAKESPEARE's *King Lear*, IV, 1, 27–28

A good many writers make the mistake of enclosing a stamped, self-addressed envelope, big enough for the manuscript to come back in. This is too much of a temptation to the editor.
>   RING LARDNER
>   *How to Write Short Stories*

The long habit of living indisposeth us for dying.
>   SIR THOMAS BROWNE
>   *The Urn Burial*

If something takes too long, something happens to you. You become all and only the thing you want and nothing else, for you have paid too much for it, too much in wanting and too much in waiting and too much in getting. In the end they just ask you those crappy little questions.

>ROBERT PENN WARREN
>*All the King's Men*

You that live in my ancestral Thebes, behold this Oedipus, —him who knew the famous riddle and was a man most masterful not a citizen who did not look with envy on his lot—see him now and see the breakers of misfortune swallow him! Look upon that last day always. Count no mortal happy till he has passed the final limit of his life secure from pain.

>Final speech by Chorus in
>SOPHOCLES' *Oedipus the King*
>translated by David Grene

Donald Barthelme

A Shower of Gold*

BECAUSE HE NEEDED THE MONEY Peterson answered an ad that said "*We'll pay you* to be on TV if your opinions are strong enough or your personal experiences have a flavor of the unusual." He called the number and was told to come to Room 1551 in the Graybar Building on Lexington. This he did and after spending twenty minutes with a Miss Arbor who asked him if he had ever been in analysis was okayed for a program called *Who Am I?* "What do you have strong opinions about?" Miss Arbor asked. "Art," Peterson said, "life, money." "For instance?" "I believe," Peterson said, "that the learning ability of mice can be lowered or increased by regulating the amount of serotonin in the brain. I believe that schizophrenics have a high incidence of unusual fingerprints, including lines that make almost complete circles. I believe that the dreamer watches his dream in sleep, by moving his eyes." "That's

---

* Copyright © 1962 by Donald Barthelme; originally appeared in *The New Yorker.* From COME BACK, DR. CALIGARI, by Donald Barthelme. Reprinted by permission of Little, Brown and Co.

405

very interesting!" Miss Arbor cried. "It's all in the *World Almanac,*" Peterson replied.

"I see you're a sculptor," Miss Arbor said, "that's wonderful." "What is the nature of the program?" Peterson asked. "I've never seen it." "Let me answer your question with another question," Miss Arbor said. "Mr. Peterson, are you absurd?" Her enormous lips were smeared with a glowing white cream. "I beg your pardon?" "I mean," Miss Arbor said earnestly, "do you encounter your own existence as gratuitous? Do you feel *de trop?* Is there nausea?" "I have an enlarged liver," Peterson offered. "That's *excellent!*" Miss Arbor exclaimed. "That's a *very* good beginning! *Who Am I?* tries, Mr. Peterson, to discover what people *really are.* People today, we feel, are hidden away inside themselves, alienated, desperate, living in anguish, despair and bad faith. Why have we been thrown here, and abandoned? That's the question we try to answer, Mr. Peterson. Man stands alone in a featureless, anonymous landscape, in fear and trembling and sickness unto death. God is dead. Nothingness everywhere. Dread. Estrangement. Finitude. *Who Am I?* approaches these problems in a root radical way." "On television?" "We're interested in basics, Mr. Peterson. We don't play around." "I see," Peterson said, wondering about the amount of the fee. "What I want to know now, Mr. Peterson, is this: are you *interested* in absurdity?" "Miss Arbor," he said, "to tell you the truth, I don't know. I'm not sure I believe in it." "Oh, Mr. Peterson!" Miss Arbor said, shocked. "Don't *say* that! You'll be . . ." "Punished?" Peterson suggested. "*You* may not be interested in absurdity," she said firmly, "but absurdity is interested in *you.*" "I have a lot of problems, if that helps," Peterson said. "Existence is problematic for you," Miss Arbor said, relieved. "The fee is two hundred dollars."

"I'm going to be on television," Peterson said to his dealer. "A terrible shame," Jean-Claude responded. "Is it unavoidable?" "It's unavoidable," Peterson said, "if I want to eat." "How much?" Jean-Claude asked and Peterson said: "Two hundred." He looked around the gallery to see if any of his works were on display. "A ridiculous compensation considering the infamy. Are you using your own name?" "You haven't by any chance . . ." "No one is buying," Jean-Claude said. "Undoubtedly it is the weather. People are thinking in terms of—what do you call those things?—Chris-Crafts. To boat with. You would not consider again what I spoke to you about before?" "No," Peterson said, "I wouldn't consider it." "Two little ones would move much, much faster than a single huge big one," Jean-Claude said, looking away. "To saw it across the middle would be a very simple matter." "It's supposed to be a work of art," Peterson said, as calmly as possible. "You don't go around sawing works of art across the middle, remember?" "That place where it saws," Jean-Claude said, "is not very difficult. I can put my two hands around it." He made a circle with his two hands to demonstrate. "Invariably when I look at that piece I see two pieces. Are you absolutely sure you didn't conceive it wrongly in the first instance?" "Absolutely," Peterson said. Not a single piece of his was on view, and his liver expanded in rage and hatred. "You have a very romantic impulse," Jean-Claude said. "I admire, dimly, the posture. You read too much in the history of art. It estranges you from those possibilities for authentic selfhood that inhere in the present century." "I know," Peterson said, "could you let me have twenty until the first?"

Peterson sat in his loft on lower Broadway drinking Rheingold and thinking about the President. He had always felt close to the President but felt now that he had, in agreeing to appear on the television program, done something slightly disgraceful, of which the President would not approve. But I needed the money, he told himself, the telephone is turned off and the kitten is crying for milk. And I'm running out of beer. The President feels that the arts should be encouraged, Peterson reflected, surely he doesn't want me to go without beer? He wondered if what he was feeling was simple guilt at having sold himself to television or something more elegant: nausea? His liver groaned within him and he considered a situation in which his new relationship with the President was announced. He was working in the loft. The piece in hand was to be called *Season's Greetings* and combined three auto radiators, one from a Chevrolet Tudor, one from a Ford pickup, one from a 1932 Essex, with part of a former telephone switchboard and other items. The arrangement seemed right and he began welding. After a time the mass was freestanding. A couple of hours had passed. He put down the torch, lifted off the mask. He walked over to the refrigerator and found a sandwich left by a friendly junk dealer. It was a sandwich made hastily and without inspiration: a thin slice of ham between two pieces of bread. He ate it gratefully nevertheless. He stood looking at the work, moving from time to time so as to view it from a new angle. Then the door to the loft burst open and the President ran in, trailing a sixteen-pound sledge. His first blow cracked the principal weld in *Season's Greetings,* the two halves parting like lovers, clinging for a moment and then rushing off in opposite directions. Twelve Secret Service men held Peterson in a paralyzing combination of secret grips. He's looking good, Peterson thought, very good, healthy, mature, fit, trustworthy. I like his suit. The President's second and third blows smashed the Essex radiator and the Chevrolet radiator. Then he attacked the welding torch, the plaster sketches on the workbench, the Rodin cast and the Giacometti stickman Peterson had bought in Paris. "But Mr. President!" Peterson shouted. "*I thought we were friends!*" A Secret Service man bit him in the back of the neck. Then the President lifted the sledge high in the air, turned toward Peterson, and said: "Your liver is diseased? That's a good sign. You're making progress. You're thinking."

"I happen to think that guy in the White House is doing a pretty darn good job." Peterson's barber, a man named Kitchen who was also a lay analyst and the author of four books titled *The Decision To Be,* was the only person in the world to whom he had confided his former sense of community with the President. "As far as his relationship with you personally goes," the barber continued, "it's essentially a kind of I-Thou relationship, if you know what I mean. You got to handle it with full awareness of the implications. In the end one experiences only oneself, Nietzsche said. When you're angry with the President, what you experience is self-as-angry-with-the-President. When things are okay between you and him, what you experience is self-as-swinging-with-the-President. Well and good. *But,*" Kitchen said, lathering up, "you want the relationship to be such that what you experience is the-President-as-swinging-with-you. You want *his* reality, get it? So that you can break out of the hell of solipsism. How about a little more off the sides?" "Everybody knows the language but me," Peterson said irritably. "Look," Kitchen said, "when you talk about me to somebody else, you say 'my barber,' don't you? Sure you do. In the same way, I look at you as being 'my customer,' get it? But you don't regard yourself as being 'my' customer and I don't regard myself as 'your' barber. Oh, it's hell all right." The razor moved like a switchblade across the back of Peterson's neck. "Like Pascal said: 'The natural misfortune of our mortal and feeble condition is so wretched that when we consider it closely, nothing can console us.'" The razor rocketed around an ear. "Listen," Peterson said, "what do you think of this television program called *Who Am I?* Ever seen it?" "Frankly," the barber said, "it smells of the library. But they do a job on those people, I'll tell you that." "What do you mean?" Peterson said excitedly. "What kind of a job?" The cloth was whisked away and shaken with a sharp popping sound. "It's too horrible even to talk about," Kitchen said. "But it's what they deserve, those crumbs." "Which crumbs?" Peterson asked.

That night a tall foreign-looking man with a switchblade big as a butcherknife open in his hand walked into the loft without knocking and said, "Good evening, Mr. Peterson, I am the cat-piano player, is there anything you'd particularly like to hear?" "Cat-piano?" Peterson said, gasping, shrinking from the knife. "What are you talking about? What do you want?" A biography of Nolde slid from his lap to the floor. "The cat-piano," said the visitor, "is an instrument of the devil, a diabolical instrument. You needn't sweat quite so much," he added, sounding aggrieved. Peterson tried to be brave. "I don't understand," he said. "Let me explain," the tall foreign-looking man said graciously. "The keyboard consists of eight cats—the octave—encased in the body of the instrument in such a way that only their heads and forepaws protrude. The player presses upon the appropriate paws, and the appropriate cats respond—with a kind of shriek. There is also provision made for pulling their tails. A tail-puller, or perhaps I should say tail *player*" (he smiled a disingenuous smile) "is stationed at the rear of the instrument, where the tails are. At the correct moment the tail-puller pulls the correct tail. The tail-note is of course quite different from the paw-note and produces sounds in the upper registers. Have you ever seen such an instrument, Mr. Peterson?" "No, and I don't believe it exists," Peterson said heroically. "There is an excellent early seventeenth-century engraving by Franz van der Wyngaert, Mr. Peterson, in which a cat-piano appears. Played, as it happens, by a man with a wooden leg. You will observe my own leg." The cat-piano player hoisted his trousers and a leglike contraption of wood, metal and plastic appeared. "And now, would you like to make a request? 'The Martyrdom of St. Sebastian'? The 'Romeo and Juliet' overture? 'Holiday for Strings?'" "But why—" Peterson began. "The kitten is crying for milk, Mr. Peterson. And whenever a kitten cries, the cat-piano plays." "But it's not my kitten," Peterson said reasonably. "It's just a kitten that wished itself on me. I've been trying to give it away. I'm not sure it's still around. I haven't seen it since the day before yesterday." The kitten appeared, looked at Peterson reproachfully, and then rubbed itself against the cat-piano player's mechanical leg. "Wait a minute!" Peterson exclaimed. "This thing is rigged! That cat hasn't been here in two days. What do you want from me? What am I supposed to do?" "Choices, Mr. Peterson, choices. You *chose* that kitten as a way of encountering that which you are not, that is to say, kitten. An effort on the part of the *pour-soi* to—" "But it chose me!" Peterson cried, "the door was open and the first thing I knew it was lying in my bed, under the Army blanket. I didn't have anything to do with it!" The cat-piano player repeated his disingenuous smile. "Yes, Mr. Peterson, I know, I know. Things are done to you, it is all a gigantic conspiracy. I've heard the story a hundred times. But the kitten is here, is it not? The kitten is weeping, is it not?" Peterson looked at the kitten, which was crying huge tigerish tears into its empty dish. "*Listen* Mr. Peterson," the cat-piano player said, "*listen!*" The blade of his immense knife jumped back into the handle with a thwack! and the hideous music began.

The day after the hideous music began the three girls from California arrived. Peterson opened his door, hesitantly, in response to an insistent ringing, and found himself being stared at by three girls in blue jeans and heavy sweaters, carrying suitcases. "I'm Sherry," the first girl said, "and this is Ann and this is Louise. We're from California and we need a place to stay." They were homely and extremely purposeful. "I'm sorry," Peterson said, "I can't—" "We sleep anywhere," Sherry said, looking past him into the vastness of his loft, "on the floor if we have to. We've done it before." Ann and Louise stood on their toes to get a good look. "What's that funny music?" Sherry asked, "it sounds pretty far-out. We really won't be any trouble at all and it'll just be a little while until we make a connection." "Yes," Peterson said, "but why me?" "You're an artist," Sherry said sternly, "we saw the A.I.R. sign downstairs." Peterson cursed the fire laws which made posting of the signs obligatory. "Listen," he said, "I can't even feed the cat. I can't even keep myself in beer. This is not the place. You won't be happy here. My work isn't authentic. I'm a minor artist." "The natural misfortune of our mortal and feeble condition is so wretched that when we consider it closely, nothing can console us," Sherry said. "That's Pascal." "I know," Peterson said, weakly. "Where is the john?" Louise asked. Ann marched into the kitchen and began to prepare, from supplies removed from her rucksack, something called *veal engagé*. "Kiss me," Sherry said, "I need love." Peterson flew to his friendly neighborhood bar, ordered a double brandy, and wedged himself into a telephone booth. "Miss Arbor? This is Hank Peterson. Listen, Miss Arbor, I can't do it. No, I mean really. I'm being punished horribly for even thinking about it. No, I mean it. You can't imagine what's going on around here. Please, get somebody else? I'd regard it as a great personal favor. Miss Arbor? Please?"

The other contestants were a young man in white pajamas named Arthur Pick, a karate expert, and an airline pilot in full uniform, Wallace E. Rice. "Just be natural," Miss Arbor said, "and of course be frank. We score on the basis of the validity of your answers, and of course that's measured by the polygraph." "What's this about a polygraph?" the airline pilot said. "The polygraph measures the validity of your answers," Miss Arbor said, her lips glowing whitely. "How else are we going to know if you're . . ." "Lying?" Wallace E. Rice supplied. The contestants were connected to the machine and the machine to a large illuminated tote board hanging over their heads. The master of ceremonies, Peterson noted without pleasure, resembled the President and did not look at all friendly.

The program began with Arthur Pick. Arthur Pick got up in his white pajamas and gave a karate demonstration in which he broke three half-inch pine boards with a single kick of his naked left foot. Then he told how he had disarmed a bandit, late at night at the A&P where he was an assistant manager, with a maneuver called a "rip-choong" which he demonstrated on the announcer. "How about that?" the announcer caroled. "Isn't that something? Audience?" The audience responded enthusiastically and Arthur Pick stood modestly with his hands behind his back. "Now," the announcer said, "let's play *Who Am I?* And here's your host, *Bill Lemmon!*" No, he doesn't look like the President, Peterson decided. "Arthur," Bill Lemmon said, "for twenty dollars—do you love your mother?" "Yes," Arthur Pick said. "Yes, of course." A bell rang, the tote board flashed, and the audience screamed. "He's lying!" the announcer shouted, "lying! lying! lying!" "Arthur," Bill Lemmon said, looking at his index cards, "the polygraph shows that the validity of your answer is . . . questionable. Would you like to try it again? Take another crack at it?" "You're crazy," Arthur Pick said. "Of course I love my mother." He was fishing around inside his pajamas for a handkerchief. "Is your mother watching the show tonight, Arthur?" "Yes, Bill, she is." "How long have you been studying karate?" "Two years, Bill." "And who paid for the lessons?" Arthur Pick hesitated. Then he said: "My mother, Bill." "They were pretty expensive, weren't they, Arthur?" "Yes, Bill, they were." "How expensive?" "Five dollars an hour." "Your mother doesn't make very much money, does she, Arthur?" "No, Bill, she doesn't." "Arthur, what does your mother do for a living?" "She's a garment worker, Bill. In the garment district." "And how long has she worked down there?" "All her life, I guess. Since my old man died." "And she doesn't make very much money, you said." "No. But she *wanted* to pay for the lessons. She *insisted* on it." Bill Lemmon said: "She wanted a son who could break boards with his feet?" Peterson's liver leaped and the tote board spelled out, in huge, glowing white letters, the words BAD FAITH. The airline pilot, Wallace E. Rice, was led to reveal that he had been caught, on a flight from Omaha to Miami, with a stewardess sitting on his lap and wearing his captain's cap, that the flight engineer had taken a Polaroid picture, and that he had been given involuntary retirement after nineteen years of faithful service. "It was perfectly safe," Wallace E. Rice said, "you don't understand, the automatic pilot can fly that plane better than I can." He further confessed to a lifelong and intolerable itch after stewardesses which had much to do, he said, with the way their jackets fell just on top of their hips, and his own jacket with the three gold stripes on the sleeve darkened with sweat until it was black.

I was wrong, Peterson thought, the world is absurd. The absurdity is punishing me for not believing in it. I affirm the absurdity. On the other hand, absurdity is itself absurd. Before the emcee could ask the first question, Peterson began to talk. "Yesterday," Peterson said to the television audience, "in the typewriter in front of the Olivetti showroom on Fifth Avenue, I found a recipe for Ten Ingredient Soup that included a stone from a toad's head. And while I stood there marveling a nice old lady pasted on the elbow of my best Haspel suit a little blue sticker reading THIS INDIVIDUAL IS A PART OF THE COMMUNIST CONSPIRACY FOR GLOBAL DOMINATION OF THE ENTIRE GLOBE. Coming home I passed a sign that said in ten-foot letters COWARD SHOES and heard a man singing "Golden Earrings" in a horrible voice, and last night I dreamed there was a shoot-out at our house on Meat Street and my mother shoved me in a closet to get me out of the line of fire." The emcee waved at the floor manager to turn Peterson off, but Peterson kept talking. "In this kind of a world," Peterson said, "absurd if you will, possibilities nevertheless proliferate and escalate all around us and there are opportunities for beginning again. I am a minor artist and my dealer won't even display my work if he can help it but minor is as minor does and lightning may strike even yet. Don't be reconciled. Turn off your television sets," Peterson said, "cash in your life insurance, indulge in a mindless optimism. Visit girls at dusk. Play the guitar. How can you be alienated without first having been connected? Think back and remember how it was." A man on the floor in front of Peterson was waving a piece of cardboard on which something threatening was written but Peterson ignored him and concentrated on the camera with the little red light. The little red light jumped from camera to camera in an attempt to throw him off balance but Peterson was too smart for it and followed wherever it went. "My mother was a royal virgin," Peterson said, "and my father a shower of gold. My childhood was pastoral and energetic and rich in experiences which developed my character. As a young man I was noble in reason, infinite in faculty, in form express and admirable, and in apprehension . . ." Peterson went on and on and although he was, in a sense, lying, in a sense he was not.

Ralph Ellison

King of the Bingo Game*

THE WOMAN IN FRONT OF HIM was eating roasted peanuts that smelled so good that he could barely contain his hunger. He could not even sleep and wished they'd hurry and begin the bingo game. There, on his right, two fellows were drinking wine out of a bottle wrapped in a paper bag, and he could hear soft gurgling in the dark. His stomach gave a low, gnawing growl. "If this was down South," he thought, "all I'd have to do is lean over and say, 'Lady, gimme a few of those peanuts, please ma'm,' and she'd pass me the bag and never think nothing of it." Or he could ask the fellows for a drink in the same way. Folks down South stuck together that way; they didn't even have to know you. But up here it was different. Ask somebody for something, and they'd think you were crazy. Well, I ain't crazy. I'm just broke, 'cause I got no birth certificate to get a job, and Laura 'bout to die 'cause we got no money for a doctor. But I ain't crazy. And yet a pin-

* "King of the Bingo Game" by Ralph Ellison, copyright © 1944 by Ralph Ellison. Reprinted by permission of the William Morris Agency, Inc.

414

point of doubt was focused in his mind as he glanced toward the screen and saw the hero stealthily entering a dark room and sending the beam of a flashlight along a wall of bookcases. This is where he finds the trapdoor, he remembered. The man would pass abruptly through the wall and find the girl tied to a bed, her legs and arms spread wide, and her clothing torn to rags. He laughed softly to himself. He had seen the picture three times, and this was one of the best scenes.

On his right the fellow whispered wide-eyed to his companion, "Man, look a-yonder!"

"Damn!"

"Wouldn't I like to have her tied up like that . . ."

"Hey! That fool's letting her loose!"

"Aw, man, he loves her."

"Love or no love!"

The man moved impatiently beside him, and he tried to involve himself in the scene. But Laura was on his mind. Tiring quickly of watching the picture he looked back to where the white beam filtered from the projection room above the balcony. It started small and grew large, specks of dust dancing in its whiteness as it reached the screen. It was strange how the beam always landed right on the screen and didn't mess up and fall somewhere else. But they had it all fixed. Everything was fixed. Now suppose when they showed that girl with her dress torn the girl started taking off the rest of her clothes, and when the guy came in he didn't untie her but kept her there and went to taking off his own clothes? *That* would be something to see. If a picture got out of hand like that those guys up there would go nuts. Yeah, and there'd be so many folks in here you couldn't find a seat for nine months! A strange sensation played over his skin. He shuddered. Yesterday he'd seen a bedbug on a woman's neck as they walked out into the bright street. But exploring his thigh through a hole in his pocket he found only goose pimples and old scars.

The bottle gurgled again. He closed his eyes. Now a dreamy music was accompanying the film and train whistles were sounding in the distance, and he was a boy again walking along a railroad trestle down South, and seeing the train coming, and running back as fast as he could go, and hearing the whistle blowing, and getting off the trestle to solid ground just in time, with the earth trembling beneath his feet, and feeling relieved as he ran down the cinder-strewn embankment onto the highway, and looking back and seeing with terror that the train had left the track and was following him right down the middle of the street, and all the white people laughing as he ran screaming . . .

"Wake up there, buddy! What the hell do you mean hollering like that? Can't you see we trying to enjoy this here picture?"

He stared at the man with gratitude.

"I'm sorry, old man," he said. "I musta been dreaming."

"Well, here, have a drink. And don't be making no noise like that, damn!"

His hands trembled as he tilted his head. It was not wine, but whiskey. Cold rye whiskey. He took a deep swoller, decided it was better not to take another, and handed the bottle back to its owner.

"Thanks, old man," he said.

Now he felt the cold whiskey breaking a warm path straight through the middle of him, growing hotter and sharper as it moved. He had not eaten all day, and it made him light-headed. The smell of the peanuts stabbed him like a knife, and he got up and found a seat in the middle aisle. But no sooner did he sit than he saw a row of intense-faced young girls, and got up again, thinking, "You chicks musta been Lindy-hopping somewhere." He found a seat several rows ahead as the lights came on, and he saw the screen disappear behind a heavy red and gold curtain; then the curtain rising, and the man with the microphone and a uniformed attendant coming on the stage.

He felt for his bingo cards, smiling. The guy at the door wouldn't like it if he knew about his having *five* cards. Well, not everyone played the bingo game; and even with five cards he didn't have much of a chance. For Laura, though, he had to have faith. He studied the cards, each with its different numerals, punching the free center hole in each and spreading them neatly across his lap; and when the lights faded he sat slouched in his seat so that he could look from his cards to the bingo wheel with but a quick shifting of his eyes.

Ahead, at the end of the darkness, the man with the microphone was pressing a button attached to a long cord and spinning the bingo wheel and calling out the number each time the wheel came to rest. And each time the voice rang out his finger raced over the cards for the number. With five cards he had to move fast. He became nervous; there were too many cards, and the man went too fast with his grating voice. Perhaps he should just select one and throw the others away. But he was afraid. He became warm. Wonder how much Laura's doctor would cost? Damn that, watch the cards! And with despair he heard the man call three in a row which he missed on all five cards. This way he'd never win . . .

When he saw the row of holes punched across the third card, he sat paralyzed and heard the man call three more numbers before he stumbled forward, screaming,

"Bingo! Bingo!"

"Let that fool up there," someone called.

"Get up there, man!"

He stumbled down the aisle and up the steps to the stage into a light so sharp and bright that for a moment it blinded him, and he felt that he had moved into the spell of some strange, mysterious power. Yet it was as familiar as the sun, and he knew it was the perfectly familiar bingo.

The man with the microphone was saying something to the audience as he held out his card. A cold light flashed from the man's finger as the card left his hand. His knees trembled. The man stepped closer, checking the card against the numbers chalked on the board. Suppose he had made a mistake? The pomade on the man's hair made him feel faint, and he backed away. But the man was checking the card over the microphone now, and he had to stay. He stood tense, listening.

"Under the O, forty-four," the man chanted. "Under the I, seven. Under the G, three. Under the B, ninety-six. Under the N, thirteen!"

His breath came easier as the man smiled at the audience.

"Yessir, ladies and gentlemen, he's one of the chosen people!"

The audience rippled with laughter and applause.

"Step right up to the front of the stage."

He moved slowly forward, wishing that the light was not so bright.

"To win tonight's jackpot of $36.90 the wheel must stop between the double zero, understand?"

He nodded, knowing the ritual from the many days and nights

he had watched the winners march across the stage to press the button that controlled the spinning wheel and receive the prizes. And now he followed the instructions as though he'd crossed the slippery stage a million prize-winning times.

The man was making some kind of a joke, and he nodded vacantly. So tense had he become that he felt a sudden desire to cry and shook it away. He felt vaguely that his whole life was determined by the bingo wheel; not only that which would happen now that he was at last before it, but all that had gone before, since his birth, and his mother's birth and the birth of his father. It had always been there, even though he had not been aware of it, handing out the unlucky cards and numbers of his days. The feeling persisted, and he started quickly away. I better get down from here before I make a fool of myself, he thought.

"Here, boy," the man called. "You haven't started yet."

Someone laughed as he went hesitantly back.

"Are you all reet?"

He grinned at the man's jive talk, but no words would come, and he knew it was not a convincing grin. For suddenly he knew that he stood on the slippery brink of some terrible embarrassment.

"Where are you from, boy?" the man asked.

"Down South."

"He's from down South, ladies and gentlemen," the man said. "Where from? Speak right into the mike."

"Rocky Mont," he said. "Rock' Mont, North Car'lina."

"So you decided to come down off that mountain to the U.S.," the man laughed. He felt that the man was making a fool of him, but then something cold was placed in his hand, and the lights were no longer behind him.

Standing before the wheel he felt alone, but that was somehow right, and he remembered his plan. He would give the wheel a short quick twirl. Just a touch of the button. He had watched it many times, and always it came close to double zero when it was short and quick. He steeled himself; the fear had left, and he felt a profound sense of promise, as though he were about to be repaid for all the things he'd suffered all his life. Trembling, he pressed the button. There was a whirl of lights, and in a second he realized with finality that though he wanted to, he could not stop. It was as though he held a high-powered line in his naked hand. His nerves tightened. As the wheel increased its speed it seemed to draw him more and more into its power, as though it held his fate; and with it came a deep need to submit, to whirl, to lose himself in its swirl of color. He could not stop it now, he knew. So let it be.

The button rested snuggly in his palm where the man had placed it. And now he became aware of the man beside him, advising him through the microphone, while behind the shadowy audience hummed with noisy voices. He shifted his feet. There was still that feeling of helplessness within him, making part of him desire to turn back, even now that the jackpot was right in his hand. He squeezed the button until his fist ached. Then, like the sudden shriek of a subway whistle, a doubt tore through his head. Suppose he did not spin the wheel long enough? What could he do, and how could he tell? And then he knew, even as he wondered, that as long as he pressed the button, he could control the jackpot. He and only he could determine whether or not it was to be his. Not even the man with the microphone could do anything about it now. He felt drunk. Then, as though he had come down from a high hill into a valley of people, he heard the audience yelling.

"Come down from there, you jerk!"

"Let somebody else have a chance . . ."

"Ole Jack thinks he done found the end of the rainbow . . ."

The last voice was not unfriendly, and he turned and smiled dreamily into the yelling mouths. Then he turned his back squarely on them.

"Don't take too long, boy," a voice said.

He nodded. They were yelling behind him. Those folks did not understand what had happened to him. They had been playing the bingo game day in and night out for years, trying to win rent money or hamburger change. But not one of those wise guys had discovered this wonderful thing. He watched the wheel whirling past the numbers and experienced a burst of exaltation: This is God! This is the really truly God! He said it aloud, "This is God!"

He said it with such absolute conviction that he feared he would fall fainting into the footlights. But the crowd yelled so loud that they could not hear. Those fools, he thought. I'm here trying to tell them the most wonderful secret in the world, and they're yelling like they gone crazy. A hand fell upon his shoulder.

"You'll have to make a choice now, boy. You've taken too long."

He brushed the hand violently away.

"Leave me alone, man. I know what I'm doing!"

The man looked surprised and held on to the microphone for support. And because he did not wish to hurt the man's feelings he smiled, realizing with a sudden pang that there was no way of explaining to the man just why he had to stand there pressing the button forever.

"Come here," he called tiredly.

The man approached, rolling the heavy microphone across the stage.

"Anybody can play this bingo game, right?" he said.

"Sure, but . . ."

He smiled, feeling inclined to be patient with this slick looking white man with his blue sport shirt and his sharp gabardine suit.

"That's what I thought," he said. "Anybody can win the jackpot as long as they get the lucky number, right?"

"That's the rule, but after all . . ."

"That's what I thought," he said. "And the big prize goes to the man who knows how to win it?"

The man nodded speechlessly.

"Well then, go on over there and watch me win like I want to. I ain't going to hurt nobody," he said "and I'll show you how to win. I mean to show the whole world how it's got to be done."

And because he understood, he smiled again to let the man know that he held nothing against him for being white and impatient. Then he refused to see the man any longer and stood pressing the button, the voices of the crowd reaching him like sounds in distant streets. Let them yell. All the Negroes down there were just ashamed because he was black like them. He smiled inwardly, knowing how it was. Most of the time he was ashamed of what Negroes did himself. Well, let them be ashamed for something this time. Like him. He was like a long thin black wire that was being stretched and wound upon the bingo wheel; wound until he wanted to scream; wound, but this time himself controlling the winding and the sadness and the shame, and because he did, Laura would be all right. Suddenly the lights flickered. He staggered backwards. Had something gone wrong? All this noise. Didn't they know that although he controlled the wheel, it also controlled him, and unless he pressed the button forever and forever and ever it would stop, leaving him high and dry, dry and high on this hard high slippery hill and Laura dead? There was only one chance; he had to do whatever the wheel demanded. And gripping the button in despair, he discovered with surprise that it imparted a nervous energy. His spine tingled. He felt a certain power.

Now he faced the raging crowd with defiance, its screams penetrating his eardrums like trumpets shrieking from a jukebox. The vague faces glowing in the bingo lights gave him a sense of himself that he had never known before. He was running the show, by God! They had to react to him, for he was their luck. This is *me*, he thought. Let the bastards yell. Then someone was laughing inside him, and he realized that somehow he had forgotten his own name. It was a sad, lost feeling to lose your name, and a crazy thing to do. That name had been given him by the white man who had owned his grandfather a long lost time ago down South. But maybe those wise guys knew his name.

"Who am I?" he screamed.

"Hurry up and bingo, you jerk!"

They didn't know either, he thought sadly. They didn't even know their own names, they were all poor nameless bastards. Well, he didn't need that old name; he was reborn. For as long as he pressed the button he was The-man-who-pressed-the-button-who-held-the-prize-who-was-the-King-of-Bingo. That was the way it was, and he'd have to press the button even if nobody understood, even though Laura did not understand.

"Live!" he shouted.

The audience quieted like the dying of a huge fan.

"Live, Laura, baby. I got holt of it now, sugar. Live!"

He screamed it, tears streaming down his face. "I got nobody but YOU!"

The screams tore from his very guts. He felt as though the rush of blood to his head would burst out in baseball seams of small red droplets, like a head beaten by police clubs. Bending over he saw a trickle of blood splashing the toe of his shoe. With his free hand he searched his head. It was his nose. God, suppose something has gone wrong? He felt that the whole audience had somehow entered him and was stamping its feet in his stomach, and he was unable to throw them out. They wanted the prize, that was it. They wanted the secret for themselves. But they'd never get it;

he would keep the bingo wheel whirling forever, and Laura would be safe in the wheel. But would she? It had to be, because if she were not safe the wheel would cease to turn; it could not go on. He had to get away, *vomit* all, and his mind formed an image of himself running with Laura in his arms down the tracks of the subway just ahead of an A train, running desperately *vomit* with people screaming for him to come out but knowing no way of leaving the tracks because to stop would bring the train crushing down upon him and to attempt to leave across the other tracks would mean to run into a hot third rail as high as his waist which threw blue sparks that blinded his eyes until he could hardly see.

He heard singing and the audience was clapping its hands.

> Shoot the liquor to him, Jim, boy!
> Clap-clap-clap
> Well a-calla the cop
> He's blowing his top!
> Shoot the liquor to him, Jim, boy!

Bitter anger grew within him at the singing. They think I'm crazy. Well let 'em laugh. I'll do what I got to do.

He was standing in an attitude of intense listening when he saw that they were watching something on the stage behind him. He felt weak. But when he turned he saw no one. If only his thumb did not ache so. Now they were applauding. And for a moment he thought that the wheel had stopped. But that was impossible, his thumb still pressed the button. Then he saw them. Two men in uniform beckoned from the end of the stage. They were coming toward him, walking in step, slowly, like a tap-dance team returning for a third encore. But their shoulders shot forward, and he backed away, looking wildly about. There was nothing to fight them with. He had only the long black cord which led to a plug somewhere back stage, and he couldn't use that because it operated the bingo wheel. He backed slowly, fixing the men with his eyes as his lips stretched over his teeth in a tight, fixed grin; moved toward the end of the stage and realizing that he couldn't go much further, for suddenly the cord became taut and he couldn't afford to break the cord. But he had to do something. The audience was howling. Suddenly he stopped dead, seeing the men halt, their legs lifted as in an interrupted step of a slow-motion dance. There was nothing to do but run in the other direction and he dashed forward, slipping and sliding. The men fell back, surprised. He struck out violently going past.

"Grab him!"

He ran, but all too quickly the cord tightened, resistingly, and he turned and ran back again. This time he slipped them, and discovered by running in a circle before the wheel he could keep the cord from tightening. But this way he had to flail his arms to keep the men away. Why couldn't they leave a man alone? He ran, circling.

"Ring down the curtain," someone yelled. But they couldn't do that. If they did the wheel flashing from the projection room would be cut off. But they had him before he could tell them so, trying to pry open his fist, and he was wrestling and trying to bring his knees into the fight and holding on to the button, for it was his life. And now he was down, seeing a foot coming down, crushing his wrist cruelly, down, as he saw the wheel whirling serenely above.

"I can't give it up," he screamed. Then quietly, in a confidential tone, "Boys, I really can't give it up."

It landed hard against his head. And in the blank moment they had it away from him, completely now. He fought them trying to pull him up from the stage as he watched the wheel spin slowly to a stop. Without surprise he saw it rest at double-zero.

"You see," he pointed bitterly.

"Sure, boy, sure, it's O.K.," one of the men said smiling.

And seeing the man bow his head to someone he could not see, he felt very, very happy; he would receive what all the winners received.

But as he warmed in the justice of the man's tight smile he did not see the man's slow wink, nor see the bow-legged man behind him step clear of the swiftly descending curtain and set himself for a blow. He only felt the dull pain exploding in his skull, and he knew even as it slipped out of him that his luck had run out on the stage.

Lawrence Sargent Hall

The Ledge*

ON CHRISTMAS MORNING before sunup the fisherman embraced his warm wife and left his close bed. She did not want him to go. It was Christmas morning. He was a big, raw man, with too much strength, whose delight in winter was to hunt the sea ducks that flew in to feed by the outer ledges, bare at low tide.

As his bare feet touched the cold floor and the frosty air struck his nude flesh, he might have changed his mind in the dark of this special day. It was a home day, which made it seem natural to think of the outer ledges merely as some place he had shot ducks in the past. But he had promised his son, thirteen, and his nephew, fifteen, who came from inland. That was why he had given them his present of an automatic shotgun each the night before, on Christmas Eve. Rough man though he was known to be, and no spoiler of boys, he kept his promises when he understood what they

* Reprinted by permission of Lawrence Sargent Hall. Copyright 1960 by Lawrence Sargent Hall. First published in *The Hudson Review*, Volume XI, No. 4, Winter 1958–59.

meant. And to the boys, as to him, home meant where you came for rest after you had had your Christmas fill of action and excitement.

His legs astride, his arms raised, the fisherman stretched as high as he could in the dim privacy of his bedroom. Above the snug murmur of his wife's protest he heard the wind in the pines and knew it was easterly as the boys had hoped and he had surmised the night before. Conditions would be ideal, and when they were, anybody ought to take advantage of them. The birds would be flying. The boys would get a man's sport their first time outside on the ledges.

His son at thirteen, small but steady and experienced, was fierce to grow up in hunting, to graduate from sheltered waters and the blinds along the shores of the inner bay. His nephew at fifteen, an overgrown farm boy, had a farm boy's love of the sea, though he could not swim a stroke and was often sick in choppy weather. That was the reason his father, the fisherman's brother, was a farmer and chose to sleep in on the holiday morning at his brother's house. Many of the ones the farmer had grown up with were regularly seasick and could not swim, but they were unafraid of the water. They could not have dreamed of being anything but fishermen. The fisherman himself could swim like a seal and was never sick, and he would sooner die than be anything else.

He dressed in the cold and dark, and woke the boys gruffly. They tumbled out of bed, their instincts instantly awake while their thoughts still fumbled slumbrously. The fisherman's wife in the adjacent bedroom heard them apparently trying to find their clothes, mumbling sleepily and happily to each other, while her husband went down to the hot kitchen to fry eggs—sunny-side up, she knew, because that was how they all liked them.

Always in winter she hated to have them go outside, the weather was so treacherous and there were so few others out in case of trouble. To the fisherman these were no more than woman's fears, to be taken for granted and laughed off. When they were first married they fought miserably every fall because she was after him constantly to put his boat up until spring. The fishing was all outside in winter, and though prices were high the storms made the rate of attrition high on gear. Nevertheless he did well. So she could do nothing with him.

People thought him a hard man, and gave him the reputation of being all out for himself because he was inclined to brag and be disdainful. If it was true, and his own brother was one of those who strongly felt it was, they lived better than others, and his brother had small right to criticize. There had been times when in her loneliness she had yearned to leave him for another man. But it would have been dangerous. So over the years she had learned to shut her mind to his hard-driving, and take what comfort she might from his unsympathetic competence. Only once or twice, perhaps, had she gone so far as to dwell guiltily on what it would be like to be a widow.

The thought that her boy, possibly because he was small, would not be insensitive like his father, and the rattle of dishes and smell of frying bacon downstairs in the kitchen shut off from the rest of the chilly house, restored the cozy feeling she had had before she was alone in bed. She heard them after a while go out and shut the back door.

Under her window she heard the snow grind drily beneath their boots, and her husband's sharp, exasperated commands to the boys. She shivered slightly in the envelope of her own warmth. She listened to the noise of her son and nephew talking elatedly. Twice she caught the glimmer of their lights on the white ceiling above the window as they went down the path to the shore. There would be frost on the skiff and freezing suds at the water's edge. She herself used to go gunning when she was younger; now, it seemed to her, anyone going out like that on Christmas morning had to be incurably male. They would none of them think about her until they returned and piled the birds they had shot on top of the sink for her to dress.

Ripping into the quiet pre-dawn cold she heard the hot snarl of the outboard taking them out to the boat. It died as abruptly as it had burst into life. Two or three or four or five minutes later the big engine broke into a warm reassuring roar. He had the best of equipment, and he kept it in the best of condition. She closed her eyes. It would not be too long before the others would be up for Christmas. The summer drone of the exhaust deepened. Then gradually it faded in the wind until it was lost at sea, or she slept.

The engine had started immediately in spite of the temperature. This put the fisherman in a good mood. He was proud of his boat.

Together he and the two boys heaved the skiff and outboard onto the stern and secured it athwartships. His son went forward along the deck, iridescent in the ray of the light the nephew shone through the windshield, and cast the mooring pennant loose into darkness. The fisherman swung to starboard, glanced at his compass, and headed seaward down the obscure bay.

There would be just enough visibility by the time they reached the headland to navigate the crooked channel between the islands. It was the only nasty stretch of water. The fisherman had done it often in fog or at night—he always swore he could go anywhere in the bay blindfolded—but there was no sense in taking chances if you didn't have to. From the mouth of the channel he could lay a straight course for Brown Cow Island, anchor the boat out of sight behind it, and from the skiff set their tollers off Devil's Hump three hundred yards to seaward. By then the tide would be clearing the ledge and they could land and be ready to shoot around half-tide.

It was early, it was Christmas, and it was farther out than most hunters cared to go in this season of the closing year, so that he felt sure no one would be taking possession ahead of them. He had shot thousands of ducks there in his day. The Hump was by far the best hunting. Only thing was you had to plan for the right conditions because you didn't have too much time. About four hours was all, and you had to get it before three in the afternoon when the birds left and went out to sea ahead of nightfall.

They had it figured exactly right for today. The ledge would not be going under until after the gunning was over, and they would be home for supper in good season. With a little luck the boys would have a skiff-load of birds to show for their first time outside. Well beyond the legal limit, which was no matter. You took what you could get in this life, or the next man made out and you didn't.

The fisherman had never failed to make out gunning from Devil's Hump. And this trip, he had a hunch, would be above ordinary. The easterly wind would come up just stiff enough, the tide was right, and it was going to storm by tomorrow morning so the birds would be moving. Things were perfect.

The old fierceness was in his bones. Keeping a weather eye to the murk out front and a hand on the wheel, he reached over and cuffed both boys playfully as they stood together close to the heat of the exhaust pipe running up through the center of the house. They poked back at him and shouted above the drumming engine, making bets as they always did on who would shoot the most birds. This trip they had the thrill of new guns, the best money could buy, and a man's hunting ground. The black retriever wagged at them and barked. He was too old and arthritic to be allowed in December water, but he was jaunty anyway at being brought along.

Groping in his pocket for his pipe the fisherman suddenly had his high spirits rocked by the discovery that he had left his tobacco at home. He swore. Anticipation of a day out with nothing to smoke made him incredulous. He searched his clothes, and then he searched them again, unable to believe the tobacco was not somewhere. When the boys inquired what was wrong he spoke angrily to them, blaming them for being in some devious way at fault. They were instantly crestfallen and willing to put back after the tobacco, though they could appreciate what it meant only through his irritation. But he bitterly refused. That would throw everything out of phase. He was a man who did things the way he set out to do.

He clamped his pipe between his teeth, and twice more during the next few minutes he ransacked his clothes in disbelief. He was no stoic. For one relaxed moment he considered putting about and gunning somewhere nearer home. Instead he held his course and sucked the empty pipe, consoling himself with the reflection that at least he had whiskey enough if it got too uncomfortable on the ledge. Peremptorily he made the boys check to make certain the bottle was really in the knapsack with the lunches where he thought he had taken care to put it. When they reassured him he despised his fate a little less.

The fisherman's judgment was as usual accurate. By the time they were abreast of the headland there was sufficient light so that he could wind his way among the reefs without slackening speed. At last he turned his bow toward open ocean, and as the winter dawn filtered upward through long layers of smoky cloud on the eastern rim his spirits rose again with it.

He opened the throttle, steadied on his course, and settled down to the two hour run. The wind was stronger but seemed less cold coming from the sea. The boys had withdrawn from the fisherman and were talking together while they watched the sky through the windows. The boat churned solidly through a light chop, flinging spray off her flaring bow. Astern the headland thinned rapidly till it lay like a blackened sill on the grey water. No other boats were abroad.

The boys fondled their new guns, sighted along the barrels, worked the mechanisms, compared notes, boasted, and gave each other contradictory advice. The fisherman got their attention once and pointed at the horizon. They peered through the windows and saw what looked like a black scum floating on top of gently agitated water. It wheeled and tilted, rippled, curled, then rose, strung itself out and became a huge raft of ducks escaping over the sea. A good sign.

The boys rushed out and leaned over the washboards in the wind and spray to see the flock curl below the horizon. Then they went and hovered around the hot engine, bewailing their lot. If only they had been already set out and waiting. Maybe these ducks would be crazy enough to return later and be slaughtered. Ducks were known to be foolish.

In due course and right on schedule they anchored at mid-morning in the lee of Brown Cow Island. They put the skiff overboard and loaded it with guns, knapsacks, and tollers. The boys showed their eagerness by being clumsy. The fisherman showed his in bad temper and abuse which they silently accepted in the absorbed tolerance of being boys. No doubt they laid it to lack of tobacco.

By outboard they rounded the island and pointed due east in the direction of a ridge of foam which could be seen whitening the surface three hundred yards away. They set the decoys in a broad, straddling vee opening wide into the ocean. The fisherman warned them not to get their hands wet, and when they did he made them carry on with red and painful fingers, in order to teach them. Once the last toller was bobbing among his fellows, brisk and alluring, they got their numbed fingers inside their oilskins and hugged their warm crotches. In the meantime the fisherman had turned the skiff toward the patch of foam where as if by magic, like a black glossy rib of earth, the ledge had broken through the belly of the sea.

Carefully they inhabited their slippery nub of the North American continent, while the unresting Atlantic swelled and swirled as it had for eons round the indomitable edges. They hauled the skiff after them, established themselves as comfortably as they could in a shallow sump on top, lay on their sides a foot or so above the water, and waited, guns in hand.

In time the fisherman took a thermos bottle from the knapsack and they drank steaming coffee, and waited for the nodding decoys to lure in the first flight to the rock. Eventually the boys got hungry and restless. The fisherman let them open the picnic lunch and eat one sandwich apiece, which they both shared with the dog. Having no tobacco the fisherman himself would not eat.

Actually the day was relatively mild, and they were warm enough at present in their woollen clothes and socks underneath oilskins and hip boots. After a while, however, the boys began to feel cramped. Their nerves were agonized by inactivity. The nephew complained and was severely told by the fisherman—who pointed to the dog, crouched unmoving except for his white-rimmed eyes—that part of doing a man's hunting was learning how to wait. But he was beginning to have misgivings of his own. This could be one of those days where all the right conditions masked an incalculable flaw.

If the fisherman had been alone, as he often was, stopping off when the necessary coincidence of tide and time occurred on his way home from hauling trawls, and had plenty of tobacco, he would not have fidgeted. The boys' being nervous made him nervous. He growled at them again. When it came it was likely to come all at once, and then in a few moments be over. He warned them not to slack off, never to slack off, to be always ready. Under his rebuke they kept their tortured peace, though they could not help shifting and twisting until he lost what patience he had left and bullied them into lying still. A duck could see an eyelid twitch. If the dog could go without moving so could they.

"Here it comes!" the fisherman said tersely at last.

The boys quivered with quick relief. The flock came in downwind, quartering slightly, myriad, black, and swift.

"Beautiful—" breathed the fisherman's son.

"All right," said the fisherman, intense and precise. "Aim at singles in the thickest part of the flock. Wait for me to fire and then don't stop shooting till your gun's empty." He rolled up onto his left elbow and spread his legs to brace himself. The flock bore down, arrowy and vibrant, then a hundred yards beyond the decoys it veered off.

"They're going away!" the boys cried, sighting in.

"Not yet!" snapped the fisherman. "They're coming round."

The flock changed shape, folded over itself, and drove into the wind in a tight arc. "Thousands—" the boys hissed through their teeth. All at once a whistling storm of black and white broke over the decoys.

"Now!" the fisherman shouted. "Perfect!" And he opened fire at the flock just as it hung suspended in momentary chaos above the tollers. The three pulled at their triggers and the birds splashed into the water, until the last report went off unheard, the last smoking shell flew unheeded over their shoulders, and the last of the routed flock scattered diminishing, diminishing, diminishing in every direction.

Exultantly the boys dropped their guns, jumped up and scrambled for the skiff.

"I'll handle that skiff!" the fisherman shouted at them. They stopped. Gripping the painter and balancing himself he eased the skiff into the water stern first and held the bow hard against the side of the rock shelf the skiff had rested on. "You stay here," he said to his nephew. "No sense in all three of us going in the boat."

The boy on the reef gazed at the grey water rising and falling hypnotically along the glistening edge. It had dropped about a foot since their arrival. "I want to go with you," he said in a sullen tone, his eyes on the streaming eddies.

"You want to do what I tell you if you want to gun with me," answered the fisherman harshly. The boy couldn't swim, and he wasn't going to have him climbing in and out of the skiff any more than necessary. Besides he was too big.

The fisherman took his son in the skiff and cruised round and round among the decoys picking up dead birds. Meanwhile the other boy stared unmoving after them from the highest part of the ledge. Before they had quite finished gathering the dead birds, the fisherman cut the outboard and dropped to his knees in the skiff. "Down!" he yelled. "Get down!" About a dozen birds came tolling in. "Shoot—shoot!" his son hollered from the bottom of the boat to the boy on the ledge.

The dog, who had been running back and forth whining, sank to his belly, his muzzle on his forepaws. But the boy on the ledge never stirred. The ducks took late alarm at the skiff, swerved aside and into the air, passing with a whirr no more than fifty feet over the head of the boy, who remained on the ledge like a statue, without his gun, watching the two crouching in the boat.

The fisherman's son climbed onto the ledge and held the painter. The bottom of the skiff was covered with feathery black and white bodies with feet upturned and necks lolling. He was jubilant. "We got twenty-seven!" he told his cousin. "How's that? Nine apiece. Boy—" he added, "what a cool Christmas!"

The fisherman pulled the skiff onto its shelf and all three went and lay down again in anticipation of the next flight. The son, reloading, patted his shotgun affectionately. "I'm going to get me ten next time," he said. Then he asked his cousin, "Whatsamatter—didn't you see the strays?"

"Yeah," the boy said.

"How come you didn't shoot at 'em?"

"Didn't feel like it," replied the boy, still with a trace of sullenness.

"You stupid or something?" The fisherman's son was astounded. "What a highlander!" But the fisherman, though he said nothing, knew that the older boy had had an attack of ledge fever.

"Cripes!" his son kept at it. "I'd at least of tried."

"Shut up," the fisherman finally told him, "and leave him be."

At slack water three more flocks came in, one right after the other, and when it was over, the skiff was half full of clean, dead birds. During the subsequent lull they broke out the lunch and ate it all and finished the hot coffee. For a while the fisherman sucked away on his cold pipe. Then he had himself a swig of whiskey.

The boys passed the time contentedly jabbering about who shot the most—there were ninety-two all told—which of their friends they would show the biggest ones to, how many each could eat at a meal provided they didn't have to eat any vegetables. Now and then they heard sporadic distant gunfire on the mainland, at its nearest point about two miles to the north. Once far off they saw a fishing boat making in the direction of home.

At length the fisherman got a hand inside his oilskins and produced his watch.

"Do we have to go now?" asked his son.

"Not just yet," he replied. "Pretty soon." Everything had been perfect. As good as he had ever had it. Because he was getting tired of the boys' chatter he got up, heavily on his hip boots, and stretched. The tide had turned and was coming in, the sky was more ashen, and the wind had freshened enough so that whitecaps were beginning to blossom. It would be a good hour before they had to leave the ledge and pick up the tollers. However, he guessed they would leave a little early. On account of the rising wind he doubted there would be much more shooting. He stepped carefully along the back of the ledge, to work his kinks out. It was also getting a little colder.

The whiskey had begun to warm him, but he was unprepared for the sudden blaze that flashed upward inside him from belly to head. He was standing looking at the shelf where the skiff was. Only the foolish skiff was not there!

For the second time that day the fisherman felt the deep vacuity of disbelief. He gaped, seeing nothing but the flat shelf of rock. He whirled, started toward the boys, slipped, recovered himself, fetched a complete circle, and stared at the unimaginably empty shelf. Its emptiness made him feel as if everything he had done that day so far, his life so far, he had dreamed. What could have happened? The tide was still nearly a foot below. There had been no sea to speak of. The skiff could hardly have slid off by itself. For the life of him, consciously careful as he inveterately was, he could not now remember hauling it up the last time. Perhaps in the heat of hunting, he had left it to the boy. Perhaps he could not remember which was the last time.

"Christ—" he exclaimed loudly, without realizing it because he was so entranced by the invisible event.

"What's wrong, Dad?" asked his son, getting to his feet.

The fisherman went blind with uncontainable rage. "Get back down there where you belong!" he screamed. He scarcely noticed the boy sink back in amazement. In a frenzy he ran along the ledge thinking the skiff might have been drawn up at another place, though he knew better. There was no other place.

He stumbled, half falling, back to the boys who were gawking at him in consternation, as though he had gone insane. "God damn it!" he yelled savagely, grabbing both of them and yanking them to their knees. "Get on your feet!"

"What's wrong?" his son repeated in a stifled voice.

"Never mind what's wrong," he snarled. "Look for the skiff—it's adrift!" When they peered around he gripped their shoulders, brutally facing them about. "Downwind—" He slammed his fist against his thigh. "Jesus!" he cried, struck to madness at their stupidity.

At last he sighted the skiff himself, magically bobbing along the grim sea like a toller, a quarter of a mile to leeward on a direct course for home. The impulse to strip himself naked was succeeded instantly by a queer calm. He simply sat down on the ledge and forgot everything except the marvellous mystery.

As his awareness partially returned he glanced toward the boys. They were still observing the skiff speechlessly. Then he was gazing into the clear young eyes of his son.

"Dad," asked the boy steadily, "what do we do now?"

That brought the fisherman upright. "The first thing we have to do," he heard himself saying with infinite tenderness as if he were making love, "is think."

"Could you swim it?" asked his son.

He shook his head and smiled at them. They smiled quickly back, too quickly. "A hundred yards maybe, in this water. I wish I could," he added. It was the most intimate and pitiful thing he had ever said. He walked in circles round them, trying to break the stall his mind was left in.

He gauged the level of the water. To the eye it was quite stationary, six inches from the shelf at this second. The fisherman did not have to mark it on the side of the rock against the passing of time to prove to his reason that it was rising, always rising. Already it was over the brink of reason, beyond the margins of thought—a senseless measurement. No sense to it.

All his life the fisherman had tried to lick the element of time, by getting up earlier and going to bed later, owning a faster boat, planning more than the day would hold, and tackling just one other job before the deadline fell. If, as on rare occasions he had the grand illusion, he ever really had beaten the game, he would need to call on all his reserves of practice and cunning now.

He sized up the scant but unforgivable three hundred yards to Brown Cow Island. Another hundred yards behind it his boat rode at anchor, where, had he been aboard, he could have cut in a fathometer to plumb the profound and occult seas, or a ship-to-shore radio on which in an interminably short time he would have heard his wife's voice talking to him over the air about homecoming.

"Couldn't we wave something so somebody would see us?" his nephew suggested.

The fisherman spun round. "Load your guns!" he ordered. They loaded as if the air had suddenly gone frantic with birds. "I'll fire once and count to five. Then you fire. Count to five. That way they won't just think it's only somebody gunning ducks. We'll keep doing that."

"We've only got just two-and-a-half boxes left," said his son.

The fisherman nodded, understanding that from beginning to end their situation was purely mathematical, like the ticking of the alarm clock in his silent bedroom. Then he fired. The dog, who had been keeping watch over the decoys, leaped forward and yelped in confusion. They all counted off, fired the first five rounds by threes, and reloaded. The fisherman scanned first the horizon, then the contracting borders of the ledge, which was the sole place the water appeared to be climbing. Soon it would be over the shelf.

They counted off and fired the second five rounds. "We'll hold off a while on the last one," the fisherman told the boys. He sat down and pondered what a trivial thing was a skiff. This one he and the boy had knocked together in a day. Was a gun manufactured for killing?

His son tallied up the remaining shells, grouping them symmetrically in threes on the rock when the wet box fell apart. "Two short," he announced. They reloaded and laid the guns on their knees.

Behind thickening clouds they could not see the sun going down. The water, coming up, was growing blacker. The fisherman thought he might have told his wife they would be home before dark since it was Christmas day. He realized he had forgotten about its being any particular day. The tide would not be high until two hours after sunset. When they did not get in by nightfall, and could not be raised by radio, she might send somebody to hunt for them right away. He rejected this arithmetic immediately, with a sickening shock, recollecting it was a two-and-a-half hour run at best. Then it occurred to him that she might send somebody on the mainland who was nearer. She would think he had engine trouble.

He rose and searched the shoreline, barely visible. Then his glance dropped to the toy shoreline at the edges of the reef. The shrinking ledge, so sinister from a boat, grew dearer minute by minute as though the whole wide world he gazed on from horizon to horizon balanced on its contracting rim. He checked the water level and found the shelf awash.

Some of what went through his mind the fisherman told to the boys. They accepted it without comment. If he caught their eyes they looked away to spare him or because they were not yet old enough to face what they saw. Mostly they watched the rising water. The fisherman was unable to initiate a word of encouragement. He wanted one of them to ask him whether somebody would reach them ahead of the tide. He would have found it possible to say yes. But they did not inquire.

The fisherman was not sure how much, at their age, they were able to imagine. Both of them had seen from the docks drowned bodies put ashore out of boats. Sometimes they grasped things, and sometimes not. He supposed they might be longing for the comfort of their mothers, and was astonished, as much as he was capable of any astonishment except the supreme one, to discover himself wishing he had not left his wife's dark, close, naked bed that morning.

"Is it time to shoot now?" asked his nephew.

"Pretty soon," he said, as if he were putting off making good on a promise. "Not yet."

His own boy cried softly for a brief moment, like a man, his face averted in an effort neither to give nor show pain.

"Before school starts," the fisherman said, wonderfully detached, "we'll go to town and I'll buy you boys anything you want."

With great difficulty, in a dull tone as though he did not in the least desire it, his son said after a pause, "I'd like one of those new thirty-horse outboards."

"All right," said the fisherman. And to his nephew, "How about you?"

The nephew shook his head desolately. "I don't want anything," he said.

After another pause the fisherman's son said, "Yes he does, Dad. He wants one too."

"All right—" the fisherman said again, and said no more.

The dog whined in uncertainty and licked the boy's faces where they sat together. Each threw an arm over his back and hugged him. Three strays flew in and sat companionably down among the stiff-necked decoys. The dog crouched, obedient to his training. The boys observed them listlessly. Presently, sensing something untoward, the ducks took off, splashing the wave tops with feet and wingtips, into the dusky waste.

The sea began to make up in the mounting wind, and the wind bore a new and deathly chill. The fisherman, scouring the somber, dwindling shadow of the mainland for a sign, hoped it would not snow. But it did. First a few flakes, then a flurry, then storming past horizontally. The fisherman took one long, bewildered look at Brown Cow Island three hundred yards dead to leeward, and got to his feet.

Then it shut in, as if what was happening on the ledge was too private even for the last wan light of the expiring day.

"Last round," the fisherman said austerely.

The boys rose and shouldered their tacit guns. The fisherman fired into the flying snow. He counted methodically to five. His son fired and counted. His nephew. All three fired and counted. Four rounds.

"You've got one left, Dad," his son said.

The fisherman hesitated another second, then he fired the final shell. Its pathetic report, like the spat of a popgun, whipped away on the wind and was instantly blanketed in falling snow.

Night fell all in a moment to meet the ascending sea. They were now barely able to make one another out through driving snowflakes, dim as ghosts in their yellow oilskins. The fisherman heard a sea break and glanced down where his feet were. They seemed to be wound in a snowy sheet. Gently he took the boys by the shoulders and pushed them in front of him, feeling with his feet along the shallow sump to the place where it triangulated into a sharp crevice at the highest point of the ledge. "Face ahead," he told them. "Put the guns down."

"I'd like to hold mine, Dad," begged his son.

"Put it down," said the fisherman. "The tide won't hurt it. Now brace your feet against both sides and stay there."

They felt the dog, who was pitch black, running up and down in perplexity between their straddled legs. "Dad," said his son, "what about the pooch?"

If he had called the dog by name it would have been too personal. The fisherman would have wept. As it was he had all he could do to keep from laughing. He bent his knees, and when he touched the dog hoisted him under one arm. The dog's belly was soaking wet.

So they waited, marooned in their consciousness, surrounded by a monstrous tidal space which was slowly, slowly closing them out. In this space the periwinkle beneath the fisherman's boots was king. While hovering airborne in his mind he had an inward glimpse of his house as curiously separate, like a June mirage.

Snow, rocks, seas, wind the fisherman had lived by all his life. Now he thought he had never comprehended what they were, and he hated them. Though they had not changed. He was deadly chilled. He set out to ask the boys if they were cold. There was no sense. He thought of the whiskey, and sidled backward, still holding the awkward dog, till he located the bottle under water with his toe. He picked it up squeamishly as though afraid of getting his sleeve wet, worked his way forward and bent over his son. "Drink it," he said, holding the bottle against the boy's ribs. The boy tipped his head back, drank, coughed hotly, then vomited.

"I can't," he told his father wretchedly.

"Try—try" the fisherman pleaded, as if it meant the difference between life and death.

The boy obediently drank, and again he vomited hotly. He shook his head against his father's chest and passed the bottle forward to his cousin, who drank and vomited also. Passing the bottle back, the boys dropped it in the frigid water between them.

When the waves reached his knees the fisherman set the warm dog loose and said to his son, "Turn around and get up on my shoulders." The boy obeyed. The fisherman opened his oilskin jacket and twisted his hands behind him through his suspenders, clamping the boy's booted ankles with his elbows.

"What about the dog?" the boy asked.

"He'll make his own way all right," the fisherman said. "He can take the cold water." His knees were trembling. Every instinct shrieked for gymnastics. He ground his teeth and braced like a colossus against the sides of the submerged crevice.

The dog, having lived faithfully as though one of them for eleven years, swam a few minutes in and out around the fisherman's legs, not knowing what was happening, and left them without a whimper. He would swim and swim at random by himself, round and round in the blinding night, and when he had swum routinely through the paralyzing water all he could, he would simply, in one incomprehensible moment, drown. Almost the fisherman, waiting out infinity, envied him his pattern.

Freezing seas swept by, flooding inexorably up and up as the earth sank away imperceptibly beneath them. The boy called out once to his cousin. There was no answer. The fisherman, marvelling on a terror without voice, was dumbly glad when the boy did not call again. His own boots were long full of water. With no sensation left in his straddling legs he dared not move them. So long as the seas came sidewise against his hips, and then sidewise against his shoulders, he might balance—no telling how long. The upper half of him was what felt frozen. His legs, disengaged from his nerves and his will, he came to regard quite scientifically. They were the absurd, precarious axis around which reeled the surged universal tumult. The waves would come on and on; he could not visualize how many tossing reinforcements lurked in the night beyond—inexhaustible numbers, and he wept in supernatural fury at each because it was higher, till he transcended hate and took them, swaying like a convert, one by one as they lunged against him and away aimlessly into their own undisputed, wild realm.

From his hips upward the fisherman stretched to his utmost as a man does whose spirit reaches out of dead sleep. The boy's head, none too high, must be at least seven feet above the ledge. Though growing larger every minute, it was a small light life. The fisherman meant to hold it there, if need be, through a thousand tides.

By and by the boy, slumped on the head of his father, asked, "Is it over your boots, Dad?"

"Not yet," the fisherman said. Then through his teeth he added, "If I fall—kick your boots off—swim for it—downwind—to the island. . . ."

"You . . . ?" the boy finally asked.

The fisherman nodded against the boy's belly. "—Won't see each other," he said.

The boy did for the fisherman the greatest thing that can be done. He may have been too young for perfect terror, but he was old enough to know there were things beyond the power of any man. All he could do he did, by trusting his father to do all he could, and asking nothing more.

The fisherman, rocked to his soul by a sea, held his eyes shut upon the interminable night.

"Is it time now?" the boy said.

The fisherman could hardly speak. "Not yet," he said. "Not just yet. . . ."

As the land mass pivoted toward sunlight the day after Christmas, a tiny fleet of small craft converged off shore like iron filings to a magnet. At daybreak they found the skiff floating unscathed off the headland, half full of ducks and snow. The shooting *had* been good, as someone hearing on the nearby mainland the previous afternoon had supposed. Two hours afterward they found the unharmed boat adrift five miles at sea. At high noon they found the fisherman at ebb tide, his right foot jammed cruelly into a glacial crevice of the ledge beside three shotguns, his hands tangled behind him in his suspenders, and under his right elbow a rubber boot with a sock and a live starfish in it. After dragging unlit depths all day for the boys, they towed the fisherman home in his own boat at sundown, and in the frost of evening, mute with discovering purgatory, laid him on his wharf for his wife to see.

She, somehow, standing on the dock as in her frequent dream, gazing at the fisherman pure as crystal on the icy boards, a small rubber boot still frozen under one clenched arm, saw him exaggerated beyond remorse or grief, absolved of his mortality.

Tillie Olsen

Tell Me a Riddle*

I

FOR FORTY-SEVEN YEARS they had been married. How deep back the stubborn, gnarled roots of the quarrel reached, no one could say—but only now, when tending to the needs of others no longer shackled them together, the roots swelled up visible, split the earth between them, and the tearing shook even to the children, long since grown.

Why now, why now? wailed Hannah.
As if when we grew up weren't enough, said Paul.
Poor Ma. Poor Dad. It hurts so for both of them, said Vivi. They never had very much, at least in old age they should be happy.
Knock their heads together, insisted Sammy, tell 'em: you're too old for this kind of thing; no reason not to get along now.

* From TELL ME A RIDDLE by Tillie Olsen. Reprinted by permission of Delacorte Press/Seymour Lawrence, Inc. Copyright © 1960, 1961 by Tillie Olson. Used by permission.

Lenny wrote to Clara: They've lived over so much together; what could possibly tear them apart?

Something tangible enough.
Arthritic hands, and such work as he got, occasional. Poverty all his life, and there was little breath left for the running. He could not, could not turn away from this desire: to have the troubling of responsibility, the fretting with money, over and done with; to be free, to be *care*free where success was not measured by accumulation, and there was use for the vitality still in him.

There was a way. They could sell the house, and with the money join his lodge's Haven, cooperative for the aged. Happy communal life, and was he not already an official; had he not helped organize it, raise funds, served as a trustee?

But she—would not consider it.

"What do we need all this for?" he would ask loudly, for her hearing aid was turned down and the vacuum was shrilling. "Five rooms" (pushing the sofa so she could get into the corner) "furniture" (smoothing down the rug) "floors and surfaces to make work. Tell me, why do we need it?" And he was glad he could ask in a scream.

"Because I'm use't."

"Because you're use't. This is a reason, Mrs. Word Miser? Used to can get unused!"

"Enough unused I have to get used to already . . . Not enough words?" turning off the vacuum a moment to hear herself answer. "Because soon enough we'll need only a little closet, no windows, no furniture, no rooms, nothing to make work but for worms. Screech and blow like you're doing, you'll need that closet even sooner . . . Ha, again!" for the vacuum bag wailed, puffed half up, hung stubbornly limp. "This time fix it so it stays; quick before the phone rings and you get too important-busy."

But while he struggled with the motor, it seethed in him. Why fix it? Why have to bother? And if it can't be fixed, have to wring the mind with how to pay the repair? At the Haven they come in with their own machines to clean your room or your cottage; you fish, or play cards, or make jokes in the sun, not with knotty fingers fight to mend vacuums.

Over the dishes, coaxingly: "For once in your life, to be free, to have everything done for you, like a queen."

"I never liked queens."

"No dishes, no garbage, no towel to sop, no worry what to buy, what to eat."

"And what else would I do with my empty hands? Better to eat at my own table when I want, and to cook and eat how I want."

"In the cottages they buy what you ask, and cook it how you like. *You* are the one who always used to say: better mankind born without mouths and stomachs than always to worry for money to buy, to shop, to fix, to cook, to wash, to clean."

"How cleverly you hid that you heard. I said it then because eighteen hours a day I ran. And you never scraped a carrot or knew a dish towel sops. Now—for you and me—who cares? A herring out of a jar is enough. But when *I* want, and nobody to bother." And she turned off her ear button, so she would not have to hear.

But as *he* had no peace, juggling and re-juggling the money to figure: how will I pay for this now?; prying out the storm windows (there they take care of this); jolting in the streetcar on errands (there I would not have to ride to take care of this or that); fending the patronizing of relatives just back from Florida (there it matters what one is, not what one can afford), he gave *her* no peace.

"Look! In their bulletin. A reading circle. Twice a week it meets."

"Haumm," her answer of not listening.

"A reading circle. Chekhov they read that you like, and Peretz. Cultured people at the Haven that you would enjoy."

"Enjoy!" She tasted the word. "Now, when it pleases you, you find a reading circle for me. And forty years ago when the children were morsels and there was a Circle, did you stay home with them once so I could go? Even once? You trained me well. I do not need others to enjoy. Others!" Her voice trembled. "Because *you* want to be there with others. Already it makes me sick to think of you always around others. Clown, grimacer, floormat, yesman, entertainer, whatever they want of you." And now it was he who turned on the television loud so he need not hear.

Old scar tissue ruptured and the wounds festered anew. Chekhov indeed. She thought without softness of that young wife, who in the deep night hours while she nursed the current baby, and perhaps held another in her lap, would try to stay awake for the only time there was to read. She would feel again the weather of the outside on his cheek when, coming late from a meeting, he would find her so, and stimulated and ardent, sniffing her skin, coax: "I'll put the baby to bed, and you—put the book away, don't read, don't read."

That had been the most beguiling of all the "don't read, put your book away" her life had been. Chekhov indeed!

"Money?" She shrugged him off. "Could we get poorer than once we were? And in America, who starves?"

But as still he pressed:

"Let me alone about money. Was there ever enough? Seven little ones—for every penny I had to ask—and sometimes, remember, there was nothing. But always *I* had to manage. Now *you* manage. Rub your nose in it good."

But from those years she had had to manage, old humiliations and terrors rose up, lived again, and forced her to relive them. The children's needings; that grocer's face or this merchant's wife she had had to beg credit from when credit was a disgrace, the scenery of the long blocks she had walked around when she could not pay them; school coming, and the desperate going over the old to see what could yet be re-made; the soups of meat bones begged "for-the-dog" one winter . . .

Enough. Now they had no children. Let *him* wrack his head for how they would live. She would not exchange her solitude for anything. *Never again to be forced to move to the rhythms of others.*

For in this solitude she had won to a reconciled peace.

Tranquillity from having the empty house no longer an enemy, for it stayed clean—not as in the days when (by the perverse logic of exhausted housewifery) it was her family, the life in it, that had seemed the enemy: tracking, smudging, littering, dirtying, engaging her in endless defeating battle—and on whom her endless defeat had been spewed.

The few old books, memorized from re-reading; the pictures to ponder (the magnifying glass superimposed on her heavy eyeglasses). Or if she wishes, when he is gone, the phonograph, that if she turns up very loud and strains, she can hear: the ordered sounds, and the struggling.

Out in the garden, growing things to nurture. Birds to be kept out of the pear tree, and when the pears are heavy and ripe, the old fury of work, for all must be canned, nothing wasted.

And her one social duty (for she will not go to luncheons or meetings) the boxes of old clothes left with her, as with a life-practiced eye for finding what is still wearable within the worn (again the magnifying glass superimposed on the heavy glasses) she scans and sorts—this for rag or rummage, that for mending and cleaning, and this for sending abroad.

Being able at last to live within, and not move to the rhythms of others, as life had helped her to: denying; estranging; taking the children one by one; then deafening, half blinding—and at last, presenting her solitude.

And in it she had won to a reconciled peace.

Now he was violating it with his constant campaigning: *Sell the house and move to the Haven.* (You sit, you sit—there too you could sit like a stone.) He was making of her a battleground where old grievances tore. (Turn on your ear button—I am talking.) And stubbornly she resisted—so that from wheedling, reasoning, manipulation, it was bitterness he now started with.

And it came to where every happening lashed up a quarrel.

"I will sell the house anyway," he flung at her one night. "I am putting it up for sale. There'll be a way to make you sign."

The television blared, as always it did on the evenings he stayed home, and as always it reached her only as noise. She did not know if the tumult was in her or outside. Snap! she turned the sound off. "Shadows," she whispered to him, pointing to the screen, "look, it is only shadows." And in a scream: "Did you say you will sell the house? Look at me, not at that. I am no shadow. You cannot sell without me."

"Leave on the television. I am watching."

"Like Paulie, like Jenny, a four-year-old. Staring at shadows. *You cannot sell the house.*"

"I will. We are going to the Haven. There you would not have the television when you do not want it. I could sit in the social room and watch. You could lock yourself up to smell your unpleasantness in a room by yourself—for who would want to come near you?"

"No, no selling." A whisper now.

"The television is shadows. Mrs. Enlightened! Mrs. Cultured! A world comes into your house—and it is shadows. People you would never meet in a thousand lifetimes. Wonders. When you were four years old, yes, like Paulie, like Jenny, did you know of Indian dances, alligators, how they used bamboo in Malaya? No, you scratched in your dirt with the chickens and thought Olshana was the world. Yes, Mrs. Unpleasant, I will sell the house, for there better can we be rid of each other than here."

She did not know if the tumult was outside, or in her. Always a ravening inside, a pull to the bed, to lie down, to succumb.

"Have you thought maybe Ma should let a doctor have a look at her?" asked their son Paul after Sunday dinner, regarding his mother crumpled on the couch, instead of, as was her custom, busying herself in Nancy's kitchen.

"Why not the President too?"

"Seriously, Dad. This is the third Sunday she's lain down like that after dinner. Is she that way at home?"

"A regular love affair with the bed. Every time I start to talk to her."

Good protective reaction, observed Nancy to herself. The workings of hos-ti-lity.

"Nancy could take her. I don't like how she looks. Let's have Nancy arrange an appointment."

"You think she'll go?" regarding his wife gloomily. "All right, we have to have doctor bills, we have to have doctor bills." Loudly: "Something hurts you?"

She startled, looked to his lips. He repeated: "Mrs. Take It Easy, something hurts?"

"Nothing . . . Only you."

"A woman of honey. That's why you're lying down?"

"Soon I'll get up to do the dishes, Nancy."

"Leave them, Mother, I like it better this way."

"Mrs. Take It Easy, Paul says you should start ballet. You should go see a doctor and ask: how soon can you start ballet?"

"A doctor?" she begged. "Ballet?"

"We were talking, Ma," explained Paul, "you don't seem any too well. It would be a good idea for you to see a doctor for a checkup."

"I get up now to do the kitchen. Doctors are bills and foolishness, my son. I need no doctors."

"At the Haven," he could not resist pointing out, "a doctor is *not* bills. He lives beside you. You start to sneeze, he is there before you open up a kleenex. You can be sick there for free, all you want."

"Diarrhea of the mouth, is there a doctor to make you dumb?"

"Ma. Promise me you'll go. Nancy will arrange it."

"It's all of a piece when you think of it," said Nancy, "the way she attacks my kitchen, scrubbing under every cup hook, doing the inside of the oven so I can't enjoy Sunday dinner, knowing half blind or not, she's going to find every speck of dirt . . ."

"Don't, Nancy, I've told you—it's the only way she knows to be useful. What did the *doctor* say?"

"A real fatherly lecture. Sixty-nine is young these days. Go out, enjoy life, find interests. Get a new hearing aid, this one is antiquated. Old age is sickness only if one makes it so. Geriatrics, Inc."

"So there was nothing physical."

"Of course there was. How can you live to yourself the way she does without there being? Evidence of a kidney disorder, and her blood count is low. He gave her a diet, and she's to come back for follow-up and lab work . . . But he was clear enough: Number One prescription—start living like a human being. When I think of your dad who could really play the invalid with that arthritis of his, is active as a teen-ager, and twice as much fun . . ."

"You didn't tell me the doctor says your sickness is in you, how you live." He pushed his advantage. "Life and enjoyments you need better than medicine. And this diet, how can you keep it? To weigh each morsel and scrape away the bits of fat to make this soup, that pudding. There, at the Haven, they have a dietician, they would do it for you."

She is silent.

"You would feel better there, I know it," he says gently. "There there is life and enjoyments all around."

"What is the matter, Mr. Importantbusy, you have no card game or meeting you can go to?"—turning her face to the pillow.

For a while he cut his meetings and going out, fussed over her diet, tried to wheedle her into leaving the house, brought in visitors:

"I should come to a fashion tea. I should sit and look at

pretty babies in clothes I cannot buy. This is pleasure?"
"Always you are better than everyone else. The doctor said you should go out. Mrs. Brem comes to you with goodness and you turn her away."
"Because *you* asked her to, she asked me."
"They won't come back. People you need, the doctor said. Your own cousins I asked; they were willing to come and make peace as if nothing had happened . . ."
"No more crushers of people, pushers, hypocrites, around me. No more in *my* house. You go to them if you like."
"Kind he is to visit. And you, like ice."
"A babbler. All my life around babblers. Enough!"

"She's even worse, Dad? Then let her stew awhile," advised Nancy. "You can't let it destroy you; it's a psychological thing, maybe too far gone for any of us to help."

So he let her stew. More and more she lay silent in bed, and sometimes did not even get up to make the meals. No longer was the tongue-lashing inevitable if he left the coffee cup where it did not belong, or forgot to take out the garbage or mislaid the broom. The birds grew bold that summer and for once, pocked the pears, undisturbed.

A bellyful of bitterness, and every day the same quarrel in a new way and a different old grievance the quarrel forced her to enter and re-live. And the new torment: I am not really sick, the doctor said it, then why do I feel so sick?

One night she asked him: "You have a meeting tonight? Do not go. Stay . . . with me."

He had planned to watch "This Is Your Life" anyway, but half sick himself from the heavy heat, and sickening therefore the more after the brooks and woods of the Haven, with satisfaction he grated:

"Hah, Mrs. Live Alone And Like It wants company all of a sudden. It doesn't seem so good the time of solitary when she was a girl exile in Siberia. 'Do not go. Stay with me.' A new song for Mrs. Free As A Bird. Yes, I am going out, and while I am gone chew this aloneness good, and think how you keep us both from where if you want people you do not need to be alone."

"Go, go. All your life you have gone without me."

After him she sobbed curses he had not heard in years, old country curses from their childhood: Grow, oh shall you grow like an onion, with your head in the ground. Like the hide of a drum shall you be, beaten in life, beaten in death. Oh shall you be like a chandelier, to hang, and to burn . . .

She was not in their bed when he came back. She lay on the cot on the sun porch. All week she did not speak or come near him; nor did he try to make peace or care for her.

He slept badly, so used to her next to him. After all the years, old harmonies and dependencies deep in their bodies; she curled to him, or he coiled to her, each warmed, warming, turning as the other turned, the nights a long embrace.

It was not the empty bed or the storm that woke him, but a faint singing. *She* was singing. Shaking off the drops of rain, the lightning riving her lifted face, he saw her so; the cot covers on the floor.

"This is a private concert?" he asked. "Come in, you are wet."

"I can breathe now," she answered, "my lungs are rich." Though indeed the sound was hardly a breath.

"Come in, come in." Loosing the bamboo shades. "Look how wet you are." Half helping, half carrying her, still faint-breathing her song.

A Russian love song of fifty years ago.

He had found a buyer, but before he told her, he called together those children who were close enough to come. Paul, of course, Sammy from New Jersey, Hannah from Connecticut, Vivi from Ohio.

With a kindling of energy for her beloved visitors, she arrayed the house, cooked and baked. She was not prepared for the solemn after-dinner conclave, they too probing in and tearing. Her frightened eyes watched from mouth to mouth as each spoke.

His stories were eloquent and funny of her refusal to go back to the doctor; of the scorned invitations; of her stubborn silences or the bile "like a Niagara"; of her contrariness: "If I clean it's no good how I cleaned; if I don't clean, I'm still a master who thinks he has a slave."

"(Vinegar, vinegar he poured on me all his life; I am well marinated; how can I be honey now?")

Deftly he marched in the rightness for moving to the Haven; their money from social security free for visiting the children, not sucked into daily needs and into the house; the activities in the Haven for him; but mostly the Haven for *her:* her health, her need of care, distraction, amusement, friends who shared her interests.

"This does offer an outlet for Dad," said Paul; "he's always been an active person. And economic peace of mind isn't to be sneezed at, either, I could use a little of that myself."

But when they asked: "And you, Ma, how do you feel about it?" she could only whisper:

"For him it is good. It is not for me. I can no longer live between people."

"You lived all your life *for* people," Vivi cried.

"Not with." Suffering doubly for the unhappiness on her children's faces.

"You have to find some compromise," Sammy insisted. "Maybe sell the house and buy a trailer. After forty-seven years there's surely some way you can find to live in peace."

"There is no help. Different things we need."

"Then live alone!" He could control himself no longer. "I have a buyer for the house. Half the money for you, half for me. Either alone or with me to the Haven. You think I can live any longer as we are doing now?"

"Ma doesn't have to make a decision this minute, however you feel, Dad," Paul said quickly, "and you wouldn't want her to. Let's let it lay a few months, and then talk some more."

"I think I can work it out to take Mother home with me for a while," Hannah said. "You both look terrible, but especially you, Mother. I'm going to ask Phil to have a look at you."

"Sure," cracked Sammy. "What's the use of a doctor husband if you can't get free service out of him once in a while for the family. And absence might make the heart . . . you know."

"There was something after all," Paul told Nancy in a colorless voice. "That was Hannah's Phil calling. Her gall bladder . . . Surgery."

"Her *gall* bladder. If that isn't classic. 'Bitter as gall'—talk of psychosom—"

He stepped closer, put his hand over her mouth and said in the same colorless, plodding voice. "We have to get Dad. They operated at once. The cancer was everywhere, surrounding the liver, everywhere. They did what they could . . . at best she has a year. Dad . . . we have to tell him."

II

Honest in his weakness when they told him, and that she was not to know. "I'm not an actor. She'll know right away by how I am. O that poor woman. I am old too, it will break me into pieces. O that poor woman. She will spit on me: 'So my sickness was how I live.' O Paulie, how she will be, that poor woman. Only she should not suffer . . . I can't stand sickness, Paulie, I can't go with you."

But went. And play-acted.

"A grand opening and you did not even wait for me . . . A good thing Hannah took you with her."

"Fashion teas I needed. They cut out what tore in me; just in my throat something hurts yet . . . Look! so many flowers, like a funeral. Vivi called, did Hannah tell you? And Lenny from San Francisco, and Clara; and Sammy is coming." Her gnome's face pressed happily into the flowers.

> It is impossible to predict in these cases, but once over the immediate effects of the operation, she should have several months of comparative well-being.
> *The money, where will come the money?*
> Travel with her, Dad, the next few months.
> Don't take her home to the old associations. The other children will want to see her.
> *The money, where will I wring the money?*
> Whatever happens, she is not to know. No, you can't ask her to sign papers to sell the house; nothing to upset her. Borrow instead, then after . . .
> *I had wanted to leave you each a few dollars to make life easier,*

as other fathers do. There will be nothing left now. (Failure! you and your "business is exploitation." Why didn't you make it when it could be made?—Is that what you're thinking Sammy?)
Sure she's unreasonable, Dad—but you have to stay with her; if there's to be any happiness in what's left of her life, it depends on you.
Prop me up children, think of me, too. Shuffled, chained with her, bitter woman. No Haven, and the little money going . . . How happy she looks, poor creature.

The look of excitement. The straining to hear everything (the new hearing aid turned full). Why are you so happy, dying woman?

How the petals are, fold on fold, and the gladioli color. The autumn air.

Stranger grandsons, tall above the little gnome grandmother, the little spry grandfather. Paul in a frenzy of picture-taking before going.

She, wandering the great house. Feeling the books; laughing at the maple shoemaker's bench of a hundred years ago used as a table. The ear turned to music.

"Let us go home. See how good I walk now." "One step from the hospital," he answers, "and she wants to fly. Wait till Doctor Phil says."

"Look—the birds too are flying home. Very good Phil is and will not show it, but he is sick of sickness by the time he comes home." "Mrs Telepathy, to read minds," he answers, "read mine what it says: when the trunks of medicines become a suitcase, then we will go."

The grandboys, they do not know what to say to us . . . Hannah, she runs around here, there, when is there time for herself?

Let us go home. Let us go home.

Musing; gentleness—*but for the incidents of the rabbi in the hospital, and of the candles of benediction.*
Of the rabbi in the hospital:

Now tell me what happened, Mother.

From the sleep I awoke, Hannah's Phil, and he stands there like a devil in a dream and calls me by name. I cannot hear. I think

he prays. Go away please, I tell him, I am not a believer. Still he stands, while my heart knocks with fright.
You scared *him,* Mother. He thought you were delirious.
Who sent him? Why did he come to me?
It is a custom. The men of God come to visit those of their religion they might help. Jew, Protestant, Catholic, the hospital makes up the list for them, and you are on the Jewish list. Not for rabbis. At once go and make them change. Tell them to write: Born, human; Religion, none.

And of the candles of benediction:
Look how you have upset yourself, Mrs. Excited Over Nothing. Pleasant memories you should leave.
Go in, go back to Hannah and the lights. Two weeks I saw and said nothing. But she asked me.
So what was so terrible? She forgets you never did, she asks you to light the Friday candles and say the benediction like Phil's mother when she visits. If the candles give her pleasure, why shouldn't she have the pleasure?
Not for pleasure she does it. For emptiness. Because his family does. Because all around her do.
That is not a good reason to? But you did not hear her. For heritage, she told you. For the boys, from the past they should have tradition.
Superstition! From the savages, afraid of the dark, of themselves: mumbo words and magic lights to scare away ghosts.
She told you: how it started does not take away the goodness. For centuries, peace in the house it means.
Swindler! does she look back on the centuries? Candles bought instead of bread and stuck into a potato for a candlestick? Religion that said: in Paradise, woman, you will be the footstool of your husband, and in life—poor chosen Jew—ground under, despised, trembling in cellars. And cremated. And cremated. This is religion's fault? You think you are still an orator of the 1905 revolution? Where are the pills for quieting? Which are they?
Heritage. How have we gone from the savages, how no longer to be savages, this to teach. To look back and learn what ennobled man, this to teach. Books in the house, will man live or die, and she gives to her boys—superstition.

Hannah that is so good to you. Take your pill, Mrs. Excited For Nothing, swallow.

Heritage! But when did I have time to teach? Of Hannah I asked only hands to help.

Swallow.

Otherwise—musing; gentleness.

   Not to travel. To go home.

The children want to see you. We have to show them you are as thorny a flower as ever.

   Not to travel.

Vivi wants you should see her new baby. She sent the tickets—airplane tickets—a Mrs. Roosevelt she wants to make of you. To Vivi's we have to go.

   A new baby. How many warm, seductive babies. She holds him stiffly, *away* from her, so that he wails. And a long shudder begins, and the sweat beads on her forehead.

"Hush, shush," croons the grandfather, lifting him back. "You should forgive your grandmamma, little prince, she has never held a baby before, only seen them in glass cases. Hush, shush."

"You're tired, Ma," says Vivi. "The travel and the noisy dinner. I'll take you to lie down."

(*A long travel from, to, what the feel of a baby evokes.*)

   In the airplane, cunningly designed to encase from motion (no wind, no feel of flight), she had sat severely and still, her face turned to the sky through which they cleaved and left no scar.

So this was how it looked, the determining, the crucial sky, and this was how man moved through it, remote above the dwindled earth, the concealed human life. Vulnerable life, that could scar.

A steerage ship in memory shook across a great, circular sea: clustered, ill human beings, and through the thick-stained air, tiny fretting waters in a window round like the airplane's—sun round, moon round. (The round thatched hut roofs of Olshana.) Eye round—like the smaller window that framed distance the solitary year of her exile when only her eyes could travel, and no voice spoke. And the polar winds hurled themselves across snow trackless and endless and white—like the clouds which had closed together below and hidden the earth.

Now they put a baby in her lap. Do not ask me, she would have liked to beg. Enough the worn face of Vivi, the remembered grandchildren. I cannot, cannot . . .

Cannot what? Unnatural grandmother, not able to make herself embrace a baby.

She lay there in the bed of the two little girls, her new hearing aid turned full, listening to the sound of the children going to sleep, the baby's fretful crying and hushing, the clatter of dishes being washed and put away. They thought she slept. Still she rode on.

It was not that she had not loved her babies, her children. The love—the passion of tending—had risen with the need like a torrent; and like a torrent drowned and immolated all else. But when the need was done—o the power that was lost in the painful damming back and drying up of what still flooded, but had nowhere to go. Only the thin pulsing left that could not quiet, suffering over lives one felt, but could no longer hold nor help.

On that torrent she had borne them to their lives, and the riverbed was desert long years now. Not there would she dwell, a memoried wraith. Surely that was not all, surely there was more. Still the springs, the springs were in her seeking. Somewhere an older power that beat for life. Somewhere coherence, transport, meaning. If they would but leave her in the air now stilled of clamor, in the reconciled solitude, to journey to her life.

And they put a baby in her lap. Immediacy to embrace, and the breath of *that* past: warm flesh like this that had claims and nuzzled away all else and with lovely mouths devoured; hot living like an animal—intensely and now; the turning maze; the long drunkenness; the drowning into needing and being needed. Severely she looked back—and the shudder seized her again, and the sweat. Not that way. Not there, not now could she, not yet . . .

And all that visit, she could not touch the baby.

"Daddy, is it the . . . sickness she's like that?" asked Vivi. "I was so glad to be having the baby—for her. I told Tim, it'll give her more happiness than anything, being around a baby again. And she hasn't played with him once."

He was not listening. "Aahh little seed of life, little charmer," he crooned, "Hollywood should see you. A heart of ice you would melt. Kick, kick. The future you'll have for a ball. In 2050 still kick. Kick for your granddaddy then."

Attentive with the older children; sat through their performances (command performance; we command you to be the audience); helped Ann sort autumn leaves to find the best for a school program; listened gravely to Richard tell about his rock collection, while her lips mutely formed the words to remember: *igneous, sedimentary, metamorphic;* looked for missing socks, books and bus tickets; watched the children whoop after their grandfather who knew how to tickle, chuck, lift, toss, do tricks, tell secrets, make jokes, match riddle for riddle. (Tell me a riddle, Grammy. I know no riddles, child.) Scrubbed sills and woodwork and furniture in every room; folded the laundry; straightened drawers; emptied the heaped baskets waiting for ironing (while he or Vivi or Tim nagged: You're supposed to rest here, you've been sick) but to none tended or gave good—and could not touch the baby.

After a week she said: "Let us go home. Today call about the tickets."

"You have important business, Mrs. Inahurry? The President waits to consult with you?" He shouted, for the fear of the future raced in him. "The clothes are still warm from the suitcase, your children cannot show enough how glad they are to see you, and you want home. There is plenty of time for home. We cannot be with the children at home."

"Blind to around you as always: the little ones sleep four in a room because we take their bed. We are two more people in a house with a new baby, and no help."

"Vivi is happy so. The children should have their grandparents a while, she told to me. I should have my mommy and daddy . . ."

"Babbler and blind. Do you look at her so tired? How she starts to talk and she cries? I am not strong enough yet to help. Let us go home."

(To reconciled solitude.)

For it seemed to her the crowded noisy house was listening to her, listening for her. She could feel it like a great ear pressed

under her heart. And everything knocked: quick constant raps: let me in, let me in.
How was it that soft reaching tendrils also became blows that knocked?
Cmon Grandma, I want to show you . . .
Tell me a riddle, Grandma. (*I know no riddles*)
Look Grammy, he's so dumb he can't even find his hands. (Dody and the baby on a blanket over the fermenting autumn mound) I made it—for you. (Flat paper dolls with aprons that lifted on scalloped skirts that lifted on flowered pants; hair of yarn and great ringed questioning eyes) (Ann) Watch me, Grandma. Richard snaking up the tree, hanging exultant, free, with one hand at the top. Below Dody hunches over in pretend-cooking. (Climb too, Dody, climb and look) Be my nap bed, Grammy. (The "No!" too late.) Morty's abandoned heaviness, while his fingers ladder up and down her hearing-aid cord to his drowsy chant: eentsiebeentsiespider. (*Children trust*) It's to start off your own rock collection. Grandma. That's a trilobite fossil, 200 million years old (millions of years on a boy's mouth) and that one's obsidian, black glass.
Knocked and knocked.
Mother, I *told* you the teacher said we had to bring it back all filled out this morning. Didn't you even ask Daddy? Then tell *me* which plan and I'll check it: evacuate or stay in the city or wait for you to come and take me away. (Seeing the look of straining to hear) It's for Disaster, Grandma. (*Children trust*) Vivi in the maze of the long, the lovely drunkenness. The old old noises: baby sounds, screaming of a mother flayed to exasperation; children quarreling; children playing; singing; laughter.

And Vivi's tears and memories, spilling so fast, half the words not understood.
She had started remembering out loud deliberately, so her mother would know the past was cherished, still lived in her.
Nursing the baby: My friends marvel, and I tell them, oh it's easy to be such a cow. I remember how beautiful my mother seemed nursing my brother, and the milk just flows . . . Was that Davy? It must have been Davy . . .
Lowering a hem: How did you ever . . . when I think how you

made everything we wore . . . Tim, just think, seven kids and Mommy sewed everything . . . do I remember you sang while you sewed? That white dress with the red apples on the skirt you fixed over for me, was it Hannah's or Clara's before it was mine?

Washing sweaters: Ma, I'll never forget, one of those days so nice you washed clothes outside; one of the first spring days it must have been. The bubbles just danced up and down while you scrubbed, and we chased after, and you stopped to show us how to blow our own bubbles with green onion stalks . . . you always . . .

"Strong onion, to still make you cry after so many years," her father said, to turn the tears into laughter.

While Richard bent over his homework: where is it now, do we still have it, the Book of the Martyrs? It always seemed so, well—exalted, when you'd put it on the round table and we'd all look at it together; there was even a halo from the lamp. The lamp with the beaded fringe you could move up and down; they're in style again, pulley lamps like that, but without the fringe. You know the book I'm talking about, Daddy, the Book of the Martyrs, the first picture was a bust of Socrates? I wish there was something like that for the children, Mommy, to give them what you . . . (And the tears splashed again)

(What I intended and did not? Stop it, daughter, stop it, leave that time. And he, the hypocrite, sitting there with tears in his eyes too—it was nothing to you then, nothing.)

. . . The time you came to school and I almost died of shame because of your accent and because I knew you knew I was ashamed; how could I? . . . Sammy's harmonica and you danced to it once yes you did you and Davy squealing in your arms . . . That time you bundled us up and walked us down to the railroad station to stay the night 'cause it was heated and we didn't have any coal, that winter of the strike, you didn't think I remembered that, did you, Mommy? . . . How you'd call us out to see the sunsets . . .

Day after day, the spilling memories. Worse now, questions, too. Even the grandchildren: Grandma, in the olden days, when you were little . . .

It was the afternoons that saved.

While they thought she napped, she would leave the mosaic on the wall (of children's drawings, maps, calendars, pictures, Ann's cardboard dolls with their great ringed questioning eyes) and hunch in the girls' closet, on the low shelf where the shoes stood, and the girls' dresses covered.

For that while she would painfully sheathe against the listening house, the tendrils and noises that knocked, and Vivi's spilling memories. Sometimes it helped to braid and unbraid the sashes that dangled, or to trace the pattern on the hoop slips.

Today she had jacks and children under jet trails to forget. Last night, Ann and Dody silhouetted in the window against a sunset of flaming man-made clouds of jet trail, their jacks' ball accenting the peaceful noise of dinner being made. Had she told them, yes she had told them of how they played jacks in her village though there was no ball, no jacks. Six stones, round and flat, toss them out, the seventh on the back of the hand, toss, catch and swoop up as many as possible, toss again . . .

Of stones (repeating Richard) there are three kinds: earth's fire jetting; rock of layered centuries; crucibled new out of the old. But there was that other—frozen to black glass, never to transform or hold the fossil memory . . . (let not my seed fall on stone). There was an ancient man who fought to heights a great rock that crashed back down eternally—eternal labor, freedom, labor . . . (stone will perish, but the word remain) And you, David, who with a stone slew, screaming: Lord, take my heart of stone and give me flesh.

Who was screaming? Why was she back in the common room of the prison, the sun motes dancing in the shafts of light, and the informer being brought in, a prisoner now, like themselves. And Lisa leaping, yes, Lisa, the gentle and tender, biting at the betrayer's jugular. Screaming and screaming.

No, it is the children screaming. Another of Paul and Sammy's terrible fights?

In Vivi's house. Severely: you are in Vivi's house.

Blows, screams, a call: "Grandma!" For her? O please not for her. Hide, hunch behind the dresses deeper. But a trembling little body hurls itself beside her—surprised, smothered laughter—arms surround her neck, tears rub dry on her cheek, and words too soft to understand whisper into her ear (Is this where you hide too, Grammy? It's my secret place, we have a secret now)

And the sweat beads, and the long shudder seizes.

It seemed the great ear pressed inside now, and the knocking. "We have to go home," she told him, "I grow ill here."

"It is your own fault, Mrs. Bodybusy, you do not rest, you do too much." He raged, but the fear was in his eyes. "It was a serious operation, they told you to take care . . . All right, we will go to where you can rest."

But where? Not home to death, not yet. He had thought to Lenny's yet, to Clara's; beautiful visits with each of the children. She would have to rest first, be stronger. If they could but go to Florida—it glittered before him the never-realized promise of Florida—California: of course. (The money, the money dwindling!) Los Angeles first for sun and rest, then to Lenny's in San Francisco.

He told her the next day. "You saw what Nancy wrote: snow and wind back home, a terrible winter. And look at you—bones and a swollen belly. I called Phil: he said: 'A prescription, Los Angeles sun and rest.'"

"You have sold the house," she cried, "that is why we do not go home. That is why you talk no more of the Haven, that is why there is money for travel. After the children you will drag me to the Haven."

"The Haven! Who thinks of the Haven any more? Tell her, Vivi, tell Mrs. Suspicious: a prescription, sun and rest, to make you healthy . . . And how could I sell the house without *you*?"

At the place of farewells and greetings, of winds of coming and winds of going, they say their good-bys.

They look back at her with the eyes of others before them: Richard with her own blue blaze; Ann with the Nordic eyes of Tim; Morty's dreaming brown of a great grandmother he will never know; Dody with the laughing eyes of him who had been her springtime love (who stands beside her now); Vivi's, all tears.

The baby's eyes are closed in sleep.

Good-by, my children.

III

It is to the back of the great city he brought her, to the dwelling places of the cast-off old. Bounded by two lines of amusement piers to the north and to the south, and between a long straight paving rimmed with black benches facing the sands—sands so wide the ocean is only a far fluted edge.

In the brief vacation season, some of the boarded stores fronting the sands open, and families, young people and children may be seen. A little tasseled tram shuttles between the piers, and the lights of roller coasters prink and tweak over those who come to have sensation made in them.

The rest of the year it is abandoned to the old, all else boarded up and still; seemingly empty, except the occasional days and hours when the sun, like a tide, sucks them out of the low rooming houses, casts them onto the benches and sandy rim of the walk—and sweeps them into decaying enclosures back again.

A few newer apartments glint among the low bleached squares. It is in one of these Lenny's Jeannie has arranged their rooms. "Only a few miles north and south people pay hundreds of dollars a month for just this gorgeous air, Granddaddy, just this ocean closeness."

She had been ill on the plane, lay ill for days in the unfamiliar room. Several times the doctor came by—left medicine she would not take. Several times Jeannie drove in the twenty miles from work, still in her Visiting Nurse uniform, the lightness and brightness of her like a healing.

"Who can believe it is winter?" he said one morning. "Beautiful it is outside like an ad. Come, Mrs. Invalid, come to taste it. You are well enough to sit in here, you are well enough to sit outside. The doctor said it too."

But the benches were encrusted with people, and the sands at the sidewalk's edge. Besides, she had seen the far rufflle of the sea: "there take me," and though she leaned against him, it was she who led.

Plodding and plodding, sitting often to rest, he grumbling. Patting the sand so warm. Once she scooped up a handful, cradling it close to her better eye; peered, and flung it back. And as they came almost to the brink and she could see the glistening wet, she sat down, pulled off her shoes and stockings, left him and began to run. "You'll catch cold," he screamed, but the sand in his shoes weighed him down—he who had always been the agile one—and already the white spray creamed her feet.

He pulled her back, took a handkerchief to wipe off the wet and the sand. "O no," she said, "the sun will dry," seized the square and smoothed it flat, dropped on it a mound of sand, knotted the kerchief corners and tied it to a bag—"to look at with the strong glass" (for the first time in years she explained an action of hers)—and lay down with the little bag against her cheek, looking toward the shore that nurtured life as it first crawled toward consciousness the millions years ago.

He took her one Sunday in the evil-smelling bus, past flat miles of blister houses, to the home of relatives. O what is this? she cried as the light began to smoke and the houses to dim and recede. Smog, he said, everyone knows but you . . . Outside he kept his arms about her, but she walked with hands pushing the heavy air as if to open it, whispered: who has done this?, sat down suddenly to vomit at the curb and for a long while refused to rise.

One's age as seen on the altered face of those known in youth. Is this they he has come to visit? This Max and Rose, smooth and pleasant, introducing them to polite children, disinterested grandchildren, "the whole family, once a month on Sundays. And why not? We have the room, the help, the food."

Talk of cars, of houses, of success: this son that, that daughter this. And *your* children? Hastily skimped over, the intermarriages, the obscure work—"my doctor son-in-law, Phil"—all he has to offer. She silent in a corner. (Carsick like a baby, he explains.) Years since he has taken her to visit anyone but the children, and old apprehensions prickle: "no incidents," he silently begs, "no incidents." He itched to tell them: "A very sick woman," significantly, indicating her with his eyes, "a very sick woman." Their restricted faces did not react. "Have you thought maybe she'd do better at Palm Springs?" Rose asked. "Or at least a nicer section of the beach, nicer people, a pool." Not to have to say "money" he said instead: "would she have sand to look at through a magnifying glass?" and went on, detail after detail, the old habit betraying of parading the queerness of her for laughter.

After dinner—the others into the living room in men- or women-clusters, or into the den to watch TV—the four of them alone. She sat close to him, and did not speak. Jokes, stories, people they had known, beginning of reminiscence, Russia fifty—sixty years ago. Strange words across the Duncan Phyfe table: *hunger; secret meet-*

ings; spies; betrayals; prison; escape—interrupted by one of the grandchildren: "Commercial's on; any coke left? Gee, you're missing a real hair-raiser." And then a granddaughter (Max proudly: "look at her, an American queen") drove them back. No incident— except that there had been no incidents.

The first few mornings she had taken with her the magnifying glass, but he would sit only on the benches, so she rested at the foot, where slatted bench shadows fell, and unless she turned her hearing aid down, other voices invaded.

Now on the days when the sun shone and she felt well enough, he took her on the tram to where the benches ranged in oblongs, some with tables for checkers or cards. Again the blanket on the sand in the striped shadows, but she no longer brought the magnifying glass. He played cards, and she lay in the sun and looked toward the waters; or they walked—two blocks down to the scaling hotel, two blocks back—past chili-hamburger stands, open-doored bars, Next to New and Perpetual Rummage Sale stores.

Once, out of the aimless walkers, slow and shuffling like themselves, someone ran unevenly toward them, embraced, kissed, wept: "dear friends, old friends." A friend of *hers*, not his: Mrs. Mays who had lived next door to them in Denver when the children were small.

Thirty years are compressed into a dozen sentences; and the present, not even in three. All is told: the children scattered; the husband dead; she lives in a room two blocks up from the sing hall —and points to the domed auditorium jutting before the pier. The leg? phlebitis; the heavy breathing? that one does not ask. She too comes to the benches each nice day to sit. And tomorrow, tomorrow, are they going to the community sing? Of course he would have heard of it, everybody goes—the big doings they wait for all week. They have never been? She will come to them for dinner tomorrow and they will all go together.

So it is that she sits in the wind of the singing, among the thousand various faces of age.

She had turned off her hearing aid at once they came into the auditorium—as she would have wished to turn off sight.

One by one they streamed by and imprinted on her—and though the savage zest of their singing came voicelessly soft and distant, the faces roared—the faces densed the air—chorded
  children-chants, mother-croons, singing of the chained;
  love serenades, Beethoven storms, mad Lucia's scream;
  drunken joy-songs, keens for the dead, work singing
    while from floor to balcony to dome a barefooted sore-covered little girl threaded the sound-thronged tumult, danced her ecstasy of grimace to flutes that scratched at a crossroads village wedding
Yes, faces became sound, and the sound became faces; and faces and sound became weight—pushed, pressed
  "Air"—her hand claws his.
  "Whenever I enjoy myself . . ." Then he saw the gray sweat on her face. "Here. Up. Help me, Mrs. Mays," and they support her out to where she can gulp the air in sob after sob.
  "A doctor, we should get for her a doctor."
  "Tch, it's nothing," says Ellen Mays, "I get it all the time . . . You've missed the tram; come to my place . . . close . . . tea. My view. See, she *wants* to come. Steady now, that's how." Adding mysteriously: "Remember your advice, easy to keep your head above water, empty things float. Float."
  The singing a fading march for them, tall woman with a swollen leg, weaving little man, and the swollen thinness they help between.
  The stench in the hall: mildew? decay? "We sit and rest then climb. My gorgeous view. We help each other and here we are."
  The stench along into the slab of room. A washstand for a sink, a box with oilcloth tacked round for a cupboard, a three-burner gas plate. Artificial flowers, colorless with dust. Everywhere pictures foaming: wedding, baby, party, vacation, graduation, family pictures. From the narrow couch under a slit of window, sure enough the view: lurching rooftops and a scallop of ocean heaving, preening, twitching under the moon.
  "While the water heats. Excuse me . . . down the hall." Ellen Mays had gone.
  "You'll live?" he asks mechanically, sat down to feel his fright; tried to pull her alongside.
  She pushed him away. "For air," she said; stood clinging to the dresser. Then, in a terrible voice:

After a lifetime of room. Of many rooms.
Shhh
You remember how she lived. Eight children. And now one room like a coffin. Shrinking the life of her into one room
She pays rent!
Like a coffin. Rooms and rooms like this. I lie on the quilt and hear them talk Once you went for coffee I walked I saw A Balzac a Chekhov to write it Rummage Alone On scraps
Shhh Mrs. Orator Without Breath. Better here old than in the old country.
And they sang like . . . like . . . *Man, one has to believe.* So strong. For what? To rot, not grow?
Your poor lungs beg you: Please. They sob between each word.
Singing. Singing. She in this poor room with her pictures Max You The Children. And who has meaning? Century after century still all in man not to grow?

"Coffins, garbage, plants: sick woman. O lay down. We will get for you the doctor."

"And when will it end. *O, the end.*" *That* nightmare thought, and this time she writhed, crumpled beside him, seized his hand (for a moment again the weight, the soft distant roaring of humanity) and on the strangled-for breath, begged: "Man . . . will destroy ourselves?"

And looking for answer—in the helpless pity and fear for her (for *her*) that distorted his face—she understood the last months, and knew that she was dying.

IV

"Let us go home," she said after several days.

"You are in training for a cross-country trip? That is why you do not even walk across the room? Here, like a prescription Phil said, till you are stronger from the operation. You want to break doctor's orders?"

She saw the fiction was necessary to him, was silent; then: "At home I will get better. If the doctor here says?"

"And winter? And the visits to Lenny and to Clara? All right," for he saw the tears in her eyes, "I will write Phil, and talk to the doctor."

Days passed. He reported nothing. Jeannie came and took her

out for air, past the boarded concessions, the hooded and tented amusement rides, to the end of the pier. They watched the spent waves feeding the new; the gulls in the clouded sky; even up where they sat, the windblown sand stung.

She did not ask to do down the crooked steps to the sea.

Back in her bed, while he was gone to the store, she said: "Jeannie, this doctor, he is not one I can ask questions. Ask him for me, can I go home?"

Jeannie looked at her, said quickly: "Of course, poor Granny, you want your own things around you, don't you? I'll call him tonight . . . Look, I have something to show you," and from her purse unwrapped a large cookie, intricately shaped like a little girl. "Look at the curls—can you hear me well, Granny?—and the darling eyelashes. I just came from a house where they had finished baking them."

"The dimples," she marveled, "there in the knees," holding it to the better light, turning, studying, "like art. Each singly they cut, or a mold?"

"Singly," said Jeannie, "and if it is a child only the mother can make them. O Granny, it's the likeness of a real little girl who died yesterday—Rosita. She was three years old. *Pan del Muerto*, the Bread of the Dead. It was the custom in the part of Mexico they came from."

Still she turned and inspected. "Look, the hollow in the throat, the little cross necklace . . . I think for the mother it is a good thing to be busy with such bread. You know the family?"

Jeannie nodded. "On my rounds. I nursed . . . O Granny, it is like a party; they play songs she liked to dance to. The coffin is lined with pink velvet and she wears a white dress. There are candles . . ."

"In the house?" Surprised, "They keep her in the house?"

"Yes," said Jeannie, "and it is against the health law. I think she is . . . prepared there. The father said it will be sad to bury her here; in Mazatlán they have a feast night with candles each year; everyone picnics on the graves of those they loved until dawn."

"Yes Jeannie, the living must comfort themselves." She closed her eyes.

"You want to sleep, Granny?"

"Yes, tired from the pleasure of you. I may keep the Rosita?

There stand it, on the dresser, where I can see; something of my own around me."

In the kitchenette, helping her grandfather unpack the groceries, Jeannie said in her light voice:

"I'm resigning my job, Granddaddy."

"Ah the lucky young man. Which one is he?"

"Too late. You're spoken for." She made a pyramid of cans, unstacked, and built again.

"Something is wrong with the job?"

"With me. I can't be"—she searched for the word—"professional enough. I let myself feel things. And tomorrow I have to report a family . . ." The cans clicked again. "It's not that, either. I just don't know what I want to do, maybe go back to school, maybe go to art school. I thought if you went to San Francisco I'd come along and talk it over with Mommy and Daddy. But I don't see how you can go. She wants to go home. She asked me to ask the doctor."

The doctor told her himself. "Next week you may travel, when you are a little stronger." But next week there was the fever of an infection, and by the time that was over, she could not leave the bed—a rented hospital bed that stood beside the double bed he slept in alone now.

Outwardly the days repeated themselves. Every other afternoon and evening he went out to his new-found cronies, to talk and play cards. Twice a week, Mrs. Mays came. And the rest of the time, Jeannie was there.

By the sickbed stood Jeannie's FM radio. Often into the room the shapes of music came. She would lie curled on her side, her knees drawn up, intense in listening (Jeannie sketched her so, coiled, convoluted like an ear), then thresh her hand out and abruptly snap the radio mute—still to lie in her attitude of listening, concealing tears.

Once Jeannie brought in a young Marine to visit, a friend from high-school days she had found wandering near the empty pier. Because Jeannie asked him to, gravely, without self-consciousness, he sat himself cross-legged on the floor and performed for them a dance of his native Samoa.

Long after they left, a tiny thrumming sound could be heard

where, in her bed, she strove to repeat the beckon, flight, surrender of his hands, the fluttering footbeats, and his low plaintive calls.

Hannah and Phil sent flowers. To deepen her pleasure, he placed one in her hair. "Like a girl," he said and brought the hand mirror so she could see. She looked at the pulsing red flower, the yellow skull face; a desolate, excited laugh shuddered from her, and she pushed the mirror away—but let the flower burn.

The week Lenny and Helen came, the fever returned. With it the excited laugh, and incessant words. She, who in her life had spoken but seldom and then only when necessary (never having learned the easy, social uses of words), now, in dying, spoke incessantly.

In a half whisper: "Like Lisa she is, your Jeannie. Have I told you of Lisa, she who taught me to read? Of the high-born she was, but noble in herself. I was sixteen; they beat me; my father beat me so I would not go to her. It was forbidden, she was a Tolstoyan. At night, past dogs that howled, terrible dogs my son, in the snows of winter to the road, I to ride in her carriage like a lady to books. To her life was holy, knowledge was holy, and she taught me to read. They hung her. Everything that happens one must try to understand why. She killed one who betrayed many. Because of betrayal, betrayed all she lived and believed. In one minute she killed, before my eyes (there is so much blood in a human being, my son), in prison with me. All that happens, one must try to understand.

"The name?" Her lips would work. "The name that was their pole star; the doors of the death houses fixed to open on it; I read of it my year of penal servitude. Thuban!" very excited, "Thuban, in ancient Egypt the pole star. Can you see, look out to see it, Jeannie, if it swings around our pole star that seems to *us* not to move.

"Yes, Jeannie, at your age my mother and grandmother had already buried children; . . . yes, Jeannie, it is more than oceans between Olshana and you . . . yes Jeannie they danced and for all the bodies they had they might as well be chickens, and indeed, they flapped their arms, scratched and hopped.

"And Andrei Yefimitch, who for twenty years had never known of it and never wanted to know, said as if he wanted to cry: but why my dear friend this malicious laughter?" Telling to herself half-memorized phrases from her few books. "Pain I answer with

tears and cries, baseness with indignation, meanness with repulsion
. . . for life may be hated or wearied of, but never despised."
Delirious: "Tell me, my neighbor, Mrs. Mays, the pictures never lived, but what of the flowers? Tell them who ask: no rabbis, no ministers, no priests, no speeches, no ceremonies: ah, false—let the living please themselves. Tell Sammy's boy, he who flies, tell him to go to Stuttgart and see where Davy has no grave. And what?" A conspirator's laugh. "And what? where millions have no graves."

In delirium or not, wanting the radio on; not seeming to listen, the words still jetting, wanting the music on. Once, silencing it abruptly as of old, she began to cry, unconcealed tears this time. "You have pain, Granny?" Jeannie asked.

"The music," she said, "still it is there and we do not hear; knocks, and our poor human ears too weak. What else, what else we do not hear?"

Once she knocked his hand aside as he gave her a pill, swept the bottles from her bedside table: "no pills, let me feel what I feel," and laughed as on his hands and knees he groped to pick them up.

Nighttimes her hand reached across the bed to hold his.

A constant retching began. Her breath was too faint for sustained speech now, but still the lips moved:
When no longer necessary to injure others
Pick pick pick Blind chicken
As a human being responsibility for action
"David!" imperious, "Basin!" and she would vomit, rinse her mouth, the wasted throat working to swallow, and begin the chant again.

She will be better off in the hospital now, the doctor said.

He sent the telegrams to the children, was packing her suitcase, when her hoarse voice startled. She had roused, was pulling herself to sitting.

"Where now?" she asked. "Where now do you drag me?"

"You do not even have to have a baby to go this time," he soothed, looking for the brush to pack. "Remember, after Davy you told me—worthy to have a baby for the pleasure of the hospital?"

"Where now? Not home yet?" Her voice mourned. "Not home yet? Where *is* my home?"

He rose to ease her back. "The doctor, the hospital," he started to explain, but deftly, like a snake, she had slithered out of bed and stood swaying, propped behind the night table.

"Coward," she hissed, "runner."

"You stand," he said senselessly.

"To take me there and run. Afraid of a little vomit."

He reached her as she fell. She struggled against him, slipped from his arms, pulled herself up again.

"Weakling," she taunted, "to leave me there and run. Betrayer. All your life you have run."

He sobbed, telling Jeannie. "A Marilyn Monroe to run for her virtue. Fifty-nine pounds she weighs, the doctor said, and she beats at me like a Dempsey. Betrayer, she cries, and I running like a dog when she calls; day and night, running to her, her vomit, the bedpan . . ."

"She wants you, Granddaddy," said Jeannie. "Isn't that what they call love? I'll see if she sleeps, and if she does, the poor worn-out darling, we'll have a party, you and I; I brought us rum babas."

They did not move her. By her bed now stood the tall hooked pillar that held the solutions—blood and glucose—to feed her veins. Jeannie moved down the hall to take over the sickroom, her face so radiant, her grandfather asked her once: "You are in love?" (Shameful the joy, the pure overwhelming joy from being with her grandmother; the peace, the serenity that breathed.) "My darling escape," she answered incoherently, "my darling Granny,"—as if that explained.

Now one by one the children came, those that were able. Hannah, Paul, Sammy. Too late to ask: and what did you learn with your living, Mother, and what do we need to know?

Clara, the eldest, clenched:

Pay me back, Mother, pay me back for all you took from me. Those others you crowded into your heart. The hands I needed to be for you, the heaviness, the responsibility.

Is this she? Noises the dying make, the crablike hands crawling over the covers. The ethereal singing.

She hears that music, that singing from childhood; forgotten sound—not heard since, since . . . And the hardness breaks like a cry: Where did we lose each other, first mother, singing mother?

Annulled: the quarrels, the gibing, the harshness between; the fall into silence and the withdrawal.
I do not know you, Mother. Mother, I never knew you.
Lenny, suffering not alone for her who was dying, but for that in her which never lived (for that which in him might never live). From him too, unspoken words: *good-by mother who taught me to mother myself.*
Not Vivi, who must stay with her children; not Davy, but he is already here, having to die again with *her* this time, for the living take their dead with them when they die.

Light she grew, like a bird, and like a bird, sound bubbled in her throat while the body fluttered in agony. Night and day, asleep or awake (though indeed there was no difference now) the songs and the phrases leaping.
And he, who had once dreaded a long dying (from fear of himself, from horror of the dwindling money) now desired her quick death profoundly, for *her* sake. He no longer went out, except when Jeannie forced him; no longer laughed, except when, in the bright kitchenette, Jeannie coaxed his laughter (and she, who seemed to hear nothing else, would laugh too, conspiratorial wisps of laughter).
Light, like a bird, the fluttering body, the little claw hands, the beaked shadow on her face; and the throat, bubbling, straining:
He tried not to listen, as he tried not to look on the face in which only the forehead remained familiar, but trapped with her the long nights in that little room, the sounds worked themselves into his consciousness, with their punctuation of death swallows, whimpers, gurglings.
Even in reality (swallow) *life's lack of it*
The bell   Summon what ennobles
78,000 in one minute (whisper of a scream)
78,000 human beings   destroy ourselves?
"Ahh Mrs. Miserable," he said, as if she could hear, "all your life working, and now in bed you lie, servants to tend, you do not even need to call to be tended, and still you work. Such hard work it is to die? Such hard work?"
The body threshed, her hand clung in his. A melody, ghost thin, hovered on her lips, and like a guilty ghost, the vision of her bent in listening to it, silencing the record instantly he was near.

Now, heedless of his presence, she floated the melody on and on.

"Hid it from me," he complained, "how many times you listened to remember it so?" And tried to think when she had first played it, or first begun to silence her few records when he came near—but could reconstruct nothing. There was only this room with its tall hooked pillar and its swarm of sounds.

An unexamined life   not worth
Strong   with the not yet in the now
Dogma dead   war dead   one country

"It helps, Mrs. Philosopher, words from books? It helps?" And it seemed to him that for seventy years she had hidden a tape recorder, infinitely microscopic, within her, that it had coiled infinite mile on mile, trapping every song, every melody, every word read, heard and spoken—and that maliciously she was playing back only what said nothing of him, of the children, of their intimate life together.

"Left us indeed, Mrs. Babbler," he reproached, "you who called others babbler and cunningly saved your words. A lifetime you tended and loved, and now not a word of us, for us. Left us indeed? Left me."

And he took out his solitaire deck, shuffled the cards loudly, slapped them down.

Lift high   banner of reason   (tatter of an orator's voice)*Justice freedom and light*
Mankind   life worthy   heroic capacities
Seeks   (blur of shudder)   *belong   human being*

"Words, words," he accused, "and what human beings did *you* seek around you, Mrs. Live Alone, and what mankind think worthy?"

Though even as he spoke, he remembered she had not always been isolated, had not always wanted to be alone (as he knew there had been a voice before this gossamer one; before the hoarse voice that broke from silence to lash, make incidents, shame him—a girl's voice of eloquence that spoke their highest dreams). But again he could reconstruct, image nothing of what had been before, or when, or how, it had changed.

Ace, queen, jack. The pillar shadow fell, so, in two tracks; in the mirror depths glistened a moonlike blob, the empty solution bottle. And it worked in him: *of reason and justice and freedom. Dogma dead:* he remembered the quotation, laughed bitterly.

"Hah, good you do not know what you say; good Victor Hugo died and did not see it, his twentieth century."

Deuce, ten, five. Dauntlessly she began a song of their youth of belief:

> *These things shall be, a loftier race*
> *than e'er the world hath known shall rise*
> *with flame of freedom in their souls*
> *and light of knowledge in their eyes*

King, four, jack. "In the twentieth century, hah!"

> *They shall be gentle, brave and strong*
> *to spill no drop of blood, but dare*
> *all that may plant man's lordship firm*
> *on earth and fire and sea and air*

"To spill no drop of blood, hah! So, cadaver, and you too, cadaver Hugo, 'in the twentieth century ignorance will be dead, dogma will be dead, war will be dead, and for all mankind one country—of fulfillment.' Hah!"

And every life (long strangling cough) *shall be a song*

The cards fell from his fingers. Without warning, the bereavement and betrayal he had sheltered—compounded through the years —hidden even from himself—revealed itself,

uncoiled,

released,

sprung

and with it the monstrous shapes of what had actually happened in the century.

A ravening hunger or thirst seized him. He groped into the kitchenette, switched on all three lights, piled a tray—"you have finished your night snack, Mrs. Cadaver, now I will have mine." And he was shocked at the tears that splashed on the tray.

"Salt tears. For free. I forgot to shake on salt?"

Whispered: "Lost, how much I lost."

Escaped to the grandchildren whose childhoods were childish, who had never hungered, who lived unravaged by disease in warm houses of many rooms, had all the school for which they cared, could walk on any street, stood a head taller than their grandparents, towered above—beautiful skins, straight backs, clear straightforward eyes. "Yes, you in Olshana," he said to the town of sixty years ago, "they would be nobility to you."

And was this not the dream then, come true in ways undreamed? he asked.

And are there no other children in the world? he answered, as if in her harsh voice.

And the flame of freedom, the light of knowledge?
And the drop, the drop of blood?

And he thought that at six Jeannie would get up and it would be his turn to go to her room and sleep, that he could press the buzzer and she would come now; that in the afternoon Ellen Mays was coming, and this time they would play cards and he could marvel at how rouge can stand half an inch on the cheek; that in the evening the doctor would come, and he could beg him to be merciful, to stop the feeding solutions, to let her die.

To let her die, and with her their youth of belief out of which her bright, betrayed words foamed; stained words, that on her working lips came stainless.

Hours yet before Jeannie's turn. He could press the buzzer and wake her to come now; he could take a pill, and with it sleep; he could pour more brandy into his milk glass, though what he had poured was not yet touched.

Instead he went back, checked her pulse, gently tended with his knotty fingers as Jeannie had taught.

She was whimpering; her hand crawled across the covers for his. Compassionately he enfolded it, and with his free hand gathered up the cards again. Still was there thirst or hunger ravening in him.

That world of their youth—dark, ignorant, terrible with hate and disease—how was it that living in it, in the midst of corruption, filth, treachery, degradation, they had not mistrusted man nor themselves; had believed so beautifully, so . . . falsely?

"Aaah children," he said out loud, "how we believed, how we belonged." And he yearned to package for each of the children, the grandchildren, for everyone, *that joyous certainty, that sense of moving and being moved, of being one and indivisible with the great of the past, with all mankind.* Package it, stand on corners, in front of stadiums and on crowded beaches, knock on doors, give it as a fabled gift.

"And why not in cereal boxes, in soap packages?" he mocked himself. "Aah. You have taken my senses, cadaver."

Words foamed, died unsounded. Her body writhed; she made kissing motions with her mouth. (Her lips moving as she read, poring over the Book of the Martyrs, the magnifying glass superimposed over the heavy eyeglasses.) *Still she had believed?* "Eva!" he whispered. "Still you believed? You lived by it? *These Things Shall Be?*"

"One pound soup meat," she answered distinctly, "one soup bone."

"My ears heard you. Ellen Mays was witness: 'Man . . . one has to believe.'" Imploringly: "Eva!"

"Bread, day old." She was mumbling. "Please, in a wooden box . . . for kindling. The thread, hah, the thread breaks. Cheap thread,"—and a gurgling, enormously loud, began in her throat.

"I ask for stone; she gives me bread—day old." He pulled his hand away, shouted: "Who wanted questions? Everything you have to wake?" Then dully, "Ah let me help you turn, poor creature."

Words jumbled, cleared. In a voice of crowded terror:

"Paul, Sammy, don't fight.

"Hannah, have I ten hands?

"How can I give it, Clara, how can I give it if I don't have?"

"You lie," he said sturdily, "there was joy too." Bitterly: "Ah how cheap you speak of us at the last."

As if to rebuke him, as if her voice had no relationship with her flailing body, she sang clearly, beautifully, a school song the children had taught her when they were little; begged:

"Not look   my hair   where they cut . . ."

(The crown of braids shorn.) And instantly he left the mute old woman poring over the Book of the Martyrs; went past the mother treadling at the sewing machine, singing with the children; past the girl in her wrinkled prison dress, hiding her hair with scarred hands, lifting to him her awkward, shamed, imploring eyes of love; and took her in his arms, dear, personal, fleshed, in all the heavy passion he had loved to rouse from her.

"Eva!"

Her little claw hand beat the covers. How much, how much can a man stand? He took up the cards, put them down, circled the beds, walked to the dresser, opened, shut drawers, brushed his hair, moved his hand bit by bit over the mirror to see what of the reflection he could blot out with each move, and felt that at any moment he would die of what was unendurable. Went to press the buzzer to wake Jeannie, looked down, saw on Jeannie's sketch pad the hospital bed, with *her;* the double bed alongside, with him; the tall pillar feeding into her veins, and their hands, his and hers, clasped, feeding each other. And as if he had been instructed he went to his bed, lay down, holding the sketch as a shield against the monstrous shapes of loss, of betrayal, of death—and with his free hand took hers back into his.

So Jeannie found them in the morning.

That last day the agony was perpetual. Time after time it lifted her almost off the bed, so they had to fight to hold her down. He could not endure and left the room; wept as if there never would be tears enough.

Jeannie came to comfort him. In her light voice she said: Granddaddy, Granddaddy don't cry. She is not there, she promised me. On the last day, she said she would go back to when she first heard music, a little girl on the road of the village where she was born. She promised me. It is a wedding—and like chickens they dance, while the flutes so joyous and vibrant tremble in the air. Leave her there, Granddaddy, it's all right. She promised me. Come back, come back and help her poor body to die.

For two of that generation
Seevya and Genya
Infinite, dauntless, incorruptible.

Death deepens the wonder

Some Questions and Problems

Three groups of questions and problems follow.

The first group comprises a series of questions for each of sixteen of the stories. These questions encourage close reading of the individual stories and are varied enough to suggest models for approaching all the stories. In some instances we present questions which lead from one to another as a guide toward mastering the form and structure of the story (e.g., questions for "That Evening Sun" and "A Shower of Gold"). In other instances the questions are not so systematic and suggest a consideration of one or two aspects of the story (e.g., questions for "First Confession," "Death of a Traveling Salesman," and "A Dill Pickle"). We have tried, in all cases, to make the questions ones for discussion, not for right and wrong answers. Almost any of these questions might be used for writing assignments.

The second, and much shorter, group of questions offers suggestions for writing assignments. Some of these are general, often involving comparisons and contrasts of stories. Some move away from close reading into wider fields of consideration. Most of them are designed to open up, not close in, ideas for writing.

The third group of questions suggests a few of the ways students may be encouraged to move from this anthology into longer, more sustained essays, involving wider reading, or into attempts at writing their own stories.

I

Frank O'Connor, "First Confession"

1. What is the most important event in the story? Is it the confession itself, or its aftermath? Justify your choice by relating it to what you consider to be the theme or main idea of the story.

2. How do the incidents leading up to the main event and the narrator's attitude toward that event enable O'Connor to get the most humor and most absurdity out of that event?

3. From the way Jack tells the story it seems that he and the priest are on one side and Nora and Gran on the other. Does this mean that O'Connor seems prejudiced in the former's behalf? Or is this a means of trying to define more clearly what the story is all about?

4. An important question which this story raises is the relationship between humor and religious subject matter: Some critics assert that one fault of a story such as this is that it mocks religion. Do you agree or disagree? Why? On the other hand, there are critics who assert that a genuinely comic story simply *can't* deal with religion. Speculate what reasons they might give for such a view. On the basis of your reading of the story, would you agree or disagree with these latter critics? Why?

William Faulkner, "That Evening Sun"

1. We never learn whether or not Jesus killed Nancy on the night Mr. Compson took the children from the cabin. But the first words of paragraph two strongly imply that the narrator could have told us, for the whole thing happened "fifteen

years ago." Is Faulkner just teasing, mystifying us, or are we asking the wrong question? In other words, what is the story about? The questions which follow point to this central question.

2. Consider the different attitudes toward Nancy's fear: Nancy's, Dilsey's, Mr. Compson's, Mrs. Compson's, the childrens'. Who believes she is in danger? Why? Why not?

3. The narrator of the story is a 24-year-old man looking back at a time when he was 9 years old. Does the older Quentin ever comment on what the younger Quentin saw and heard? Judging from details and comments, are we more aware of the innocent and ignorant child or of the older man looking backward? Does the narrator know more than the young Quentin? Support your answer with relevant details.

4. How do these items in the story relate to the main idea: the three opening paragraphs, the paragraph on Mr. Lovelady at the end of section V, the attempted suicide of Nancy, and the attitude of the jailer?

5. Why does Nancy fear Jesus? What specific impressions of him do we as readers have? Is he a villain? An enigma? A victim? The narrator does not comment, but what do we feel about him in the one brief scene (in section I) where he appears? Throughout the greater part of the story he may or may not be present; if he is, he is invisible. Think about this, and ask yourself: why Faulkner chose to name him as he did. At what specific point in the story is it clear that the name may have more than literal meaning? Can you see any connection between the choice of this name and Nancy's comment about herself in the last sentence of section II? Exactly how would you describe Nancy's attitude toward Jesus' threat: Does she regard it as unavoidable? Is she seeking to escape it? To put it off? Or what? Show, by analyzing specific passages, why you think as you do. What does her behavior at the end of the story imply about this question?

6. Notice particularly the dialogue with which the story closes. We might say that it leaves us at a high point of sus-

pense; does it? What is the dialogue about? What do you think it contributes to the story's meaning?

7. We might argue that Faulkner's choice of point of view heightens the impact of the story. In what ways is this true? Is that, however, enough reason to explain the choice of point of view? We learn a lot more about the behavior of the children than we need to know if the story is "about Nancy." Is Faulkner, then, uneconomical, or are the children important in their own right in the story? Why does Nancy seek out the children? Where does the story suggest differences between understanding facts or evidence and knowing the truth?

8. What *is* the theme of the story? Why is Nancy's story so important in relation to this theme? Why does Faulkner's narrator create a whole complex community in this brief story: children, adults, members of the white establishment, and various blacks? Is innocence simply a question of age? Or does it have something to do with the social attitudes and values of a particular society?

Katherine Mansfield, "A Dill Pickle"

1. Katherine Mansfield has usually been praised for her use of selective specific detail to create atmosphere, illuminate character, and/or suggest theme. In the light of the foregoing, what use does Miss Mansfield make of the following: the Japanese vase of paper daffodils, the Christmas tree, the pot of caviar, the tea?

2. Since the title suggests that the pickle may be more important than the other details, just what do you think it contributes to the story's atmosphere, characterization, and/or theme? Do you agree with those critics who assert that the dill pickle is really a symbol of the male member and that the story therefore concerns frustrated sexuality? Why or why not?

3. While much of what we know about the man in the story derives from the girl's subjective response to him, yet there

are other evidences to reveal his character—his speech, his actions, and his reactions to the girl. What kind of portrait emerges—what is he like? Does this figure bear any resemblance to the one the girl creates for us by her impressions and reactions? Does it at all differ? Why or why not?

4. Do you think Miss Mansfield sides with the girl in the story? What evidence is there to support your answer?

5. At the very end what does the man's speech and behavior toward the waiter indicate about his character? Does it reveal anything about the failure of the love relationship?

J. F. Powers, "The Valiant Woman"

1. One of the delights of this story is the deft, incisive manner in which the author brings to life the characters and suggests their subdued hostilities. The description of the dinner and Father Firman's silence reveals much about the priest and his relationship with Mrs. Stoner. Analyze the first few paragraphs and show what they reveal about their relationship with each other. What role does Father Nulty play in this relationship? Is he just an observer? An innocent victim? A foil?

2. Another delight of the story is the use the author makes of the mosquito. How does Father Firman's reaction to it reveal facets of his character and his relationship with Mrs. Stoner?

3. When Father Firman begins to compare his housekeeper with those of other priests (such as Cronin) he concludes that Mrs. Stoner is not so bad. Is he just rationalizing or is he simply recognizing that much of the time he overdramatizes his own plight? To answer this question, consider what the card game reveals concerning Father Firman's plight. Is he just a hapless victim or does he contribute to his own misery by his ploys?

4. Are the particular plot episodes on which the story centers—the birthday dinner and the card game—crucial in them-

selves or do they simply serve as examples of what constitutes a typical day in the life of Father Firman?

D. H. Lawrence, "Two Blue Birds"

1. The opening of this story, "There was a woman who loved her husband but she could not live with him—" reminds us of a literary form we are all familiar with from our early childhood. As further clues, we mention a later reference to the husband as Prince Charming and to the wife as a wolflike figure. To use elements of such a literary form may seem odd, especially in a story as sophisticated in tone as this one is. But in thinking about the story, ask yourself what is *real* about a fairy tale. Cinderella and Prince Charming are not realistic, everyday characters, but *what* is it they embody in human experience that is real? Comparably, we may better understand the husband, wife, and secretary if we think of them not as characters we may meet in everyday life but as having a reality analogous to that of fairy tale characters.

2. For example, is there anything childlike in their behavior —the husband's relation to his secretary, the wife's idea of marriage, the secretary's idea of devotion to her employer? Pursuing the analogy further, what in the story corresponds to evil or evil forces and to the ominous atmosphere or tension we often find in a fairy tale?

3. On the other hand, we also pointed out that the tone of the story—the narrator's attitude toward his characters and the way the characters often speak—is sophisticated, that is, it is witty, urbane, even blasé Consider, for example, the paragraphs on page 116, beginning with, "However, they were awfully kind—" and ending with, " 'but the crystallizing out'— what did that signify?" Analyze these paragraphs and show what is sophisticated here. What is the relation in the story between the childlike fairy tale elements and the adult sophistication as an explanation of the relationship between husband, wife, and secretary?

4. Often in fairy tales certain animals becomes symbolic. That is, they exist literally and at the same time they represent

something beyond that, such as associations or concentrated feelings or ideas. In the light of the foregoing, explain what you think the title means. Make particular use of the discussion about bluebirds between husband and wife on pages 124–125.

5. What does Lawrence think of the people in this story? Does he side with the wife, the husband, the secretary? Or does he disapprove of all of them? Or is he just detached from them all? Or would you describe his attitude differently? On what evidence in the text do you base your answer?

Katherine Anne Porter, "THE JILTING OF GRANNY WEATHERALL"

1. Describe the point of view maintained in this story. What are the special advantages Miss Porter derives from her manner of presenting the story?

2. Because the story is presented in the manner referred to in Question 1, the reader has to deduce certain important facts. Trace the references to these three characters and show how you arrive at your conclusions as to their importance in Granny Weatherall's life: George, John, Hapsy.

3. What role do the following play in Granny's life and in her attitude toward life: work, order, resignation? Point out passages that support your conclusion.

4. In making her story, Miss Porter gives metaphoric power and resonance to several images; among these images *light* and *food* are of great importance. Show how each of these two images takes on metaphoric meaning in the story.

5. In the last paragraph we read, "For the second time there was no sign. Again no bridegroom and the priest in the house." What does *bridegroom* mean here? (You might read Jesus' parable of the virgins, *Matthew* 25: 1–13.) What discovery do we and Granny make about her view of her life in this paragraph? What does Granny's last remark, "I'll never forgive it," mean to you? With what kind of feeling does Granny "blow out the light" at the end?

6. What meanings develop around the word *jilting*? The name *Weatherall*? How do you feel about Miss Porter's choice of a name for Granny? Since Granny's discovery about herself and her life comes at the very end, does the discovery invalidate, make useless, her apparently full, rich, and fertile life? (This is surely a question for discussion rather than one which can be intelligently answered with a yes or no.)

Joyce Carol Oates, "In the Region of Ice"

1. What evidence is there that almost from the beginning Sister Irene has strongly ambivalent feelings toward the student, Allen Weinstein? What is the basis of this ambivalence, and how does it affect what happens subsequently?

2. What does the conversation between Sister Irene and Sister Carlotta reveal about Sister Irene's dilemma in the story? How would you interpret this remark from that scene: "Sister Irene acquiesced with a smile, but of course she did not think so: only reality is real." (Page 192.) Is there anything ironical in her remark (that is, that *we* see implications in it that *she* doesn't see)?

3. What does Weinstein's long harangue about Humanism reveal about his state of mind and his problems? What does it reveal, if ironically, about Sister Irene's state of mind and problems?

4. After Weinstein has finished his harangue and is preparing to leave, he glances at Sister Irene, who is terrified "at what he was trying to do—he was trying to force her into a human relationship." (Page 195.) Why is this so terrifying? Does he force her into a human relationship? Why or why not?

5. Notice this line: "She wanted to cry out in fear that she was being forced into the role of a Christian, and what did that mean?" (Page 196.) What does it mean for Sister Irene? Why does it frighten her?

6. What in Weinstein's letter makes Sister Irene realize how desperate his condition is? What is the significance of the

speech from *Measure for Measure*? (You might, besides studying the speech, read it in context in Shakespeare's play.) Notice that Mrs. Oates takes the title of the story from this speech; it must, presumably, function to reveal something about Weinstein, Sister Irene, and the story as a whole. What does it reveal?

7. What light do Weinstein's parents throw on his problem? Do we have any sympathy for them? Why or why not?

8. Why does Sister Irene finally refuse to help Weinstein? Notice particularly this passage from their last interview: "She stared at him as if he had asked her to do something obscene." (Page 203.) What has he asked her for? Is that all he wants?

9. Why does Sister Irene keep repeating that she can just be "one person"? What light does Mrs. Oates' comment on her story throw on her intentions? On the story? What particularly does the last sentence of the story make us feel about Sister Irene: "If she could have felt guilt, she thought, she might at least have been able to feel something." Could Sister Irene have helped Weinstein?

Eudora Welty, "DEATH OF A TRAVELING SALESMAN"

1. Choose three or four passages—almost at random—which demonstrate that, though the details of what Bowman sees are precisely and exactly presented, the *atmosphere*, the *effect*, of what he sees is strange, unusual. How is this effect, this atmosphere, achieved? How do we account for it? Is it just that Bowman is physically ill? Or are there other reasons?

2. The image of a bed recurs through the story: where does a reference to a bed first appear? Notice all the references to bed (or cradle) you can. Is the image of a bed usually or invariably related to some other image? The central perception of the story (see Question 4) is preceded by Bowman's discovery that the woman is young, Sonny's wife not his mother. Is this confusion about her age and relationship to Sonny made likely? Is it accounted for only by Bowman's state of

health and mind? Was it just a trick on Miss Welty's part to name the young man Sonny, or does this choice of a name accentuate for the reader the role that the woman plays in the story?

3. Besides the image of the bed, notice when and where other images seem to gather meaning by their recurrence: for example, *professional, guide, fire, the lamp.* How many of these images come together in the scene at the supper table?

4. Bowman's central perception of the story is reported in this passage: "Bowman could not speak. He was shocked with knowing what was really in this house. A marriage, a fruitful marriage. That simple thing. Anyone could have had that.

"Somehow he felt unable to be indignant or protest, although some sort of joke had certainly been played upon him. There was nothing remote or mysterious here—only something private. The only secret was the ancient communication between two people." What is simply true and what is ironical about this passage? Are the words *traveling* and *salesman* in the title just descriptions of Bowman's work or do they also become relevant images?

5. Why does Bowman leave the house? We read of "explosions" in his heart at the end; is this chiefly a metaphor for a physical experience, or is it something more?

Ambrose Bierce, "CHICKAMAUGA"

1. Bierce's selection of a central character is crucial to his story. Why does he conceal the boy's disability until the end —is it just a shocking trick, a surprise ending? Has it been prepared for or hinted at? At what places?

2. Of what use is the boy's disability and Bierce's concealment of it? Is the boy really the central concern of the story, or is he the chief instrument for getting at the central concern of the story? What does Bierce want to create for us?

3. The story moves from a child's game to a reality. How does the child's sword signal this movement? The reader's

perception of the difference between game and reality moves at a different pace from the child's: show that this is so by examining the difference between your response to several of the episodes and the child's response.

4. Is the final scene too sensational and grisly, or is it successful? Does your discussion of Question 3 throw any light on this question?

Harris Downey, "THE HUNTERS"

1. Once you have read through the story, note again the first paragraph and the last sentence of paragraph three. Explain just what the narrator is revealing to us about the nature of the big soldier in the last half of the paragraph, particularly the implications of *beast* and *hunter*. Does Private Meadows share this insight, or does he still see the big soldier differently? (Notice the difference between *loneliness* and *solitariness*.) What does *lost* mean in the story?

2. The other soldier Private Meadows meets also says he is lost: "*I'm* lost." What is the difference between him and Private Meadows? What is similar and what is different about their being both lost?

3. There are three main episodes: the German paymaster, the goats, and the parachutists. Compare and contrast Private Meadows' feelings and attitudes in his response to each of these. We are told Private Meadows' feelings and attitudes, but we must deduce those of the other soldier. What are the differences?

4. Read the paragraph in which the big soldier finds out where his company is and leaves Private Meadows. What is accomplished in this paragraph, especially in the last half? What is the distinction between "solitariness" and "loneliness" made in the last sentence of the paragraph?

5. Is Barr's information about the flyers at the end of the story necessary to complete the story? Would it have been better to leave this matter in doubt? Discuss whether or not

this detail weakens the effect of the story by becoming too explicit.

6. What does the title mean? In what ways does the story become a parable, or at least, hint at parabolic meanings? That is, although this is clearly a realistic narrative about episodes during World War II, is there any reason in the story to see the possibilities of extending its implications so that the war itself becomes a metaphor for social and political action? Von Clausewitz, the early nineteenth-century Prussian military scientist, remarked that war is just an extension of peacetime behavior; does this story seem to suggest a similar kind of relationship between peace and war? Or is war something different, something special?

Flannery O'Connor, "REVELATION"

1. About seven-tenths of the story is the scene in the waiting room. Why is this scene so long in proportion to the rest of the story? What are some of the most important things about Mrs. Turpin revealed in this scene? Three times in the course of the scene we learn that Mrs. Turpin has conversations with Jesus; what do these conversations reveal about her?

2. Trace the stages of Mrs. Turpin's awareness of the "ugly" girl: how does her growing awareness of the girl qualify or tend to undermine our image of Mrs. Turpin's complacency and sense of superiority?

3. The violent outburst and attack of the "ugly" girl is irrational and never explained. Why do you suppose Flannery O'Connor chooses not to give any more information than she does about this matter?

4. "She had been singled out for the message"; this is how Mrs. Turpin responds to the girl's "Go back to hell, you wart hog." Whom does Mrs. Turpin regard as her antagonist? Notice that in the last three scenes of the story it is not the girl who disturbs Mrs. Turpin; she sees the girl as an instrument, a bringer of a message. How have we been prepared for this response of Mrs. Turpin's?

5. Mrs. Turpin's antagonist—as she sees it—becomes clearer in the last scene of the story, after she leaves the Negro laborers and goes to the pig parlor. Read this last scene carefully and discuss the implications of the following passages:

"She had the look of a woman going single-handed, weaponless, into battle."

" 'If trash is what you wanted why didn't you make me trash?' "

" 'Who do you think you are?' "

"The question . . . returned to her clearly like an answer from beyond the wood."

6. How does Mrs. Turpin's vision at the end resolve the story? Notice particularly the passage describing those bringing up the end of the procession; what seems to be the truth Mrs. Turpin now has about her virtues?

7. Flannery O'Connor has rigorously limited the point of view in this story. Although the voice of the narrator guides us, we see things as Mrs. Turpin sees them. We do not, therefore, have to agree to the interpretations Mrs. Turpin makes of everything. We can, finally, wonder: is "Revelation" an admonitory parable about the conversion of Mrs. Turpin? Is she a "better" woman at the end of the story? Or is this the story of a disturbed woman who goes mad? (In discussing these possibilities it might be most helpful to return to Questions 3 and 4. Suppose one just saw the "ugly" girl as spiteful or mad. Must we accept Mrs. Turpin's interpretation of the girl's outburst as the "correct" one?)

Albert Camus, "THE GUEST"

1. Since most of the story comes to us through Daru's eyes, it is useful to ascertain what kind of person he is. What are his traits of character? His beliefs? His attitude toward other men? Towards the countryside in which he lives? What are his first impressions of the Arab? Do they change at all? If so, in what respects?

2. What is Balducci's role in the story? Is he simply a

device in the plot in order to bring the Arab to Daru or does he represent views in some ways different from those of Daru? Explain.

3. Camus implies but does not make explicit the political and historical context of the story: Both Daru and Balducci are of European origin and live in Algiers. The time, as we know from the story, is after World War II, just before the outbreak of hostilities between Algerian nationalists and French colonists. Is this background important to the story? If so, in what ways? What connection does it have with the difficulties of Daru with Balducci and the Arab?

4. Is Daru's final disposition of the prisoner consistent with his actions and attitudes as revealed early in the story? During his night with the Arab? Or does Daru change in some ways? Does Daru finally just get the Arab off his hands—that is, refuse to act? Or does he perform a genuine action? Just what does he offer the Arab? Support your answer by careful consideration of the farewell scene with the Arab.

5. "And in that slight haze, Daru, with heavy heart, made out the Arab walking slowly on the road to prison." Although we never see into the Arab, can we explain why he chooses the prison road? Or is his choice important only as it affects Daru? And why is Daru's heart "heavy"?

6. Why is Daru, as the last words of the story tell us, *alone*? Has he changed in the course of the story? Why or why not? What light does the message on the blackboard throw on your answers to the foregoing questions?

7. This story is translated from French; the original title, "*L'Hôte*," may mean either "guest" or "host." How does this ambiguity, impossible to render in English, extend the implications of the story?

Anton Chekhov, "Rothschild's Fiddle"

1. Upon first reading, many readers find this story rambling and perhaps pointless. Why might this be so?

2. Chekhov tells us a good deal of what goes on in the mind of Yakov and he presents several episodes in which Yakov appears. Choose one such episode early in the story, and show what kind of person Yakov is—his personality, his attitudes, the things he thinks about. What are his conflicts? Does he change in his thinking and attitudes? Consider one of the later episodes on which to base your answer.

3. Chekhov has been called an "impressionist"; that is, he presents a series of details—episodes, responses, thoughts—but he doesn't explain or show the connections between the series. One brief example in this story is when Yakov sees the lady at the bathing-shed. What is the point of this episode? How does it connect with the rest of the story thematically?

4. Perhaps the most crucial example of this impressionistic technique in this story is the third paragraph from the end. How are the details of this paragraph connected with each other and with the story as a whole? Is it enough to say that Yakov repents for his earlier treatment of Marfa and Rothschild, or is there something more profound, less obvious going on?

5. Why does the story need the last paragraph? Why is it named for the fiddle? What does the giving of the fiddle have to do with Yakov's frequent thoughts about gain and loss?

6. How would you characterize the tone of this story—sad, tragic, comic, rueful, or what? Why?

Heinrich Böll, "Murke's Collected Silences"

1. Why does Böll concentrate so particularly on machinery —such as the elevators, tape recorders, sound equipment—in this story? Is it simply that *that's* what the story is about, or does the machinery play a symbolic role in the story?

2. What role do Murke's silences play as an affirmation of a metaphysical or religious viewpoint? What is the viewpoint and what is its relationship to those of others in the story such as Bur-Malottke?

3. What is the connection between God and silence as Böll presents the two? Is this a story that affirms God or does it seem to suggest that "God is dead"? Or is there some other view that better describes the story's presentation of God? Explain.

4. Or is the real focus or center somewhere else? Why does Böll give us so much detail about the intellectual, social, and moral characteristics of the world in which Murke lives? What are those characteristics? Is there any evidence that that setting in a Germany one generation removed from Nazism is a crucial factor in the story? Or is the world of the story one whose characteristics are familiar to you?

Donald Barthelme, "A Shower of Gold"

1. We might describe this story as just a series of episodes, but there is a unifying action, introduced in the first sentence. What is that action? At what points are we reminded of it between the first and last sections of the story?

2. The next to the last episode closes with Peterson's phone call to Miss Arbor. How have his experiences since his interview with Miss Arbor led him to make the phone call? What do the scenes with Jean-Claude, with his barber, and with the girls from California contribute to our understanding of the world in which Peterson lives? How are the scenes with the President and the cat-piano player like and unlike the other three scenes?

3. Technically "A Shower of Gold" is unusual or out of the ordinary in at least two noticeable ways; this question and the next one draw attention to these two ways. In the first place, dialogue is not conventionally divided so that each speaker has a separate paragraph. Is this merely a gimmick, an eccentricity of Barthelme's, or does the appearance of the dialogue on the page help to control our attitude toward the speakers and what they are talking about? Explain.

4. A second way the story is unusual is in the predominance of allusions and high-sounding phrases: allusions to Gia-

cometti, Rodin, Neitzsche, Pascal, Nolde, etc., and phrases of "absurdity," "I-Thou relationship," "possibilities of authentic selfhood." Are these allusions and phrases just a tour de force or do they relate to the story's meanings? Do their density i.e., frequency, and the way they are used by the speakers reveal anything about the relation of these allusions and phrases to meaning?

5. Much of the story is given over to dialogue. Turn your attention to the descriptions of action and to the observations and comments. What kinds of actions occur? Are they expected? Rational? How do they accord with the things that the characters talk about? Compare, for example, the dialogue of the barber with his actions and with the images by which Peterson observes the barber.

6. Examine the first paragraph carefully. How do each of the last two sentences of the paragraph work as satiric anticlimaxes? What kind of intellectual, emotional, and moral order is implied by the way the paragraph makes a pattern out of money, TV, opinions, experiences, and knowledge? Do succeeding paragraphs have a similar pattern? Do they tend to be organized in the same way?

7. What is Peterson talking about at the very end of the story? How important is the word *alienated* to the story? What meaning does the story give to the word? What has happened to the implications of the title of the story at the end? (If necessary, consult a dictionary of classical mythology for the story of Danaë and Perseus, and also read *Hamlet*, II, ii, 290 ff.) What does the narrator mean by the last sentence?

Lawrence Sargent Hall, "The Ledge"

1. Hall's handling of point of view is important to examine. There is no question that the fisherman is the central character. Yet do we identify with him, or do we remain somewhat detached from him? Explain your answer by analyzing passages in which the author enters his mind. On the other hand, we are also told what other people feel: the wife; the

boys, especially the son; the fisherman's brother; the townspeople. Is this a weakness on Hall's part or does it help us to answer the question as to where the point of view lies? What is the significance of the character's being unnamed?

2. Consider the details we learn about the fisherman—other peoples' attitudes, direct comment by the narrator, the fisherman's words and actions. Is he a sympathetic character, one we admire or about whom we feel concern? His fate may be said to arise from his self-reliance; if this is so, what do we *feel* about self-reliance? Admire it? Distrust it? Question it? Why?

3. The first and last paragraphs might suggest that the ideas *cold* and *warm* are important ones. Notice the way the two ideas are used throughout the story. In what sense is the fisherman a cold man? Explore this idea carefully by studying passages where images of *cold* and *warm* appear.

4. Although the sequence of episodes is amazingly simple, yet the tension becomes tremendous up to the last paragraph. What makes for suspense, especially if we agree that it is not a hope of rescue? Are we ever in doubt about the outcome? *Could* another boat have appeared in time?

5. Why does Hall call the story "The Ledge"? True, it is the scene of the episode, but does naming it as the title in any way contribute to the total meaning? If so, how? What role does the natural world play in the story? How does it contribute to the meaning? Can you suggest how the natural world, the other characters, and the fisherman are interrelated in the story? Does this interrelationship give us any clues as to the real conflict? In the light of all these questions now look carefully at the last paragraph of the story.

II

1. Three of the stories in the first group, "What Was Innocence?" tend to reinforce the idea that innocence is something peculiar to children and that a child's loss of innocence is a sad but necessary consequence of growing up. But

Elizabeth Bowen's "A Queer Heart" suggests a very different idea about innocence: her innocent character is a grown woman and a mother. Compare and contrast the implied attributes and values attached to innocence in "A Queer Heart" with those of one or more of the other stories in the group. (The quotations from Elizabeth Bowen and Graham Greene at the beginning of this group of stories might be helpful.)

2. Discuss any of the stories in the second group, "This Thing Called Love," as a love story. None of these is a conventional "romantic love" story—boy-meets-girl, boy-gets-girl; and none of them, even the comic one, "Childybawn," can be called happy. What, then, does any one of these stories, suggest about that vague, diffuse, and too often mindlessly stereotyped concept called *love?*

3. Do you think it is merely facetious or, perhaps, scandalous to include "The Valiant Woman" among a group of stories about marriage? Of course, it is humorous to do so, but it is part of Powers' point: read, in the Douay translation of the Bible, *Proverbs* 31: 10–31. (Compare the translation of the first verse in this passage with the translations of the King James Version and the Revised Standard Version.) Discuss "The Valiant Woman" as a story about marriage. If you are familiar with Neil Simon's play (or the movie) *The Odd Couple,* you might discuss how both Powers and Simon say something about marriage without being merely facetious or scandalous although the couples in neither work are married.

4. Joyce Carol Oates' brief comment on "In the Region of Ice," immediately following the story in this text, suggests an interesting topic for discussion. Read Sophocles' play *Antigone;* what in the story, especially in Sister Irene, seems to have been suggested by Sophocles' play?

5. Although Flannery O'Connor never, so far as we know, made this connection, a reader of her story "Revelation" might be reminded of the book of *Job* in the Bible. Read *Job* and discuss ways in which Mrs. Turpin might be seen as a variant on the character of Job *and* his comforters.

6. Five of the stories in this volume present a character fac-

ing death: "The Jilting of Granny Weatherall," "Death of a Traveling Salesman," "The Ledge," "Tell Me a Riddle," and "That Evening Sun." (Questions on "That Evening Sun" raise the question of focus in that story, but it can be considered here nevertheless.) Examine how any one or two of these stories develop the theme that the way we confront death reveals our feelings about the meaning and values of life.

7. Akutagawa's "In a Grove" (which provides the central plot of the Japanese movie *Rashomon*, which in turn was the basis for the American western movie *The Outrage*) has been interpreted in two ways. One, that truth is relative and, therefore, does not really exist; two, that truth exists but cannot be determined because men—and even ghosts—are fundamentally liars, protecting themselves. Discuss whether the story upholds either of these conclusions. Are there merits in both views? Or would you suggest other interpretations? Why or why not?

8. The importance of a title may vary from work to work, but twentieth-century writers generally rely more on the necessity of an accurate title than early writers did. Sometimes it has seemed that a twentieth-century short story (or poem, or play, or novel) would be incomprehensible or uncertain in its focus, without its title. This has seemed especially true when the author of a story tends to remove the narrator's voice from the story (see the comments on point of view in the Introduction). Whatever the accuracy of these comments, several of the stories in this collection do depend, for the real thrust of their meaning, on the title; others, while not relying so heavily on the title for point, profit by a forceful and particularly suggestive title. Discuss the role the title plays in your understanding of such stories as the following: "That Evening Sun," "A Dill Pickle," "Two Blue Birds," "Fracture," "The Jilting of Granny Weatherall," "The Home Stretch," "Defender of the Faith," "The Ledge," "Tell Me a Riddle," "A Shower of Gold."

Many of these titles are allusions. "That Evening Sun" is a quotation from the first line of W. C. Handy's song, "St. Louis Blues"; "Defender of the Faith" is a phrase with several associations in the history of the Roman Catholic Church; the phrase "Oh Jerusalem" alludes to the great Psalm 137; and for "The Valiant Woman" see Question 3 in this section. Show how these intentional references to other works also help to extend the implications of the stories, sometimes directly, sometimes indirectly, and even negatively. (Or investigate any one in a brief essay.)

9. Obviously, many—maybe most—of these stories might be placed in a different group from the one chosen. Choose one of the stories and discuss the appropriateness of considering it in another group as well as the one where it appears. For examples: "Childybawn" might appear under the heading, "To Speak of Marriage . . ."; "The Jilting of Granny Weatherall" under "What Can a Man Believe In?"; "Death of a Traveling Salesman" under "What Can a Man Believe In?" That many of the stories may be viewed from various perspectives does not invalidate the arrangement in this book; it is rather evidence that the richness and suggestiveness of good literature allow for multiple perspectives.

10. Study the comments about fiction and about their own stories made by several of the writers included in this anthology: Chekhov (quoted at the end of the Introduction) and the following (quoted at the end of their respective stories): R. V. Cassill, Thomas Churchill, Nancy Huddleston Packer, Joyce Carol Oates, Harris Downey, Flannery O'Connor, Doris Lessing, and Jordon Pecile. Can you discover, among these writers, any common or similar ideas about the making of fiction? the intentions of writers? attitudes toward readers?

III

1. Further reading in any one of the authors included in this anthology can be rich and rewarding. Here are six suggestions for possible projects.
    a. Joyce's "An Encounter" is the second story in his collection, *The Dubliners.* This enormously influential book is at once a collection of discrete stories and a cunningly arranged fictional anatomy of a world in paralysis; it

should be read as a whole. You might compare and contrast "An Encounter" with some other stories in *The Dubliners*, discussing how the stories present differing perspectives on a similar view of life in a modern city. Or you might discuss what part "An Encounter" plays in the pattern of the book as a whole.

b. Before her early death Flannery O'Connor had completed two short story collections and two short novels (*see* Biographical Notes). Read at least one of these volumes and write an essay on the kind of world Miss O'Connor presents in her fiction: setting, social and character types, religious themes, use of violent actions.

c. Read more stories by Frank O'Connor (*see* Biographical Notes) as well as one or both of his autobiographical volumes, *An Only Child* and *My Father's Son*, and his fine book of criticism, *The Lonely Voice*. Write an essay centering on the role of autobiography and of the autobiographical method in his stories. Or write an essay on the uses O'Connor makes of life in Ireland in his stories.

d. William Carlos Williams was an enormously prolific writer. (Only a few of his works are mentioned in the Biographical Notes.) You might read his autobiography and more of his short stories and write an essay on one of the themes or interests which recur in his work. Or read also his *In the American Grain*, some of his poems, and his long poem *Paterson*, and write an essay on his deep absorption with *place*, with regionalism.

e. "Two Blue Birds" is an interesting example (on one level) of D. H. Lawrence's satiric side. You might read an entire novel in which a satiric method dominates, *Aaron's Rod*, and discuss Lawrence's satire. Or you might consider Lawrence's treatment of love, sex, and marriage in several of his short stories (the group collected in *The Portable D. H. Lawrence* [Viking Press] is convenient), or in novels like *The Rainbow* or *Women in Love*.

f. Read more of the short stories of Donald Barthelme (*see* Biographical Notes) and the brief essay by Nancy Huddleston Packer following her story, "Oh Jerusalem." What might Mrs. Packer's view of Barthelme's stories be? Why do you think it would be her view? What do *you* think about the stories?

2. We have included a number of war stories. You might ask yourself (in a longish paper) what actual feelings about war are generated in you by these stories. Do you tend to hate it; do you want to join one? Or you might consider a longer paper (and perhaps with the help of more reading of fiction and fact) on the question, "Can war and warfare be educated out of men or do they play some necessary role?" You might start with William James' classic essay, "The Moral Equivalent of War."

3. Try an essay based on your readings and feelings about "brotherhood." Do you feel ironical or despairing or hopeful about the prospect of men achieving this kind of closeness? What do your own experiences contribute to your responses? If you feel it *could* be achieved, would you want it? Why or why not? How could it be achieved? What do the stories collected here contribute to your thinking?

4. At this time, in our country, the idea of "brotherhood" must remind us of the living together or apart of whites and Blacks. Read widely in the stories included in these two paperback anthologies of stories by Black writers, and write an essay on how the world looks from the perspectives offered by the stories you have read: Hughes, Langston, ed., *Best Short Stories by Negro Writers* (Little, Brown & Co.) and Clarke, John Henrik, ed., *American Negro Short Stories* (Hill and Wang).

5. Try writing a story of your own. The question "Who Am I?" is usually an important one for a student. You might find it profitable to pursue that theme in a fictional form, transforming material from your own life into fiction as several of the writers in this anthology have done.

Biographical Notes

(These notes are selective. In most cases we have listed only a few representative titles. Notes for such writers as Joyce, Faulkner, and Chekhov, are somewhat extended to allow us to suggest something of the career and influence of such important figures. We have not tried to list all the honors and prizes that the writers have received, only a few of the most notable.)

AKUTAGAWA, RYUNOSUKE (1892–1927) Born in Tokyo, Akutagawa graduated from the University of Tokyo, taught a short while, worked on a newspaper, and wrote about a hundred stories. His first publications were Japanese translations of William Butler Yeats and Anatole France. Akutagawa was opposed to the naturalism of the confessional and autobiographical fiction popular in his day. His stories, often reworkings of traditional tales, usually set in the past, found little favor; he was attacked as irrelevant, overly interested in style, and unpleasantly bitter in theme and tone. He committed suicide in 1927. Renewed interest in his stories and the first English translations of several of them can be attributed to the phenomenal success, during the early

1950's, of the film *Rashomon;* the title of that film and its framing story derive from a similarly titled story by Akutagawa, but the main plot is based on "In a Grove."

BABEL, ISAAC (1894–1941?) Born and raised in the Jewish ghetto of Odessa in the Ukraine, Babel was in appearance, temperament, and training an intensely withdrawn, scholarly, pacifistic intellectual. His first few stories received the encouragement of the great writer Gorky, who advised Babel to see more of life. Babel's service in the Russian army and his subsequent enrollment in a Cossack regiment during the Soviet's 1920 campaign in Poland were, therefore, in violent contrast to his normal inclinations. This was especially so since the Cossacks—wild, almost savage, warriors—were not only antithetical types to him but had long been notorious as the instruments of the frequent official persecution of the Jews in Russia. One volume of Babel's short stories, *Red Cavalry* (1926), from which "Crossing Into Poland" comes, memorializes this experience. During the Thirties Babel fell from favor in Stalin's Russia; in 1937 he was accused of political crimes, was imprisoned in a concentration camp in 1939, and died sometime later—his death certificate was dated 1941. Two translations of his stories have appeared: *Collected Stories* (1955) and *You Must Know Everything: Stories 1915–1937* (1969).

BARTHELME, DONALD (1933–   ) Born in Philadelphia, Barthelme grew up in Texas, attended the University of Houston, and has worked as a museum director and as an editor of the magazine *Location.* Besides a novel, *Snow White* (1967), he has published three collections of short stories—*Come Back, Dr. Caligari* (1964), *Unspeakable Practices and Unnatural Acts* (1968), and *City Life* (1970).

BIERCE, AMBROSE (1842–1914?) After a childhood of mean poverty and family discord in Ohio and Indiana, Bierce served in the Union Army during the Civil War, rising from drummer-boy to brevet major. He moved to San Francisco after the war and, except for brief stays in London and Washington, D.C., lived there until 1913. Primarily a journalist, he became a prominent literary figure during the 1880's and 1890's. His married life was miserable: his wife died soon after a divorce ended years of discord; one son died an alcoholic; another was shot in a barroom brawl. Bierce's bitter and sardonic writings seemed grounded in his life. In 1913 he resigned—for the last time—from his position in William Randolph Hearst's newspaper empire, joined the staff of Pancho Villa, the northern Mexican revolutionist, as a press observer, and disappeared in Mexico. When and how he died are unknown, but many legends sprang up about the event. His best stories were collected in *In the Midst of Life: Tales of Soldiers and Civilians* (1891); his other most celebrated work is *The Devil's Dictionary,* or, as it was first called, *A Cynic's Word Book.*

BÖLL, HEINRICH (1917–) A leading voice in postwar West Germany and associated with an influential writers' league known as Group 47, Böll is a Catholic, born in Cologne. He returned to his native city after having been drafted into the army during the Second World War, in which he was wounded several times before he was taken prisoner. His first novel was published in 1949 and he is a prolific writer, but American translations of his works did not appear until the Sixties. Among his best works are *The Train Was On Time* (1949, translated 1965), *Billiards at Half-Past Nine* (1959, translated 1962), and *The Clown* (1963, translated 1965). A translation of some of his short stories, *18 Stories,* appeared in 1966.

BOWEN, ELIZABETH (1899–) Miss Bowen lists her home as the city of Cork in Eire, but she has always divided her time between Ireland and England. She was born of an Irish Protestant family whose history she recorded in *Bowen's Court* (1942), was educated in England and married an Englishman, Allen Charles Cameron. She was widowed in 1952 and during the later years of that decade worked with student writers in several American universities. Besides writing novels and short stories, she has written many literary essays and edited several books. Among her most highly praised novels are *The House in Paris* (1935), *The Death of the Heart* (1938), and *The Heat of the Day* (1948). Some critics believe she is at her best as a short story writer, of which the best-known collections are *The Cat Jumps* (1934), *Look at All Those Roses* (1941), and *The Demon Lover* (1945). Among her many honors was nomination to the Order of the British Empire in 1948; she is also an Honorary Member of the American Academy of Arts and Sciences.

CAMUS, ALBERT (1913–1960) By the time of his fatal automobile accident, Camus, only 46 years old, was one of the most influential writers of Europe. He was born in the then French colony of Algiers and during his youth was active in promoting provincial theater. After the fall of France in 1940 he left Africa to become active in the French underground, chiefly as one of the editors of the underground newspaper *Combat.* After the liberation of France in 1944, his short novel *The Stranger* (1942) and his essay *The Myth of Sisyphus* (1942) swiftly became classics of the popular existentialist movement which swept Europe and America in the postwar years. Camus' later writings include the novels *The Plague* (1947) and *The Fall* (1956), a short story collection, *The Exile and the Kingdom* (1957), and the philosophical essay, *The Rebel* (1951). Among his several dramas perhaps the best-known and the most successful is *Caligula* (1938, revised 1945). In 1957 he received the Nobel Prize for Literature.

CASSILL, R. V. (1919–   ) Born in Iowa, Cassill studied at the State University of Iowa and has taught at the Writers' Workshop there, as well as at several other colleges; he now teaches at Brown University. He has also studied art and worked as an art teacher in the early 1940's. His short stories have been collected in three volumes: *15 x 3* (1957), *The Father* (1965), and *The Happy Marriage* (1966); among his several novels are *Clem Anderson* (1961) and *The President* (1964).

CHEKHOV, ANTON (1860–1904) Chekhov's father was a grocer, his grandfather a serf who had bought his freedom. When his father went bankrupt, Chekhov, who had already begun to study medicine at the University of Moscow, undertook to support his family as a free-lance writer for comic newspapers. He completed his medical studies but practiced medicine very little after graduation. Instead he devoted most of his energies to writing fiction and theater pieces, and he became fairly wealthy. Always in frail health, by 1897 he recognized that he was fatally ill from tuberculosis and most of his last years were spent in various health resorts all over Europe. In 1901 he married the leading actress of the Moscow Art Theater which he had helped to establish. He died in 1904 in the German health resort of Badenweiler. Although he wrote a few novels, his mastery is most evident in shorter fiction; his practice and his influence amounted to a virtual redefinition of the short story as a modern form. He shifted emphasis away from the patterned plot onto the illuminating power of apparently trivial details of behavior, attitude, and circumstance. Readers of Russian find translations of Chekhov notoriously inadequate; the wonder is that so much of his skill and his vision are available to English readers. There are many translations of selections of his enormous output; the largest, but far from complete, collection is the thirteen volumes of *Tales*, translated by Constance Garnett (1913–1922). Chekhov's lifelong interest in writing for the theater was climaxed by the four great plays completed at the end of his life: *The Sea Gull* (1896), *Uncle Vanya* (1899), *The Three Sisters* (1901), and *The Cherry Orchard* (1904).

CHURCHILL, THOMAS (1934–   ) Mr. Churchill was educated at the University of Washington and taught English at Western Washington State College, the University of British Columbia, and the University of Connecticut. He has written a number of stories, articles, and reviews and is currently working on a long "narrative." With his wife and two sons he has spent much of his time recently crossing the United States from one coast to the other looking for the Good Place, which he does not expect to find.

DOWNEY, HARRIS Born in Baton Rouge, Louisiana, Downey studied at Louisiana State University and New York University, and now lives in Louisiana. His novels include *Thunder in the Rain* (1956), *The Keys to My Prison* (1964), and *Carrie Dumain* (1966). "The Hunters" is his best-known story, having been widely anthologized and translated.

ELLISON, RALPH (1914–   ) Born in Oklahoma City, Ellison attended Tuskegee Institute in Alabama, majoring in music; he then came to New York to study sculpturing and worked with the Federal Writers Project. "I never wanted to be a writer," he said on the evening he was received into the National Institute of Arts and Letters; "I only wanted to be a musician. I wanted to be a composer. It simply didn't work out that way." What worked out was that in 1942 he became editor of the *Negro Quarterly*, and he published some stories and worked on a novel. The novel, *The Invisible Man* (1952), won the National Book Award; no American novel published since 1940 has been more highly praised or seems so certain of permanence. Ellison has been a teacher in Austria and Germany and in such schools as Bard College, the University of Chicago, and Yale University. His short stories have not been collected; his second novel, on which he has been long working, is expected soon; in 1964 *Shadow and Act*, a collection of essays on literature, music, and the American Negro, received high praise.

FAULKNER, WILLIAM (1897–1962) Faulkner lived most of his life in Oxford, Mississippi—the seat of Lafayette County and of the University of Mississippi. His life as a citizen, writer, and—as he occasionally insisted—a farmer of Oxford was interrupted by a few sojourns in other places: in 1918 he went to Canada to enlist in the Royal Flying Corps and saw service in France; in the early Twenties, after a few years at the University, he lived for a while in New Orleans; during the Thirties and Forties he was occasionally in Hollywood, where he worked as a screenwriter; in the late Fifties he was writer in residence at the University of Virginia. But almost all his most enduring fiction is based on the history, legends, and traditions of the people in Oxford and Lafayette County, places which appear in his writing as Jefferson and Yoknapatawpha County. It is generally agreed that though financial rewards and critical acclaim did not come until after World War II, Faulkner's greatest works were published in the late Twenties and Thirties:

besides several volumes of short stories, these most admired books include *The Sound and The Fury* (1929), *As I Lay Dying* (1930), *Light in August* (1932), *Absalom, Absalom* (1936), and *The Hamlet* (1940). Public honors for Faulkner were climaxed in 1950: in that year his *Collected Stories* received the National Book Award; the National Institute and American Academy of Arts and Letters (of which he became a member) presented him with the William Dean Howells Medal, an award made only once every five years; and he received the postponed 1949 Nobel Prize for Literature. A second National Book Award came for *A Fable* (1954), an allegorical treatment of an episode in the French army during the last year of World War I. Although Faulkner worked many years on *A Fable* and professed to regard it as his most important work, his secure reputation as one of America's greatest writers rests on the novels and stories that create the history of Yoknapatawpha County and of the Indians, Negroes, farmers, aristocrats, and townsmen who lived in that often tragic, often uproariously comic, world.

HALL, LAWRENCE SARGENT (1915–   ) A New Englander, born in Massachusetts, educated at Bowdoin College and Yale University, Hall now makes his home on Orr's Island, Maine. He has owned and operated a boatyard, but his chief occupation has been a college teacher; he teaches at Bowdoin College. Besides short stories and essays, he is the author of a novel, *Stowaway* (1961), and a literary study, *Hawthorne, Critic of Society* (1942).

JOYCE, JAMES (1882–1941) Educated at Jesuit schools and at University College in Dublin, Joyce briefly entertained the idea of studying medicine. He taught school for awhile, then, in 1904 he left Ireland with his wife, Nora Barnacle, whom he did not legally marry until 1931. Between 1904 and 1912 he lived mostly on the continent, teaching English at language schools in Yugoslavia and writing, returning to Ireland on several occasions. In 1912, however, an Irish publisher's reluctance to publish his short story collection, *Dubliners*, brought to a climax his disgust with the Catholic Church, the nationalism, and the middle-class mores of Ireland; in that year he decisively left Ireland for good. *Dubliners* was published in England in 1914. Joyce lived in various places in England and Europe, chiefly France, devoted almost all his time to writing, frequently receiving financial help from various patrons and friends. His eyesight steadily failed and his family life was marked with disaster. Notoriety and increasing critical acclaim attended the publication of his books. He died in Zurich, Switzerland, having left France after the German invasion. Besides two small volumes of poetry and a play, Joyce published three other books: *A*

Portrait of the Artist as a Young Man (1916), *Ulysses* (1922), and *Finnegans Wake* (1939). The list is deceptively small, for it is no exaggeration to say that these three works and *Dubliners* make up the most influential as well as the most original and accomplished body of fiction by any writer of English in the twentieth century.

LAWRENCE, D. H. (1885–1930) Lawrence's childhood and early life in the coal mining region of Nottinghamshire were transformed into autobiographical fiction in his third novel, *Sons and Lovers* (1913). His father was a barely literate coal miner, his mother an educated and evangelical former school teacher. Lawrence was a biology teacher until his first novel was published in 1911. In 1912 he eloped with a married woman who was not free to marry him until 1914; this scandal, the fact that she was German-born, Lawrence's indifference to World War I, and the censorship scandal over his fourth novel, *The Rainbow* (1915), all made Lawrence's name one of the most notorious among writers during his lifetime. As a writer he continued to shock large segments of the public; his last novel, *Lady Chatterley's Lover* (1928), was banned from publication in its original form in England and the United States, a ban which was observed until the late 1950's. During the last decade of his life Lawrence traveled all over the world, seeking out nonindustrialized, primitive societies in Italy, southwestern United States, Mexico, Ceylon, and Australia. He died of tuberculosis in Italy. He was a prolific writer; his passionate outcry against a civilization that severs mind and body, his feeling for the natural world, his scorn for conventional sexual mores and over-intellectualism inform all his work. Besides the three novels already mentioned, *Women in Love* (1920) is among his best. His several volumes of short stories and novelettes, beginning with *The Prussian Officer and Other Stories* (1914), were collected in 1955. Although primarily known as a master of fiction, his mastery is also evident in *Collected Poems* (1928), travel books like *Sea and Sardinia* (1921) and *Mornings in Mexico,* (1927) and the brilliant if eccentric literary criticism of *Studies in Classic American Literature* (1923).

LESSING, DORIS (1919–   ) Born in Persia, daughter of an English army captain, Doris Lessing moved to Southern Rhodesia and lived there until 1949, when she moved to London. Life in British colonial Africa provides the setting for many of her novels and stories— *The Grass is Singing* (1950), her first novel; *Children of Violence,* the collective title of a series of novels completed in 1969; *This Was the Old Chief's County,* a short story collection. Probably the best-known of her many novels is *The Golden Notebook* (1962). Other short story collections are *The Habit of Loving* (1958) and *A Man and Two Women*

(1963). Her essays on a return visit to Africa, *Going Home* (1957), and her documentary novel, *In Pursuit of the English* (1960), reflect her intense concern with several critical political, social, and economic issues of our time.

MANSFIELD, KATHERINE (1888–1923) Born Kathleen Beauchamp in New Zealand, where she lived until 1903 when her father sent her to study music at Queen's College in London. She adopted the name Katherine Mansfield when she began to publish her stories. Her family insisted that she return to New Zealand in 1906, but in 1908 she persuaded them to let her leave once more for England, which became her home until her death. After a very brief marriage in 1909, while trying to sell her short stories she augmented her allowance from her family by singing in a touring opera company. In 1911 her first volume of short stories, *In a German Pension*, was published. She met, worked for, and eventually married the distinguished editor and author, John Middleton Murry. Attacks of arthritis and then tuberculosis caused her to spend her last years in increasing pain and attacks of despondency. She died in a sanatorium outside Paris. Her two other collections of short stories were *Bliss and Other Stories* (1920) and *The Garden Party and Other Stories* (1922). All of her stories, published and unpublished, were collected in 1937, as *The Short Stories of Katherine Mansfield*.

MAUPASSANT, GUY DE (1850–1893) Regarded as one of the founders of the modern short story, de Maupassant was born in Normandy and began a career as a clerk in a government office. Gustave Flaubert, author of *Madame Bovary* and de Maupassant's godfather, encouraged him to write and served as his master. In 1880 he was asked to contribute a short story to a new collection; this, his first published work, was "Boule-de-Suif" (Butter-Ball" or "Ball of Fat"), immediately acclaimed as a masterpiece. In the decade 1880–1890 de Maupassant wrote several plays, six novels, and about three hundred stories. The prodigious energy implied in this activity and the notorious incontinence of his private life led to a collapse in 1890; in the next three years he suffered frequent violent attacks of general paresis and he died in an institution for the insane. If de Maupassant's concern for the invention of clear, forceful, and retellable plots accounts for the common feeling nowadays that he is an old-fashioned writer, it is also true that his genius for inventing appropriate and memorable plots has made several of his stories among the most familiar works of Western literature—"Boule-de-Suif," "The Necklace," "The False Gems," "The Piece of String."

OATES, JOYCE CAROL (1938–   ) Born in the state of New York, Mrs. Oates studied at Syracuse University and did graduate work at the University of Wisconsin. She now teaches at the University of Windsor in Ontario, Canada. Her books include two short story collections —*By the North Gate* (1963) and *Upon the Sweeping Flood* (1966)—and four novels—*With Shuddering Fall* (1965), *A Garden of Earthly Delights* (1967), *Expensive People* (1968), and *them* (1969). It is a measure of the critical regard in which Mrs. Oates is held that the last three novels were nominated for the National Book Award in 1968, 1969, and 1970, respectively; *them* received the award.

O'CONNOR, FLANNERY (1925–1964) When she was little more than five, Mary Flannery O'Connor appeared in a newsreel shown all over the country with her pet bantam rooster because the rooster could walk backwards. In 1961 Flannery O'Connor published an essay in *Holiday* about the peacocks she raised on a farm in Andalusia, Georgia. While still a student at the Women's College of Georgia, Mary Flannery O'Connor exercised her talents as a cartoonist and an artist and thought she might become an artist. She continued to paint and draw all her life. But a fellowship to the Writers' Workshop at the University of Iowa helped her to focus on the talent which she mastered and which made her, by the time of her early death, one of the outstanding writers of her generation. In 1950 she discovered that she had lupus, the same destructive disease from which her father had died in 1941, but in her case the spread of the disease was arrested for several years by a new drug. During her last years, weakened by the disease and the drug, she had to use crutches constantly, but she was not entirely confined to the Georgia dairy farm where she lived with her mother. She lectured and gave readings frequently, traveled to the shrine at Lourdes, France, and in 1963 received an honorary degree at Smith College in Massachusetts. Although a devout Roman Catholic, Miss O'Connor chiefly wrote about the fundamentalist Protestants of her native state in the small body of distinguished fiction she published: two short story collections—*A Good Man Is Hard to Find* (1955) and *Everything That Rises Must Converge* (1965)—and two short novels—*Wise Blood* (1952) and *The Violent Bear It Away* (1960). *Mystery and Manners*, a collection of her essays and lectures, appeared in 1969.

O'CONNOR, FRANK (1903–1966) Michael O'Donovan, born in Cork, Ireland, wrote under the pseudonym Frank O'Connor. He first took the pseudonym while fighting with the Irish Republican Army during the Irish Revolution and during the Civil War in the years following the First World War. The experiences of these years, including a year in a British prison camp, formed the basis for his first collection of short stories, *Guests of the Nation* (1931). He was, by profession, a librarian, and was also a director of Dublin's famous Abbey Theatre, but the core of his life's work is the more than twenty volumes of short stories he published. During the Fifties and Sixties he lived and taught in the United States, but he died in Dublin. As a man of letters, he published not only short stories: a study of the novel, *The Mirror in the Roadway* (1956); a study of the short story, *The Lonely Voice* (1963); a novel, *Domestic Relations* (1957); two splendid autobiographical volumes, *An Only Child* (1961) and *My Father's Son* (1969), and many others. In the United States many of his short stories are available in three volumes, *The Stories of Frank O'Connor* (1952), *More Stories by Frank O'Connor* (1954), and *Collection Three* (1969).

O'FAOLAIN, SEAN (1900–) Like Frank O'Connor, O'Faolain was born in Cork and fought with the Irish Republican Army. He studied at the National University in Dublin and was a student and fellow at Harvard University. He has lived and taught in both the United States and Ireland and is now retired in Ireland. He has been a prolific writer, chiefly known for his short stories; *Finest Stories* (1957) is a convenient sampling. No student should fail to read his critical study, *The Short Story* (1951) or his wonderful anthology-textbook, *Short Stories* (1961).

OLSEN, TILLIE (1913–) Born in Omaha, Nebraska, Mrs. Olsen now lives with her husband and children in San Francisco. Before 1950, when her first story was published, she had worked as a typist, a transcriber, and a secretary. She has received several honors; in 1962–1963 she was a resident at the Radcliffe Institute for Independent Study. *Tell Me a Riddle* (1961), a collection of four of her stories, is her only book to date.

PACKER, NANCY HUDDLESTON (1925–) Mrs. Packer was born in Birmingham, Alabama, and studied at Stanford University, where she is now a member of the celebrated Stanford Creative Writing Staff, and where her husband, Herbert Packer, is Dean of the Law School. Her stories appear in various magazines and anthologies but no collected volume has yet appeared.

PECILE, JORDON (1931–) Born in Pennsylvania, a graduate of Cornell University, Pecile was awarded a Fulbright grant to Florence, Italy in 1954. After service in the Navy as a teacher at the Academy and on duty in the Antarctic, he began graduate work at Princeton but changed to the Iowa Writers' Workshop in 1965. He now teaches at Mt. Holyoke. In 1970 he was awarded a second Fulbright to Aix-en-Provence, France, and hopes "to bring back a novel."

PIRANDELLO, LUIGI (1867–1936) The outstanding Italian writer of the first half of the twentieth century, Pirandello was born to wealthy parents in Sicily, earned a doctorate in German studies at the University of Bonn, and published his first volume of short stories, *Love Without Love*, in 1893. His father's financial reverses necessitated Pirandello's becoming a professor of Italian literature in Rome, a post he reluctantly held from 1897–1921. He published hundreds of short stories, nine novels, much literary criticism, and several volumes of poetry. But his international reputation is chiefly based on his plays; of the more than forty he wrote from 1910 until his death, four have been especially important: *It Is So (If You Think So)* (1916), *Six Characters in Search of an Author* (1921), *"Henry IV"* (1922), and *As You Desire Me* (1930). In 1934 he received the Nobel Prize for Literature. Relatively little of his vast output, except for his plays, has been translated into English, but a few volumes of selected short stories are available in paperback editions.

PORTER, KATHERINE ANNE (1890–) Born in Indian Creek, Texas, a direct descendant of Daniel Boone, Miss Porter attended convent schools in Texas and Louisiana. She moved to New York in 1920 and worked as a journalist and free-lance writer, and traveled widely in the United States, Mexico (her "much-loved second country"), and Europe. She did not seek to publish her stories until relatively late and her collected fiction comprises very few volumes, but her extraordinary craftsmanship and artistry have made this body of work one of the most highly praised in modern American fiction. Two collections of short stories and four short novels (a form in which she is one of the few masters) were published between 1930 and 1944: *Flowering Judas and Other Stories* (1930, enlarged 1935), *The Leaning Tower and Other Stories* (1944), *Hacienda* (1934), *Noon Wine* (1932), *Pale Horse, Pale Rider* (1939), and *Old Mortality* (1939). She published a collection of essays, *The Days Before*, in 1952, but not until 1962 did she bring out another volume of fiction; this was the celebrated allegorical novel, *Ship of Fools*, on which she had worked for many years and parts of which had already appeared in print. She has received many awards and has held several distinguished posts at various American colleges and universities. In 1965 all of her short fiction was gathered into *Collected Stories*, which received the National Book Award. Miss Porter is a member of the National Institute of Arts and Letters and of its guiding body, the American Academy. *Collected Essays and Occasional Writings* appeared in 1969.

POWERS, J. F. (1917–) Born in Illinois, James Farl Powers worked at the traditional odd jobs of the developing writer—chauffeur, door-to-door insurance salesman, bookstore clerk, etc.—before his first story was published in 1943. In the early 1950's he was on the staff of a publishing house, and he has taught writing in colleges, but he is now mainly a writer. He has lived in County Wicklow in Ireland. Although chiefly known for his stories about the life of the American Roman Catholic clergy, some aspects of Midwest American life also provide him with subject matter. His first novel, *Morte D'Urban* (1963), won the National Book Award; his short story collections have included *Prince of Darkness* (1947), *Presence of Grace* (1956), and *Lions, Harts, and Leaping Does* (1963).

ROSENFELD, ISAAC (1918–1956) A student at the University of Chicago during one of its most stimulating periods, Rosenfeld went to New York in 1941 to begin study for a Ph.D. in philosophy, but he broke off studies to become a writer, especially as a contributor to, then an editor of, *The Partisan Review*. During the Forties he became one of the most admired essayists of the time, publishing essays, reviews, and short stories in various magazines. He taught part time at New York University; between 1952 and 1954 he taught at the University of Minnesota; from 1954 until he died of a heart attack he taught at the University of Chicago. In 1951 he published an autobiographical novel, *Passage From Home;* a second novel, *The Enemy*, was completed in the same year but has never been published, although three sections have been published as short stories. "The Brigadier" is one of those sections. His short stories have been collected in *Alpha and Omega* (1966), and a collection of his reviews and essays, *An Age of Enormity*, appeared in 1962.

ROTH, PHILIP (1933–   ) Born in New Jersey, educated at Bucknell University and the University of Chicago, Roth has been a teacher at several universities, including a tenure as writer in residence at Princeton. His first book, a collection of several short stories and one short novel, which gave the volume its title, *Goodbye, Columbus* (1959), received great critical acclaim, won the National Book Award, and was immensely popular. Since then he has published three novels—*Letting Go* (1962), *When She Was Good* (1967), and *Portnoy's Complaint* (1969), the last another extraordinarily popular and critically acclaimed work.

WELTY, EUDORA (1909–   ) Born in Jackson, Mississippi, which is still her home, Miss Welty graduated from the University of Wisconsin and attended the Columbia University School of Advertising. During the Thirties she worked for the United States government in rural areas of her home state. Although she has exhibited her work as a photographer, her chief work is her fiction, most of which is set in the southern Mississippi Valley—past and present. Her first two collections of short stories, *A Curtain of Green* (1941) and *The Wide Net* (1943), are among the most distinguished volumes of their kind in modern American letters. Her most recent collection is *Losing Battles* (1970). She has also published novels, including *The Robber Bridegroom* (1942), *Delta Wedding* (1946), and *The Ponder Heart* (1954). A member of the National Institute of Arts and Letters, Miss Welty received the William Dean Howells Medal in 1955.

WILLIAMS, WILLIAM CARLOS (1883–1963) From 1910 until his death, Williams practiced as a pediatrician in the city of his birth Rutherford, New Jersey. He had earned an M.D. at the University of Pennsylvania (1906) and had done postgraduate work in Germany. Best-known as one of the most original, accomplished, and influential poets of twentieth-century America, Williams received the National Book Award in 1950 and the Bollingen Prize for Poetry in 1952; his many volumes of poetry have been gathered into several volumes, *Collected Poems* (1934), *Collected Later Poems* (1950), and *The Desert Music and Other Poems* (1954); in 1958 he published the last of the five parts of a long, impressionistic poem, *Paterson*, a masterpiece on which he had been working for more than a decade. Because he ranks so high as a poet, his distinguished achievements in other forms of literature have not yet been properly appraised: plays, novels, an autobiography, literary and cultural essays (*In the American Grain* [1925] and *Selected Essays* [1954] are especially important), and two collections of short stories, *Make Light of It* (1950) and *The Farmer's Daughters* (1961). He was a member of the National Institute of Arts and Letters and of its guiding body, the American Academy.